WITHDRAWN

AFRICAN RELIGIONS:
A SYMPOSIUM

African Religions:
A Symposium

Edited by

Newell S. Booth, Jr.

NOK Publishers, Ltd.

New York • London • Lagos

NOK Publishers, Ltd.
150 Fifth Avenue
New York, New York 10011

© Copyright by Newell S. Booth, Jr. 1977

Library of Congress Catalog Card Number 73-88062
International Standard Book Number 0-88357-012-2

Printed in the United States of America

Table of Contents

Contents—*continued*

Preface

The collection of articles appearing in this book has developed out of a Colloquium on African Religion sponsored by Western College, Oxford, Ohio, and supported by funds supplied by the Consortium for Higher Education Religion Studies, Dayton, Ohio. Sessions of the colloquium were held during the academic year 1969-1970 at Western College and also at United Theological Seminary, Dayton, and Payne Theological Seminary, Wilberforce, Ohio.

The articles by Barrett, Janzen, Koech, M'Timkulu, Sieber, and the first two by Booth were originally papers presented to the colloquium. Although they have been extensively revised, it should be noted that basically they represent the views of the authors in 1969-1970. The articles by Brown and Chappelle, Rieber, Sturm, Thomas, and the third and fourth by Booth were added to provide greater variety and coverage.

No attempt has been made to "cover the field" or to present examples of all types of African religious expression. The subjects dealt with were at least partly determined by the accidental factor of the competencies of those available as contributors. In spite of this nonrational aspect of the selection process we believe that the book provides a good introduction to African religion through the eyes of a variety of observers. It is not intended to replace introductions which deal in a more general way with African religion as a whole but to supplement them by providing concrete examples.

One advantage of this kind of book is that it need not be read in any particular order. Although arranged in what seems to be a logical sequence, for some purposes the articles might well be read in a different order. For example, one might begin with the impact of African religion in the Americas and then move back to its African source. Thus it is hoped that the book will meet the needs of a variety of persons with scholarly or general interest in Africa. The annotated bibliography at the end is intended as a guide to further reading.

As director of the colloquium and editor of the book, I wish to express my thanks to the present and former members of what was first the Planning Committee and then the Editorial Committee:

Charles Brown, United Theological Seminary, Dayton
Yvonne Chappelle, formerly of Wright State University, Dayton
Calvin Rieber, United Theological Seminary, Dayton
Willis Stoesz, Wright State University, Dayton (formerly of Western College)
Fred Sturm, University of New Mexico, Albuquerque (formerly of Western College)
Ann Weisenborn, formerly of Western College

Appreciation is also due to my wife, Mary Lou Booth, who served as secretary and typist, to Western College for various facilities which were provided, and especially to the Consortium for Higher Education Religion Studies which not only supported the Colloquium but made further funds available for editorial work.

Delay of several years in publication has not reduced the value of the articles, as they do not deal with "current events." However, the authors have continued to learn and to think and would undoubtedly write some things differently now.

Newell S. Booth, Jr.

Miami University
Oxford, Ohio
February, 1977

Illustrations

1) A Kilumbu (prophet-diviner), Baluba. Photographed in Kamina, Zaïre, by N. Booth, 1972.

2) Egu Orumamu. Chief mask of the Igala. H-23", wood. Carved about 1941. Photographed in Ikeja, Nigeria by R. Sieber, 1958.

3) Do. Purification mask of the Aowin. Photographed in Dadiaso, Ghana, by R. Sieber in 1967.

4) Reliquary figure, Bakota, Gabon. H-21½", wood and brass. Courtesy of the Indiana University Art Musuem.

5) Reliquary figure, Fang, Gabon. H-24", wood. Courtesy of the Indiana University Art Museum.

6) Bom Bosh, 96th King of the Bakuba, Zaïre. Courtesy of the Brooklyn Museum.

7) Funerary terra cotta of the royal high priest of Bruku. Photographed in Kwahu-Tofo, Ghana, by R. Sieber, 1964.

8) Possession by *preto velho*, Brazil. Photographed by F. Sturm, 1971.

9) His Excellency Mr. Diangienda, son of the prophet Kimbangu, leader of the Church of Jesus Christ on Earth through Simon Kimbangu. Photographed in Kinshasa, Zaïre, by N. Booth, 1972.

10) Mosque, Bagamoyo, Tanzania. Photographed by N. Booth, 1969.

AFRICAN RELIGIONS:
A SYMPOSIUM

1

An Approach to African Religion

Newell S. Booth, Jr.

An early Portuguese visitor to the southern coast of Africa reported that "The people are all Hottentots and they have no religion." He was wrong on both counts, but at least on the latter point his mistake was understandable. After all, he was from Europe, where the presence of religion is manifested in church buildings, priests, and sacred scriptures. Perhaps he was on his way home from India where comparable phenomena would have been seen. In that part of Africa, however, he saw no identifiable religious buildings, no distinctively religious functionaries, and certainly no scriptures. Therefore, "they have no religion."

A parallel may be found in traditional China, which has also been said to have been "a country without religion."[1] C.K:Yang has shown, however, that in China religion has been very important, not so much as a separate institution as in "diffused" form, "with its theology, rituals and organizations intimately merged with the concepts and structure of secular institutions...." In this "diffused form, religion performs a pervasive function in an organized manner in every major aspect of Chinese social life."[2]

What Yang has said of Chinese religion may also be said of Sub-Saharan African religion; it is not identifiable as a separate institution but permeates the whole society. For example, Colin Turnbull's book, *The Forest People,* is not specifically about the "religion" of the Bambuti pygmies, yet in describing their daily life he certainly describes their religion. For them the forest, their natural environment, is where God is found.[3] The "sacred" is encountered in the high points of their everyday life. While the Bambuti are hardly "typical" Africans, the unity of religion and life among them provides what is perhaps an extreme example of that which is generally characteristic of Africa.

It is precisely this omnipresence of religion that makes it difficult to get a secure grip on the subject; in fact it was this that misled the Portuguese traveler into thinking that Africans had no religion. The distinction between all-pervasive religion and no religion at all is rather difficult to make and may depend on the perspective of the observer and the definition of religion with which he begins—consciously or unconsciously.

Given the pervasive nature of African religion, it is not surprising that most of the useful information available on the subject comes from the anthropologist. Typically it is to be found in a monograph on a specific group which the anthropologist has come to know through long and close contact. The monograph may include a chapter on religious beliefs and ceremonies, but information on the basic religious orientation of the community is probably spread throughout the book—which is as it should be where religious phenomena are spread throughout daily life. The anthropologist can tie together kinship terminology, agricultural methods, royalty, and the ancestors in one coordinated package; thus he has an advantage over the political scientist, the economist, or the historian of religions, who tries to lift out one aspect of the culture for special attention but finds it thoroughly entangled with everything else.

The historian of religions certainly appreciates the material provided by the anthropologist; often he has little else available. His purpose, however, is somewhat different, namely, to focus on religion as a phenomenon to be studied on its own terms, the understanding of which is a valid end in itself. Yet he faces a real problem: how is it possible to *focus* on that which is pervasively present in the whole society?

Africa has not been neglected by historians of religions. In their writings we frequently find supreme gods, initiation rites, and spirit possession cults from Africa rubbing shoulders with similar phenomena from Siberia, Central America, and Polynesia. This is undoubtedly useful for comparative purposes, but precisely because the phenomena are separated from their context there is danger of losing sight of that which is most distinctively "African."

Even accounts of "African religion" in general are based on information from many different areas, taken out of local context. The author must constantly *remind* the reader of the pervasive nature of African religion; this pervasiveness is not inherent in his presentation as it is in a good anthropological account.

The tendency to separate religious phenomena from their context may be partly responsible for premature generalizations regarding "African religion" and also for overly hasty identification of African and non-African phenomena. Beliefs and practices abstracted from the whole of which they are parts may have quite different appearances from those which they have in context. One might suggest as an analogy the way in which a collection of African masks in a museum gives us very little understanding of the significance of any particular mask in the context of a whole outfit worn in a dance celebrating some event of communal significance.

Perhaps we could sum up the problem of the study of African religion as follows: in anthropological writings that which is *religious* may be "lost" in the larger social context, while in writings by historians of religions the essential "Africanness" tends to be obscured by the concern for "religion" as such. The solution is to have the two approaches informing and supplementing each other. Perhaps the ideal would be one scholar trained in both fields or collaboration between scholars in the two fields; lacking this we at least need both kinds of study. The perspectives supplied by students of art, literature, and history are also essential.

A question which may be raised at this point is whether African religion can properly be spoken of in the singular or only in the plural. Our reading and observation turns up a profusion of phenomena to which we may attach such labels as "supreme gods," "nature spirits," "ancestor rituals," "initiation practices," "divine kings," "secret societies," "sorcerers," and "demons," with considerable variety from place to place. Perhaps we will decide that there is no such thing as "African religion," but only "African religions." As the various ethnic groups do not by any means have the same beliefs and practices, it may seem best to reduce our range of vision from "Africa" to certain limited areas in Africa where close similarities can be observed. One difficulty with this, however, is that the differences do not necessarily follow geographical divisions nor do they always coincide with the linguistic or other cultural distinctions. Thus we may find common features as far apart as Sierra Leone and Swaziland which are not found in some intermediate areas, while there is often no obvious reason for significant differences in belief and practice between neighboring and otherwise closely related peoples.

Any valid approach to African traditional religion must begin with careful studies of specific ethnic groups by scholars who have closely associated themselves with these groups. Here is where the African scholar studying the religion of his own people or a closely related people is especially valuable. However, outsiders who are prepared to put themselves in the position of not only looking *at* but also *with* the people they are studying can make significant contributions. This has in fact been done by a few anthropologists and missionaries, but not, so far as I know, by anyone clearly identifiable as a "historian of religions." [4] Of course, anyone who has tried to understand the religion of a given group on its own terms has been acting to some extent as a historian of religions, whatever his professional label may have been.

Wilfred Cantwell Smith has focused our attention on the new phase in the study of religions which results from the "personalization" of such study. We have moved, or are moving, he holds, from dealing with religion in terms of "it," "they," or even "you" to an approach in which "we" is the distinctive pronoun. [5] It is no longer enough to talk *about* people of other religions, or *to* them; now we must talk *with* them. [6] The historian of religions, ideally, is one who recognizes "that we—all of us—live together in a world in which not they, not you, but *some of us* are Muslims, some are Hindus, some are Jews, some are Christians." Perhaps, Smith continues, it will be possible to add, "some of us are communists, some inquirers." [7] Can we also add, "some of us are African traditional believers?"

Smith maintains that "anyone who writes about a religion other than his own today does so, in effect, in the presence of those about whom he is speaking," and goes on to say that "no statement about a religion is valid unless it can be acknowledged by that religion's believers." [8] He refers here not primarily to statements about "external data" but to the "meaning that the system has for those of faith." [9] Surely this can—and must—be applied to the study of African religion. To do so will help to overcome the objections of many Africans to the way Western students of Africa—historians of religions, anthropologists, and others—exploit Africa for their own academic or ideological purposes. One African scholar puts it this way:

> Throughout the long history of Western scholarship African religions have never been the object of study in their own right. African deities were used as mercenaries in foreign battles, not one of which was in the interest of African peoples. [10]

The non-African student of African religion must examine carefully his motivations and presuppositions. Especially he must avoid any conscious or unconscious assumption of superiority. As Smith says, "One cannot study religion from above, only from alongside or within...." [11] Anyone who tries to study African religion from an assumed position of superior revelation or superior rationality will only produce distortions. Of course, one does not have to accept the truth of a religion in order to study it, but one must respect it as a system of belief and practice which makes sense to people who are as intelligent and honest as oneself.

In this connection, it is important to avoid terms such as "superstition," "pagan," "fetish," "primitive," and "animism." Some of these may originally have had valid, non-judgmental meanings; today they have little clear content but strong suggestions of inferiority and are rightly resented by Africans. Thus an African scholar says, "There are no 'animists' in Africa"; "animism" is a product of "the Western mind." [12]

It also appears that the description of religion in terms of a "sacred" reality which is opposed to the "profane" is based on non-African ways of thinking. If an important characteristic of African religion is its pervasive quality, then there are few phenomena that can be identified as distinctively sacred in the sense that they are separated from the rest of life. The whole of life is sacred in that it is "saturated with being." [13]

The need to prove certain points, positively or negatively, distorts accounts of African religion. Today the need to compensate for past negative judgments may lead to positive generalizations made without adequate foundation in careful examination of the facts. There is also the danger of attempting to justify African religion on alien standards. For instance, it has been suggested that some African scholars have "over-reacted in the face of the arrogance and insults of western scholarship" and have tried to present African beliefs in terms acceptable to Western thought. [14]

A new phase in the study of African religion is made possible by the appearance of African students of African religion. They are able to work at least partially from "within" the tradition they are studying, even when they are themselves Christian or Muslim. Their criticisms of the work of non-Africans must be taken with great seriousness. However, it is apparent that they do not always agree among themselves. Some African scholars, for instance, have emphasized the monotheistic character of African religion, [15] but it has also been suggested that this is due to their Western Christian orientation. [16] The important point is that this is a controversy between *Africans,* reminding us that even disagreements in the study of African religion must now be understood in an African context.

It is especially important that any generalizations about African religion be made from a standpoint *within* Africa rather than from an outside perspective. The "personalization" of which we have spoken also requires that such generalizations be made on the basis of sympathetic knowledge of one local group. From this perspective it is possible to look over the larger scene and identify continuities as well as discontinuities. All treatments of "African religion" are undoubtedly written from the perspective of one part of Africa; this however, is not always made clear to the reader, perhaps because it is not clear to the author. It is inevitable that African religion be approached from the perspective of a local position within West Africa, East Africa, or South Africa; the fact of this perspective should be in the conscious awareness of both writer and reader. Thus, one may make Akamba-based generalizations, Yoruba-based generalizations, Luo-based generalizations, or, as I porpose to do, generalizations based primarily on what I know of the Baluba.

Generalizations about African traditional religion have frequently been made in terms of beliefs and practices: "otiose high gods," "ancestor worship," "secret societies," and "initiation rites." Phenomena that have been called by these names can undoubtedly be found in various parts of Africa. The search for similarities on this level, however, though it may be moderately successful, does not seem to be the most appropriate way to proceed, partly because it tends to obscure the "pervasive" quality of African religion. I propose instead to suggest some unifying concepts which underlie specific beliefs, myths, symbols, and rituals. These are intended, not as conclusions, but as suggestions of areas in which further investigation may be fruitful.

Taking this approach, the first concept I would propose is that of vitality or *life-power*. In African thought true being is dynamic; "to be" is to possess the power which makes "being" possible. Tempels, whose generalizations are also based primarily on his experience among the Baluba, says that "being is that which has force." [17]   While some of Tempel's generalizations may be questioned, this one at least seems to provide a basis for further exploration.

There are many centers of power which have the potential of affecting life positively or negatively: natural phenomena, animals, mediums, spirits. Behind or beyond these there may be one central source of power. It is, however, the power manifested in human life which is most significant. Mbiti and p'Bitek, who disagree on many other things, agree that in Africa God or the gods seem to exist "for man." [18]

The second basic concept which I propose, then, is *humanism;* African religion is centered more in man than in God or in nature. Ideally, man has within his power the means for a happy and significant life.

Kenneth Kaunda, the President of Zambia, expresses and

celebrates the humanism of Africa in these words:

> To a certain extent, we in Africa have always had a gift for enjoying Man for himself. It is at the heart of our traditional culture, but now we see the possibility of extending the scale of our discovery by example to the whole world. Let the West have its Technology and Asia its Mysticism! Africa's gift to world culture must be in the realm of human relationships. The Colonialists may talk condescendingly about the things they have taught us, yet I honestly believe that we have been all the time much nearer to the heart of things that really matter than our Western teachers. After all, don't the scientists tell us that Africa was the cradle of Man? The way things are going, Africa may be the last place where Man can still be man....
>
> I believe that the Universe is basically good and that throughout it great forces are at work striving to bring about a greater unity of all living things. It is through cooperation with these forces that Man will achieve all of which he is capable.[19]

African humanism, we should note, is not individualistic; it is a communal humanism. This brings us to the third concept, that of *wholeness.* In Africa the sacred is manifested not so much by separation as by unity. It is appropriate to recall that even the English word "holy" is related to the word "whole." In Africa it is undoubtedly true that the whole is the holy. Thus man finds his fulfillment not as a separate individual but as a participant in a family and a community. Relationships with other people are of utmost significance. Troubles of almost all kinds are due to breakdowns in human relationships; the well-being of each individual depends on the preservation or restoration of these relationships.

Although the human community is primary, man is also related to the physical environment, especially to the land from which comes nourishment for life and in which the deceased members of the community are buried. As one author puts it, African society "is not only an organization of human relationships, but...includes also the relationships of people with the earth as a whole, with their own land, and with the unseen world of constructive forces and beings in which they believe."[20]

This sense of wholeness transcends time in a *continuity* which unites the present with the past and also the future. It has been suggested that Africans have a strong sense of the past but virtually none of the future.[21] Perhaps it is better to say that the future is assimilated to the past, that the two are not distinguished from each other in the same way that they are in some other cultures. *Distance from the present* is more important than *direction.* In fact, thinking of past and future as two opposite "directions" from the present is probably alien to African thought. In Kiluba, for instance, the same word, *keshya,* can be translated either "yesterday" or "tomorrow." The present is the center of time but it has meaning only in the context of a larger reality which extends outward from it, in whatever "direction." The living community is the link which unites the ancestors and the unborn generations. The idea of "reincarnation," present in some African societies, is one way of affirming the time-transcending continuity in human existence.

The four concepts of vitality, humanism, wholeness, and continuity meet in a fifth, *health.* Healing, in Africa, has to do with preservation or restoration of human vitality in the context of the community as a whole. The English word "heal," it may be noted, is also related to the words "whole" and "holy."

When I asked a Luba friend where he would begin an account of the traditional religion of his people he replied, "I would begin with the situation of a man who is ill and searching for healing."[22] He went on to suggest that on procedure for dealing with sickness is for each person in the village to bring one stick to a common fire on which food is cooked. This food is then taken to the intersection of two paths and given as an offering to whatever spirit has been offended. Here we see clearly that healing power depends on right human relationships and harmony with the whole enviornment, including the time-transcending spirit world.

The centrality of the concern for healing can be demonstrated all over sub-Saharan Africa. It appears not only in the traditional religions but also in the new "independent churches." One of the attractions of Nkamba, the "New Jerusalem" of the Kimbanguist Church in Zaïre, is the healing power found in the sacred stream and even in the sacred soil of the place where the Prophet Simon Kimbangu himself preached and *healed.* Significantly, the prophet's body is buried at Nkamba and his son is the leader of the community.

Although there is a strong practical element in African religion, it is not concerned exclusively with attempts to "get something"; it also involves *celebration* of that which is already possessed or experienced. Of course, celebration not only affirms wholeness and healing; it contributes to them. Festivals, feasts, dances, artistic expression, and the recitation of myths celebrate the communal existence and at the same time strengthen the community against evil influences. When I asked a member of the Balunde dancers among the Baluba the reason for his dancing he said at first,

"Simply for entertainment". Further discussion, however, revealed that he believed this "entertainment" served to protect and enhance the community. Thus no clear line can be drawn between the functional and celebrative elements in traditional African religion.

The approach we have taken helps us to understand the position and significance of Islam and Christianity as African religions. If one thinks of "religion" in terms of specific doctrines and practices, there obviously is considerable difference between these two religions and traditional African religions. But Islam and Christianity have been successful in Africa very largely because they have been understood in terms of the basic underlying concepts of African religion. Thus they have become "African religions" or, perhaps, new expressions of the African way of being religious. Speaking of three Christian groups and the traditional believers among the Budjga portion of the Shona people, Murphree says that each group is "best understood as a modality on a religious spectrum which they must all share. . . . Budjga religion is the complete religious spectrum itself, of which they are only related parts." [23]

Christianity and Islam make their appeal in Africa in terms of new possibilities of power, humanity, wholeness, continuity, healing, and celebration. Africans frequently see them as supplementing rather than replacing their traditional beliefs and practices. A Luba chief with an ancestral shrine in front of his house and a Luba diviner both told me that they were "Methodists." I believe they were sincere; they found in Methodist Christianity certain resources that they did not find in their traditional beliefs, but the reverse was also true. Among the Yoruba the vast majority today identify themselves either as Muslims or Christians; the vast majority also practice some aspects of their traditional religion. In a University class in religion only one out of some thirty Yoruba students thought there was anything wrong with this.

In general, Islamic leaders in Africa appear to accept this situation while Christian leaders have been more inclined to try to force a choice between the new and the old. Christianity has been appreciated as a new source of power, especially in the fields of education and medicine; there has also been resentment of attempts to destroy the old ways. One reason for the growth of many independent churches would appear to be the desire to have the best of two worlds: contact with new sources of power and, at the same time, preservation of a sense of communal wholeness.

There is also, of course, a strong movement in churches originally founded by Western missionaries toward the "Africanization" of worship, organization, and theology.[24] In fact, it has been suggested that African thought forms are closer to those of the Bible than are the thought forms of the contemporary West. Thus Christianity, as well as Islam, must be studied in its African context as an expression of the African way of being religious.

People of African descent in the Western hemisphere also appear to have preserved much of what is basic to African religion, even when they express themselves in terms of Christian belief. (As suggested above, the African heritage probably provides at least as good a base for Christianity as does any other tradition.) The study of Afro-American religion is not only significant in its own right but also can serve as an interesting and useful approach to the study of religion in Africa; the reverse is also true.

To study African religion on its own terms requires that we look at it not primarily as a collection of doctrines and rituals but as a basic attitude towards life which may be overtly expressed in a variety of ways. Because one of these basic attitudes is the sense of wholeness in life, African religion can only be understood properly through a "wholistic" approach, involving the cooperation of several disciplines.

Much of what has been said regarding the nature of African religion may also be true of religion in other cultures. As was suggested earlier, there are interesting affinities between African and Chinese traditional religion. Thus a study of African religion may contribute not only to an understanding of Africa but also to the understanding of religious phenomena as such.

The early Portuguese visitor could not identify anything "religious" in Africa because religion was so integrated into all of life. The modern student of African religions seems to face a similar difficulty but turns it into an opportunity; the very pervasiveness of the religion provides a clue both to the method of study and to the nature of the religion.

NOTES

1. Hu Shih, "Ming Chiao" (The Doctrine of Names), in *Hu Shih wen ts'un*, Shanghai, 1928, Vol. I, p. 91. Quoted in C.K. Yang, *Religion in Chinese Society*, Berkeley: University of California Press, 1967, p. 5.
2. Yang, *Religion in Chinese Society*, p. 20.
3. Colin Turnbull, *The Forest People.* New York: Clarion Books, n.d. (original copyright, 1961), p. 93.

4. African historians of religion, such as Dr. Christian Gaba, are doing this kind of work.
5. Wilfred Cantwell Smith, "Comparative Religion: Whither and Why?" in Mircea Eliade and Joseph Kitagawa, eds., *The History of Religion: Essays in Methodology*, Chicago: The University of Chicago Press.
6. *Ibid.*, p. 47.
7. *Ibid.*, p. 58.
8. *Ibid., p. 42.*
9. Ibid.
10. Okot p'Bitek, *African Religions in Western Scholarship.* Nairobi: East African Literature Bureau, 1971, p. 102.
11. Smith, "Comparative Religion: Whither and Why?", p. 55.
12. p'Bitek, *African Religions in Western Scholarship.* p. 57.
13. Mircea Eliade, *The Sacred and the Profane.* New York: Harper, 1959, p. 12.
14. p'Bitek, *African Religions in Western Scholarship,* p. 7. See also pp. 41, 46f.
15. See E. Bolaji Idowu, *Olodumare: God in Yoruba Belief.* New York: Praeger, 1963; John Mbiti, *African Religions and Philosophy.* New York: Praeger, 1969; and *Concepts of God in Africa,* New York: Praeger, 1970.
16. p'Bitek, *African Religions in Western Scholarship,* p. 47.
17. Placide Tempels, *Bantu Philosophy.* Paris: Presence Africaine, 1959, p. 35.
18. Mbiti, *African Religions and Philosophy,* p. 92; p'Bitek, *African Religions in Western Scholarship,* p.109.
19. Kenneth Kaunda and Colin Morris, *A Humanist in Africa.* Nashville: Abington Press, 1966, p. 22f.
20. Robert Parsons, *Religion in an African Society.* Leiden: E. J. Brill, 1964, p. 176.
21. Mbiti, *African Religions and Philosophy*, p. 17.
22. Dianda Kalesa, personal communication.
23. Marshall Murphree, *Christianity and the Shona.* London: The Athlone Press, 1969, p. 151.
24. See, for instance, Kwesi Dickson and Paul Ellingworth (eds.), *Biblical Revelation and African Beliefs*, Maryknoll, New York: Orbis Books, 1962; and E. Bolaji Idowu, *Towards an Indigenous Church,* London: Oxford University Press, 1965.

2

Some Aspects Of Zulu Religion

Donald M'Timkulu

A fundamental concern in the study of the sociology of Africa is to trace the factor of change. We usually confine the change we are looking for to that which is a consequence of the impact of Western culture on African societies, and we disregard the fact that change was going on within these cultures also in response to internal developments. In other words, we are not dealing with static communities, but societies which had a cultural dynamic of their own. While there are fundamental concepts which are common throughout Africa, there are also differences, sometimes minor, sometimes deeply embedded, which arise from the geographic, social, and cultural conditions in which a particular group found itself when the changes occurred.

Among the Zulus especially there are two important aspects of social change which produced distinctive social concepts which are part of their religious system. First, the Zulus were the vanguard of a large migratory movement. Not so long ago we believed the migration was from the central lakes of Africa southward, but more recent research seems to indicate that it began in the west, came right across the continent, and turned southward between the great lakes and the sea. This vast movement of peoples took place over very many centuries. Religious ideas at their deepest develop and become formalized among a settled people, as they begin to cultivate the arts of peace. In the migration of the groups sometimes referred to as the Southeastern Bantu there are indications of a change in their social systems which arose from the fact that they had been a people on the move for so many centuries. They settled here or there and then moved on; thus a constant movement has long been a feature of these societies. This is one, reason for the particular interest which the social and religious concepts of the Zulus have for us, especially in contrast to the more settled populations of West Africa. They give us interesting material for the study of what happens to a society on the move that had started with what may well have been the same kind of religious ideas as the more settled populations which remained in the homeland.

Another instrument of change in the southern Bantu situation, of which the Zulus are an example, is that at the time of their contact with Western cultures they had just gone through another cataclysmic change within themselves. That famous military genius, Shaka, in a short space of time, had succeeded in welding a multi-tribal nation out of the numerous tribes of Natal and Zululand. The very act of absorption, which was a part of the Zulus' deliberate policy, produced changes in the social structure of both the conquered and the conquerors. Whenever the Zulus moved into a new area and established themselves, the able-bodied men were immediately taken into and spread throughout the armies and the women were absorbed through marriage into the Zulu groups. Thus a new nation was born which has outlasted the military power on which it was based. The result of this hammering together of a great empire was a disruption of the old stabilities of the societies as well as a setting in motion of a mighty snowball of tribal movements throughout south and central Africa. Such a social climate is conducive neither to the growth of religious ideas nor to the creation of a philosophy of life in regard to man's relationship with the supernatural powers.

This last phrase suggests a general definition of the term "religion," which might be thought of as the creation of a philosophy of life in regard to man's relationship to the supernatural powers— the creation of the "sacred." The other aspect of religion is that which concerns man himself. What does man think of himself and of his place in the universe? To sociologists this question is basic for the development of religious ideas. When man begins to think of his place in the universe—"Who am I and what am I here for? What is the rest of the 'here' in which I am?"— he is beginning to develop religious concepts, and these are the origins of religion itself.

Let us look at the Zulus under these two aspects of the general definition we have proposed. The Zulus had an idea of a Creator, a God whom they called by several names. The most common was "the Great Great One." The Zulu language repeats the adjective to indicate the superlative in certain cases. And so Nkulunkulu, the "Great Great One," is their term for the Creator. God, after creating the world, withdrew himself from it to some extent, leaving it to go on its own momentum, so to speak. He was not constantly in touch with, or part of, Creation.

But there were certain outflows from his act of creation. God remained interested in two particular aspects of it, in relation to which he now and again became concerned and revealed himself. He was concerned first with relationships between man and man. The concept of *ubuntu,* the recognition of the other person as a person, is basic to the ethics of all the southern Bantu. They regard it as basic because it is one of the Creator God's concerns. If anyone or a group deviates too far from this basic and expected relationship of man to man, then there occurs one of the few occasions in which the Creator himself immediately intervenes.

God is also interested in the coherence of society. African religion is to a very large extent a "family" religion. The relationships within the family, within the clan, between clan and clan, and so on, are all important, and God is interested in the continuing coherence of the group so that it doesn't break up. If, for instance, we seek to use the Christian term "sin" in the context of Zulu society, we could only mean that which breaks up the coherence of the society. Something more serious than ordinary antisocial conduct would be recognized by such a term. This may be illustrated by a look at the way "murder" is treated in the Zulu legal system. When an instance of one man killing another occurs there is always careful inquiry to see whether it might be a case of justifiable homicide. When a man begins to break up the God-given coherence of society he may be removed and it is not a murder, for he has ceased to be a man. Many a time in a chief's court one will hear a defendant giving as his reason for beating or killing a man that the victim was "no man," meaning he had denied himself all the qualities of *ubuntu* and was the type of fellow who disrupts society. It might happen, then, that the fine could be simply one ox or a penalty which gives some kind of compensation to the family, but not of such an extent as a penalty for an offense against sacred human life would require. A man may lose his sacred quality if he goes beyond the bounds of humanity and begins to disrupt society.

From this interest of the Creator in what is going on in the world (from which he has become somewhat removed) three things flow. First, he is interested in the cycle of human life. For instance, he arranged death to be part of the experience of mankind. We have several stories about this. A very good one, which is still being used among people in the villages, is about the chameleon. God sent a chameleon to man on earth, with the message, "All right, man, I've heard about all your troubles. I now decree that you shall not die."

The chameleon went hesitantly along the road with the message. God didn't hear any response for a long time from mankind, because the chameleon was taking such a long time to get to the end of his journey. So God became angry and sent the lizard dwon with a new message. The lizard quickly whipped the journey through with the message, "All right, man, you shall die." Long afterward, the chameleon arrived with his message: "God says you shall not die." Then man replied, "Oh no, we'll stick with the word of the lizard." From this story comes the common saying in Zulu to express the idea, "We'll stick with what you said first of all"— the Zulus say, "We'll stick with the word of the lizard." God's directive came to man in a way which showed He was a little doubtful about the matter. Still, the arrangement of the whole cycle of the life of man is in God's hands. It is something far beyond man's control.

But God was not only interested in creating man and his cycle of life. He was also interested in seeing that man was able to live. Therefore the fertility of both soil and beast is one of God's gifts and the Zulu shares with the Christian the belief that if there is a drought he can pray to God about it. When there is a break in fertility he refers back to God since it is an area of God's continuing interest in man.

Another gift of God has to do with the making of decisions. This concept is basic and unique enough to have special names which are not used for anything else. Man is left, Zulus believe, with two "spirit forces," sometimes called "two hearts." One is called *unembeza*. This is a witness for good which exists in every man's heart. Man knows what is good because *unembeza* is there to guide him. The opposite to this is called *ubovane*— that which impels a man to act against the law of right. These are both natural in man. The Zulu in a period of indecision may say, "My one heart says, 'I should do this.' My other heart says, 'I should do the other.'" There is a constant struggle for the good in man because there are the two aspects of man, both God-given.

Fourth, God is the only one who is able to control whatever is beyond man's control. The Zulu believes that he lives in the midst of forces, some of which he can control and many others which he cannot. To refer to them by the phrase "supernatural forces" would be a poor translation of what is meant. The issue is confused if it is assumed that magic and religion are the same in traditional society or, at least, among the Zulus. Rather, magic is a misuse of forces within the supernatural world, and this misuse is not in God's hands at all. God himself has other controls here. That which is beyond man's control, that which is present in the great crises of life, is always in God's hands. When there is a tremendous crisis, such as floods all over the country so that hundreds of people die, or when there is drought and starvation, the Zulu does not turn to the manipulator of charms or to the "witch doctor."* He turns to the diviner, who, as a real "shaman," has God-given spiritual forces to make contacts with Him and with the ancestors. This is the kind of man who is sometimes able to lead the total society to particular acts of reconciliation when such tremendous crises take place. In Zulu thinking there is a kind of fatalism which is part of the outlook on life. There may occur events one cannot do anything about or even understand at all; these are regarded as acts of God. The Zulu lapses into fatalism about them. Even the ancestors can do nothing, for it is the Great Great One himself acting, perhaps out of his anger against the total society. One just doesn't know, for God is not always very consistent, as can be seen in the story about life and death. Then one just leaves matters as they are and it is one's duty to accept what has happened either as a chastisement from God for some reason or other, or simply as an incomprehensible anger from the Great Great One.

All these aspects of the outflow of God's interest in man provide a context in which the future life in relationship to God may be understood. In Zulu religious thinking there is a belief that man is both flesh and spirit. The spirit in him is something that endures, is indestructible, and lives after death. This ontology of man, as composed of body and spirit, is basic to the African's acceptance of dreams. Dreams are the context in which the spirit, or soul, or shadow, sometimes leaves the body and goes to live temporarily in other sections of the spiritual world from which it may then bring back a message. Dreams can thus be very important sources of information and guidance; they provide one situation in which living human beings have contact with the spirit world.

Those who have died are not subject to the limitations of this world; because the spirit can leave the body and take on a more strictly spiritual existence it has a great deal more power than humans have in ordinary existence. The connotations of the word "spirit" or "soul" are different for the Zulu than for the Christian who uses the same word. The Zulus believe that the spirit or, one

---

* This is a phrase we ought not to use because it mixes two very different ideas. The witch is the man who misuses supernatural forces in dangerous and evil ways, while the doctor is one who heals.

might say, the "breath," only leaves the body at some time after death. In true Zulu fashion when we mean that the man is really dead we say "the spirit has gone out." It has then left its bodily habitation and gone to live in the spirit world. It is not clear just where this world is. As part of the Christian intrusion people have now and again thought of it as "up in the heavens," but Zulus mean no more than "just around," wherever this may be.

There is no conception at all that the spirit in any way suffers after death for actions in its bodily life. It is thought, however, to leave the body with a large part of its personality intact. If there is a fractious, angry father who dies, one expects him to be a rather fractious, angry ancestor. Families who have had a crusty old gentleman as their head become particularly careful in making certain that after he is dead he is not annoyed, because he always was a man who got annoyed easily; on the other hand, a more placid head of a family would not arouse so much concern among his descendants since he always was a jolly fellow with whom it was easy to deal.

One aspect of life after death is that one carries one's human personality forward into the next life, and another is that the common Zulu village is recreated in its social organization in the next world. The whole social organization in terms of relationships of people is carried on there, including the prestige and standing of one group in relation to another. This has certain repercussions. For instance, in the matter of what is often called "ancestor worship,"* those who have little status in this life would have little status in the next. This would include younger sons within the family or an older son who had not married.

One of the important concerns of the Zulus is that a person ought to get married so that his name will be carried on. They often use the phrase "carrying on my name." By this they mean more than merely the bearing of one's name by future descendants. It expresses a concern that if a man were to leave this world without leaving behind any progeny he would have no status in the spirit world. Therefore it is a tremendous responsibility for a son to get married in order to make sure that his father has status when he goes into the other world, for without children one is not able to "carry on one's name."

It is interesting to note that this way of thinking makes it difficult for the Zulu to understand what the Christians mean by "eternal

*The term must be used with some care, for ancestors are always to be "remembered" with "veneration." This is the major part of the ritual and not "worship."

life." For them, "eternal life," is this continuum of life between the present state in the body and that in the spirit world. This leads us to a fundamental concept of Zulu society and of African societies elsewere: society is one and consists of the living and the dead; the community is a continuum without a break. The interest of the elders in their children not only springs from this concern for the welfare of the children themselves but also from a concern for their own welfare and the welfare of their ancestors who are now dead. They are concerned with the continuance of life of both the dead and the living as one, and even the continuance of those who are yet unborn. This is why it is such a catastrophe in Zulu society when a wife is infertile, since one could not then expect the "spirit" part of one's self to be carried through. A break in the line has occurred.

This tremendous life force of the dead has an effect not only in the carrying on of the name; sometimes the personality of the dead ancestor can be carried on. There is a kind of reincarnation in Zulu religion. It isn't reincarnation as the Greeks or Hindus understand it, but it is an impress of the personality of the dead ancestor. In Western society one might look at a child and say, "He's the very image of his father." But in Zulu society one waits until the child has a personality to talk about. It is only when the young man begins to do things that one might begin to say, "He really is his father." There can be a personality so strong in the ancestor that it reincarnates itself in the next generation. This is another reason why one must have children: for a continuum of life. Sometimes the personality of the ancestor could be looking for a descendant through whom the particular qualities which made him the man he was can be carried on within the family. An interesting thing that may happen with a chief, for instance, is that the impress of the personality of the ancestor is not in the eldest son. It can be in any one of his progeny, so that in conflicts over succession to the chiefship the elders might say, "This is the man who is his father, and not that fellow."

In considering these general aspects of Zulu religion we must go further into the question of so called "ancestor worship" since it is at the central core of their religious ideas. It consists really in the relationships of the living and their departed senior relatives. Not everybody who dies, not even all older people, are revered as ancestors. It is only those who have descendants and who are senior heads of families who may have this status. For instance, one of the reasons for the veneration of a living grandfather is the fact that he is sure to join the important group of ancestors simply because he is a grandfather. When he dies, he is still the head of a unit which is continuing. The spirits of the departed, therefore, to whom divine functions are attributed, are selected spirits rather than all of them, and it is these to whom the African turns with any plea for help when his own strength has reached its limits, or when he is faced with crisis factors in his life or work over which he has no control. The belief in ancestral spirits who afford this possibility is both the backbone and content of the religion of all African tribes. The details of the ritual may vary from tribe to tribe, but since the concept is basically identical it is one reason we may speak of African religion rather than African religions.

These ancestral spirits are the extra-human forces which are personal, and a person lives in intimate contact with these extrasensory forces. They must be consulted on all important occasions. One must be very watchful about their manifestation in any form, lest one bring about personal or community disaster. The increase of power which the departed spirit has, because it is in closer contact with the life forces than it was during its bodily life, is always used for the sake of the community or of the society as a whole. The ancestor is not interested only in the family of his own particular descendants, but in this family as part of a continuing society, among both the living and the dead.

This importance of "ancestor worship" as a matter of community welfare means it is more than simply a matter of individual protection. There are anthropologists and church-related writers who in discussing ancestor worship emphasize the aspect of protection, citing the individual who wears a charm in the belief that he will escape some individual injury. This may occur, but it is a deflection of ancestor worship, a misuse of it, even in terms of the individual himself. It would be like the Christian who never prays at all except when he is in some trouble which affects him personally and not society as a whole. This deflection does occur, but in large measure ancestor worship is always a communal affair.

Ancestor worship is concerned with society, with the total group, and any deviation by the individual becomes dangerous for the whole group because it affects everyone. The group's harmony may be disturbed by a single person, as for example when a calamity such as a blight on the crops is regarded as the result of one person's deviance. It then becomes important to reconcile the whole community— important enough to call home the head of the family who, in the tremendous mobility in Africa these days, may be working 800 or more miles away. Without him the ceremony would have no meaning for the total community of the living and the dead.

There are three kinds of rites, occasions of special ritual remembering, which are undertaken in ancestor worship. The first has to do with concerns which may arise in the daily round of life. The individual lives his religion in Africa; it is not something to which he is converted. The ancestors are interested in whatever is being done in the continuing processes of life. Therefore it may be continually necessary to make certain they are not annoyed by anything going on at any time. In some families, to be sure, there may be very little reference to the ancestors until some crisis takes place, but in others, because of a current need or because of the personality of particular ancestors, there is continual reference to them in daily life. It becomes a matter of importance that they be remembered and be made to feel they are still a continuing part of the family. If they have been neglected they may "turn their backs" on the living so that they no longer use their powers of mediation or their own intensive forces to make certain there is harmony and well being within the family. Certain rites of propitiation and reconciliation are then necessary in order to get them to "turn their faces" once more toward the living. These are carried out either by the head of the family or, in important cases, by the head of the clan or even the tribal "shaman," who has the most detailed knowledge of the spirits.

There are also rites which are connected with the great crises of personal development. A large part of African worship is concerned with rites of birth, puberty, marriage, and death, the four great passages of life. These are always surrounded with a great deal of ceremony appropriate to the occasion, and the whole family or the whole socity or village must directly participate in them.

Third, there are rites connected with some calamity or suffering on a national scale. These too are part of the rites of worship within the ancestor group.

Finally, in gaining perspective on the role of ancestor worship, one should take account of the fact, as is not always done by scholars, that the ancestors are not in themselves either omniscient or omnipresent. In fact, now and again they must be "awakened." They may even get lost or go to the wrong place. This helps us to understand why the Zulu is so unwilling to leave what he calls his "ancestor's graves." If he moves away and then begins to give his offerings and rites, the ancestor may not know him, because he has changed locality and moved to areas unknown by the ancestors.

Though they have great power since they are in contact with life forces, this power depends on being remembered. Zulus think of Nkulunkulu as having a court somewhat like the courts of Zulu kings, and the hierarchy of prestige and standing in it is as severely maintained as it is in Zulu military life.* The place the ancestor takes in this court depends on how much remembrance he is effectively receiving. The ancestor will resent any loss of status in the spirit world and will work out his anger by withholding his good will and protection from his descendants.

This has a bearing on understanding some of the disruptive consequences of the great mobility which industrialization has brought about in modern Africa. Two may be mentioned. The first is the widespread breakdown in the total concept of the continuum family. The fact that the core of the family is not located in one place where the generations can easily get together at any time and perform the necessary worship rites has made for a breakdown in the social structure of the extended family system which has its roots in this religious concept. To the extent that it is possible for a man to work in a distant place and go back home, he may still try to keep this tradition alive; nonetheless there has been, as a consequence of labor policies, serious erosion of the solidarity of the family and its religious life. This is partly the cause of what has often been referred to as a sense of confusion in the urbanized African. He has a sense of loss, of feeling that he is not secure, not sure of himself. The roots of his security, which depend on a feeling that the world is under control, that he is not on his own but a part of a secure system, have been cut.

This is one of the reasons for the widespread growth in the belief in charms in urbanized African society. In the ordinary traditional society charms are really not very important because people have a sense that things are under control and therefore they do not have to be constantly worried about protecting themselves. Once, however, a person is in a situation where he knows that, if troubles come, he cannot immediately get the necessary means to save himself, he looks for something which can help. This may be illustrated by the birth ceremonies among many urbanized Zulus who cannot go through all the old rituals having roots in the traditional way of life. For instance, the feeling is rife among semi-urbanized Zulus that babies must not be brought into large groups too soon or they will pick up all sort of diseases. In the old society this did not matter, for

*Zulu kings were traditionally regarded as inaccessible and remote from the ordinary man.

the necessary birth rituals were all undertaken within the extended family unit with little chance of outside and dangerous forces being brought in. But the new Christian urbanized Zulu goes to an *inyanga* (the doctor who can control evil forces) and says, "I'm going to baptize my child in two weeks' time and you know what happens when you have large crowds. Can you do something?" The result is a ceremony among the urbanized called "smoking the child," *nkutungisa.* The *inyanga* puts certain charms in an open bowl and the fumes are allowed to envelope the child for a short period, the child being moved up and down. This was not done in the old society. It is a new form of protection for a new need which has arisen because Christianity demands infant baptism in the presence of large congregations composed of strangers.

The result is not a return to old patterns, but rather a search in the new situation for the old securities, now adapted to fit new conditions. It is an instance of a society building itself and adapting to a changed environment. Though the change has occurred as a result of the impact of Western culture, it indicates a going forward and not a going back.

One of the significant phenomena in the changing African situation during the last twenty to twenty-five years has been the tremendous growth of what have variously been called separatist churches, independent churches, or messianic movements. Let us look at an instance of this development in the southeastern part of the continent and see what some of its significant aspects are and what comparisons are possible to similar phenomena elsewhere.

In much of the discussion about "indigenous churches" there is expressed a concern to relate the Christian church to its African environment. The concern is often to find ways in which the church can take on more of an African character in its physical and conceptual aspects. "Indigenization" here means the church's search for renewal in African soil. Many of the so-called separatist churches in Africa are of this type. An effort is made by a group or by one man, generally called a prophet, to break away in search for greater African identification. In the process a church is formed which is more African in spirit and in its procedures, but it is still a Christian church trying to put on new garments.

An interesting and fruitful approach to the study of separatist churches was first made by Sundkler in his book *Bantu Prophets.* He suggested that there is an aspect of these separatist churches which does not arise from a desire for "indigenization," but from what he calls "deprivation." According to this view, the rise of religious movements in the context of culture contact can be attributed to stress and deprivation resulting from this contact. This becomes applicable not only to the growing number of separatist churches in Africa but also to all sorts of nationalistic movements. The movement away from the established church in this respect becomes an aspect of the rise of national consciousness among a people living under conditions of stress and deprivation within a dominant and overpowering culture.

In many such situations conditions may prevail which engender, among individuals and groups, such a sense of deprivation as to give rise not only to a complete rejection of old patterns but to lead to the creation of something new. In situations of extreme deprivation, when it begins to be felt that improvement is effectively blocked and there is no obvious means of alleviating or terminating deprivation, there occurs a rebellion of the human spirit. In less extreme situations man tends to buttress his own sense of identity by falling back on a belief in a glorious past which has been lost, or by fashioning a set of hopes for the future which are not likely to be realized.

Such movements may arise within the church, or within society as a whole. They may be called by various names, but all of them belong to the same genre. The hope for the future or the remembrance of the past may be entirely subjective and nonfactual; it is enough that people think them to be true. "We Zulus think we are wonderful fellows. Other people may not think so, but we think we are." As Zulu schoolboys, when hearing from a white history teacher that Shaka was "that great murderer who killed women and children," we would raise a great murmur of dissent. That was not the picture we had of "Shaka, the builder of the nation." We thought he was a marvelous man who unified the people and established a great empire. In the present-day conditions of the Zulus as a subject people, this was a glorious past to remember. Could the Zulus recover their positive glory? All indications seem to be against it. Within a society when such hopes for the future begin to get dimmer and dimmer, the response is to find identity and dignity through the one institution which would not be subject to an immediate political crackdown— the creation of a separatist church with its roots deep in the past.

One clear illustration of this kind of development is a separatist group in South Africa called the "Shembites." Initially they called themselves the "people of Shembe," rather than a "Shembe church." This group is not a breakaway from anything at all, which is an interesting aspect of it. It began in the early 1930's when people were beginning to feel the effects of the Great Depression, especially in the urban areas. In the early years of the decade the African people were beginning to move more and more into jobs made possible by a degree of industrial development in South Africa. They had begun to hope for an improving economic base which would provide a better future. But then came the frost of the depression and these hopes were killed.

At this time a man called Shembe who had been working on the farms and in the small town areas of the Free State found himself "called" to go back to his people in Natal, the home of the Zulus, to give them the teachings which had come to him as part of his dreams.

His particular emphasis was to find some salvation for his people during the difficult times. He had one great gift which came to him when he received the dream message from God. This was the gift of healing. Not only Africans but also whites and Indians would come to him and he would "lay hands" on their sick, breaking through racial differences. Shembe as a nominal Christian was struck by the similarity of his power of healing to that of Jesus. This convinced him even more of the importance of the message he had received in his dream. Initially his movement contained several aspects of the traditional prophet movements. His concern, however, was not so much to preach the gospel or to establish a new Church as to provide a measure of economic security for his people. The essential basis of the Shembe group was a cooperative one. They banded together, first of all, to buy land in order to gain more security at a time when individual purchase of land was being steadily denied to Africans. They would also live in a new way as a communal group.

It is interesting that they did not go back to the New Testament apostles as models. Theirs was an entirely new structure centered in the kind of world that Shembe knew well — the world of employment. His common sharing meant a pooling of wages. Everyone living in the common village worked and contributed his wages and the head of this common family was able to buy land which then the members of the group really owned. They would not be pushed around by the white man any more: The community had a religious structure in which Shembe emphasized living together on the basis of *ubuntu*; but, even more, he began to stress aspects closely linked to the urban situation which he knew. He sought to move out of the city as soon as possible because there was a feeling that "the town cannot be home." Just at this time South Africa had passed a series of acts making it impossible for any African to buy property in town. This was the infamous Urban Areas act which to a large extent established *apartheid* long before it became an official policy. The main effect of this was to close the African out of the process of urbanization by denying him property rights in the cities. In the late 1920's this act had been amended in various ways which tightened this exclusion. In 1927 there had also been passed the Color Bar Act which made it possible to exclude Africans from skilled jobs.

It was for this mounting deprivation during the decade before that the Shembe movement sought to provide an answer. The Shembites looked for a place outside the city because there they could still buy land which would be home for them. They would establish a community which would enable them to look after themselves. As a matter of fact, as the sect began to grow they not only bought the land on which they lived but also farms all over which they began to work for themselves. Belonging to this community gave the individual a sense of economic security but, even more, it gave him a sense of pride and achievement because he had been able to do this all on his own against tremendous odds.

This interesting reaction to deprivation is an exact counterpart to the development of Father Divine in the United States at about the same period. Shembe, seeking security and a future, established hope in terms of a rural corporate community, while Father Divine sought it in the urban situation, providing through a sharing of wages the things which the individual could not get for himself, such as his famous "Sunday chicken dinners" for the poor, his hotels and his lakeside resorts. The differences lay mainly in the nature of the societies within which each of these men was working. Both of them were responses to deprivation giving hope for the future to their people at a time when they had begun to believe there was no hope.

The Shembe movement, though it had an economic base, still had to develop within a religious setting. In this also may be seen a parallel to the Father Divine movement. The most important conclusion Shembe had drawn from his reading of the Bible was the hope of establishing a community of equals who would be concerned with a common destiny. This goes back also to the African concept of the worth of man and his work, and the conviction that the coherence of society must never be broken. Shembe saw that it had been broken, and that people must again work together to be able to produce. Entry into this society was purely on the terms of being willing to put wages into the hands of the "Father," as he had come to be called.

He was always called "Baba," "Father," and never "prophet," for this was going to be a large new family which, like the old family, would give a sense of security, of purpose, and of a future. He used the Christian religion at this point, though it is interesting to note that while the concept of a common people is very important in the New Testament, he drew his ideas mainly from the Old Testament. One finds that in many of these prophet groups the concepts of the good life as given by Jesus and particularly the concept of the Holy Spirit as a guide and as part of the Holy Trinity present so many difficulties that they tend to ignore the New Testament while interpreting very literally the Old Testament.

Thus, the religious ideas that undergirded the Shembite movement and bound its people together were mainly from the Old Testament. A large part of Shembe's exhortations to the people was in terms of a new Moses who was creating a new people of Israel. At one time they even called themselves "Israelites," until there was another group with this name which got into serious conflict with government, not many years after the Shembites began.

The Shembe movement grew phenomenally, particularly in the thirties and forties and even into the fifties. It spread especially among semi-urbanized groups. The ordinary Zulu out in the kraal, who was still able to have his land from his chief where he could grow sufficient crops and have sufficient cattle, and whose sons could go to the city to work and bring in money to buy still more cattle, was very satisfied with things as they were. The politicians, for instance, have found such people very difficult to deal with, for they will not believe that they are oppressed! It was among the urbanized and semi-urbanized, who had a strong sense of deprivation and who were prepared to make sacrifices to correct this wrong, whether in political, national, or church life, that the spearpoint of the development of the people would be found.

Another aspect of these movements is that they are shunned by the educated classes. They are movements of the semi-educated and semi-urbanized. A kind of prestige discrimination takes place so that within them there arises what we may call a "natural" leadership. The leaders do not have the education or the training that is comparable to that of the leaders in other spheres of society. They are men who have a natural wisdon of their own and to a large extent the growth of the movement depends on this. The educated classes generally think of indigenous church movements as something beneath them and as a waste of "good material" which could be used for national regeneration, though they do take a certain amount of pride in the new societies that these movements create.

The Shembe movement now has a very large membership; estimates of its size vary from 120,000 to 150,000. They have much land, and after the depression they even put up their own stores and their own cooperative units for buying fertilizer, seed, etc. They were very progressive due to their policy of employing the educated people to run their economic enterprises. The Shembites themselves, or at least Father Shembe, did not stress education for his people, although many of them (including Father Shembe himself) did send their sons to schools and colleges.

An interesting issue was raised when his eldest son, who was a university graduate, wanted to come back and be the leader after his father's death. While his father was still alive he remained a Shembite but took a teaching job. He would go back home occasionally for the great festivals but did not otherwise participate in the group life at this time. He expected his main job would be to organize and look after the economic side of the movement while the "natural" leaders would look after the religious side of it. But when his father died he soon found this easy division of leadership did not work. During Shembe's lifetime it had already become obvious that the son, though quite a worthy person in many ways, lacked the charismatic gifts of his father; nor could he be the medium through which his father could speak after his death. New mediums had to arise. They were women, called "angels," who began to say they could hear the vibrations of Father Shembe. The younger Shembe himself did not believe this but the pressures on him were heavy. It was important for the group to feel that the great strong figure of the Father was still with them and so he had to accept the "angels" even though conflicts began to arise.

Although the Shembe group could create a new society with economic securities and social solidarity, it incorporated into its beliefs a large part of the beliefs of the old traditional society. One of these was the belief in the great power of the ancestors. According to tradition Shembe after his death would be a powerful ancestral spirit and it was expected that he would continue to be the guide and the power which directed the whole society. The "angels," therefore, fulfilled an essential role as the channels of communication.

For a time the son had resisted the pressures on him, some of which took the form of seeking to make him take a second wife (polygamy being an approved pattern within the group). He already had a wife, but members of the group felt he should have more wives so that the spirit of the father could be in many more children. About a year after the father died, the angels reported a message from Father Shembe urging him to take a second wife. Six months later, when he had done little about it, an angel repeated the message, adding, "The Spirit of Father Shembe commands you to marry me." These pressures toward the ways of the old society from which the religious basis of the new society derived its strength led the educated son to marry not one but at least five more wives.

Another aspect of the Shembites' interaction with the wider society has to do with their relation to the Christian tradition. As was stated above, Shembe's basic religious ideas were almost all from the Old Testament. So much was this the case that at the beginning they did not even celebrate Good Friday and Easter. They did however, celebrate Christmas because it was an important national holiday. But the dream visions of Father Shembe had begun during Good Friday week, so the group used to go out into the countryside annually, thousands of them in their white robes, to celebrate the great day of the anointing of the prophet. With the growth of education and the influence of some elders of the group who had a Christian background, there began to be a certain amount of conflict. The feeling grew that they ought to give some place to Jesus Christ in their teachings.

This was something that came in almost as an afterthought, but some interesting changes took place. First, the star looking very much like the Star of David, with which they had marked all their great villages, was quietly replaced by a cross. The great festival when they went up into the mountains to celebrate the anointing of the prophet began to incorporate aspects of the Christian Easter festival, and they began to baptize their converts by total immersion. Mainly for political reasons (in order to be registered as a religious organization by the government) they now call themselves the Zulu National Baptist Church.

Many of these changes were already taking place during Father Shembe's lifetime. It would seem that many of them came about as a result, not so much of outside pressure, as of a wish to be accepted by other churches, to have "standing" with them. Contributing factors were the apartheid laws which led to their desire to be recognized as a religious and not a political or economic group.

Several elements of continuity with the earlier society may be mentioned in addition to those already given. They have continued the kind of worship service instituted among the early Shembites. The worship service consists entirely of dances and was held in earlier days on a Saturday, though now it has been shifted to Sunday. Father Shembe organized the people into various groups: the married men, the young men, the married women and the marriageable maids, and finally young girls and boys, all in different uniforms. They performed ritual dances which began at eight o'clock in the morning and carried on through the day into the late afternoon. The whole village would get into the act with the drummers and dancers all in a coordinated disciplined movement. Father Shembe in instituting this form of worship drew support from the Old Testament "Rejoice before the Lord."

A great deal of teaching took place in smaller groups led by the elders. In fact, the old village ways remained so much a prototype within the group that even the question of who gets married to whom was decided, or at least had to be approved, by Father Shembe himself. The dances of the marriageable groups were the usual occasions for matchmaking.

The drift toward the incorporation of the teachings of the New Testament has continued. In talks that are given to small groups there are now texts used from the New Testament, unknown twenty years ago, and the Shembites are even thinking of sending promising young men preparing to be elders off to Bible schools.

What is happening is that there is movement here from a society whose basic ends were social improvement into a religious organization. In their latter days the Shembites are beginning to look, in some aspects, very much like the usual separatist church. The development of this group thus serves as one illustration of the relationship between religious and social change in African society.

3

The View from Kasongo Niembo
Newell S. Booth, Jr.

"Kasongo Niembo" is one of the two major kingdoms of the Baluba Katanga or Baluba Shankadji; it is a title that may be used to refer to the king as well as to the land comprising the kingdom. The capital, or residence of the king, Kinkunki, is located near Kamina, the major commercial and transportation center of the north Shaba (Katanga) area of the Republic of Zaïre (Congo). It lies about nine degrees south of the equator in an area of grasslands and forests, cut by the many streams and rivers which flow into the upper Lualaba and thus eventually into the Zaïre (Congo). Rainfall is plentiful from October through April; by July everything is dry and fires race through the tall grass.

The Baluba live in villages, usually composed of members of several patrilineal families. The traditional economy is based on subsistence agriculture, with cassava as the staple crop. Because the soil is relatively poor and quickly exhausted, fields are moved frequently and traditionally villages were relocated about every twenty years. Hunting, fishing, weaving grasscloth, wood carving, pottery, and iron working also contributed to the economy.

Kasongo Niembo is in the heart of Bantu-speaking southern Africa. According to Guthrie, it is in Kiluba (the language of the Baluba), and in the languages of some neighboring peoples, that the highest percentage of common Bantu roots is found. He concludes that it was in this area, "the bush country to the south of the equatorial forest midway between the two coasts," that "Proto-Bantu" was spoken, and that this was the center from which the Bantu-speaking peoples dispersed.[1] Although there are problems with this theory, at least it can be said that the territory of Kasongo Niembo is in a region that has as good a claim as any to be "typically Bantu."

Archeological excavations have provided evidence of people very much like the present-day Baluba living in the same area as early as the eighth or ninth century.[2] The Baluba themselves tell of Kiubakaubaka (the great builder) and Kibumbabumba (the great potter), the first man and woman, who lived at some indefinite time in the past. According to other Baluba the first man was Kyomba, to whom the Creator gave the knowledge of fire and of agriculture.[3]

The really significant beginning for the Baluba, however, was the founding of the Luba empire.[4] Historians generally suggest some time around 1600 as a likely date for this event, but the Luba traditions, while undoubtedly containing historical information, are more concerned with significant relationships and the validation of roles and customs.

The story begins with a chief named Nkongolo or Nkongolo-Mwamba. This is the name of a dual spirit, dwelling in two serpents, one male and one female, who live in different rivers but on occasion come together in the sky forming the rainbow, also known as Nkongolo. The child Nkongolo is said to have received this name because the rainbow-serpent spirits were responsible for his birth or because of his reddish color.

By cunning and violence Nkongolo established his rule over a considerable area, but he lacked noble blood and noble qualities. These were brought by Mbidi Kiluwe ("Mbidi the Hunter"), the son of a chief somewhere to the east, who wandered into Nkongolo's territory, married his sisters, and departed, leaving them pregnant. His son, Nkongolo's nephew, Kalala Ilunga ("Ilunga the Conqueror"), after a series of adventures, defeated and killed his uncle, and then extended his empire. The defeated Nkongolo became a guardian spirit of the new dynasty but its noble blood and customs were derived from Mbidi Kiluwe, who is said to have been "the first Muluba." The *balopwe* or "kings" of the Baluba result from this union of two traditions. Some of the stories of the founding of the empire may also reflect the transition from a matrilineal to a patrilineal society.

The root -*luba* is found in the verb *kuluba,* which means to be lost or deceived. One explanation is that Mbidi Kiluwe and his associates were "lost," separated from their place of origin and strangers in a new land. Thus they were *Baluba,* the "lost ones." The name is still understood to refer in the strictest sense to the king and the nobility associated with his court. In a more general sense it has come to be applied to all the inhabitants of the area which came under the rule of the descendents or associates of Kalala Ilunga.

It is clear that the Baluba are not all of one ancestry but "an agglomeration of elements which have acquired, under the influence of various factors, a certain unity of culture and language." [5] They are closely related to the Basonge to the north, the Aruund' ("Balunda") to the west, and the Balamba and Babemba to south and east. Thus the Baluba are part of a larger group of peoples in southern Zaïre, eastern Angola, and northern Zambia with interrelated traditions and customs. In many areas linguistic and cultural transitions are gradual rather than abrupt so that clear boundaries are not easily drawn. [6]

This paper is based on first-hand information from the area around Kamina and from the territory of the Bene Nsamba to the southwest, supplemented by written sources, some unpublished, from various Luba areas, and from closely related neighboring groups.

When I asked Dianda Kalesa where he would begin in giving an account of the traditional religion of his people, he said, "With the situation of a man who is ill and searching for healing." Certainly the problem of sickness and health provides a significant unifying theme for our study. By "health," of course, more is meant than simply the opposite of physical disease, although this is an important part of it. Also included are healing— or "wholeness"— of mind and spirit and of the society.

Father Placide Tempels, whose work *Bantu Philosophy* is based largely on his experience among the Baluba, states that the essence of Bantu religion has to do with "a practical solution of the great problem of humanity, the problem of life and death, of salvation or destruction." [7]

My father, who lived for a number of years among the Bene Nsamba, put it this way:

> The Bene Nsamba find themselves surrounded by too many troubles. There are pain, sickness and death. The crops fail. The hunt is not successful. The presence or absence of certain phenomena of nature brings disaster. Other people are hostile. There is so much to fear. In religion they seek the help of unseen forces in averting or overcoming these calamities. There is so much mystery which cannot be explained. Causes are not evident for the effects which are seen. Religion gives courage to face these unknown mysteries of life and death....
>
> To the Bene Nsamba religion is a means of getting what they want. In groups the people ask the spirits for victory in conflict, for rain, for fertility in land and animals, for salvation from diseases and wild beasts, for successful hunting and fishing, for the right

choices in communal life as to building sites, succession of rulers, etc. As individuals they seek boons from the Spirits in deliverance from all sorts of ills and in success with every imaginable kind of venture. [8]

We should note that one of the most meaningful words in Kiluba, *bwanga* (plural, *manga*), is usually translated as "medicine." This is a correct translation if we remember that the Luba concept of medicine is broader than that of the modern West. *Bwanga* can refer to almost any kind of power available to achieve some human purpose. It is the power which is effective in counteracting disharmony or, sometimes, in a negative way, power which disrupts harmony.

Tempels suggests that *bwanga* may be translated as "magical remedy," but goes on to point out that what we call "magic" is to the Baluba "nothing but setting to work natural forces placed at the disposal of man by God to strengthen man's vital energy."[9] It is an attempt to control the environment for human purposes. Jason Sendwe defines *bwanga* as "all substances intended to heal or relieve human beings" and goes on to say that "Bwanga is the primordial ideal for the African, for the prolongation of his earthly existence."[10] Any object or action which can be used either to enhance or to diminish human life may be called *bwanga*. The function of *bwanga* is that of "supporting and fusing together or breaking up and splitting asunder whole sections of Luba society."[11]

The religion of the Baluba is thus primarily concerned with life and with the power that protects and enhances life, not only the life of the individual but especially the life of the community. If religion is defined in terms of "ultimate concern," we may say that for the Baluba this is focused on the enhancement of human existence rather than on the natural world or on the divine. A Luba scholar states that "The Bantu start from the principle of life and existence in order to analyze their philosophical conceptions."[12] He is here speaking of *human* life, supporting the view that Luba religion is best understood as a form of religious humanism.

It is not, however, an individualistic humanism but a social or communal humanism, a concern for the enhancement of human values in the context of family, tribe, or nation. Furthermore, although the human factor is preeminent, the community cannot be separated from the total environment in which it exists.

Bantu psychology cannot conceive a man as an individual existing by himself, as unrelated to the animate and inanimate forces surrounding him. It is not sufficient to say he is a social being; he feels himself a vital force in actual intimate and permanent rapport with other forces—a vital force both influenced by and influencing them.[13]

"Man" stands at the center of things; he participates both in nature and in supernature, both in the material and the spiritual. He is aware of a "fundamental unîty underlying and conditioning the many forms and shapes of reality as a whole."[14] A person cannot separate himself from this unity and his religion involves right relationships with it. These relationships, however, are not ends in themselves, they are means toward the enhancement of human life.

The Kiluba word usually translated "person" or "man" is *muntu*, composed of the root *-ntu* preceded by *mu-*, the singular prefix of the first class of nouns. The plural prefix is *ba-*, giving *bantu*, the word now used to designate the speakers of the large family of languages which includes Kiluba.

There has been considerable discussion of the meaning of the root *-ntu*, based on the writings of Father Placide Tempels, the Abbé Alexis Kagame, and Janheinz Jahn. It is first necessary to observe that the root is found not only in *muntu* and *bantu* but also in *kintu* (plural, *bintu*) meaning "thing," or "inanimate object," in *buntu*, meaning "humanity" or "manliness," in *pantu* (or *hantu*) which has a prepositional sense suggesting "place where," and in other combinations. The question of the meaning of *-ntu* would not normally be asked by the ordinary Muluba, for it is not properly a "word" by itself, apart from its determinative prefixes. Yet we must not deny the African philosopher the right to draw out the theoretical implications of his speech. One Muluba puts it this way:

> The particle 'ntu' is the key to the arch of Bantu philosophy, theology, and politics. It has an ontological meaning and signifies 'being,' 'existence,' or 'that which exists...' ntu is the vital element possessed by every being.[15]

Tempels says that *muntu* signifies "vital force, endowed with intelligence and will."[16] If *-ntu* means "being," it must be understood as dynamic— "being" as energy or force.

> The Bantu speak, act, live as if, for them, beings were forces....Force is the nature of being, force is being, being is force.[17]

Muntu, then, is "human being," not in a static, completed sense, but in an active, dynamic sense. If it is true that "Existentialism is the view that the verb 'to be' is transitive,"[18] then in this sense, at least, the Baluba are existentialists; "to be" is not only to exist but to act.

Here, perhaps, is the basis of the statement that the central theme of Bantu philosophy is the contrast between life and death.[19] At the risk of pushing speculation too far we might suggest that life is an activity, while death is only a state or condition, lacking dynamic quality. This is consistent with Sendwe's insistence that the dead are not *bantu,* they lack the quality of active existence:

> The term 'muntu' is never applied to the dead. It designates living human beings, and only these. It is the opposite of the noun 'mufu' [the dead]. [20]

Sendwe takes this position in direct opposition to Tempels' view that *muntu* is the inner self, that which is eternal in man, which at death is separated from the body.[21]   Other Baluba generally support Sendwe's view against that of Tempels, and we should note that even Tempels observes that while "the dead also live . . . theirs is a diminished life with reduced vital energy." [22]

Muntu—person—differs from all other beings in having a "spirit," *muya.* This word also means "breath," and can be used to refer to the steam from a kettle. [23] When a person dies it is essentially the same thing to say that his breath has left him and that his spirit has left. When *muya* departs one ceases to be Muntu and becomes *mufu,* a dead person, for "he no longer has the strength to dwell in the world of the living." [24] *Muya* is present only in the living, it is a quality of *muntu.* Neither a corpse nor a disembodied spirit is *muntu,* for *muntu* is a unity of *ngitu,* "body," and *muya,* "spirit" or "breath."

Muntu properly refers only to one who is whole or healthy. A sexually impotent person is not *muntu* but *mufu,*[25] which reminds us that for the Baluba the most significant thing about a person is his participation in the continuity of the community. One who does not or cannot so participate is, for all practical purposes, "dead"; he is not in the true sense *muntu.* Neither is a deformed or handicapped person *muntu* in the full sense. Such a person "is classed among the *bintu*—things" and "is designated by the name of the infirmity of which he is a victim." [26]   It is also doubtful whether a person of radically different appearance or habits, such as a European, is properly termed *muntu.*

Sendwe maintains that the Baluba have a monistic view of man; "the 'muntu' forms an indivisible whole.".[27] He does, however, have certain distinguishable aspects, namely: *ngitu,* "the body"; *nenyi,* "wisdom"; *tunango,* "intelligence"; *dishima,* literally, "the liver," but used as we use "heart"; *muya*, "the soul" or "the breath"; and *mwelevwe*, "the shadow." This latter is divided into the external shadow, which is a projection of the living person, and the "life-shadow" which survives death (and is hardly distinguishable from *muya*, the soul).[28]   During sleep, and perhaps at other times, the shadow can be separated from the person and can wander about independently.

Dishima is the core of man's personality which determines his character and differentiates him from others. It is the center of emotions, reason, and judgement, and thus the seat of *nenyi* (wisdom) and *tunango* (intelligence). In fact, it can be said to be the essence of that which distinguishes *muntu* from *nyema* (animal).

Tunango (intelligence) has to do particularly with a good memory and ability to transmit the traditional lore of the community, while *nenyi* (wisdom) is primarily the ability to live with others according to the rules of the community.[29]   Thus, that which is significant about a person is his relationship to the ongoing society in which he participates.

To be *muntu* is in a sense to be constantly in the process of becoming *muntu*. According to the Luba view a man "must ceaselessly augment his powers."[30]   Three major crises in this process are birth, puberty, and death.

Becoming *muntu* begins with birth but the infant is *muntu* more in hope than in actuality. When he receives a name—typically that of a deceased ancestor — he is more fully a participant in the ongoing community. Sometimes through dreams or a process of divination it will be determined that a particular ancestor-spirit is "following" a pregnant woman in order to be "reborn." In this case the child will carry the name of this ancestor, who will be known as his *ngudi*. Because a name is more than just a convenient label, identity of name carries with it a certain identification of being. Sometimes the child is identified with the ancestor whose name he bears to the point where there may be a certain reluctance to punish him as this would do violence to the forefathers.[31]   Thus the life of a new-born child is not totally new but is in some important sense continuous with the communal past; the name he bears is a symbol of this continuity.

The greatest crisis between birth and death is puberty, for it is at this point that the young person achieves the power of participating in the process of reproduction, thus becoming a link in the continuity of the community. However, the rites and celebrations associated with this event do not necessarily take place at exactly the age of puberty; a boy may be initiated any time between the ages of seven and sixteen.

The male initiation ceremony is called *mukanda* by the Baluba and several neighboring groups. The details vary somewhat in different parts of the Luba area; here I follow the account of Jason Sendwe.

A time near the beginning of the dry season — May or June — is selected. "On the specified day the atmosphere of the village is somber; the drums give forth dismal sounds and the dances are sorrowful." [32]

The participants in the ceremony are the circumciser (*ngongo*) the hyena-man (*kiminga*), the wolf-man (*kavwidji*), the guides or shepherds (*walubenji*), and other aids. The mothers say goodbye to their boys and are given discouraging predictions by a "bad guide." He leads the crowd in a song which proclaims that the boys will never return because they will be caught by the hyenas and wolves. A good guide, however, gives encouraging predictions.

Near the place of circumcision the boys are seized one by one by the wolf-man and the hyena-man, who take them to the *walubenji*. These encourage the boys and turn them over to the circumcision aides, who prepare them for the operation. When this is performed a rifle is shot and there is dancing by the ceremonial assistants. The *walubenji* return to the village to reassure the parents.

The boys then spend three months in the bush during which time they undergo various hardships and are not allowed to see any women. Their mothers bring them food, but this must be left at a distance and can contain neither salt nor oil. A teacher instructs them in sexual matters and in traditional stories and songs.

When the wounds are healed and the lessons learned a great hunt is organized for the benefit of the circumciser. Having killed an appropriate animal, the boys approach the village singing and deliver the meat to the house of the circumciser. Then they return to the bush where they wash and put on new clothes before their final grand entrance to the village as full adult members of the community, an event celebrated by dancing and feasting.

The ceremony of circumcision, although according to some a relatively recent import from outside the Luba area, [33] has great importance as a time of "death and rebirth," out of which comes a "new man," no longer a child, but a full participant in the communal life.

Among the Baluba there is also a ceremony for girls, known as *butanda*, which normally takes place a little before actual puberty.

It was traditionally believed that a girl who did not go through this ceremony would be likely to bear deformed or retarded children.

The ceremony is conducted by an older woman, known as the *inamutanda*. First comes the "entrance into *butanda*" when "the girl is carried out of her hut in the evening and laid on a mat, where she must stay, covered by a cloth." The next morning the *inamutanda* kills a fowl, gives the girl the *dishima* (liver or heart) raw, telling her that "she has received a woman's heart." The rest of the fowl is cooked whole and the girl shares it with the *inamutanda*, being careful not to break any bones as it is believed that, "if she breaks a bone, her offspring will be born with broken bones." The girl remains on the mat until evening when she is free.[34]

A year now passes in which the girl is in a state of suspense between childhood and maturity, during which she is not allowed to do any work. She receives training for several weeks or months in sexual and other matters relevant to the responsibilities of a mature woman.

The "coming out" from *butanda* traditionally took place after the girl had given clear evidence of her maturity by having three menstrual periods.[35]   A festival of beer drinking and dancing was held to mark the entrance of the girl into full womanhood and readiness for marriage.

In general, the initiation rites involve three stages: separation from the past, a period of suspended existence, and reintegration into the community as an adult member. The person's role as either "man" or "woman" is clearly affirmed through the appropriate ritual. Up until this time his existence, though certainly human, has not been fully integrated into the community. He has not been able to undertake fully his social obligations. Most especially, he has not been able to participate in the ongoing continuity of life; he has not been capable of becoming an ancestor. Although initiation does not necessarily coincide exactly with sexual maturity there can be no doubt of the close relationship. Initiation thus recognizes the existence of new forces which have important social consequences. There are also clearly religious aspects of this transition, for the continuation of human existence in community is surely the "ultimate concern" of these people.

Marriage is often closely associated with the puberty rites and may be seen as simply their natural culmination. Among the Baluba — and generally in Africa — not to marry would be an unheard of deviation from the normal course of life. Marriage provides the context for parenthood, by which the continuity of life is assured. To become a parent for the first time is a significant step forward in a person's status, as indicated by the fact that parents are often called by the name of their oldest child, prefixed by *sa-* for the father and *ina-* for the mother. To be childless is to be cut off from the continuity of life, to be a "dead-end." Not only does one's life then lack significance, one has also failed the ancestors who were counting on descendants to enhance their heritage. "To live is above all to procreate." [36] This importance of children is one reason given for the practice of polygamy.

The true or complete *muntu* can now be identified as the mature person, fully participating in the life of the community, especially in its continuation through the propagation of children. To become a grandparent is an especially clear assurance of a person's significance and prominence. In general, to reach old age is evidence that a man has successfully enhanced his powers — although in some cases the achievement of longevity may lead to the suspicion that one has improperly gained control over powers rightly belonging to others.

Survival and success are seen as evidence of true personhood as long as they are not based on exploitation of others. Personal achievement must always be in the context of the welfare of the community as a whole, and the successful man is responsible for helping those who have fallen behind. No one has the right to get too far ahead of the group; a certain balance and harmony must be maintained. This ideal is difficult to maintain in the context of new economic conditions but is widely held even in contemporary Luba society.

The final crisis of life is death, which can be seen as a failure of the positive forces and a disintegration of *muntu* into his constituent parts. In another sense, however, death is the passage into a new stage of life. Interestingly enough, there are striking resemblances between the death rites and puberty rites; both are significant stages in the process of becoming an ancestor, that is, of becoming not simply a dangling dead-end of life but a link in the continuity of existence which unites the past and future through the present.

Burial of the dead takes place as soon as it is possible to make contact with all significant relatives. Places especially appropriate for burials are crossroads and the immediate vicinity of anthills and streams, all of which may be understood as symbols of renewal or continuity of life. The body is usually placed in a crouching or "pre-natal" position, surrounded by various personal objects: clothing, decorations, implements. There are special places and methods for the burial of particular kinds of persons such as chiefs, diviners, hunters, twins, lepers, and albinos.

At the burial the mourners disclaim all responsibility for the death and implore the deceased not to disturb them. Much of the shrieking and extreme display of grief at the time of death and burial may be intended "to impress the spirit with the respect that the living have for him, that he may thus be well inclined, and not bring sickness or calamity to the village."[37]   After the funeral the participants wash in the river to cleanse themselves. Sometimes one man will build a small fire in the path which the others, returning from washing, step over, "believing that in this manner they shake off the spirit which may be following them."[38]

The realm of the dead is Kalunga, a word which also has the meaning of "sea" or of the "the waters under the sea." It has been defined as "the space which cannot be filled, which possesses a superior power which subjugates us, against which nothing can be done."[39]   Among some of the neighbors of the Baluba to the southwest, Kalunga is used as a name for the supreme God, while among the Ndembu it may simply mean "the grave."[40]

The association of water with the dead is manifested in several ways. For instance, water must be crossed to reach the realm of the dead. There is a ferry man who receives a toll from those he carries so that "at burial the mouth and hands of the corpse are filled with beads for the payment of this ferry man."[41]   Streams are often said to be the places of departed spirits, and dead chiefs were commonly buried in the beds of streams. There is a Luba saying that "dry land is death but water is life";[42]   thus the association of water with burial and death may symbolize the rebirth that follows death.

Kalunga, as the place of the dead, is divided into two major parts. Kalunga-ka-Niembo is the abode of the *bankambo*, the benevolent ancestors who take an interest in the welfare and behavior of the living, warn them of dangers, and give aid in time of trouble. They are thought of as living much as men do on earth, following ordinary occupations in a familiar environment.

On the other hand there is Kalunga-ka-musona, a sort of "hell" of "eternal obscurity," sometimes referred to as Kalunga-kalala-mashika — "Kalunga of coldness." The inhabitants of this realm are the *bikidji*, spirits who are cut off from any positive association with the living, and who, therefore, may be vindictive and dangerous. They include childless people, those who have been antisocial, such as witches, and those for whom proper burial procedures have not been carried out. It has been suggested that Europeans when they first appeared were probably thought of as *bikidji.*

As indicated before, the dead man is no longer properly referred to as *muntu* but rather as *mufu.*

> The difference between a 'muntu' and a 'mufu' resides in the fact that the latter has already lost the 'ntu,' which we recall constitutes the vital element, while the muntu still possesses it. This force animates the life of the living, while that of the dead is 'idling.' [43]

Death is a negative and basically unnatural phenomenon, the origin of which is frequently attributed to some kind of carelessness or weakness. According to one story, the Creator

> knew that both Life and Death...would pass along the path in order to reach the people, so he appointed Dog and Goat between them to guard the path in order to allow Life to pass but not Death.
> The two argued with each other as to whether or not they would go to sleep and in the process Goat felt insulted and left Dog alone. Dog did in fact go to sleep and Death slipped by him on the Path. [44]

According to a Kaonde account, Lesa (God) sent three sealed gourds to man by Mayimba, the honey-guide bird.

> "Go, take these," he said, "to the man and woman whom I have created, and open them not on the way. When you hand them to the people, say unto them, 'Thus says Lesa: Open this one and that one which contain seeds for sowing, so that you may have food to eat; but the third one you shall not open until I come. When I come I will instruct you as to the contents of the third package." Mayimba took the gourds, but his curiosity as to their contents was great, and he stopped to open them. In the first two he found seeds of corn, bean, and other foodcrops, and having examined them he replaced them, closing the gourds as they had been closed before. He then untied the third gourd, inside which were death (lufu), sickness, and all manner of carnivora and death-bringing reptiles. As soon as he opened the gourd these escaped and Mayimba could not catch them....Thus it was that death, sickness and fear came to man. [45]

Although death is a negative phenomenon, in some ways the dead have more power and influence than the living. They manifest themselves on special occasions and in particular phenomena. The night and noonday are times when spirits are likely to be about, as is the time of the new moon. Springs, pools, streams, and waterfalls are frequently the abode of spirits — reminding us again of the close connection of water and the spirit world. Trees may be associated with spirits, as may such ephemeral phenomena as whirlwinds. The dead are also manifested in animals, especially snakes, leopards, and lions. When such an animal frequents the neighborhood of a village it may be thought to be the reincarnation of a chief; therefore it should not be killed even if it harms the village.

The departed spirit may become a *mukishi* (plural, *bakishi*), an invisible being who "follows" the living, serving as a "guardian spirit" and especially assisting in the hunt. The term is a rather flexible one; at times it seems to refer not so much to the spirit of the deceased person himself as to a kind of spiritual influence associated with him. A man may be said to "inherit" the *mukishi* of his *ngudi*, the ancestral spirit whose name he bears. One Muluba told me that the *bakishi* are "in the wind," not on earth or in the sky, meaning apparently that they "hover" between the human and the superhuman and also that they are like the wind, mysterious and illusive—they cannot be seen, though their influence can be felt.

There are various types or classes of *bakishi*, for instance, *mundele*, a water spirit; *mwadi*, a female spirit; *kamwadi*, a male spirit; and hunting spirits such as *buyanga* and *kiluwe*. One cannot properly say whether each of these names refers to one spirit or many spirits; they are collective names like "wind" and "water."

The Baluba prepare carved or molded objects as dwelling places for the *bakishi*; these are called *bankishi* (singular, *nkishi*). When a spirit is believed to be present in one of these the total phenomenon of "spirit in object" may be referred to as *mukishi* while the object alone is simply *nkishi*.

Almost every man in traditional Luba society is said to have his own *mukishi*, in the sense of a guardian spirit. Usually he builds a small hut near his home in which his *mukishi*—as "spirit in object"— can be kept. Food and drink offerings are brought here and requests made for assistance. A man invoking his *mukishi* will kneel before the little hut, rub himself with *mpemba* (white clay), and make his needs known.

There has been considerable discussion of the proper term to use in speaking of the approach to the spirits of the dead. Earlier writers spoke of "worship" and, in fact, described the basic religion of African peoples as "ancestor worship." African scholars, however, generally find such terminology inappropiate because the spirits of the dead are not "gods" but simply invisible members of the family. "Communion with the ancestors" has been suggested as a better expression. "Invocation of the spirits" also seems quite appropriate, precisely because it has a certain ambiguity. One may invoke both gods and lesser beings — or even impersonal concepts. Also, "invocation" carries the suggestion of "arousing," which is in keeping with Luba terminology.

It is frequently said that the Baluba and other Africans believe in "reincarnation," but this is misleading. As we have seen, a new-born child may have the name of an ancestral spirit, his *ngudi*. He may be said to have the *mukishi* of his *ngudi*, but he does not have his *muya* ("spirit"). Thus in a sense he fills the communal vacancy left by the deceased but his being does not include all that survives of the being of the ancestor. Evidence of this is the fact that more than one person can have the same ancestor-spirit as *ngudi* and that at the same time the ancestor may be said to be in "in Kalunga." The essential point is that one cannot understand the living apart from the dead. The latter may manifest their presence in a variety of ways: in their namesakes, through man-made objects, in animals and natural phenomena. Luba beliefs regarding the spirits of the dead are complex and may appear contradictory to outsiders. The problem is that Luba thought is not analytical but, as one Luba scholar puts it, "global." [46] If we keep in mind the fact that the Luba concern with spirits is more "existential" than theoretical, we will not expect one systematic, coherent account, but rather a diversity of expressions of the conviction that the dead are not absent but very much involved in affairs of the living.

For instance, they are interested in the places inhabited by their descendants. In fact, this interest may be unbearable at times; traditionally it was the custom to move the village whenever a chief died. (Of course, there were also practical reasons for moving every few years, having to do with sanitation and worn-out soil.) Whenever a village is moved it is essential that the spirits of any earlier inhabitants of the new site be consulted. as well as the ancestral spirits of the present village. Diviners must make contact with the spirits and if the result is unfavorable an alternative location must be selected.

The ancestral spirits are also very much concerned with the moral standards of their descendants. Those who fail to follow the traditional customs are a danger to the whole community, which includes its deceased members. Such transgessors may expect negative attention from the ancestral spirits.

The relationship of the living and the dead is a two-way street; the dead depend on the living for their continued existence. A man without a male heir has no point of contact and apparently either ceases to exist or becomes a homeless, wandering spirit, who may cause trouble for the living and have to be disposed of by some special procedure. Those who are ancestor-spirits normally take a benevolent interest in their descendants, warning of dangers and giving help in trouble; but if their desires are left unfulfilled they too can be vindictive and destructive, bringing illness and even death.

While death in general is attributed to an act of God — direct or indirect — particular deaths are usually understood as due to the action of some human agent, living or dead. Dissatisfied or adverse spirits may manifest their hostility by causing disease, accident, or suicide. Death as a punishment for breaking the rules of the community may be inflicted by basically benevolent spirits acting as guardians of tradition.

Death, disease or other misfortune may also be caused by witch-craft, *bufwishi*. Belief in this possibility is based on the concept of the "shadow-self" or "dream-self," which is able to leave the body, wander about, and engage in various activities. The witch (*mfwishi*) is one who has a "bad heart," a solitary, introverted person who does not relate well socially. This disposition is present in the person even when it is not the basis of overt action. The Baluba do not distinguish verbally between a witch, who disrupts and destroys life because of some inherent quality over which he or she has no control and of which he or she may even be unconscious, and a sorcerer, who consciously chooses to be antisocial. Both may be called *mfwishi*, or, in the case of a woman, *nkinda*.

The concept of witchcraft is closely related to that of death; in fact, the word *mfwishi* is derived from the same root as *kufwa*, to die, and *mufu*, the dead person. It is interesting to note that *mufu* can refer especially to a spirit which engages in antisocial acts; among the neighboring Ndembu it refers to "dangerous ghosts rather than moral ancestors." [47] The root meaning of these words would seem to have to do with that which diminishes life and disrupts harmonious relationships; it sums up all that is most feared by the Baluba.

Having looked at that which is for the Baluba the human ideal, summed up in the term *muntu*, and that which threatens this ideal, summed up in the related words *mufu* and *mfwishi*, we may now observe that the practical concern of the Baluba is to protect life by warding off that which destroys it.

One cannot deal with the threat to life in general terms; in each case one must identify the particular source of the evil. When disease or death strikes it is assumed that there is an underlying cause that must be brought to light. The belief that death or illness is caused by some personal agent does not necessarily rule out a material cause; for instance, the idea that certain diseases are caused by germs might well be accepted. But the more important question would remain: "Why did the germ affect *this* person at *this* time?" A pill or some other form of Western medicine may be welcomed to counteract the germ, but this is only a kind of "first aid." A real cure depends on the identification of the personal agent responsible and then use of the proper procedure to counteract his influence. To put it differently, right relationships must be restored in order to bring true healing.

The first step in the restoration of right relationship involves identification of the problem by means of divination. The simplest form of divination is that in which the object used (*lubuko*) is the *kashekesheke*, a small piece of wood usually having one end carved to resemble a human head. The diviner (*umbuki* — one who owns or uses a *lubuko*) holds one side while the person consulting him holds the other. A stool is between them. The problem is presented by the diviner in the form of questions, most of which can be answered "yes" or "no." If the answer is affirmative, the instrument moves up and down, causing it to knock on the stool below. If the answer is negative the instrument moves sideways in a kind of sweeping action. Other types of movements may indicate more specific answers. All these movements are believed to be caused by some spirit, although the specific spirit need not necessarily be identifiable. Anyone who cares to try his hand at it may make himself such an instrument and seek initiation from an established practitioner. Once he gets the "feel" of it, he begins practice on his own. Although a particular spirit may be said to be guiding the instrument, the diviner himself is not believed to be possessed by a spirit nor does he have any prestige apart from whatever reputation he may establish.

The successful *kashekesheke* paractitioner is undoubtedly one who is sensitive to human relationships and who, during the consultation, when he and the consultant are both holding the instrument, is able to feel the other's reactions and reflect them as the interpretation develops. It should be noted that the *kashekesheke* is not only consulted to discover the personal cause of sickness but also frequently to get a clue regarding the whereabouts of a lost article. It is the lowest and least complicated form of divination.

A somewhat more complicated form is *ngombu*, in which, among the Bene Nsamba, the *lubuko* or instrument is the skin of a civet cat through which a piece of wood has been placed with the head of a man carved on it. The diviner (*umbuki wa ngombu*) holds the head of the skin while the one seeking help holds the tail. The diviner asks question in response to which the skin moves up and down to indicate affirmation and back and forth to indicate negation.

Among the Bakaonde, *ngombu* refers to a type of divination in which pieces of wood (*mpingo*) are placed in a calabash and shaken in front of those gathered for the test. When the diviner comes opposite to the guilty party or names him the *mpingo* is said to stand on end instead of lying flat. [48]

In these forms of divination in which the material object (*lubuko*) plays a central role it is also assumed that spirits are involved in the response given. Thus the *lubuko* is defined as "an instrument which...permits [the diviner] to communicate with the ancestors and consequently to analyze with precision the case of a person bringing a complaint." [49] The word *lubuko* is related to *kubuka*, a verb which means "to consult the spirits."

Divination implies a world view in which all things are bound to each other in a "web of relationship," so that a condition existing anywhere in the cosmos may be reflected elsewhere. A rupture in the fabric of human relationships may be expected to produce its identifiable counterpart in the material world. Whether or not we accept this view, we may at least note that the way in which the material objects are used provides the sensitive diviner with clues as to the points at which a rupture may have occurred within the community. No doubt the successful diviner is also well-informed regarding the habits and hostilities of all those who may be his potential clients.

The distinction between "divination" that uses material objects and "prophecy" that relies on direct communication with or possession by the spirits is not absolute, for the diviner is at least indirectly in touch with spirits and the prophet frequently uses certain objects. The difference is real but relative.

One type of practitioner on the borderline between divination and prophecy is the *kitobo* (plural, *bitobo*). He is associated with a particular location, usually close to water, where he receives answers to his questions by observing the behavior of fish, snakes, or crocodiles, or the movement of waters in caverns or hot springs.

One that I observed used catfish in a forest pool. He could not actually divine for us as we had not given him sufficient notice; if we had been able to stay overnight he would have proceeded in the proper fashion the next morning. As it was he could only demonstrate the process of divination. He "called" his catfish and showed us how he would receive the answer to questions by the way they responded, making it quite clear to the spirits involved that this was not a proper divination but only a demonstration.

The most common type of "prophet" or spokesman for a spirit is the *kilumbu* (plural, *bilumbu*). (Fig. 1) He is a special kind of person who adopts an unusual life style. When under the influence of the spirit he speaks in an abnormal voice, stares in a peculiar manner, and whistles through his teeth. He wears a colorful and impressive costume which includes grass cloth, skins, beads, and feathers. A *kilumbu* frequently, though not always, is the son of a *kilumbu*, but, in any case, his own vocation must become clear through dreams or a disease which can only be healed by initiation as a *kilumbu*. One who acts in a "crazy" manner may be thought to have received *bulumbu*, the quality of being a *kilumbu*.

Consultation with a *kilumbu* involves careful preparation, often beginning the previous evening and requiring the cooperation of his wife or wives. He proceeds by asking a series of questions: "Is it illness? Is it death? Is it inability to have a child?" When he hits on the correct problem those consulting him cry out "Vidye Kalombo!" enthusiastically accepting his statement. He then discovers more about the problem by further series of questions, until the whole matter is clearly revealed through a kind of "dialogue" between himself and his consultants. To an outsider it might appear that no supernatural powers are required and that the major function of the *kilumbu* is that of providing therapy by giving his clients an opportunity to state their own problems. The significance of the consultation is emphasized by the beating of drums and the ringing of bells at appropriate points.

The *kilumbu* does not rely primarily on physical objects to give a message, but may have a basket containing such things as chalk, horns, dried fruits, bones, stones, or the head of a chicken. He is believed to be possessed by the spirit of some great hero of the past, a *vidye*. In fact, when under the influence of the spirit he is no longer himself and must be addressed as "vidye" rather than by his own name. Because of his connection with the ancestors he is especially involved in problems which concern them.

The *kilumbu* is not only a diagnostician; having brought to light the problem, he makes a prescription in terms of appropriate offerings or sacrifices to be performed or *bwanga* to be secured. He may, in fact, provide the *bwanga* himself, thus acting as a *nganga* or "medicine man." According to one *kilumbu*, God reveals to him the appropriate medicine for each situation.

Although a *kilumbu* may act as a *nganga*, the two functions are not the same. One seeks the cause of disruption, disease, and death, while the other seeks to reorient the appropriate powers in such a way that wholeness will be restored. The business of the *nganga* is with *bwanga,* or

> spiritual efficacy, and he believes this efficacy is associated, in a varying degree, not only with the entire animal, vegetable and mineral worlds, but also with words, actions, times of day and night, indeed every physical and spiritual property is teeming with spiritual influences, good and bad... [50]

The *nganga* frequently has an extensive knowledge of herbs, many of which would be recognized by science as having objective healing properties, while others would be classed as objectively "useless." This distinction, however, is not very significant for the *nganga.* The real power of *bwanga* is more in the realm that we would call "spiritual" than in that of the "physical" (although the distinction would not be made in this way by the Baluba). Because the real basis of disease is in the area of personal relationships among the living, and between the living and the dead, the real cure is one that overcomes whatever powers are disturbing the communal harmony. Thus such a clearly physical act as setting bones is understood essentially as a kind of "first aid," given while the real cause of the difficulty is being dealt with at a deeper level.

> A woman has had an accident, and she goes to the medicine man badly burned. He sees that the case is beyond his powers, and so he gives the husband a magic bracelet called a "nasambakanya" telling him to take his wife to the white man, where she will be made well. At the Government dispensary, she is handed over to the doctor's care, while the husband, apparently without thinking, gently rubs the magic bracelet up and down his forearm. The woman is housed, fed and doctored, all free of charge, and at a cost to the state of say 200 francs, yet when she is healed, she goes off without even a "thank you." Was it not the "dyese" of the medicine-man which had so wonderful a result? Thus immediately she reaches home, her husband takes a big present to the medicine-man for curing the wife's wounds. The "nsambakanya" bracelet gets all the praise. As for the government doctor, he is very clever, no doubt, but only a tool in the hands of the medicine-man, and under the spell of his "blessing." [51]

We should understand that the healing power is not so much present in the physical objects as in the person of *nganga.* That is, healing for the Baluba is more personal than material; the material objects "are said to bring healing largely because of the · ower of the medicine-man's hand, received at his initiation" by an already established member of the profession. [52]

The *nganga* is a very important, powerful person in the community, believed to be the "guardian of public health, safety and welfare of the whole community, from birth and before, until death and after." [53] Thus it is very unwise to be on bad terms with him; even when he is suspected of "malpractice" it often seems wiser not to expose him.

The only proper sense in which the *nganga* is a "witch doctor" is that he seeks to counteract the influence of witches. He is not himself a witch, any more than a psychiatrist is psychotic. It is of course, conceivable that a psychiatrist could be psychotic and, in like manner, a *nganga* could be a witch, but in both cases this condition would undoubtedly hamper their therapeutic efficiency. It may also be true that both the psychiatrist and the *nganga* are more effective if they have enough affinity with those with whom they deal to be able in some way to "think like them." The *nganga* may thus have certain characteristics in common with the witch and perhaps be under special temptation to become a witch. Another analogy may be that of the policeman who must to some extent be able to think like the criminal he wishes to catch and may even use some of the same methods. Policemen may, in fact be under special temptation to become criminals. Nevertheless, in spite of abuses, the policeman's function is to protect the community from those who would destroy it. This is also the function of *nganga*. Thus the attempt of a government to supress witchcraft by outlawing the *banganga* would be seen by traditional Baluba much as most Americans would see an attempt to rid society of crime by disbanding the police force.

One particular kind of *nganga* is the *bwana mutombo*, who is particularly concerned with the collection and preparation of medicines. He is a kind of "pharmacist" who knows all the appropriate medicines and constantly seeks for new ones. He may also carve statues through which spiritual powers are manifested. Traditionally he was associated with the society of the Bayembe or Bakasandji; who were said to dig up corpses in order to produce strong medicines. At the court of Kasongo Niembo—and of other chiefs—there is a *bwana mutombo* who might be considered the "Minister of Health" for the kingdom.

A person accused or suspected of disrupting the social harmony by witchcraft, causing illness, death, or other distress, may be required to undergo a trial by ordeal, normally conducted by a *bwana mutambo* or a *kilumbu*. Such a trial is referred to as *mwavi* after a somewhat rare tree whose bark is used in one form of the ordeal. In order to prove guilt or innocence, the accused person, standing opposite his accuser, drinks water in which a piece of this bark has been placed. The accuser says, "If you have stolen (or whatever his supposed crime may have been), then die of 'mwavi'; but if not, then vomit." [54]

According to Burton, most people vomit. Those who do not will confess quickly and make amends, hoping thus to escape death; only rarely does a person actually die. The poison, apparently, is a weak one, and perhaps is most likely to take effect when the person has a guilty conscience and expects it to kill him. A pigeon may undergo the ordeal in place of the human suspect. Because of the Luba view of the "interaction of forces" it can be held that what happens to the pigeon reveals the truth regarding the guilt or innocence of the human being. The human force dominates that of the pigeon so that the latter can represent the former. [55]   There are other forms of ordeal, such as licking a hot ax-head. If the tongue is not burned, innocence is established. [56]

As disease and death are generally attributed to the activity of some personal being, living or dead, the Baluba look to their *banganga* for protective medicine that will ward off such effects. One of the most common forms is the *kilambo*, a small antelope horn filled with appropriate ingredients and worn about the neck in order to ward off evil and give strength and good fortune. Other forms of protective medicine may be placed in the house and around the village.

The selection of items for use as medicine is not arbitrary but based on a clearly understood principle:

> [T]he medicine-man is attracted by some unique feature in an animal, root, or other object, believing that which produced such a feature in the animal will (a) produce the same in a human being if used raw, (b) bring about a more concentrated effect if dried and scraped or ground, and (c) that it will have exactly opposite result if burnt. [57]

The most powerful medicines normally contain something taken from a human being, living or dead. [58]

Healing is sought not only by the use of *bwanga* but also through maintaining right relationships with the spirit world. The Baluba say, "I do not call only on *bwanga,* but I also invoke the *mukishi,* for both have the same purpose." [59]   In fact, the Baluba do not distinguish clearly between the healing power of *bwanga* and that of spirits. In the abstract it might be said that the former is impersonal and the latter personal but in practice the two are inextricably mixed together. The carved image which provides the locus for a spirit may be called "*bwanga*" as well as "*mukishi.*" As noted before, the concern of the Baluba is not with theoretical distinctions but with practical methods of enhancing life.

No method, of course, is foolproof. In fact, it is recognized that in the end all will fail. Thus it is said, "Death is the great one; medicine deceives," and "Death does not know the doctor; even the doctor himself dies." [60]

The *bakishi*, along with *manga*, are involved in the preparations for planting and harvesting, hunting and fishing, and the smelting of iron. These are all activities in which significant forces, personal and impersonal, are intimately involved. For instance, the change of condition from ore to metal could get out of control and disrupt the harmonious balance of power in the community; therefore the procedure must be carefully surrounded by prohibitions and restraints. The smith who brings about the change is obviously in communication with unusual powers and is thus a special kind of person who must follow certain prescribed patterns of behavior.

The clay and stick kiln is built in the form of a kneeling woman, complete with breasts and tatoo marks, and the extraction of the metal from the ore is considered to be a birth. Those involved observe special taboos and carry out the work under the influence of unusual powers. They shout "to the spirits to give them many axes and hoes," or challenge the evil spirits "to do their worst, for they cannot resist the powerful charms of the forge." [61] Father Tempels states that "coppersmiths and blacksmiths think that they will not be able to smelt the ore, thereby changing the nature of the material treated, unless they dutifully appeal to a higher force which can dominate the vital force of the 'earth' which they claim thus to change into metal." [62] In some areas the smelting of metal was such a critical event that it could not take place without the death of a human being.

A concept that is central in the religion of the Baluba is that of *vidye* (plural, *bavidye*). The term is probably best translated as "lord" or "superior being." Frequently it refers to the spirits of the great heroes of the Luba past, especially those associated with the founding and spread of the kingdom. Among the Baluba Kasai it is said that *mvidie* refers to the original founding ancestor of a kinship group. [63] The terms *vidye* and *mukishi* are not mutually exclusive designations; in general, *mukishi* is the more comprehensive term for spirits associated with the dead, while *vidye* refers specifically to a more limited group of great spirits who are guardians of the whole community.

The term *vidye* may also be used in reference to living persons associated with these great spirits. Thus, a *kilumbu* when in the state of possession is a *vidye* and in certain contexts kings or the heads of secret societies may be considered as *bavidye* because of their close relationship to the great spirits. In present day Luba practice, *vidye* is actually used as a term of respect in addressing anyone, somewhat as "sir" might be used in very polite English. Basically, however, it refers to one possessed of superior vital power (*buvidye*) associated with the heroic past.

Although perhaps once living humans, the *bavidye* also are associated with natural phenomena, especially lakes, but also rivers and mountains. An interesting case is Nkongolo-Mwamba, mentioned above, who is the rainbow, a dual serpent, and also the ancient chief who was defeated and killed on earth but remains powerful in the spirit world. Nkongolo is sometimes referred to as *mutwe wa bavidye*, the "head of the great spirits." [64]

Often the *bavidye* are in pairs, such as Monga and Umba, who "live" in the Kalunga forest near the Lovoi River. They were responsible for the establishment of the chieftainship in their area. The king received from them *mpemba,* the sacred white chalk, which was to protect him "against sickness and the attacks of enemies, guarantee him the fidelity of his wives, make hunting fruitful and abundant for him..." [65]

At the place of Monga and Umba there is a *kitobo* or "diviner," who receives and interprets the message of the spirits to those who come for consultation. The great reputation of this center attracts people from all over Luba territory who need supernatural guidance beyond that which can be secured from local practitioners.

Another important pair of *bavidye* is Panga and Banze, who "live" at Kalui and have a special association with the chieftainship of Kasongo Niembo. It is to them that the great chiefs go to validate their claims and to them in times of crisis that they turn for guidance. Here, too, a *kitobo* interprets the message of the *bavidye,* but only to the chief or his representative.

We have already discussed the *bilumbu* (plural of *kilumbu*) who are possessed by the *bavidye* and, in fact, are addressed as "vidye" when so possessed. When one consults the *kilumbu* one is actually consulting the *vidye* who possesses him. These *bavidye* who speak through the *bilumbu* are, in fact, the same kind of spirits as those consulted by the *bitobo* at sacred centers such as that of Monga and Umba. The difference is that the *kitobo* is not himself possessed and must consult the spirits at one particular location while the spirit "follows" the *kilumbu* wherever he goes. Also, the same spirit may possess many *bilumbu* while it has only one sacred center.

The *bavidye*, as hero-founders of the society, are especially concerned with affairs of the chieftainship and of the community as a whole. Thus both the *bilumbu* and the *bitobo* have special relationships with the chiefs and must observe similar customs, such as that of eating in a special place apart from ordinary people. They are, in a sense, representatives of the dead chiefs.

It is in connection with the concept of *vidye* that we can best understand the religious meaning of chieftainship or kingship for the Baluba. The chief or king (*mulopwe*) is both the symbol of communal health and its active defender and promoter. "Normally the living chief, as visible head of the community, is owner of everything and everybody. He is responsible for their welfare and demands their loyalty." [66] It is important that he be able to trace his ancestry and thus his authority back to the period of the foundation of the kingdom. From Nkongolo, Mbidi Kiluwe, and Kalala Ilunga is derived the *bulopwe* or "sacred quality vested in the blood...which gives chiefs the right and supernatural means to rule." [67] The *bulopwe* itself may be said to have come "from the east" with Mbidi Kiluwe, and to have been established among the central Baluba "on the tutelary power of Kongolo's ghost." [68]

The senior line of Luba rulers is now represented by Kasongo Niembo and Kabongo. These, along with other "paramount chiefs," such as Mutombo Mukulu of the Bena Kalundwe, may properly be called "kings," and within their territories the term *mulopwe* is reserved for them. In other Luba areas, such as among the Bene Nsamba, where there is no one supreme ruler, the title is given to local village chiefs. Strictly speaking, *bulopwe* is "one and indivisible"; [69] those who possess it do not have a "part" of it but rather "participate" in its undivided wholeness.

There is an objective quality to kingship or chieftainship that does not depend on actually having authority over a significant number of people. Thus, most of the people of the village of Kanene have been moved by the government to a site on the main road, several miles away. But Chief Kanene remains on the land of the ancestors, maintaining the tradition, even if not the authority, of the past. This suggests that the primary function of the chief may be not so much to rule as to represent the continuity between past and present. The chief receives his authority from the ancestors and holds the communal lands on their behalf.

The king or chief, as symbol of the health or wholeness of the community, is not supposed to manifest any signs of weakness or even to have the needs of normal men. For instance, traditionally he is not to be seen eating, presumably because he does not require ordinary nourishment like other mortals. (The possibility of poisoning may also be a practical factor.) A special enclosure is thus provided where he retires to eat.

The chief must not flee from his enemies; if he does this indicates that the "spirit of the chieftainship has left him" and he must be killed. [70] Any kind of deformity makes a man ineligible for the chieftainship.

> Some of the Luba chiefs are considered unworthy of the position if they continue ill more than four days. It is then the duty of the chief's sisters to poison him. Thus, however ill a chief may be, on the fourth day he will get up and stagger about his harem, or go out to receive the greetings of his people, pretending to be well. He is especially active and anxious to display his vigour if he hears that his sisters are in the neighborhood. [71]

Among the Bene Nsamba the chief cannot die wearing the *lukano*, the bracelet which is the sign of chieftainship, because it is associated with life. Thus when death threatens it must be removed.

Extensive ceremonies are carried out at the time of the installation of a new king, with the purpose of putting him into proper relationship with supernatural power. Until these take place, a man is not really king, even though he has been chosen for the role and may be exercising authority.

These ceremonies are a kind of "rite of passage" for the whole society. When the chief is dead the society is dead until brought back to life by the installation of a new chief. Thus "each change of rule provokes a veritable return to origins." [72]

One of the ceremonies takes place in the *kobo ka malwa*, the "hut of misfortune" in which the new chief communes with the relics of his predecessors and has "incestuous" relations with his niece. The meaning of this latter act is variously interpreted; we can at least say that, as something normally forbidden but at this point required, it has a sacred significance.

Traditionally, human blood was required in carrying out the rites of installation. It has been suggested, in fact, that the title *mulopwe* originally indicated one who was consecrated with human blood. [73] With the abandonment of this practice the question may be raised as to whether a fully valid installation is still possible.

After his time in the hut with his niece, the new king performs a special dance, the *Kutomboka*. The only other time this dance occurs is in connection with the male initiation rites, suggesting again that the installation of the chief is to be seen as a kind of "rite of passage."

There are various types of "royal emblems" among the Baluba: bracelets, necklaces, headdresses, axes, staffs, stools, and skins. Very important are the *makumbo* (singular, *dikumbo*) of the paramount chiefs, baskets containing the preserved heads or genital organs of their predecessors. The *dikumbo* of Kasongo Niembo is said to have originated with the kead of Nkongolo, cut off and preserved by Kalala Ilunga. When a king dies it is first said only that he is ill, for the body cannot be buried until his successor has obtained possession of the *dikumbo*, thus validating his claim to supernatural powers. [74]

The new king does not take over the enclosure of the old king, but establishes a new one. The old enclosure, if it includes the grave, may become the headquarters of the *mwadi*, the woman to whom the spirit of the departed king has returned. She is also said to be the "wife" of the dead king. A miniature kingdom, complete with a staff of counselors, is set up in the vicinity of the king's grave. The *mwadi* rules as the continuing representative of the king on earth. These *bitenta* (plural of *kitenta*) of important former kings may be maintained for many generations; that of Nkongolo himself is still in existence.

The king or chief can, in a sense, be considered as "priest," that is, he serves as a mediator between the living members of the community and their ancestral past. He is responsible to the ancestors for the communal welfare and especially for the land which they have cultivated and in which their bodies are buried. In times of communal crisis he presents to the ancestors the needs and petitions of the living. While he may not himself have the powers of divination or prophecy he is the patron of those who do.

We have seen that *buvidye*, the quality associated with the *bavidye* or superior spirits, is manifested at special places, in possessed persons (*bilumbu*) and through chiefs (*balopwe*) whose authority goes back to the heroic period. It is also manifested in the groups sometimes known as "secret societies." One of the most important of these is that of the Bambudye, whose origins go back to the heroic period in which the Baluba themselves originated. "It is the national society *par excellence*." [75]

The main public activity of the Bambudye is dancing at the new moon, at funerals, and at the initiations of new members. When dancing they are said to be possessed and thus changed into something more than their normal human personalities.

The Bambudye of a group of neighboring villages have their own headquarters or lodge where meetings and rituals are held. Traditionally it is "a long low building...back in the forests, and the only path to it is guarded by three rows of five gates." [76] Anyone who ventures into the sacred area must join the society. The members of the lodge are supposed to "share their beer, food, entertainment and women..." [77] (Women as well as men may join the society.) The members are treated with respect by the general population and the society as a whole apparently has exercised considerable political and economic authority in some Luba areas through a combination of supernatural sanctions, threats, bribes, and a close alliance with local chiefs.

Another important society is—or was—that of the Bakasandji or Bayembe. They are believed to rob graves and eat corpses, not because they enjoy eating human flesh but because of the power which can thus be secured. Parts of the bodies are also said to be made into strong medicines. It may be, however, that their participation in such activities has been deliberately exaggerated by members of the society in order to frighten people. [78] As in other societies, dancing is an important aspect of their activities; when masked and decorated and engaged in their own particular dance they are believed to be possessed by the spirit *Muyembe*. This society, like the Bambudye, is open to both men and women.

The Balunde are another dancing society. When asked the reason for their dancing a member at first said "simply for entertainment," but when pressed suggested that the dancing strengthens the community against hostile spirits. They also care for the sick, preparing medicines from trees and roots which they rub on the diseased portions of a patient's body.

It should be noted that all of these societies have a close connection with medicine (*bwanga*); their members may be referred to as "medicine men" (*banganga*). In fact, a society as such, with all its practices, is sometimes spoken of as a kind of *bwanga*, so that entering into a society may be spoken of as "entering into *bwanga*." The essential function of the societies, like that of *bwanga* generally, is to protect and enhance human life.

Today the old societies are for the most part dead or dying, but new ones arise to meet the needs of people in a changing world. Luba religion is certainly not static; new practices are copied or invented while the underlying purpose of enhancing human life in the communal context remains.

We have observed that Luba religion is primarily concerned with the actions of persons and personal spirits but that these are sometimes associated with natural phenomena—water in various forms, mountains, plants and animals. One part of nature that is very important to the Baluba is the moon, which is thought of as masculine, with two wives, the evening and morning stars.

According to the Luba account the moon was as bright as the sun until the two fought and the sun threw mud on the moon, obscuring its light. In spite of this the moon fills a more important position in Luba belief and ritual than does the sun.

The most significant periodic event for the Baluba is the new moon. Literally it is new; every month a different moon is born, grows, and then slowly dies. The appearance of the new moon is an especially critical time, for the moon is associated with the cycle of birth and death, the menstrual cycle of women, and the cycle of the seasons. It is a particular moon that brings the rains and another that brings the dry season with its hunting. The day of the new moon is the "day of the spirits" when no work is to be done and various rituals must be carried out. It is the day when the *manga* and the *bakishi* are taken out doors to be purified and strengthened and the secret societies dance. Twins, who are "children of the moon," and their mothers, who have the title *inakwezi*, "moon mother," receive special recognition at this time. The coming of the moon marks a new beginning in life; "the moon was dead and now reborn and with it all the forces of fertility in man and nature." [80]

The "working religion" of the Baluba, as we have seen, is concerned with the protection and strengthening of human life, not only in individuals but in the community as a whole. The beliefs and practices related to *bwanga*, the *bakishi*, and the *bavidye* can all be understood in these terms.

There is, however, a belief which appears to be on a somewhat different level and which has few practices related to it. It is a more theoretical belief, although certainly very strongly held, in a being who is the ultimate source of the various powers which may be used to enhance life. The Baluba have many names for this being, some shared with neighboring peoples. Their own most distinctive tradi-

tional name for him is Vidye Mukulu, which is best translated as
"Great Lord."

What is the relationship between Vidye Mukulu and the *bavidye*?
The words used might suggest that Vidye Mukulu is the greatest
among the *bavidye* but not essentially different from them in
nature. Because *mukulu* may mean "old" as well as "great," it has
been suggested that Vidye Mukulu is an original ancestor, a "first
father." It has also been reported that some Baluba state that
"Vidye i muntu mukatampe," [81] "Vidye is a big (or great) man." As
used here without qualification, "Vidye" should probably be
understood to refer to Vidye Mukulu.

In spite of all this, careful attention to what the Baluba say and do
leads to the conclusion that Vidye Makulu is a unique being rather
than one of a class.

The statement that "Vidye is a great man" can probably best be
understood as a "manner of speaking," suggesting the personal
quality of the deity, rather than as a literal identification of him with
man. Sendwe states that, taken literally, such a statement would be
a "flagrant abomination" that could never be accepted by the
Baluba, [82] and Kagame holds that in the Bantu languages generally "The root 'ntu' does not suit God." [83]

The *bavidye* as a class are not clearly distinguished from men;
many of them were in fact heroic human figures. Also, they possess
living men in such a way that these men can be said to become
bavidye. The Baluba insist that Vidye Mukulu never was a man;
certainly he does not possess men. Theuws holds that the word
"Vidye" without any qualification originally referred to the Supreme
Being and that its use for other spirits and for living people
associated with them is secondary. [84] The *bavidye*, then, would be
those who share something of the power of Vidye *par excellence*.
Although this cannot be proven, it appears to be more consistent
with the evidence than the opposite view, that originally there were
many *bavidye*, heroic, superior, yet originally human beings, one of
whom gradually came to be thought of as the greatest of all.
According to Theuws, the use of the same names for God and for
certain men may be due to a desire to glorify the latter or to describe
God in terms of great men but "it is not a question of an
identification of an ancestor with God." [85] Of course, in this, as in
other aspects of their belief, the Baluba are not concerned with
clearcut philosophical distinctions; thus their statements about
Vidye Mukulu do not always point consistently in the same direction. Also, there are a number of names that are used more or less

interchangeably with Vidye Mukulu but sometimes in different contexts so that it is hard to say whether or not they are really synonymous.

Perhaps the most widely used traditional name after Vidye Mukulu is Shakapanga, "father of creation" or "father-creator." It is reported that some Baluba refer to God as *Shakapanga upanga na kupangulula*, meaning "the father-creator who creates and un-creates."[86] Among the Kaonde God may be referred to as *Chipangavije*[87] (the equivalent of *Kipangavidye* in Kiluba), meaning "creator of Vidye." There is a Luba saying: "The Creator, he created Mpanga and he created Banze, he created Nkulu and he created Yumba"[88]; Mpanga, Banze, Nkulu, and Yumba are all *bavidye*. God is also Kipanga Mutombo, "creator of Mutombo." "Mutombo" is a common Luba name; here it may suggest "Everyman" or, at least, the Baluba in general. The root *-panga* in all these words refers to the action of creating which is carried out by God alone; it "is never used to designate...any human work whatever."[89] The root *-longa* is used to refer to the making of anything by man; the use of these two words clearly separates the works of God from, the works of man. Another name sometimes used for God is Sendwe, "Craftsman."

Creation does not seem to be *ex nihilo*; the existence of some kind of world is assumed. What is required is that it be put in order for man's use. As in the second chapter of Genesis, the central interest is not in cosmology so much as in man and his requirements. The supreme gift of God is life; "God created the first man and woman and gave them life" and this life "has been handed on from generation to generation."[90] Not only human life but the life of all living things comes from the one creator. God is the "Father of all" who, through his intermediaries, transmits life to all creatures.[91]

God is frequently spoken of in connection with events which have some overwhelming, dramatic quality and thus seem beyond the power of men, living or dead, to explain or deal with. Perhaps there is some similarity here to the legal category of "acts of God." Presumably God, who established the natural order of things, is the only one who can go against it.

Thus death in general, which is seen as contrary to the original and proper order of things, comes as the result of the carelessness, curiosity, or greed of some created being. Although the actual deaths of specific individuals are usually accounted for in terms of the actions of man or of various spirits, in certain special cases they are attributed to God. Thus, death by lightning and from smallpox and leprosy are attributed directly to God, as are widespread epidemics or disasters affecting a whole community, in contrast to individual troubles that have a different source. Unnatural extremes of heat or cold, flood or drought are seen as coming from God. The birth of twins is also something which can only be explained by the direct ac. ̇n of God, and in some areas twins are referred to as, in a special sei.ṣe, "children of God."

On the other hand, we should note that certain very natural events are also attributed to God. Thus when an extremely old person dies naturally and peacefully there is no attempt to fix the blame on any human agent; it is said that "God called him."

A name for God that is not originally Luba but is now in fairly common use, especially among Christians, is Leza. This name is used in Zambia and as far south as the borders of the Kalahari; it probably came to the Baluba through the Babemba. Various suggestions have been made regarding the meaning of this word; some of which are rather farfetched and none of which can be conclusively demonstrated. In general, Leza seems to be associated with the sky and things which come from it, such as rain, wind, and lightning. Smith and Dâle go so far as to say that for the Ba-Ila, "Leza is the sky and that which comes from it." [92]

The distinctive name for the Supreme Being among the eastern Baluba or "Baluba Hemba" is Kabezya Mpungu, while among the western Baluba or "Baluba Kasai" it is Nzambi, a name used by the Aruund' and all over the western part of Bantu Africa, from the Herero of Namibia to the Fang of Gabon.

The Supreme God is not prominent in the daily religion of the Baluba. It has been suggested that he is "more of a cosmological figure than a religious one." [93] There are stories of how God, disturbed by some activity of men, withdrew from the world and is now relatively inaccessible. There are also stories of how man has attempted to find God, such as the following, reported from the Bakaonde:

> Away back in the world's history our ancestors were occupied in building a great tower to reach the heavens. While they built the white ants were at work on their wooden pillars, and down they came, one after the other. They struggled on, adding pillar to pillar, but the white ants were more successful than they, and after years of labour, down came their tower.... [94]

This sense of distance between God and man is widespread. The Baluba have a saying: "God cannot be seen with the eyes; otherwise I would ask him many things." [95] Direct prayer to the Supreme

Being is rare but there are, or at least used to be, occasions when it took place. According to one account the chief and people gathered "at the foot of the tree planted once upon a time by the ancestors" to pray to God for rain.[96] The following is an example of a prayer that might be given in a time of emergency:

> Oh Vidye, Father;
> Father of the dead, Father of the living,
> We are dying with our children.
> Now all the food is dried in the fields.
> What shall we eat?
> Change! Notice us!
> It is you, Father who does not give to one alone.
> Who gives to the great, who gives to the small.[97]

Prayers need not always be in an emergency, however, as in the case of the following, reported from the Baluba Kasai, which sums up the faith of the Baluba:

> Lord God
> Give me life, a strong life
> Give me well-being
> That I may marry and have children
> That I may raise chickens and goats
> That I may have money, all sorts of goods
> That I may flourish in health and life
> My daughters belong to God
> My sons are his children
> All that I have is his
> He is their Master.[98]

Normally, however, God is approached through the ancestors. As senior members of the human community they must speak on behalf of their descendants. As noted before, this does not mean that God is simply the "First Ancestor." In theory God clearly differs from other beings in essential nature, not only in degree. The fact that one prays to God through the ancestors, however, may lead to difficulty in maintaining the distinction in practice. Perhaps the very attempt to express the relationship between God and the ancestors in such a way that it could be visualized in terms of an "organizational chart" is to do violence to the Luba view.

God, for the Baluba, is not only distant, he is also very near. This paradox is well expressed by the saying "God is not far away—when you call to Him He answers, but if you run after Him you cannot catch up to Him for night will overtake you."[99] The names for God that we have mentioned may suggest distance and otherness; there are also names by which he may be addressed in a more intimate and personal way, such as Kalemba Namaweji and Kungwa Banze.

He is also said to be known as Wamanene, interpreted as "the sorrowful or suffering one." [100]

Perhaps the lack of frequent reference to God, often understood to indicate his distance from man, may also, paradoxically, suggest that he is so overwhelmingly present that he can usually be taken for granted. Ordinarily he need not be specifically addressed in prayer because he is already present in everything. There is a sense in which absolute otherness and absolute nearness are closely connected.

The relationship between the Supreme God and other beings has not been worked out in clear theoretical fashion by the Baluba and some of their statements may seem to the outsider to be inconsistent with each other. Perhaps, however, these statements indicate that the Baluba, like many other peoples, have experienced the Divine both as transcendent and as immanent, both as one and as many. There is one Divine Power, "Father of Creation," who is discontinuous with his creation. And yet this same Divine Power manifests himself in or through created beings, especially through the great forces of nature on the one hand and, on the other hand, through the great ancestral heroes of the past. Thus Leza may be that which comes from the sky, but his reality is not exhausted by these phenomena. Vidye Mukulu may be associated with the ancestors and for some purposes he may even seem to be identified with an ancestor but this is not all that is to be said of him. In different contexts divine power may be spoken of in different ways; the consistency of these ways of speaking is not so much theoretical as functional.

This brings us back to the basic point that life for the Baluba is a whole; there is no "religion" separated from life. The protection, enhancement, and celebration of life necessarily involves the whole human community, living and dead, the natural environment and God the Creator. There are distinctions: the dead are not the living, nature is not human, God is other than that which he has created. But the distinctions are not separations; for the Baluba they exist only within a functional whole.

Luba religion has the capacity to change, discarding old elements and accepting the new. In regard to certain practices it is difficult to know whether to speak in the present or past tense. Much of what has been described above is now in the past for a great many Baluba, yet the old ways are still widely influential, if not in terms of specific practices, at least in an underlying attitude. Many have accepted Christianity as an important new source of power but continue to hold much of the traditional outlook and to participate in those traditional practices that still seem relevant to their needs. Luba religion is not necessarily tied to any particular outward manifestations; new terminology and ceremonies may replace the old but continue to express the underlying concern for the enhancement of human life in a community of the living and the dead.

NOTES

1. Malcolm Guthrie, "Some Developments in the pre-History of the Bantu Languages," *The Journal of African History*, III, 2 (1962), p. 280.
2. Robert Cornevin, *Histoire du Congo*. Paris: Editions Berger Levrault, 1966, p. 26 ff.
3. le Reverend Pere Colle, *Les Baluba*. Bruxelles: Institute Internationale de Bibliographie, 1913, Vol. I, p. 354. This work deals with the Baluba Hemba, the eastern Baluba.
4. The correct name of the people is *Baluba*, one person is a *Muluba*, the language is *Kiluba*. Strictly speaking, it is incorrect to use the root *-luba* without a prefix but it is frequently so used when serving as an adjective modifying an English word. Although incorrect in Kiluba, this is easier in English; therefore I will continue the practice.
5. Edmond Verhulpen. *Baluba et Balubaises du Katanga*. Anvers: L'Avenir Belge, 1936, p. 10. In this and all other French sources, the translations into English are my own.
6. See Olga Boone, *Carte Ethnique du Congo: Quart Sud-est*. Tervuren: Musee Royal d'Afrique Centrale, 1961, especially pp. 50, 115f, and 145f.
7. Placide Tempels, *Bantu Philosophy*, tr. Colin King. Paris: Presence Africaine, 1959, p. 13.
8. Newell S. Booth, "Teaching a Bantu Community," Unpublished Ph.d. dissertation, Hartford Seminary Foundation, 1936, pp. 40, 42
9. Tempels, *Bantu Philosophy*, p. 31.
10. Jason Sendwe, "Traditions et coutumes ancestrales des Baluba-Shankadji," *Bulletin du Centre d'étude des problèmes sociaux indigènes*, No. 24. Elisabethville (Lubumbashi), 1954, p. 106. Mr. Sendwe came from the family of chiefs of Mwanza, was a "medical assistant" in charge of dispensaries, became Vice-Premier of the Congo and was Governor of North Katanga until his assassination in 1965.
11. Theodore Theuws, "Outline of Luba Culture," in *Cahiers economiques et sociaux*, II, 1, 1964, Leopoldville (Kinshasa), p. 15.

12. Edouard Sendwe, "L'Homme dans la Genèse et l'homme chez les Bantu," unpublished thesis. Montpelier: Faculté Libre de Théologie Protestante, 1963. Mr. Edouard Sendwe is the son of Jason Sendwe. He now goes by the name Sendwe Ilunga.
13. Placide Tempels, *Bantu Philosophy,* p. 68f, as quoted in Edwin W. Smith (ed.), *African Ideas of God.* London: Edinburgh House Press, 1950, p. 20.
14. Theuws, "Outline of Luba Culture," p. 14.
15. E. Sendwe, "L'Homme dans la Genèse,", p. 47f.
16. Tempels, *Bantu Philosophy,* p. 37.
17. *Ibid.,* p. 33.
18. Emmanuel Levinas, in Jean Wahl, *A Short History of Existentialism,* tr.Forrest Williams and Stanley Maron. New York: Philosophical Library, 1949, p. 51.
19. E. Sendwe, "L'Homme dans la Genèse," p. 67.
20. *Ibid.,* p. 50.
21. Tempels, *Bantu Philosophy.*
22. *Ibid.,* p. 43.
23. E. Sendwe, "L'Homme dans la Genèse," p. 66.
24. *Ibid.,* p. 67.
25. E. Van Avermaet, *Dictionnaire Kiluba-Francais.* Tervuren: Musée Royale d'Afrique Centrale, 1954, p. 153.
26. E. Sendwe, "L'Homme dans la Genèse," p. 50.
27. *Ibid.,* p. 51.
28. Theuws, "Outline," p. 10, and Van Avermaet, *Dictionnaire,* p. 128.
29. E. Sendwe, "L'Homme dans la Genèse," p. 58f.
30. *Ibid.,* p. 63.
31. W. F. P. Burton, *Luba Religion and Magic in Custom and Belief.* Tervuren: Musée Royal de l'Afrique Centrale, 1961, p. 56.
32. J. Sendwe, "Traditions et coutumes," p. 94.
33. Van Avermaet, *Dictionnaire,* p. 227.
34. Burton, *Luba Religion,* p. 152.
35. *Ibid.,* p. 153.
36. Syphorien Bamuinikile-Mudiasa, *La mort et l'au-dela chez les Baluba du Kasai.* Lubumbashi: Centre d'étude des problemes sociaux indigenes, 1971, p. 33.
37. Burton, *Luba Religion,* p. 42.
38. *Ibid.,* p. 38.
39. Van Avermaet, *Dictionnaire,* p. 387.
40. Merran McCullogh, *The Southern Lunda and Related Peoples.* London: International African Institute, 1951, p. 72.
41. Burton, *Luba Religion,* p. 40.
42. *Ibid.,* p. 43.
43. E. Sendwe, "L'Homme dans la Genèse," p. 50.

44. Agnes Donohugh and Priscilla Berry, "A Luba Tribe in Katanga," *Africa*, V. 2 (London), p. 181.
45. Frank H. Melland, *In Witch-Bound Africa*. London: Seeley, Service and Co., 1923, p. 158.
46. Bamuinikile-Mudiasa, *La mort*, p. 67.
47. V. W. Turner, *Chihamba: The White Spirit*. Manchester: Manchester University Press, 1962, p. 6.
48. Melland, *Witch-Bound Africa*, p. 224.
49. E. Sendwe, "L'Homme dans la Genèse," p. 63
50. Burton, *Luba Religion*, p. 81.
51. *Ibid.*, p. 89.
52. *Ibid.*, p. 84.
53. Burton, *Luba Religion*, p. 92.
54. *Ibid.*, p. 68.
55. E. Sendwe, "L'Homme dans la Genèse," p. 75.
56. Burton, *Luba Religion*, p. 69.
57. *Ibid.*, p. 105.
58. Colle, *Les Baluba*, Vol. II, p. 471.
59. J. Sendwe, "Traditions et coutumes," p. 117.
60. Van Avermaet, *Dictionnaire*, p. 153.
61. Burton, *Luba Religion*, p. 119.
62. Tempels, *Bantu Philosophy*, p. 59.
63. Bamuinikile-Mudiasa, *La mort*, p. 25.
64. Theuws, "Outline," p. 7.
65. Verhulpen, *Baluba*, p. 166.
66. Burton, *Luba Religion*, p. 63.
67. Jan Vansin, *Kingdoms of the Savanna*. Madison: University of Wisconsin Press, 1966, p. 34.
68. Theuws, "Outline," p. 7.
69. *Ibid.*, p. 8.
70. Burton, *Luba Religion*, p. 19.
71. *Ibid.*
72. Stephen Lucas, "Baluba et Aruund." Unpublished dissertaion, Paris: E.P.H.E., 1968, p. 142.
73. Van Avermaet, *Dictionnaire*, p. 369.
74. Burton, *Luba Religion*, p. 19.
75. Colle, *Les Baluba*, Vol. II, p. 568.
76. Burton, *Luba Religion*, p. 154.
77. *Ibid.*, p. 155.
78. Van Avermaet, *Dictionnaire*, p. 181.
79. *Ibid.*, p. 26.
80. Theuws, "Outline," p. 37.
81. Tempels, *Bantu Philosophy*, P. 37.
82. E. Sendwe, "L'Homme dans la Genèse," p. 49.
83. Alexis Kagame, "La place de Dieu et d'homme dans la re-

ligion des Bantu," *Cahiers des Religions Africaines,* vol. II. Kinshasa, 1968.

84. Theuws, "Outline," p. 37.
85. Theodore Theuws, "Textes Luba," *Bulletin du Centre d'étude des problemes sociaux indigenes,* No. 27, Lubumbashi. 1954, p. 30.
86. Dugald Campbell, *In the Heart of Bantu Land.* Philadelphia: J. B. Lippencott Co., 1922, p. 245. Lippincott
87. Melland, *In Witch-Bound Africa,* p. 154.
88. Theuws, *Textes Luba,* p. 73.
89. E. Sendwe, "L'Homme dans la Genèse," p. 48.
90. Melland, *In Witch-Bound Africa,* p. 154.
91. Theodore Theuws, "Le reel dans la conception Luba," Zaïre 15, 1 Bruxelles, 1961, p. 22.
92. Edwin W. Smith and A. M. Dale, *The Ila-Speaking People of Northern Rhodesia.* London: Macmillan, 1920, vol. I, p. 205.
93. Booth, "Teaching a Bantu Community," p. 39.
94. Campbell, *In the Heart of Bantu Land,* p. 266.
95. Theuws, *Textes Luba,* p. 76.
96. *Ibid.,* p. 34.
97. *Ibid.,* p. 85f.
98. Bamuinikile-Mudiasa, *La mort,* p. 30f.
99. Burton, W. F. P., *Proverbs of the Baluba,* Elisabethville (Lubumbashi): Editions de la Revue Juridique, n.d., p. 53.
100. Campbell, *In the Heart of Bantu Land,* p. 245.

4

The Tradition of Renewal in Kongo Religion

John M. Janzen

INTRODUCTION

This essay is an interpretation of Kongo religion around the theme of process and renewal within a cultural tradition. While ample justification for this approach is found in the abundant historical documentation from the Lower Zaïre dating back to the sixteenth century,[1] much of the ethnographic literature on Kongo traditional religion focuses on its degeneration in the face of slavery, colonialism, and foreign missions. The classic monographs all project a sharp break in Kongo culture history around the turn of the last century and accordingly deal either with the "pure tradition' before that break, with the colonial degradation itself, or with the reaction to the colonial impact. Although it must be acknowledged that slavery, colonialism, and Christian missions did influence Kongo society profoundly, there is good reason to deal with the history of Kongo religion from the viewpoint of internal continuity rather than that of disruption from without.

The need for such an approach is more apparent after ten years of post-independence synthesis—actually beginning in Lower Zaïre about 1945—during which individuals who have grown up in their own society have been resolving for themselves issues of religious form and meaning. An enhanced historical record, the result of recent discoveries of documents, has also contributed to the possibility of analysis on the basis of continuity instead of discontinuity.

The perspective of continuity or process is not altogether lacking in existing works but it is not systematically developed; it is often replaced by a more static theoretical perspective. Doutreloux, for instance, notes that the BaKongo have a remarkable facility of adaptation, of partial obliteration of their tradition and the substitution of a new feature that says the same thing another way; nevertheless, he goes ahead elsewhere to construct a static metaphysic of Kongo magic.[2] Balandier also is aware of the renewal historically of Kongo religion and can point in his writing to episodes of the discarding of the *minkisi* (sacred medicines, singular *nkisi*), but he fails to relate this in any systematic way to other dynamic features of the religion which he studies, such as "messianism." [3]

The matter of the creation and the destruction of the *minkisi* is of particular interest, for nowhere more than here do we have specific and observable evidence of the dynamic character of Kongo religious tradition. It will be useful to take up this problem briefly, and to draw theoretical significance from it.

Judaism and Islam, largely on the basis of the second commandment banning "graven images," are religions devoid of "icons." "The People" or "the Word" in these traditions become the visible vehicles for the expression of Divine Will; images simply do not appear. It may come as a surprise to some readers that Kongo religious culture respects this canon as well insofar as God is concerned. Nsemi Isaki, an early twentieth-century catechist wrote, "Of Nzambi-God, we only speak his name; we have not seen an *nkisi* bearing His name." [4] Alongside this restraint before a Divine Being who cannot be represented, the proliferation of statues, medicine bundles, and the like stands in sharp contrast. The threshold between the absence of visual representation of divinity in Kongo culture and the proliferation of representation is found in origin tales such as that of the god of twins, Funza, who was responsible for the first *nkisi*. We shall see later that this threshold has on occasion been evident in historical moments of renewal when the ritual reliquary has been abandoned for a renewed worship of God.

There is an interesting parallel to the *nkisi* in the Eastern Orthodox Christian concept of the icon. The special quality of an icon "is its expression of the formula by which man might represent God without fear of blasphemy and which might satisfy the devotional needs of the faithful without fear of idolatry." [5] The icon is a thing, but also a memory symbolizing a religious experience. The church may sanctify the icon in a special rite at which a holy link is established between the image and its prototype, between that which is represented and the representation itself. [6]

In terms of their origins the icons are often the artistic and material manifestation of visions given to certain persons. "As such, these visions received by the Church through the icon, become a new revelation, a source of theological ideas (e.g., Divine Wisdom) and from it there emerges an iconographic theology." [7] It is, in effect, a sort of iconographic dispensation which becomes a religious canon not unlike that of the written word which, while based on traditions, has a place for development and renewal, combining an ancient vision with an interior truth.

The parallels with Kongo *nkisi* tradition are remarkable. Nsemi puts it this way, in telling about the origins of the *minkisi*: "The first *nkisi* called Funza originated in God. After Funza there followed a series of many *minkisi* distributed out over the whole land each with its representative powers, governing over its particular domain." [8] He goes on to tell of the first ancient who dreamed of plants and other medicines he must mix together to relieve pain and hunger. Many such accounts tell of particular *minkisi* and their founders, and of the cult that has been developed by subsequent devotees.

My purpose in comparing the *minkisi* with icons is to develop a theory of ritual symbols that will facilitate the analysis of Kongo religious culture as process. The Ba-Kongo, no less than the Orthodox Christians, are quite aware of the separateness of the material "host" of the *nkisi* and its object, the spirit or force symbolized. Never is an *nkisi* itself the object of worship. Yet while the Orthodox Church apparently has been able to accept the icon as compromise between those who would do away with images of the supernatural and those who require them, the BaKongo have, on the whole, rested less easily with their *minkisi*. Not only do *minkisi* seem to require inventing from time to time, but they become obsolete and are discarded. Thus they manifest the unsure hold of the invisible upon the material in Kongo thought and belief. The reason for this was not always the intervention of the European. Nsemi notes the widespread tendency of people in 1915 to disregard the rules of *nkisi* making.

> The construction of an nkisi—the ingredients and the songs—must follow the original model. If you put the ingredients together helter-skelter you injure the nkisi and it will become angry over your failure to arrange it properly. An nkisi's strength is rooted in how it was discovered originally; the ingredients are put in as they must be, else it loses its strength and gets confused. Some people do not understand what kind of plants are capable of curing. Then also there is the kind of person who makes an nkisi not learned from his own people, or perhaps he has no access to the parents of twins. Others will know that such an nkisi has been designed by the person himself, and they will ridicule him as incompetent, for his nkisi is not authentic—it does not originate with the ancestors. So many people do not come in possession of powerful medicines, and this is a shame. [9]

In his way Nsemi has given us the key to the *nkisi* as a symbol: the relationship of the original model (literally, *bukatombila*, "as it arose") with the ingredients and songs that are in fact pronounced.

When this association is imperfect, or helter-skelter, the *nkisi* gets angry, confused, and loses its "power." We have here an excellent portrayal of "symbolic loss" or "semantic drift."

An interesting comparison can be found in Roland Barthes' discussion of why fashions change in modern salon-inspired apparel. [10] The original model is continually recreated by the clothing actually worn, by commentary in the fashion books, and by pictures (icons). These reproductions are not synonymous with the original; they are "secularized" versions, manifestations of "the world" as opposed to "*la mode.*" Fashion change, with the assistance of built-in obsolescence, is assured. A new style replaces the old and for a time enjoys the power of originality.

Kongo religious ritual is not produced in the salons of *haute couture*, but in the tensions, aspirations, and routines of daily life. In certain times and sectors of the society, religious paraphernalia are created in the context of cult life. In the dynamic balance between the original model and the reproduction, between the devotee and the iconoclast, we have an interesting matrix in which to study the tradition as processed.

In the first section below I shall look at the history of Kongo iconoclast movements, which attack the *minkisi* and order the people to return to the true worship of ancestors and God. Next I turn to the esoteric cults which appear to have endured throughout the foregoing upheavals, and which are *iconorthostic* rather than *iconoclastic* ("-orthostic" meaning "to originate," as "-oclastic" means to "to destroy"). [11] The third section examines the social structural characteristics that contribute to human tension, and the conventionalized ways that have developed to take care of these, and to define the lines of society. In the final section I analyze renewal of the word, the verbal icon which appears in song, ritual, and prayer, and its relationship to the quest for a just and orderly community.

TRADITION AND ICONOCLASM:
A HISTORIOGRAPHY OF KONGO RELIGIOUS RENEWAL

An appropriate point of entry to the history of Kongo religion is that most controversial event of 1921, the Kimbanguist movement, which is widely held to have given the death blow to tradition. Let us see it first as related by the keeper of the holy city of Nkamba-Jerusalem, the second son of the prophet Kimbangu, Dialungana Salomon, addressing the faithful in a recent theological pamphlet:

Know this, that we the black race are the most dishonoured of all races whom God created in this earth. And especially in this black body we were given by God our Father. We could not finish telling the torments imposed upon us by the white man, especially the government white man. Think how we were transported by the peoples of Europe, how many blacks were put in ships like sardines in cans. Many times, a'small number managed to arrive in America and other countries of the white man, but even those few fell into unlimited suffering. Those who remained to work in Kongo were put to death for any little thing, specially while they carried loads from Matadi to Leopoldville. From Leopoldville to Matadi, thousands and thousands died!

Then the people of this country were put to digging the railroad from Matadi to Leopoldville. Multitudes crowded to their death. Note also that in the year in which World War I ended, 1918, a serious epidemic occurred; in all Kongo there remained no village and no house without a corpse. A little more and the black race would have entirely disappeared....

Then·it was that the missionaries came to shine light among us here in Kongo and among all nations of the earth, following the Commandment of Jesus as given in the Bible they themselves brought (Matthew 28 : 19). But they did not care to obey the words of the Lord Jesus, taking them over only to fabricate deceits to enrich themselves in the name of Jesus. For they were hired men, and cared not for the sheep (John 10 : 12-13) ...

Because the missionaries did not obey the voice of the Lord Jesus, they taught the people that having left their sins it was in the missions that they would find Christ their saviour. But only a small number believed; many villages showed not a single convert. When the missionary travelled in the villages, the elders would impress upon their juniors to hide in the forests lest the white man catch them by witchcraft and send them to Europe. The people as a whole did not leave their wickedness; fetishism, dancing, drinking and witchcraft continued among them.

But see the great thing that happened on 6 April 1921!

In Nkamba a man appeared who had never studied at a mission station, but he was a believer and had learned to read and write a little from a village teacher. His name was Simon Kimbangu. He raised the dead, caused the paralysed to stand upright, gave sight to the blind, cleansed lepers, and healed all the sick in the name of the Lord Jesus. But he chased away those who practised witchcraft.

In the twinkling of an eye this news spread, and the whole country went wild. Like dust the news spread that in Nkamba had appeared a Prophet who was raising the dead. From that time Nkamba was called the New Jersalem.

Note two astonishing things!

1.   The Prophet.
2.   The New Jerusalem.

Think well on both of them.

When the prophet was revealed, the dead in stretchers and the sick of all kinds were brought to the Prophet of God. But in everything, whether raising the dead, healing the sick, or giving a blessing in the name of Jesus, first there must be prayer, then hymns, and then a teacher must read the Bible and teach doctrines that change hearts, in order that all men should leave their wickedness; for if that does not happen, then these blessings you have come to get become as fire to you. Believe in the Lord Jesus, he who saves you from your sins. For I am in obedience to him.

Now God our Father and his Son Jesus Christ are returned to us, so cease your wickedness....

Now see how all the villages hastened to abandon their fetishes; see all the roads littered with fetishes of all kinds. People confessed their sins. Drums were broken, dancing forsaken. People struggled to seek out teachers. Churches were built overnight in all the villages. Those who had not cared to pray to God fought for places in church, and those who had had no use for schools fought to enter the classroom.

Thus the words of Jesus were fulfilled....

Because Simon Kimbangu obeyed the voice of Jesus, all things promised by Jesus were fulfilled in him, the work of Jesus was revealed, and the names of God the Father and of the Lord Jesus were glorified. Since the coming of the missionaries it had never happened that the dead arose, the lame walked, and the blind saw; or that people of their own free will threw away their fetishes, or wanted to pray to God. And only then did we the people of Kongo know that God and Jesus remembered us. The grief and suffering of our fathers were heard by God the Father, and the tears of us the black people were wiped away in Kongo. [12]

Kimbangu was arrested in 1921 and sentenced to death. The sentence was commuted to life imprisonment and he was sent to exile in Katanga where he remained until his death in 1951. In 1960, concurrent with the independence activities in the Congo, Kimbangu's mortal remains were brought back to the Lower Congo and a mausoleum was opened at his home village, Nkamba, today called Nkamba-Jerusalem, the holy city of the Kimbanguist church. On every 6th of April the "return of the prophet" is commemorated and pilgrims come to the mausoleum to deposit prayers and to renew their ties with the memory of Kimbangu. The Bethesda Pool in a nearby stream, where Kimbangu in 1921 sent people to wash after he blessed and healed them, is also a place of prayer and meditation.

The three sons of the prophet lead the church, known as the "Eglise de Jesus Christ sur la Terre par le Prophet Simon Kimbangu" (EJCSK). They shape the direction of the worship and belief of a claimed three million members in Central Africa, the majority in Zaïre, but some in Zambia, Uganda, and West African countries. The youngest son, Joseph Diangienda, (Fig. 9) is a skilled public speaker who can hold his audience in attentiveness hours on end, speaking to them about the mission of the church and the meaning of the prophet's teaching and the challenge of Kimbanguism in contemporary Africa. Early in 1970 he successfully led the EJCSK to admission in theWorld Council of Churches.[13]

While the sons of Kimbangu have undefined, and thus unlimited, authority in such matters as healing, it is the Bantumwa ("the sent"), the apostles, who bless the many members and followers of Kimbangu. They are the remaining individuals who were followers and workers with Kimbangu in 1921, most of whom spent the intervening years in exile in other places in the Congo in colonial labor camps or in village arrest.[14]

Kimbanguism is active not only at the holy city of Nkamba-Jerusalem but also in hundreds of villages and cities in Zaïre. It is a way of life complete with schools where children are occupied in marching and presenting religious messages through choreography. Music plays an important role in the church and, although Kimbangu ordered certain types of drums broken in 1921, other types are used in the music and liturgy of the movement. Liturgy and choreography alike are an adaptation, bringing together traditional Kongo cosmological motifs and Christian idioms out of the common life of people from all walks of life. The forms of this worship and the ideas informing it reveal that Kimbanguism, like a strong plant, has sprouted and grown in fertile soil. The plant looks strangely Protestant, the soil, the flowers, the scent, familiarly African. What here is continuity? What discontinuity? Although I shall not deal in any detail with Kimbanguism as such, I want to look at the "fertile ground" of Kongo religion in a manner that should assist in a better comprehension of Kimbanguism and similar bodies.

One trend in the recent sociological study of African religious movements is represented by Balandier,[15] who deals with Kimbanguism and other religious movements in terms of a "before-colonialism," and "after-colonialism" with the present (pre-1960—the sociological present) consisting of a kind of transitional phase. "Before-colonialism" (up until about 1890 or 1900 in this part of Africa) was a style-period often described as the ethnographic present. This is basically the approach of structural functionalism in anthropology and sociology; the implicit orientation toward religion is that a society is a coherent whole, with religion serving to maintain it. Colonialism enters the picture, according to this perspective, and upsets the balance; a new balance is attempted which includes the messianic or nativistic movements which are reactions to the colonial presence and lead to a synthesis which we then see in such movements as Kimbanguism.

The colonial governments used this perspective of a coherent society to which their administration could simply be attached and tried to maintain the society at its earlier functional stage and to keep everybody happy by convincing them that they needed only to look back and do things as their forefathers did. It is a conservative model of government which necessitates the suppression of any kind of movement pointing toward change, renewal, or independence.

Already in the latter years of the colonial presence in Africa, in the 1950s, the functionalist's model of society was being challenged. Maquet, who had worked in the Congo, criticized the functionalist's bias for supporting the colonialist outlook on society but also, from a strictly methodological standpoint, as leading to an erroneous understanding of the dynamics of society and religion. [16]   He suggested that an approach to the study of religion and society would be necessary which (a) was not based on a stasis model of society and (b) allowed the student of society to integrate history with an analytic approach.

Bohannan's essay on the Tsav cult among the Tiv of Nigeria followed this more historical approach. [17]   Bohannan was interested in this anti-witchcraft cult because of its pattern of repetition in Tiv history. Concerned with reforming society, destroying a pseudohierarchy, and reestablishing an egalitarian basis among people, it was discovered, after consulting the historical record, that it reappeared every generation or so, although not on a scheduled basis. Bohannan argued that, if one takes the standard functionalist view of the Tsav cult, it is difficult to incorporate it into a logically coherent picture. Error might easily creep in if one were only around long enough to witness one Tsav cult appearance which would appear to be a reaction to the impact of colonialism. Bohannan argued that social science has often mistakenly looked at every little indication of change or movement in African society in terms of reaction to the colonial presence. It was a temptation, to be sure. Very often there was thought to be no history available in the study of a particular African society, so it was very difficult to know whether something like the Tsav cult had occurred in the past or not.

In this respect the study of Kongo religion can be very instructive. We have a more or less documented history, dating back to the arrival of the Portuguese in 1482, which can be brought to bear in explaining a movement like Kimbanguism. Taking the surface evidence of Dialungana's remarks, the characteristics of Kimbanguism that strike us as interesting are these: the feared extinction of the Kongo people, misery in the early colonial setting, an epidemic in 1918, disease and conflict. We also note that Kimbangu taught the destruction of the *minkisi*, the worship of the true God, and the restoration of general morality. As a matter of course Kimbangu also taught monogamous marriage, no smoking, and no drinking. These, one would think on first analysis, are items he got directly from the British Baptist missionaries of the area.   But it is precisely in drawing the apparently obvious conclusion regarding such matters that we fall in greatest danger of missing the mark. Kimbangu's reason for judging idolatry wrong and for ordering the destruction of the *minkisi* is not in the final analysis the same as that of the missionaries.

We are faced at this point with the choice of two alternative and diverging courses of explanation which Bastide has spoken of as "internal causality" and "external causality."[18]   Without the utilization of deep historical knowledge we may rely on a single dimension history for the movement and call Kimbanguism either a reaction to colonialism and an acceptance of foreign religious models, thereby confirming the "external causality" of the movement; or, we may assert the internal causality of the event, assuming, as did Bohannan with the Tiv Tsav and Bastide in his work with Afro-Brazilian revitalization movements, that we can find historical antecedents to the event that suggest a continuity of structures and values. Bastide insists that what is important in analyzing the meeting of two civilizations is not so much the exchange of ideas as the process of handling and transforming these ideas and types. The internal-external causality dichotomy may also correspond to the past-present or future-present dichotomy, since tradition and *telos* alike are important in determining events. As the criteria for our rapid backtracking in Kongo history of the past 400 years we expect the ambiguous contemporary occurrences such as the destruction of the *minkisi*, the occurrence of disease and conflict, and the restoration of "godly" as opposed to "sacramental" morality, to serve us well in indicating to what extent there is a continuity of structures and values.

Our first example from Kongo history will be the reign of the famous Christian Kongo king, Affonso I, who was invested in 1506. The Portuguese explorers arrived in Kongo first in 1482 and returned frequently in later decades, establishing ties between the Court of Portugal and Kongo, and promoting missions and schools in Kongo staffed by Portuguese priests, while Kongo youths frequented schools and the royal court in Portugal. Before 1500 the king Nzinga Nkuwu and others of the royal family were baptized into the Christian faith. The king and his son Mpanzu a Kitima however, renounced Catholicism sometime between 1494 and 1506, whereas the queen and another son, Affonso, remained Catholic. Mpanzu, the pagan prince, had remained in the capital before 1506 while Affonso, in the traditional manner of the chosen prince, was sent off to become the governor of the Nsundi provincial capital before succeeding to the throne. So when Nzinga Nkuwu died in 1506 the conflict for succession between the pagan Mpanzu a Kitima and Affonso the Christian ensued. [19]

A battle between the two brothers took place around or within the capital with Affonso's supporting troops numbering far fewer than those of Mpanzu a Kitima. Documents suggest that Affonso defended the capital city from within and Mpanzu attacked from without. The first assault by Mpanzu's troops was repulsed, tradition relates, in a manner that Affonso was not even aware of at the time; his troops were said by the enemy to have been accompanied by a dazzling white female figure, together with a mounted cavalier, riding upon a white charger carrying a red cross. The pagan troops took flight because they could not face up to this celestial knight and the white woman.

Mpanzu attacked again the following day, but again the celestial couple came out and stopped them. Seeking to enter the city by another manner, Mpanzu stumbled against poisoned stakes that had been planted by Affonso's defenders and died, whereupon Affonso's troops chased the pagan troops and defeated them soundly. When Affonso heard that the rout of Mpanzu was due to the celestial protection received from the virgin mother of God and the celestial rider St. James, he regarded it as a clear mandate for his reign. This was to be not just another succession, but the beginning of a new era with Christianity as the validating principle confirmed and undergirded by victory in battle.

Affonso ordered a church erected on the capital hill, naming it the Church of the Holy Cross; he himself laid the first stone at the center of the cross in the church. He then assembled all his nobles and ordered them publicly to forward to him whatever the Christian religion forbade in the nature of traditional reliquary; statues and masks and all sorts of ritual objects were collected. The king then had wood brought to the very place where he had defeated his brother with the help of the celestial warriors and there he burned the ritual objects and distributed crosses and statues of the saints brought by the Portuguese to all the noblemen, ordering them to re- turn to their provincial towns, to build churches, and to set up crosses as he had done at the capital. Affonso had founded a new era of Christianity, complete with the advantages of education. He himself was able to read and write. He set up schools, sent princes to Europe, brought in missionaries, and enjoyed a long and peaceful reign until 1543. It was marred in the end, however, by an increas- ing interference in his own government by the Catholic Church and the Portuguese government and the gradual increase in slavery.

The ascent of Affonso to the throne and his order to destroy the traditional reliquary marks the first of a series of such events known in Kongo history. The next outstanding known example dates from the early eighteenth century, almost 200 years later.

After Affonso's reign the Kongo kingdom had its vicissitudes. The king had formerly controlled the sources in the ocean from which shell currency was secured but Portuguese pirates found other sources and inflated the currency. Also, the Catholic Church had forbidden by canon law "royal incest" in the Kongo kingdom. Cousin marriage in the royal context in Kongo kept the number of princes and factions that would vie for power down to a minimum. The queen mother would be the only one that could give birth to contender princes, while the king might have other wives. As royal incest, or cousin marriage, came to be forbidden, the number of direct contenders to the throne increased sharply as did the rivalry between the two houses of Kimulaza and Kimpanzu. Strong per- sonalities surrounded by their kinsmen constituted the focal points of an increasingly fragmented authority, until a vicious circle of allying and fighting developed among the nobility. [20]

An eyewitness report by a Father Bernardo da Gallo, an Italian Capuchin priest who spent some time in the capital city, gives vivid details. [21]   He relates how he found himself in 1702 in a mountain fortress with the Kimulaza faction—that of King Pedro IV, who was in hiding. He also visited a Don Pedro Constantino (Chibengo), of the rival Kimpanzu house. The capital lay in ruins; both sides want- ed to use Father da Gallo in claiming the throne.

Rumors reached da Gallo of irregular rituals in the Church. It was being said that a child had received a vision from the Madonna that if the kingdom were not restored immediately God would punish the people. Another rumor of 1704 was that an elderly woman had seen the Madonna who had told her that Mount Chibangu, where the king was in hiding, would be destroyed by celestial fire if the king did not go to the capital and restore the kingdom. This woman diviner had acquired the reputation of a saint in certain circles. She burned *minkisi* and healed, either with the sign of the cross or with the name of the Holy Trinity. If her own work was not enough, she considered herself to be the precursor of a younger woman who called herself "Sainte Antoine" or "Dona Beatrice." Da Gallo tried to combat her heresy and she, in turn, criticized him, so that for months a veritable religious battle went on, with Father da Gallo saying Mass for the king at his fortress hideout and down below in the valley Sainte Antoine (Dona Beatrice) burning and destroying all kinds of *minkisi* and hearing confessions and healing. What scandalized the Father most in the activity of the prophetess is that she was burning all kinds of sacred objects brought to her, including crosses.

> She kneeled before me and touched the ground three times with her forehead, hesitated a bit as if to pray, then rose up and circled three times about me. I asked the counselors the meaning of this act and they said it was a sign of joy and that she had done the same thing with the king. The interpreter added that she seemed to be 'stupid' (possibly possessed) because she had been dead and had been resurrected. [22]

She walked about on the tips of her toes, hardly touching the ground, and moved her whole body in the manner of an adder with her neck stiff as if she had lost her spirit and with eyes exorbited, speaking in a frenetic manner, so that it was impossible to understand her. Upon inquiring, he learned that she had entered her ministry after being gravely ill and at the point of death and seeing a Catholic brother dressed like a Capuchin appear to her with the message that the Kongo people should repopulate the abandoned capital.

While da Gallo vied for the allegiance of the king in his refugee hideout, Dona Beatrice moved with her entourage to the abandoned capital and erected a small grass shack against the wall of the gutted cathedral. She tried to enthrone Chibengo with a kind of investituary bull called the "Santissimo Papa," which the king had inherited originally from the Pope in Rome, but Chibengo refused it.

Out of the camp of Chibengo, she drew a large following and in short order, with the aid of miracles, she had the capital filled with people before whom she was suddenly the restorer-liberator, a Kongolese Joan of Arc.

Chibengo, meanwhile, was being manipulated by the king and by da Gallo against Sainte Antoine. Chibengo was given authority to move back into the capital at the head of the king's army, or what was left of it, in order to rout out Sainte Antoine, but in the process he declared himself the king, and Beatrice, Sainte Antoine, his spiritual counterpart. But by various forms of subterfuge Beatrice was arrested in 1706. At first the king did not grant Father da Gallo permission to deal with her as he wanted. But da Gallo eventually intervened before the king and Dona Beatrice was burned at the stake in July 1706, on charges of heresy and crimes against the throne and the faith.

The vacuum of documentation during the late eighteenth and early nineteenth centuries represents a loss of interest by Europeans in Kongo civilization; it is the height of slavery in Kongo, and the times must have been a nightmare. Oral tradition in the early twentieth century suggests that Kongo religious culture persists throughout. In about 1850-1860, the kingdom much reduced in scope, King Nerico Lunga acquired power and had the *minkisi* destroyed. There followed a period still remembered in 1920 as "the peace of the royal throne." [23]

There was another movement called the "Kioka" ("the Burning") in 1890 when *minkisi* were again collected and burned and the paths leading up to the cemeteries were cleaned and various other indications appeared of an attempt at a restoration of morality, proper social structure, and peace.

It is apparent from this sketch of antecedent examples of destruction of the *minkisi*, renewal of the faith, and restoration of morality and of the kingdom from 1506, 1706, 1850, and 1890 (and more that are undocumented) that not every thing in Kimbanguism in 1921 was new and had to do with either a reaction to colonialism or the influence of British Baptist Christianity. We can conclude that in a fundamental way religious renewal is one of the available traditional options, so much so that we must speak of Kongo cultural history as dealing with religious renewal as an institution.

If renewal then is a traditional option that is available in Kongo life, if destruction of the *minkisi* is there as a kind of iconoclastic tradition with people destroying their religious paraphernalia in order to recreate the intangible truths behind the symbols which are no longer meaningful, then I think we can with profit look elsewhere and at other levels for this same theme.

Thus, in the remainder of the essay, I shall search for episodes, themes, and acts of symbolic embodiment as well as renewal and revitalization in various dimensions of Kongo life as they appear on a more day-to-day basis. We will now look at life within the smaller units of society, at the clan level rather than the national level. Arthur Darby Nock sees religion as something which occurs "at a time when extensive disorganization, forced disruption or despondency has hindered the normal function of meaningful institutions." [24] If this be so, revitalization or renewal is actually what religion is all about at whatever level it appears, national or individual. Episodes of renewal constitute a special case within the overall historical function of a religious system. Our search for renewal at various levels then takes the form of looking for those areas of life where the active principal of religion resides under conventional circumstances.

THE ESOTERIC CULTS OF
KONGO: KIMPASI, KHIMBA, LEMBA

To gain a better perspective of these episodes of *iconoclastic* renewal in the history of Kongo religion we must look at the quite inverse, yet related, *iconorthostic* cults that seem to have thrived through the period. "Iconoclastic", of course, refers to the destruction of outward ritual objects to which the first part of the essay is devoted. "Iconorthostic" as already suggested, refers to the counter process of creating a new ritual object or relation out of discrete pieces of experience and perspective. The casual connection between the two is apparent if we note that it is Kimbanguism, not mission Christianity or the moralistic influence of the colonial powers, that is often perceived by the BaKongo to have dealt the cults of Kimpasi, Khimba, and Lemba the crucial defeat in the Lower Congo of 1921.

Already in the sixteenth-century literature there is mention of Kongo "boys in white," referring to the smearing of white clay over the bodies of the initiates to the cults. In the eighteenth century we have better evidence: Father da Gallo identifies one cult by the name of Kimpasi, noting that it is designed for the healing of the ill and other "pagan" purposes that he dare not describe. He relates how he once set out to destroy the huts of the Kimpasi camp "and they chased me away by force with rocks, with cries and menaces armed with bows and arrows." [25]

In the late eighteenth century near Angola another source describes the various "superstitions" and "idolatries" of the "circum-

cision" camps, and the camps women go to for sixty days before
their marriage and the forest houses "they go to to die and be
resurrected." "They do all other idolatrous acts and worship the
devil" and these houses are called "Quimpaxi" (Kimpasi). [26]

A symptom of the difficulty scholars have encountered in studying the Kongo cults is their seeming haphazardly scheduled
seances. They do not meet periodically; rather they seem to lapse
into nonexistence over a period of ten, fifteen, and sometimes
twenty years, then all of a sudden they are there again in full force.
Following the accounts of missionaries and some of the early ethno-
graphers, it becomes apparent that only one or two of the writers
understand the principle which triggers a periodically recurrent
event. Van Wing noted at the beginning of this century that the
Kimpasi is considered a remedy for generalized evils and ills which
strike the society, such as widespread sterility, epidemic, or a high
rate of abortion. Any or all of these factors may precipitate a new
seance. [27]   Father Bittremieux, speaking about the Khimba in
Mayombe, says it is held in view of the "rampages of witches," and
that during this time people build new villages.[28] He notes the
sporadic recurrences of the Khimba, but does not suggest any
reason. With great disparagement he states, "We think we have
them stamped out and then they pop out all over again and we're
nowhere. The schools are empty, the people leave and introduce
themselves to the Khimba and we're just where we were when we
started."

Another observer, British missionary Weeks, suggests that these
are not exclusively cult groups, but that they have the aspect of
guilds and exist to keep tyrannical chiefs and upstart nobles in
check. [29]   Also they may protect people from false charges of witchcraft and actually rid the land of witches. Weeks sees these "guilds"
as having some relationship with authority on the one hand and
witchcraft on the other, but his account is descriptive rather than
dynamic.

The Lemba, which was located north of the Congo river, is mentioned briefly by Laman, a Swedish missionary-linguist, as having to
do with healing and with setting up a pattern for marriage. A
Manianga healer, himself initiated in his youth to the Lemba, says it
was entered into after an illness which had brought one near death,
but from which one had miraculously recovered, much in the manner of votive offerings, masses, and monuments in traditional
European Christianity. [30]   A given saint there would be called upon
to receive the gratitude and recognition of the recovered; in Kongo

one would substitute for the saint an ancestor or spirits such as the Nkita of Water (Kimpasi), the androgynous Mahungu (Lemba), or Mbumba Luangu, the rainbow, (Khimba), and for the votive offering the initiation into the cult.

After several individuals in a community had been referred by the diviners to the initiation the sponsoring persons would be contacted. In connection with the Lemba there is strong emphasis upon the patrilateral kinsmen as sponsors. If one's own father is a member, then the obligation rests on him. If he is not, then one of his matrilineage; if this does not produce a Lemba member, then one looks in the father's matriclan, where surely there is a Lemba member. The significance of the patrilateral ties to a cult association in a matrilineally recruited society is quite evident; it provides a principle of alternation whereby the cult stands separate from the clan and lineage, crosscutting the particularistic ties of the former.

The cults, then, would hold seances because of an epidemic, rising mortality, sterility of women, famine, or all of these, abstractly characterized by the rising level of witchcraft; or because of any breakdown in social relations evident in the rise of the level of feuding. Also they could be called into existence by diviners who were in a position to recommend ritual initiation to individuals and clans. Once a diviner had recommended a cult the chiefs of an area would set about to sponsor an initiation. All the conflicts in the community would need to be resolved before the cult could really begin and one of the songs that stems from this period of pre-cult preparation recommending all that must be done goes as follows:

> He who hides sorcery in his heart must give it up or be ostrasized. The village is tranquil and thus it must stay. All quarrels must be resolved. No one can be fined or held for outdated grievances. Knives will be sheathed and no guns will be seen on the paths, and delinquents will be burned. [This last is a reference to witchcraft.] [31]

We have here a straightening out of all the social ills that have been accumulating, somewhat in the manner of the seven-year practice in ancient Judaism of resolving or absolving all debts. Here conflicts of any sort seem to be included in the program.

As opening time approaches, priests or diviners propagate a mystique of anticipation and fear. People are going to be "dying" and there will be strange goings-on out in the forests; awe, mystery, and anticipation are encouraged.

The seance as such, while quite diversified both between the several cults and within each, can be charted out in comparative fashion following Van Gennep's standard threefold stages of separation, transition, and combination. In the Kongo cults the first stage, that of entrance, was heavily accentuated with the "death of entrance" and took place either in a market or in a village. "Death into the cult" is a theme analogous to the allegation of Dona Beatrice who was in the habit of dying and rising from the dead.

The Khimba "death" ritual described by Bittremieux began when the novices were given a narcotic drink (a *bonzo*). Out of his satchel the priest took a packet, blessed by the ancestors, composed of white clay, red clay, various seeds, small fruits, and other things. The novice, after ingesting these, had a white line traced on each arm and upon his chest. He then twirled the Mbumba Luangu statue around the house three times until he fell upon the ground, and the cry went out that he was dead. Two or three of the veterans of the cult carried the "cadaver" to the Khimba enclosure in the forest. [32]

In the Kimpasi the death of entrance followed a similar pattern, although at night. The novices were undressed and then were told to lie down. It was then said that the Nkita patron spirit had devoured them and the song around the dead continued:

"Oh mystery of mysteries, my friend; well, don't we die the Nkita death?" "Mystery of mysteries, my friend; don't we die the Nkita death; here is the day of glory, sleep in the sleep of death—mystery of mysteries. Here is the day of glory; sleep in the sleep of death. And you, the profane, close your houses well. We in the Kimpase are among ourselves. The profane doesn't sleep in the sleep of death, but we in the Kimpase, we dance." [33]

So it goes on, suggesting that the death ritual is the point of entrance. Again the setting up symbolically of a ritual group that is distinct from those that are left behind in society brings out certain underlying contrasting conditions by the very ritual. The use of white clay in connection with death is noteworthy, as is the nakedness of the novices in contrast to those remaining in society who are clothed.

In the Lemba, according to Fukiau's reconstruction, the first stage of initiation consisted in a blessing of the novice by an *nganga* priest. A crossroads was chosen for this purpose. The fledglings were taught in song that man owed his life to Mahungu, patron spirit of complementarity and fertility. But as the initiates were anointed with red and white, the presence of Nzambi-Mpungu, God Almighty, was invoked.

Bow down,
That God may pass,
On the back as on the stomach,
The face as on the stomach,

A rooster was burned over a fire between the outstretched legs of the initiates, and the fat droppings rubbed over his body. Three times the master bounded his student by the hand (making an invisible line around him) and three times he made him pass between his legs. Spitting on the green leaf of the *kimbansia* grass, the masters consecrated their charges in the Lemba. [34]

The second identifiable stage of the cult initiation concentrates on foods; in the Lemba it involves a lavish banquet of pig offered by the neophytes to their masters, but with all apparently participating. [35]
In the Khimba and Kimpasi the analogous phase is one of privation, during which the initiates are forbidden to eat meat and to drink palm wine; they are given many prohibitions, e.g., to talk only in a low voice as befitting the dead. They must execute very strenuous dances and they sometimes must lie out in the sun half of the day, which in Zaire is quite an accomplishment. They are not only "dead," but they are the suffering dead. [36]

The time for suffering and trial in the Khimba and Kimpasi is followed immediately by the deeper entrance into the cult. A new world has opened on the cult side as opposed to the outside and within this cult world they are defining terms as if this were a world in its own right. The initiates are taught the oaths and the secrets of the cult. In the Lemba a set of moral restrictions is now spelled out to the initiate: the Nganga-Lemba may not fight with others; he may not drop palm wine on the ground; he may not quarrel; he may not commit adultery; when he eats, drinks, or speaks, all are quiet; the Nganga-Lemba may never reveal what he has seen in the Lemba initiations. [37]

Following upon the instructions comes a final sort of consecration into the esoteric symbols of the cult. In the Khimba there is a consecration of the *diyowa*, a cross-shaped trench, the "holy of holies." Derived from the verb *yowa*, to wash or to cleanse, it characterizes the place of purification, the place of initiation.

Water is placed in the *diyowa* trench in the ground, and the initiate kneels down before it. Pointing his finger to the double statue Thafu Maluanga, who represents the rainbow, he chants, "You Thafu Maluangu, all that I see here I will not tell a soul, neither to a woman or man, to a profane person, nor to a white man, else swell me up and kill me." [38] This oath of secrecy and the instructions of the *diyowa* is the apparent heart of the cult.

The equivalent Lemba stage was "the Descent to Lemba," an approach by the initiates down into a valley near a stream where they could come upon their masters, masked in an abstract array of highly charged symbols uniting man, the ancestors, and God. Having thus come face to face with the terrifying power of Mpemba, the "White," the new Lemba initiates would swear by what he had seen. [39] Thereupon would follow a "hilltop" phase of the Lemba in which the initiates would face their masters across a cross trench (like the Khimba *diyowa*), inside a circle decorated with a small tree, a sharp knife, and a packet of red and white clay. Then all entered into the oath ceremony as the initiate rubbed his face in the palm wine-moistened mud of the crosslike trench. Throughout, the order of Lemba and the patron spirit Maluanga is invoked. [40]

In the Kimpasi an analogous stage offers the final oath around the crosslike trench, and the invocation of the Nkita water spirits. [41]

Each of the three seances is closed with a feast, with master and initiate, sharply separated at the outset, now intermingling because they are common members of the cult. The exit back into society, in the case of the Lemba, was uneventful. In the Kimpasi and Khimba, where younger persons rather than the Lemba priest and his wife are concerned, there is more to do. The exit is characterized by the inverse of entrance. The Kimpasi graduates shave the hair on the head, the armpits, and the beard, and they once again smear themselves with white clay before emerging into society in this state. In other areas they return as the "dead" and are considered not to be aware of their kinsmen; they do not know their names, and they commit crimes and licentious acts for several weeks because the dead are not supposed to come back to life and immediately know what their social identity is. [42]

Having examined in only sketchy manner the several stages of the historic Kongo cult seances in the Kimpasi, Khimba, and Lemba, we are convinced of a direction in Kongo culture quite the opposite of that sketched in the first part of the essay. There renewal was exhibited through a sloughing off of material sacrament; here, renewal is concerned with recharging symbols and the creation of the material sacrament (*nkisi*): the iconorthostic process.

Central to the understanding of this process are the several modes of symbolic operation and expression drawn from the referents in the natural and the human world as they are combined in the cults.

Of particular importance are three operational modes. The first can be called the singling out of oppositional relations such as male and female and their complementary repiecing together into a harmonious interexistence. The second, related to the first in the sense of being an extension of it, can be termed the ritual inversion of a situation or relation; here rite inverts hierarchy, and plays a significant role in recreating complementary balance in a situation of threat or imbalance. Third, there are those operations in the ritual expression in the cults which can be called unifying or totalizing in their message; not just a fragile balance, but a wholeness is established, a form most significant in healing rituals. The play of opposites and complementarity from the cult context is best il-lustrated in the Khimba *diyowa*, the place of purification, the holy of holies, a trench dug out in cross form and filled with water. Along with it we have the androgynous statue of Thafu Maluangu, representing the rainbow and also male and female, as an available sharp complementary opposition of two cooperating forces in the universe. This becomes very interesting when we see that the sexual complementarity of the human universe is framed and rounded out by a floral counterpart. One plant that is used, *lemba-lemba*, is seen as a calmant, a symbolic "tranquilizer." But *sisia-sisia*, on the other side, is a violent poison. [43] So we have here a poison-tranquilizer opposition. This does not necessarily stand in homology to the two sexes, but represents the undercurrent of de-finition that generally goes along with the male-female distinction. The male is believed to be strong and works immediately, whereas the female also is strong but works slowly. Male and female are also associated with a dichotomy of another sort in the plant world where one is a violent poison and the other is a calmant.

This suggests that the holy of holies in Kongo cult expression is concerned with bringing together opposites and controlling and di-recting and using the power that is generated in the process. When you bring male and female together, the result is procreation; when you bring two plants together the result is a third kind of combina-tion, something more than the sum of its parts. The traditional Kongo ritual manipulators discovered this and used it to considerable advantage, so that wherever certain plants were brought together they could constitute a cure or a poison, a blessing or a curse, and the power that was generated was known to be use-ful both for good and for evil, both for blessing and for cursing.

Thus there appears to be in Kongo symbolic manipulation a persis-tent effort to combine opposites in the universe. In the example to follow such oppositions as black and white, and the opening of the rainy and dry seasons, are used in complementary fashion to create a symbolic union between various dimensions giving the impression of an entire universe bound up in one symphony of antiphonal harmony.

Initiation to the Kongo "crown chiefship" is a way in which a man may be honored by his patrifilial children. They "elect" him after he has recovered from an illness. It also can take on hereditary dimensions so that it is carried within the clan from one generation to the next; the children of the clan collectively find another father to honor. Dimensions of this priesthood can also be understood as a way of celebrating the ancestor cult. But of direct interest here are the ingredients is the asperge used to anoint the "chief." First, there are the juices of *lemba-lemba* leaves. This plant, as suggested earlier, has the connotation of calmness. It is often planted behind the house of a woman who has twins because such mothers are supposed to be very calm in the face of all the ambiguous and therefore dangerous aspects of twinship. Second, its complement is *mpoko*, a plant that tends to be associated with the inauspicious side of life. The other two plants used in the asperge are a root of the palm tree and a particular mushroom. But why use this particular combination in connection with honoring your father?

To understand this we must penetrate the idiomatic message of plant symbolism. The mushroom is of a kind that is underground most of the year—in other words, invisible. It comes out at the beginning of the rainy season for a few weeks and then disappears again. The palm root is white in color and goes deep into the ground in search of water. The palm tree gives a white sap that rises from deep down in the bottom of the palm tree. The best wine and the most wine made from it comes up at the beginning of the dry season. Just as the mushroom comes up through the ground at the beginning of the rainy season, so the sap of the palm tree comes up at the beginnning of the dry season. What occurs in this ritual manipulation is not only the association of opposable plants, but elements of other dimensions as well- calendrical and chromatic. The mushroom that is underneath most of the year but comes up with the rain and the palm root which is underneath most of the time but comes up during the dry season are brought together as complementary opposites in the universe. [44]

The appearance of color in the foregoing example of ritual complementarity is not fortuitous. It is part of a very rich Central

African ritual color symbolism, greatly employed in the Kongo cults. In the Kimpasi opening as the seance moves from outside to inside the cult, the color red is used most often. In the Khimba there is use of both red and white. As the cult progresses the use of the color white increases, and in the Khimba the adepts exit into society using exclusively white whereas in Kimpasi, contrariwise, there is the use of the color red again as adepts approach exit. Following the Kimpasi, for example, we see that the transition from "life" into ritual "death" is symbolized by the color red, represented all across Central Africa by the ground-up bark of the camwood tree; and as we get to the heart of the secrets in Kimpasi the color white comes to the fore to symbolize transcendent purity. In the Khimba, white (river clay) seems to dominate and the play on both red and white is not as apparent.

There is a third color to this scheme. On the final day when the cult initiates are supposed to show everything they have learned they use red and white along with black, usually represented in charcoal. In Central Africa red tends to indicate transition mediation, and white the inner part of the secrets, truth. Black is used at the end in the making up of a total sacrament in which the complete color triad is called into play. In other areas in Central Africa and in other contexts in Kongo white, represented by river clay (*mpemba*), is generally considered to connote the beyond, the liminal. For example, people will speak of death as "going to the white" (to *mpemba*). Death and white bring into association water; clear water is called *maza mampemba*—white water. It is really not white that is being characterized here; it is clearness, openness, truth, and visibility of mystery.

White, red, and black are also associated with the body, such that white, being the clear, the beyond, is the inside of the body and the black, the outside. White may then denote, for example, the beginning of a cure and black the finish, just as in a fire black is the finished product of the fire. Red is most interesting here in that red is in many cases between white and black. Red is the transition of going into the Kimpasi and of coming out. Red is the ambiguity between white and black; it is process, transition.

It should be evident that the color spectrum engaged in Central African religious ritual as briefly portrayed here provides for more than a simple unification of complementary opposites. It does this symbolically in the white-red, white-black combinations in ritual. But it does more. It provides the ritual expert with a multivalent sensory referent that can express the transition from one thing or condition to its opposite. In other words, it can express inversion.

The very existence of the cults, based on the theme of "death from conventional life" should alert us to the profound characteristics of ritual inversion, and its purposes. An excellent case study in this regard is the figure of Mother Ndundu, female overseer in the Kimpasi. It is somewhat difficult to know whether the term Ndundu, literally "albino," means that Mother Ndundu must always be an albino. She was, at any rate, also an old woman who was already past child-bearing age, and a woman who had not given birth to many children—or if she had given birth to children it was better for ritual purposes if her children had died. So Mother Ndundu was a most unfortunate kind of female figure in ordinary life; yet in the context of the cult she was lifted to an elevated position and all the negative features of her sterile being brought into the cult and given central roles. Mother Ndundu was made the mother of the cult members and her role was sung about as follows:

> "Mother, Ndundu, powdered in red, is the ground in which chiefs germinate. Mother Ndundu is the source of peace and not of excitation. As the water nymphs she ranges about not to excite but to appease. By *lembe* she calms those who thrash about. The women are restless but Mother Ndundu is the paragon of peace." [45]

Mother Ndundu, therefore, is sterile but is made the mother of chiefs. She is white, but she is powdered in red; she is calm, other women restless; she is thus given a completely inverted and incongruous casting here from what normally would be the role of a woman; in other words, combinations are put together here which are the reverse of what they would be expected to be in normal life. Sterility is made into fertility in the ritual context. Mother Ndundu's partner, the "father" of the cult, is called "Nakongo," "King of Kongo" and "Father of God" in a kind of vaunting inversion of status which indicates the ritual language is that of defining something by an inversion of what it would be in conventional life.

This characteristic of ritual inversion, really more widespread than Kongo society, by which life and death, society and cult, clothed and naked, orderly and disorderly, sterile and fertile, etc., are first put into complementary opposition, then inverted status from the normal, has an important renewal function. By presenting the mirror image of life, proper relations are signaled. Like Durkheim's assertion of the necessity of "crime" to define the norm, or Douglas's perception of ritual prohibition as a signal of boundaries of a system, so ritual inversion reconfirms the convention of limits of thought and society—after having "stretched" them, made them more resilient, so to speak. [46] The awesome and incongruous combination of Mother Ndundu defines earthly fertility by her "white" otherworldly sterility. Likewise Father Nakongo, the "Father of God," we may imagine, provides a sort of sacred obscenity defining the magnitude of God along with his accessibility.

Ritual inversion has a further function that relates it to the core of the argument of continuity in Kongo religion, the hypothesis of renewal. Ritual inversion has very significant incorporative qualities as a mode of symbolic operation that makes it particularly suited to embrace new or alternative directions of thought. By rebound, so to speak, the outside, threatening, cruel, or unexpected situation or element, can be incorporated to a world view if it can be made to contrast complementarily to the inside, secure, old, and routine areas of existence. This has profound significance for an interpretation of Kongo religious history, and the entire range of problems attendant to the "Christianization" of African religion. Let us examine a specific example.

In one of the urban cults that took place in Matadi in 1915, there is a very interesting sequence reported. [47] During a ritual meal the leaders go to great lengths to mimic the Catholic priest. The sole prohibition placed upon the participant group at this time is that they are not to tell him of their meeting. I think we have to say they are doing this very much in the same way that our political cartoonists by negative instance inject an ironic appraisal into a current event. A Mother Ndundu who is old and sterile and haggard now becomes, by inversion of her normal station in life, the mother of chiefs. If we bring the Catholic priest into the ritual in a similar manner and prohibit people from telling the Catholic priest that we are doing this, then we are really defining our position as being one in which the Catholic priest is no more powerful than we are. We are absorbing him into our ritual symbolism so that we can cope with him.

I would prefer not to call this acculturation but to suggest that the very process of incorporation by ritual inversion is a way of strengthening the flexibility of the incorporating tradition. This is where we can say that the Kongo religious condition by its very nature is self-renewing because it does have, traditionally, this element of incorporating the outside, the new, the alien, so as to strengthen and update its contents. Certainly there will be an acculturation and assimilation at one level, but the very fact that contemporary Kongo religion accommodates many Christian forms does not mean that it is not also traditional Kongo religion. The longer one participates in Kongo society and speaks Kikongo, the more one realizes that the manner of perceiving reality has not changed even though people can come to church on Sunday morning and be baptized and say the right words. One can find sermons that come close to genius in fitting the two traditions together so perfectly that if you are on the one side it serves your purposes and if you are on the other side it serves your purposes. Thus what we have is renewal and, at the same time, the continuation of the old.

The rich symbolic heritage in which complementarity and inversion ritual made the incorporation of new elements of the universe a science finds its fulfillment, as it were, in the totalizing symbolic syntheses of healing and body imagery. These, in turn, are radiated on to social relations.

Just how this further aspect works is illustrated again in the choice of floral categories in a cure for madness. The cure is an effective sedative ingested in liquid form, made from the juices of four plants mixed together, each of which carries the name *lemba* (to calm). The first is the favorite, *lemba-lemba*, a domestic plant which is grown in the village. The second plant is *lemba-ntoko*, a wild plant which grows only in the forests. Two other plants are "white" *kilembe-lembe*, sometimes called "male" *kilembe-lembe*, and "red" or "female" *kilembe-lembe*. [48] Thus we have in this particular cure the combination in complementary association of village and forest, and, by implication, of the world of man and the world of the dead, because the dead are associated with the forest; a clan cemetery is invariably a forest, an old village. Then there is the complementary association of the domestic and the wild. We also have male and female, but in a different kind of complementarity, one not associated with village and forest, or domestic and wild, but with its own kind of duality standing independent and yet each intercepting the other. This cure embodies the ideals of traditional herbalism; it calms the body, and it also combines complementary opposites in the universe.

One prominent Lower Zaïre healer takes the color scheme of red, white, and black, applying it to the body with the following association: white as the inside of the body, black as the outside, and red being the periphery of the body—in other words, the skin. Popular classification adds to this the male-female dichotomy of the body; the left side is the female side, the right side is the male side. The body becomes a veritable analogy of the universe and society, with passages through the body metaphorizing passages through the social system as it is set up in the village or in the clan or in any corporate order.

One would then expect a certain amount of play back and forth from body imagery and body allusions to social symbolism and social allusions. The study of curing becomes very interesting when you are aware that people are either consciously or unconsciously saying social things with body manipulations or else saying body things with social manipulations.

Certain ritual seances tend to be associated with constipation, stomach swelling, and certain kinds of eye problems, which can be compared with poison in the social sense which is caused by bad intention. Now which is cause and which is effect is sometimes exceedingly difficult to say, but symbolically the two are related. It follows in Kongo thought that the cure for poisoning, outside hostility, is usually a good strong purge. This is the same purge that is recommended after having foolishly eaten bad food. We have here several levels in which symptoms attributed to poisoning, to bad social relations, are reflected in harmful physical processes, thereby providing a close symbolic correlation between society and body. The need for bodily cleansing due to physical pollution or discomfort is also attributed to an individual's slovenly care of his own body. The symptoms are the same as above, but the cause now is evil directed inward by the person upon himself, rather than from outside. But both outside evil intention and self-ignorance are mirrored in body perception and symbolic traditions on the body.

Both body and society are susceptible to harmful outside forces and must be protected. A host of practices, some widespread, others localized, act to shield the fragile points of an individual's life and the boundaries and junctures of society. A child, in some areas of Kongo, is given three enemas in early life; the first just after birth to counteract harmful air taken in while learning to eat; the second after a month when the child develops "elephant stomach," a "stuffing" or "choking" condition; the third at the time of weaning around age two. The three enemas in fact demarcate the progressive social entrance into the world at three dangerous moments in early life of the child when his status is especially ambivalent, or when his body is in jeopardy. In this same connection I heard of a Kongo sailor who after sailing the high seas for several months would come home and take a good strong enema to strengthen himself before visiting his friends and relatives.

The point to be emphasized in all this is simply that even today, fifty years after the abandonment of the old esoteric cults, the icon-orthostic process of signification of experience continues to enrich the homologies of body, society, and universe. The process is possibly more fragmented and individualized than in the days of Kimpasi, Lemba, and Khimba, which had accumulated meanings for centuries, but it is still based on most of the same cosmological foundations, and thrives in the same social soil, as we will see presently.

BLESSINGS AND CURSES:
DAILY RELIGION AT THE JUNCTURES OF KONGO SOCIETY

The corporeal *symbolique* sketched above lives on in Kongo daily events, offering an available set of images in which to frame several modes of social relationships. Nowhere is this more strikingly manifested than in the way an alliance between two clan groups hinges upon the issue of fertility. Within this context the *esoteric* symbolism fostered in the cult tradition appears in an *exoteric* setting at the most important juncture of society: marriage.

Infertility is attributed to the malefic intentions of kinsmen—through alliance and descent—upon the body of the female in question. In the idiom of bodily openings and passages it is referred to as "the womb being tied up," the first suspected origin of which is that the marriage relation has not been adequately arranged. By this same token the most important spiritual prerequisites of marriage are the blessing of all sides of one's social person: father, mother, father's father, and mother's father. The immediate paternal blessing is of particular importance because it is the father who, having raised the girl and given her his spiritual birthright, expects a symbolic gauge from the groom in the form of a bride payment. Although all sides of the bride's social person receive a share of the bride payment, that to the father's matrigroup is the most substantial.

The importance of the paternal blessing hints at the relatively greater importance of the spiritual qualities channeled patrilineally as against other lines of descent. In terms of residence rules alone this can be seen already. An individual grows up in the father's habitation. Young men at puberty are transferred to the tutelage of their mother's brother, and in times past went to reside with him. Today school, job, and other factors interfere. A girl joins her husband upon marriage; yet here too the mother's brother remains the legal custodian. Because material and social identity accrues from this half of a person's social self the matrikin relations are often beclouded with struggles for authority and competition regarding money. It is not surprising that witchcraft accusations are greater within the matrilineage and even considered to be a congenital matrilineal trait by many.

In an important sense, then, although the uncle's blessing is sought, the father's is more significant since it stands as a counter-manding influence to the encumbrances of internal matriclan affairs. Although in incidental events the tables may be turned and the patrilateral relationship become murky with witchcraft accusa-tions and suspicions, the overall structural relations in Kongo social norms preclude this by and large.

Thus when a woman has difficulty with infertility, or difficulty in giving birth her husband will frequently send her to her paternal matriclan to receive their blessing. In one such typical case I witnessed, the wife of an urban judge had had difficult deliveries. There were four children, the second and the fourth born by Ceaserean section—the fourth stillborn. The husband suspected problems between the wife's father's and mother's families as a source, so he sent her back to her village to get the blessings of the fathers. Her troubles were analyzed by a local prophet-diviner to be due to the father's clan not having "eaten" (received for its use) its share of the bride price, while the bride's maternal family "ate" the entire sum. Although the paternal and maternal blessings had been given at the time of marriage, it was suspected that they were no longer good and that the "fathers'" envy and discontent had "closed her womb." Thus the social imagery bears directly on the body. After bargaining the case, the husband added to the bride payment, so that his wife's father's clan could get their due share. Three elderly women of the father's clan blessed the woman, each doing the *dumuna* jump ritual with her three times, after which the paternal blessing was extended. The village deacon closed the event with hymns and prayers.

The rationale of fault and its solution is not hard to uncover in the foregoing case. Blessings are given where the assurance of confid-ence and good will is desired. Or, where malice and envy is known to exist, the impediment to confidence is corrected, as here with the supplemental payment of the bride price.

Behind this single case, and in keeping with the whole back-ground of bodily symbolism as social referent, lies a more systematic world view through which disease, misfortune, and ordinary experience is understood. There are diseases and mis-fortunes that result from "natural causes" spoken of as "diseases of God." On the other hand, there are diseases caused by man. This dichotomy is pressed into service whenever a clan is in a situation

where misfortunes or diseases must be accounted for. Either with
the help of a diviner or by internal arguing and discussing, the
group will determine whether the problem is "of God" or "of man."
If the former, then they know that God is in control of the universe
and that all is well, even though they have had a misfortune.
Generally an old person's illness is said to be caused by God. When
a young person is ill and the disease is not immediately curable,
they will start to look for the manmade cause. If lightning strikes a
tree and nobody is under it, this is God's lightning; if there was a
person under it who was killed, they will usually look for a human
cause.

One Zaïrois writer has formalized the relationship of the two
causal modes in terms of "death within the will of God" and "death
outside the will of God." [49] This does not specify the chaos of un-
willed death as necessarily of human origin, but permits it to result
from forces which are outside and beyond order, a type of explanation of evil that relates cosmic chaos to evil intention. Most often,
however, a dichotomy is drawn between "God-made disease and
misfortune" and "manmade disease." It is interesting and most
useful for us to look closely at the "manmade diseases" said to result
simply from the condition of disorder within the social group.
Lingering arguments that have not been resolved can have as a
consequence the proxy affliction of an individual. Thus a child may
be believed to become ill because of an argument between his
parents, even though the child has not sinned.

When people talk about diseases caused by man, they do not risk
calling people witches outright; in fact, the witchcraft cases that
enter court are always cases of libel where people take their op-
ponent to court for having accused them, often obliquely with
synonyms, of being a witch. By saying, "Don't talk so much," you
are not saying a person is a witch who must be killed, but suggesting that too much talking can serve an antisocial, debilitating function in society. Gossip or "whispering" is also a form of witchcraft.
In other central African groups one occasionally runs into the notion
of the "breath of man" being a synonym for witchcraft. Another
term that is currently in vogue in Lower Zaïre is the French
"mystere," for any bizarre turn of events, including misfortune and
disease. You ask what has caused this person's illness and the
answer will be "mystere." You ask, "What is going on in this clan
that they are always sick or having trouble?" and a neighbor will
shrug his shoulder and say "mysteres." So it has to do with linking
an obvious consequence with an invisible cause. The chains of

causality are basically mysterious. The way in which people proceed to figure out how a misfortune which is very concrete is linked up with the condition of the clan or of the society is a process of discovering or revealing the *"mystere."*

Misfortune, illness, general hardship, and other problems are explained in terms of evil intention and conflict within the group, irresponsibility on the part of leadership and by the members of the clan. This kind of causality works in such a manner that it protects the group, using misfortune or negative events in a positive way to stabilize the clan. If, for example, there is crop failure or disease or epidemic or business failure, this serves as an occasion for the group to get together to rally around a negative event and to examine its collective conscience so as to determine where the weakness is, where the misunderstandings are, where the evil intentions are lurking, and to bring these out and thus to eliminate as much as possible the psychic and the social difficulty.

Once evil intentions within the matrilineage are suspected as being at the root of disease or misfortune, one of several paths toward rectification may be sought. Under normal conditions the lineage headman will convene his fellows and they may try among brothers to resolve the issue. Many of the day-to-day problems of village or city life are resolved in this manner. These are usually unspectacular, but when they become acute, when suspicion breeds countersuspicion and violent thought gives rise to further violent thought, the very existence of the orderly group is jeopardized. It is then that outside help is sought from a diviner, seer, or other inspirational figure who in modern times is often called a prophet, *ngunza.* He will guide them through to a solution, either by open discursive debate (a form of group therapy) or by invoking mystical sanctions such as an oath of purity, confession of guilt before the misfortuned, or (in the past) something as severe as the traditional poison ordeal.

Outside help may be forthcoming without the clan or lineage seeking it. The patrifilial "children" (*bana bambuta*) of clan men frequently come to the aid of their "fathers." [50] In all rituals having to do with death, e.g., burial, lifting of mourning, succession of authority, the clan "children" who are not of the same matrilineage intervene as guards or, as I was told once, "policemen," not only to keep the houses of the patrilateral clan together, but to serve as mediators between the living and the dead of their fathers' clan. In this way the "children's" role is seen not just as practical, but as priestly as well, crucial to what is often called the cult of ancestors, but could more appropriately be called the "children's cult" to their fathers. The symmetry of the paternal blessing upon the child and the children's conciliatory and priestly role vis-a-vis their fathers is apparent.

The *nkasa* poison ordeal of old—it was largely discontinued with colonial times—constitutes another good example of the matriliny in search of mystical sanction to its internal anxieties. Because it was administered much like a purge, with all the attending symbols of social purification, the ordeal brought bodily imagery and ritual-mystical sanctions together nicely. Why was it administered? General apprehension, a rash of deaths or illnesses in a village or clan of the sort that were thought to be beyond the will of God was one important reason. The *nkasa,* according to theory, would trace out the provocator of the crime, with illness causality linking members of the kin group in such a way that certain persons would be structurally suspect, and judge the intention of the crime as much as the suspected act. In a case where circumstantial evidence was not available the ordeal would be there to judge hidden intentions of the group involved. It is a very shadowy thing to judge intentions rather than actions, but necessary in a society that has no rigid hierarchy, such as much of Kongo society is at an operational level. Mechanisms are found whereby one can judge and guide and direct the intentions of people and not just their actions. The *nkasa* ordeal was there to get people that were grumblers and people who were in their hearts witches. The mystical connection believed to link the perpetrator of a mystical crime with a victim had to be revealed. The ordeal was a perfect mechanism, for it worked even by not working.

Thus the poison ordeal is reported to have been used early in testing the fidelity of the spouse or concubine and to try criminals and state traitors. Early Kongo kings used it to examine the fidelity of their vassals, although the vassals had the right to send proxies to take the test. It was also used in lawsuits where lying was suspected and in adultery cases. [51]

Usually the ordeal was preceded by what must have been days or even weeks of bargaining between accuser and accused, two factions of a clan, and by an agonizing appraisal of how to focus the vague sense of anxiety upon one of several suspects. As in most other corrective rituals, divining played the crucial role in this thinning down of the field to an ordeal candidate. Often resolution was achieved at this stage and the suspect would pay a fine such as a pig in damages. Only as a last resort, one gets the impression, was the ordeal used. Even then, great variations were still the rule.

In those areas where the social structure was more decentralized a doctor would mix and administer the potion, usually *nkasa*, [52] to an individual suspected by a diviner of witchcraft or antisocial tendencies. An individual himself might also be honor bound to offer to drink the *nkasa*; someone accused in court of being a witch might proffer the line "No, I am not, and I'll take the *nkasa* to prove it." And it is not impossible that the doctor who administered the *nkasa* combined the functions of judge and executioner.

In areas where the social structure was decentralized, in a case of conflict between several clans or in a case where one single individual would be challenged to take the ordeal, close kinsmen of the father's, the suspect's own, and his wife's clan would send out representatives both to mix and to take the ordeal along with the principal subject, so that everything was done in the most objective manner possible. Thus it was the several contenders in a dispute who together underwent the ordeal to determine guilt.

A generalized account of North Kongo ordeals, told to me by men, some of whom had drunk *nkasa* and lived, goes as follows. The *nkasa* bark was prepared in front of the crowd of onlookers and subjects for the ordeal. Those chosen came to the center of the circle and those who had prepared the drink themselves drank a modest amount to verify that there was no vicious poison in the *nkasa*. Then the trial subjects each drank the same amount, ranging anywhere from one to two liters. They then dressed in a brief loincloth and sat within the circle of onlookers who danced about them. The dancing went on, first in the village of one party that had taken *nkasa* and then in the village of another one of the subjects, throughout that day and night. My informants generally agreed that a true witch would not last through the first dancing place. In some ordeals with collective representation all the subjects would come out alive, while at other times some died. The practice seems to have been that a person who defecated, or soiled the cloth, or fell into syncope during the daylight hours, would either be killed or have to pay severe fines. Those who escaped the guilt of these signs were considered pure, confirmed non-witches.

The theory behind the ordeal hinged on the belief that the evil substance defecated—*kundu*, a gland-like place in the intestines—incriminated the witch. This *kundu*, hereditary or acquired, was the evidence of active "hot" witchcraft. When the ordeal fell into disuse the *kundu* notion lost some of its physiological connotations. But, because the main lines of social organization did not change much through the years, *kundu* remained as a leading theory of cause in social stress and crisis, and as an explanation of misfortunes.

Kundu played an important role in the ritual of Munkukusa ("rubbing"), which appeared as a purification cult in 1951-1953, to rid the land of witchcraft. [53] Everybody in a matriclan had to be present when the Munkukusa was done, or send a piece of paper with his name on it to be represented by "proxy." The idea was to submit to a rigid oath not to engage in witchcraft acts. It was claimed this was necessary in order for individuals to be safe from disease and death so that once again they would enter into harmonious relations with each other. At the same time the animal excrements and the dirt were swept away from the cemetery, and in the middle of the designated night each clan would send a delegation to the place where they bury their matrilineal forefathers. One person only of the clan itself was chosen, with all of the "children" of that clan.

As already suggested earlier, the "children" serve as the line of association between their living fathers and the deceased matrilineal relatives of these latter; the children also represent a buffer or arbitrator between their "fathers," who may be in conflict with each other, and so it is the "children" generally who intervene to keep their fathers from breaking down into debilitating argument. Here the oath and accompanying rites were administered by the children. (The "children"—patrifilial children—of course are members of their own matriclan, so each person is simultaneously "child" and "father.")

When the "children" and a representative from among the "fathers" went to the graves in the middle of the night, those who stayed behind in the village continued commemorating in song. A sense of danger was felt at this moment of transition. Those who went to the grave could not look behind them or they would disappear, turn blind, or go mad, it was said. When they arrived they must choose a grave of an individual who had never heard the "bell of God," an ancestor whose customary life was not changed radically by colonialism or by the missions. Such an early individual stands at the apex genealogically of the clan and therefore would be in a structural position to integrate the living of that clan. The "children" encircled his grave, and then one of the "children," acting as representative, enters the circle and offers greetings:

"We are here of the city of such-and such which you left us. Our troubles are truly many. The children are dying, the young men are dying, the old men are dying, and therefore you fathers, we have come. You must return to the city of the living. Come to judge this affair for us. Whoever is guilty, let him die." [54]

When the "child" has spoken these words, the clan headman pours wine upon the head of the grave and creates a muddy place. With the mixture of ancestral earth and palm wine he anoints all the "children." Taking the remaining mud he puts it in a dish and gives it to one of the "children" to take up to the village. A "child" fires a gun salvo and then they sing, "We implore you, come in strength, come in strength." The return march to the village with the mud begins with the dead following.

Thus the clan "children" lead a cortege of their paternal ancestors up to the village. Another gun salvo marks the entrance to the village; when the people in the village hear the shot all immediately come to wait at the entrance of the village and when those coming from the cemetery arrive all go into the church. There the one who was carrying the ancestral mud proceeds to put the plates with it upon the altar, at the place where the Bible rests when the catechist instructs. This procedure was followed by all the clans who had sent someone to the graves of the village. The night was finished with dancing outside to celebrate the coming of long-deceased ancestors to bind up the witches and to extend their benediction upon the village.

The time has now come to do the *kukusa* —the purification. First, a cross in the form of a trench, exactly in the form of the Khimba *diyowa* described above, is dug just before the front doors of the church. A second cross, of wood, is prepared. These two crosses plus a Bible, some nails, and a hammer constitute the ritual paraphernalia. The grave mud in the church is dumped into the cross-trench *diyowa* and is again moistened with palm wine.

The head of the lineage leads in doing the *kukusa* (the rubbing) as he recites the following:

"It is thought of me that I am a witch. If I have been a witch, if I have devoured my elders then let my sign be my death."

Repeating this three times, he kneels over the cross of wood and says,

"If I have fallen back into witchcraft, then the nails," [55]

and then he pounds the nails; all the people there reply, "Strike the nail" ("*Koma!*"). The one doing the *kukusa* takes the hammer and drives the nail into the wooden cross. [56]

Throughout the participants keep their eyes fixed toward the interior of the church, for therein are the dead, who were brought from the cemetery to "bind" the witches, while the cross is said to "carry away" the evil intentions of people. The one doing the *kukusa* leaps over the two crosses and the Bible three times each way. Then he kneels down and puts his face into the mud and immediately rises with his entire face covered with grave mud.

After all the clan members have done the *kukusa* (rubbing on mud), a night watch follows. In the morning the "children" go to draw barrels of water for the stage known as "throwing out the *kundu*." A huge accumulation of material wealth is brought together and laid out in one big heap in the center of the village: harvests of beans, corn, avocados, oranges, bread, manioc, mangoes, coconuts, money, and eggs. Even French texts and the notes from school lessons—anything that constitutes a source of contention—is thrown in. In tattered rags the people encircle this place. They pour water on all of this and then trample and dance and walk over it, thereby "crushing the *kundu*." Others take a pan of water and throw it on those who are trampling, thereby washing the mud of the *kukusa*. The mud on the faces is washed and the water mixes with the things that are being trampled. All that has been collected and is now being trampled takes on the name "*makundu* of the witches." As the food and riches are absorbed by the mud, the "*makundu* of the witches" lose their strength. Mud and contents are placed in a large basket, and the entire contents—the neutralized evil of the community—are thrown out into a hole in the forest and thereby the *makundu* have been expelled from the village and the society purified.

This description of the Munkukusa suggests similarities with the poison ordeal. Bargaining before a diviner, the actual ordeal, and invocation of the clan ancients and God, all give evidence of inviting a ritual sanction to point out the source of clan divisiveness. The structure of the rite tells us much more. Bringing back into the village and memory of the living a clan ancestor who stands beyond the divisiveness of the present is a strong affirmation of unity. The fact that it is the patrifilial children doing the rite, rather than the clan members among themselves, points to the unifying intent of the symbolism involved. At the same time another symbolic unification is being effected, that between ancestors and church. By bringing the ancestors into the church, and applying the merged ancestral-Christian force of judgment in the *diyowa* before the church a new integrated symbol was consolidated. A more collective notion of *kundu* (evil, power, bad intention, divisiveness) seems to have evolved at the same time. As in the poison ordeal, at the climax of the purification the *makundu* are expelled from the body—in the one case physical and social, in the other, social and religious.

We must ask at this point whether the matriliny in Kongo society is indeed as unable to resolve its internal intensions on its own as appears to be the case. All instances of ritual rectification investigated— the paternal blessing, the invocation of the poison, the "children" bringing the ancestral presence into the midst of the living—impose a corrective from the outside. The ideology of curses and blessings would seem to suggest that at least the BaKongo often see this as being the case. Witchcraft is believed usually to be inherited matrilineally, and only rarely patrilineally. The paternal blessing is emphasized, by contrast, above that of the matrilineal side. But it must be emphasized that the tables can be turned in respect to blessings and curses where indebtedness or slavery to the paternal side is involved.

It is thus not matriliny per se which must be investigated most closely in looking for the nexus of the issue; rather it must be seen that matriliny in Kongo society is merely the principle of recruitment to the major corporate group. It is in fact corporate structure, rather than simply matriliny, which involves certain kinds of tensions and stresses. But since rights to land, resources, and the like are matrilineal, the putting in order of relations usually involves the infusion of the matrilineal corporate structure with the breath of spiritual renewal, often in the idiom of father-child ties.

One of the several Kongo notions of governance, found in the verbal category *sika*, indicates to what extent a corporate head can go without laying himself open to charges of abuse or laxity. *Sika* means to be solid, firm; it implies the projection of a law, to command, or to take a resolution to do something, to determine, verify, or promise. In this same sense, it is the duty of the lineage headman, *mbuta*, to *sika* his group as one whole, to keep the various sections from separating or falling into divisiveness. Every Kongo clan, by extension, has its *minsiku*, rules, prohibitions, or interdictions (*nsiku* being the substantive derivation of *sika*). Handed down from the ancestors these may bear upon such matters as who is to be buried in the cemetery, or as when trees can be cut from the clan forest. All Kongo corporate organizations have their *minsiku*, interdictions, binding upon the membership. The point to be emphasized in the relation of *sika*, the act of governing, to the *minsiku*, the interdictions, is that the former is more essential while the latter is incidental, symbolic of the integrity of the former. Thus the community head who cannot maintain order by his dynamic governance cannot do so by arbitrary prohibitions.

Contrasting sharply with the authority of corporate chiefship as described above is that of a variety of types of exterior authority: the patrifilial children, the diviner whose outside position contributes to clarity of insight, or the authority of appeal in such things as the poison ordeal or an oath administered by an outsider. No single title embraces the roles that accomplish this "outside" authority, although the various types of *banganga* (magicians, doctors) and *bangunza* (seers, prophets) in one form or another are usually consulted. Most important among the *banganga* of yesteryear was the *nganga ngombo*, the diviner, who was first consulted by the individual or matrilineage in time of crisis. He it was who would, as we have seen, perform the pre-ordeal bargaining to determine which member of a clan would take the poison. The diviner would also be the one to suggest which esoteric cult or curative measure an individual or clan would need to undergo to stabilize internal affairs.

In recent decades, however, the role of the *ngunza* whom we may call an "inspirational diviner," has taken an increasingly important place in Kongo life. *Nganga*, on the other hand, has come to refer to plant-using curers, and to a variety of professional ritual experts who, as in the past, dispense fabricated powers for a price. For the most part, the cosmology touched upon in describing the esoteric cults and the Munkukusa is known to them. Markets in all large Kongo cities stock the floral and faunal and mineral substances they need. There is a certain degree of overlap between *nganga* and *ngunza*, magician-doctor and seer, and one does hear the title *nganga-ngunza* used occasionally. But whereas *nganga* essentially refers to a ritual manipulator, a "doer," *ngunza* applies to the individual positioned outside of society able to see its clandestine entanglements; the prophet-seer in Kongo is also a medium, possessed by an outside spirit. A certain amount of the disrepute that adheres to the term *nganga* can be attributed to Kimbangu and later Kongo messianic figures who in many instances superceded the *banganga*. But *ngunza* as a role term does have its own independent etymology.

In the seventeenth and eighteenth century *ngunza* was used to describe a warrior who, smeared in red, ventured out to protect society. This is the contemporary use of the term among such Kasai groups as the Pende where *ngunza* denotes the warrior "caste" who also work iron. More recently in Kongo, but still before Kimbangu, *ngunza* applied to the seer who would stand at the outskirts of the village and break into a trance, and while he was thus in ecstasy he would reveal within the village where malicious medicines (*minkisi*) had been hidden. In Kimbangu's time the term meant essentially seer of the hidden; but with him it also took on the meaning of one who can heal and raise from the dead through the power of the Holy Spirit.

In contemporary times an image of the *ngunza* has consolidated into the picture of several things: an ecstatic seer of the hidden in human affairs; a worker of miracles who traces his calling to a spectacular intervention of the other-natural world in his life, such as an episode of raising from the dead; an individual, male or female, who works with a clientele to divine their problems, and sometimes to look for a cure; by contrast, also a specialist that does not divine, but prays and lays on hands; or, most radically, someone who gathers a following of the dispossessed and as chief ascetic constructs a New Jerusalem. These seemingly contradictory modes of character in Kongo are all called *kingunza*, the gift of the prophet.

THE STRUCTURE OF SPIRIT IN KONGO RELIGIOUS THOUGHT

The contrast between the clan notion of governance and the appeal outside to corrective authority presents a structural interpretation of renewal in Kongo society. Yet the impression left of this is that clan means repression and the appeal outside means liberation or redemption; as such this view is misleading. We need to look more carefully at the intention expressed in the verbal concepts equated with the "inside" corporate act of governance, *sika* (only one of many useful terms chosen for simplicity), and the appeal to "outer" authority, *mpeve*. The simple structural interpretation is misleading, since both notions are terms of renewal, although the manifestation of the first is a prohibition (*nsiku*) and that of the second, possession, trembling, or some act of individual sanction. We can examine the use of these two notions best in the context of the Kongo independent churches where we are outside of the conventional clan structure but still faced with history, ritual symbolism, and corporate society. (I must emphasize that these two represent only two typical threads running through the fabric of Kongo religious thought. Other verbal categories might also serve well for a similar analysis.)

One of the songs that Kimbangu is said by eyewitnesses to have sung with his enthusiasts in 1921 implores the Spirit to descend upon the people:

O Spirit come,
    Come, come to help us!
    Many ills beset us here below.
    But let us continue praying till the end
O Spirit come,
O Spirit come,
    You, all my friends,
    The insignificant as well as the whitemen,
    Continue praying till the end.
O Spirit come,
O Spirit come.

These lines came to be considered as an important theme song of the 1921 messianism of the Lower Congo and as such, with the perceived threat the movement evoked in colonial eyes, was considered provocative to the authorities. Many people claim to have been arrested for singing *O Spirit Come*. Thus the notion of *mpeve* early in this century came to be associated with daring defiance of foreign authority and liberation from suffering.

Yet this is not the most important connotation it had. Before Kimbangu *mpeve* specified the vital principle or attribute of every individual. Its verbal root, *veeva*, meant to blow, to breathe, or implied the breeze responsible for the fluttering of a cloth or flag. [57] One traditional curing specialist, the *nganga kipeka*, would wave raffia cloth before a sufferer to create *mpeve* and heal, a therapy later incorporated into the rituals of a contemporary independent church, as we shall soon see. All these are manipulative rituals to express and in some measure channel *mpeve*. But the interior manifestation of *mpeve* in Kongo thought is trembling, ecstatic manifestation accompanied usually by glossalalia and exorbited eyes. This too, a mark of Kimbangu reported by eye witnesses of his work in 1921, existed before that as a sign of possession. Here and there in the historical and ethnographic literature there is evidence of it. The eighteenth-century Kongo prophetess, mentioned in the first section of the essay, was described as trembling with eyes exorbited, prone to shouting, "*Yesu, Yesu,*" an expression often heard in North Kongo Protestant glossalalia. But other ritual specialists, on a more conventional basis, trembled ecstatically. The *mfumu mpu*, the *nkita* specialist, and the traditional *ngunza* who would "smell out" malific medicines, all trembled as a mark of possession by clairvoyant spirits.

With Kimbangu however, the mark of trembling was brought into the Christian setting, and generally the spirit, *mpeve*, thought to possess adepts, was the missionary's Holy Spirit. By coming under possession of the Holy Spirit, and manifesting this through trembling in ecstasy, many Kongolese believed they had thus obtained the spiritual power and redemption withheld from them by mission Christianity. This significance of Kimbangu in Kongo Christianity today is well expressed by one man who said that Kimbangu made it possible for him, a Kongolese, to be Christian—i.e., with the validifying symbols of Kongo tradition, ecstasy and speaking in tongues.

Despite the disclaimer by authorities in various independent and mainline churches that trembling is the only manifestation of the Spirit, and statements to the effect that Spirit indwelling is possible without trembling, ecstatic trembling is today in Kongo a good indication of the manner in which spiritual authority operates. And it is in this respect that a comparison of *mpeve* and *nsiku* becomes possible. I shall briefly compare the distribution of ecstatic trembling—the structure of spirit— in several groups: the Church of the Holy Spirit, where trembling is widespread, the Church of Jesus Christ on Earth by the Prophet Simon Kimbangu, various mission-founded Protestant churches, and, in passing, the Catholic churches.

The Church of the Holy Spirit, Nzieta branch, traces its spiritual genealogy back to Kimbangu through several prophetic individuals. While it thus has spiritual legitimation from a central source, and places some emphasis on the symbol of the staff (*nkawa*, from chiefly staffs of old) as indicator of the prophetic role, in fact, the rituals reveal that all male prophets (members of the group) come under possession. In the "blessing" rite the male members bless the women and children; in the "healing" the male members heal each other and the women and the children; in the "weighing of spirit" rite the male members, beginning with the first ranking, tremble and then go through a rite analogous to the paternal blessing *dumuna* described earlier. The men in turn "weigh" one another, and then the women, while the latter do not tremble. Failing to grasp the hand of the "weigher" is a sign of guilt requiring confession to a senior male prophet. This rite, which has a strong confessional quality, reveals the equalitarian "priesthood of spirit" among males and their general status superiority over females within the group.

The doctrine of spirit held by this group appears formally to follow many canons of tradition although the better educated and recognized spokesmen of the group affirm that their belief in Spirit is Christian. The word *mpeve* is used independently of its adjective "holy" at times, although within prayers, sermons, and certain benedictions the term is explicitly *mpeve a nlongo*, "Holy Spirit." A pamphlet by Pastor Makanzu—who is not exactly an apologist for the Church of the Holy Spirit, but who is prone to long and ethnographic descriptions—gets close to the crux of the issue by his analysis of the term *dikisa*, used by the prophets of the movement in question to discuss the nature of spirit. Makanzu writes,

> The words dikisa mpeve are synonymous with the phrases "to give a person spirit" or "to cause a spirit to enter a person." Many times when an individual—one who has been ill and subsequently healed by a prophet—is to be infused or, entered by the spirit, the prophet will say to him: "Now pay attention! You are ill because you have lacked the spirit; you have been eaten by witches..."
>
> However, when an individual has been infused with the spirit, and has learned to tremble, the matter has not ended there. The spirit of such an individual does not possess sufficient power to heal the sick or to know matters hidden in the spirit. His power is also not adequate to comprehend signs and visions and to know their meaning. For this reason the spirit that comes quickly upon him who is learning must be measured, just as we can measure peanuts on a scale and know their value. [58]

From this text we learn that *mpeve*, spirit, resides both in every man and "out there" as well. Spirit within every person in some way emulates and replicates spirit which can be *dikwa*, "infused." Now *dika*, the verb of importance in the passage, is the factative form of *dia*, to eat, and in its causative form, *dikisa*, means to nourish an ill person, to force him to eat, or to oblige him to take medicine or poison. Thus *dikisa nkasa* is used to describe the administration in olden times of the poison ordeal. *Dikisa mpeve* has reference to the role of the prophet in guiding the novice into direct relation with higher "spirit" while at the same time thereby stirring to life a more vital being within him.

While mention of spirit, explicitly the Holy Spirit, is common in the Kimbanguist church, and the *O Spirit Come* theme song of the 1921 movement is heard occasionally, actual ecstatic trembling as manifestation of spirit possession is considerably different from the Church of the Holy Spirit. Although Kimbangu is acknowledged to have trembled in his 1921 ministry and to have provoked mass trembling among his early followers, today the ordinary Kimbanguist is discouraged from doing so. Only the sons of the prophet, who head the corporate body, and the "apostles" (*bantumwa*, "the sent") who were with Kimbangu in 1921 are permitted to tremble openly before the masses of members as manifestation of possession by the Spirit. Healing by spiritual power is similarly curtailed; only those who take orders from the church hierarchy are permitted to manifest spiritual gifts openly within the context of the church.

On the April 6 commemoration of the "return of Kimbangu to Nkamba" the apostles conduct a dispensation of the spirit rite in which they stand behind a wooden railing and carry on a sustained controlled trembling as they lay their hands on and bless the hundreds of pilgrim-adepts who file by one by one. The April 6 festivities at Nkamba also mark the time when pilgrims are permitted to file through Kimbangu's mausoleum. Hundreds of pilgrims stand in line awaiting their chance. Here too, from time to time, ecstatic seizure occurs in the presence of the prophet's mortal remains, and the church leaders are obliged to take note of this spontaneous expression of "spirit." How do they fit the phenomenon into the organization of the church? On one occasion when hundreds of pilgrims were awaiting entrance to the mausoleum whose only key is in the hands of the prophet's son, a man was seized just as he entered the compound. Of his own initiative, he rushed out to escape from the crowd, but was caught and brought back. Shortly thereafter it was spoken about in the crowd that he had been seized by the prophet's spirit for attempting to enter the holy presence with sin in his heart. Yet in the afternoon of the same day a woman was similarly seized ecstatically as she entered the mausoleum. Contrariwise to the earlier case, her seizure was interpreted as a sign that she had been blessed by the prophet. She was brought out before the crowd by the head of the church and introduced. The head himself took the direction of the band playing outside and led them into a frenzied continuation of the song they were playing to extend the moment until they could play no longer. Thus he was able to maximize the impact of the woman's spirit possession yet through his own actions legitimize her gift to his own authority. People said that Kimbangu had been working on that day.

The dilemma of keeping· a large corporate establishment together, yet spiritually vital, is an increasingly serious one for the leadership of the Kimbanguists. If it is to maintain the schools, seminaries, and legal apparatus it must have to keep pace with the missions, then the charisma of the prophet will have to be channeled and routinized within this structure. The corporate model of the matriclan fits increasingly and the structure of prohibition, *nsiku*, is the model of governance. Yet the more bureaucracy is made efficient—and Kimbanguist bureaucracy is quite efficient—the more there will be spiritual alienation.

There is evidence to suggest that the quest for spiritual renewal within the Kimbanguist group follows not the style of *O Spirit Come* of 1921, but the appeal analogous to that made before a clan head to govern (*sika*) wisely. On a number of instances while attending Kimbanguist services I have seen informal appeals made by lowly individuals to the church authorities or in prayer and song to God to reinforce the instructive presence of the law, to make the law manifest. During the April 6 celebrations at Nkamba mentioned above, the choir director at one point left his stand and quite impulsively knelt before the spiritual leader to beseech him

> ...today we have come to the sixth of April, We pray to you to safe-guard (sikidikisa) this day. Look at the group of young men and women who need to be helped, but the world does not care (ka sikila ko). Therefore you must watch over (sikidika) them. There is no one else to do (sikidika) it. If not you yourself, or you the leaders, then all our hope is shattered, for there is no one else in whom we can place our trust.[59]

In another similar use of the plea for authority, this time in a much less auspicious regional Kimbanguist meeting, and addressed not to the head of the church but to God on High, a noticeably unsuccessful worship provoked the plea. The musical background of the youth in Kimbanguist schools and the elders were different. Whenever a Kimbanguist hymn was introduced, the older members invariably fell back into the local harmonies that clashed severely with the youths' singing. The young pastor, recently out of the theological school at Nkamba, took the youths aside after the formal service and directed them in a drum-accompanied, rousing, ever-crescendoing rendering of the song *Sikidikisa Nz'amvimba* ("Undergird the Whole World"). From stanza to stanza, the quest for just authority, for righteousness, was projected upon the individual, to the church, to clans and nation, and finally to the entire world. Each stanza rose in pitch and volume, until the song itself became an affirmation of the transcendent order longed for. And yet no one broke into ecstatic trembling.

The religious quest for transcendent justice and order is often a quest for solidarity that makes itself evident in Kongo worship wherever Kongolese are in charge. (Europeans seldom emulate the style.) It is as if only through unity of the human group can unity with the divine occur. The ritual context for this is the word, spoken or sung. In song, it is common to repeat over and over in increasing crescendo, as described above. At the climax of these singing-out sessions the difference between various church organizations is noticed. The Pentecostal-type Churches of the Holy Spirit channel ecstasy and make it the center of their worship ritual. The Kimbanguists, with a firm control of Kimbangu's charisma, limit it severely. Protestant groups, particularly in the North Kongo, find trembling and ecstasy appearing at any climax in song or sermon, whereas in the south such outbursts are frowned on. Among Catholics, except for the cell groups such as Jaama, ecstatic trembling is unknown; this does not mean that there are no Catholic prophets locally.

It is not so much the search for a particular cultural form that characterizes Kongo religion, but an exit altogether from the encumbering structures of society and symbol. The aptness of given forms such as trembling to manifest spirit, and the father-child relation to channel blessing are greatly appreciated. But the leaders of the Pentecostal-like spirit churches insist that ecstatic trembling, while the core of their rites of "blessing," "weighing," and "healing," is not a prerequisite to being infused or indwelled by the Holy Spirit. They know their Bibles too well. When asked why they emphasize trembling, they answer it is an enjoyable and meaningful form—an apt form. An analogous observation must be made of the father-child relationship. While the prototypic relationship of blessings is that by the paternal clan, and the priestly role in approaching ancestors that of the clan "children," these very social channels can also become obstructed with evil intentions, possessiveness, jealousy. Religious renewal in Kongo is not then limited to a particular form, but broadly exists in finding the right alternative form to redeem the situation. This dialectic is the only constant underlying the perplexing wealth of Kongo ritual diversity, both *iconorthostic* and *iconoclastic, esoteric* and *exoteric.*

NOTES

1. "Kongo" refers to the ethnic or linguistic group, the BaKongo (speaking KiKongo) living in what is now the Republic of Zaïre (formerly Congo-Kinshasa), the Congo Republic (Brazzaville), and Angola. "Congo" refers to the present area of Zaïre when it was called the Belgian Congo or the Democratic Republic of Congo. "Lower Congo" or "Lower Zaïre" refers to the area inhabited by the BaKongo along the lower reaches of the Congo or Zaïre river.

2. Albert Doutreloux, "Introduction à la culture Kongo," in *Miscellanea Ethnographica* (Tervuren 1962), No. 46, p. 120.
3. Georges Balandier, *Sociologie actuelle de l'Afrique noire.* Paris: Presses Universitaires Françaises, 1963.
4. Isaki Nsemi, unpublished notebook. Laman Collection, Svenska Missions-forbundet Archieves, Lidingo, Sweden. n.d. (ca. 1915).
5. John Beckwith, *The Art of Constantinople.* New York: Phaidon, 1961, p.2.
6. Serge Boulgakoff, *L'Orthodoxie.* Paris: Balzon, d'Allonnes & Cie, 1958, pp. 195-196.
7. *Ibid.*, p. 197.
8. Nsemi, unpublished notebook, n.p.
9. *Ibid.*
10. Roland Barthes, *Systeme de la mode.* Paris: Le Seuil, 1967. Barthes' general theory of semiology is worked out in an earlier work, *Elements de semiologie,* in *Communications,* 4 (1964), pp. 91-135.
11. I am indebted for the discovery of this Greek term, whose meaning Kongo material so bountifully fulfills, to Hugh Laurence.
12. Dialungana Salomon, in Wyatt MacGaffey. "The Beloved City: Commentary on a Kimbanguist Text," *Journal of Religion in Africa,* II, 2, (1969). pp. 136-139.
13. See William H. Crane, "The Kimbanguist Church and the Search for Authentic Catholicity," *Christian Century,* LXXXVII, 22, (June 1970).
14. *Nsadula ye Ntwadusulu ya Dibundu dia Kimbanguisme* (Methodes et Principes). Brazzaville: Imprimerie nouvella, n.d., p. 51.
15. Balandier, *Sociologie actuelle de l'Afrique noire. passim.*
16. Jacques Maquet, "Objectivity in Anthropology," *Current Anthropology* (January 1964).
17. Paul Bohannan, "Extra-Processual Events among the Tiv of Nigeria." *American Anthropologist,* 60 (1958), pp. 1-12.
18. Roger Bastide, "La causalité externe et la causalité interne dans l'explication sociologique," *Cahier international de sociologie,* XXI, 3 (1956).
19. Jan Vansina, *Ancient Kingdoms of the Savanna.* Madison: University of Wisconsin Press, 1965, pp. 36-37.
20. *Ibid.*, p. 118.
21. Louis Jadin. "Le Congo et la secte des Antoniens," *Bulletin de l'institut historique Belge de Rom,* Fasc. XXXIII, 1961, vol. XII; pp. 411-615.
22. *Ibid.*, p. 498.

23. J. Van Wing, *Etudes Bakongo*. Bruxelles: Nauwaelerts, 1959, p. 569.
24. Arthur Darby Nock, in Talcott Parsons' *The Structure of Social Action*. Glencoe: The Free Press, 1949, p. 424.
25. Jadin, "Le Congo et la secte des Antoniens," p. 464.
26. Louis Jadin, "Apercu de la situation du Congo en 1775," *Bull, de l'institut hist. Belgè de Rom,* Fasc. XXXV, 1963, XII, p. 383.
27. Van Wing, *Etudes Bakongo*, p. 176.
28. Leo Bittremieux, *La société secrète des BaKhimba au Mayombe*. Bruxelles: Institut royal colonial Belge, 1936. Sect. des sciences morales et politiques, Tome V, fasc. 3, pp. 32-33.
29. John A. Weeks, *Among the Primitive BaKongo*. London: Seeley, Serince, and Co., 1914, p. 159.
30. Lenz Kriss-Rettenbeck, *Das Votivbild*. Munich: Verlag George D. W. Callway, 1961.
31. Van Wing, *Etudes Bakongo*, p. 430.
32. There is no indication just what the "narcotic" was in this report. Normally now *bonzo* refers to the "opener" drink in a cure. The reference is from Bittremieux, *La société secrète des BaKhimba au Mayombe*, p. 49.
33. Van Wing, *Etudes Bakongo*, p. 447.
34. Fukiau-kia-Bunseko, *N'Kongo ye Nza yakun'Zungidila/Cosmogonie-Kongo*. Kinshasa: Office Nationale de Recherche et du Developpement, 1969. Recherches et Synthèses, No. 1, pp. 134-136.
35. *Ibid.,* pp. 136-137.
36. Van Wing, *Etudes Bakongo*, p. 451.
37. Fukiau, *N'Kongo ye Nza yakun'Zungidila/Cosmogonie-Kongo,* p. 137.
38. Bittremieux, *La société secrète des BaKhimba au Mayombe,* p. 52.
39. Fukiau, *N'Kongo ye Nza yakun'Zungidila/Cosmogonie-Kongo,* pp. 138-140.
40. *Ibid.,* p. 142.
41. Van Wing, *Etudes Bakongo*, pp. 466-467.
42. *Ibid.,* pp. 470-471; Weeks, *Among the Primitive BaKongo,* p. 167.
43. *Lemba-lemba* is *Brillantesia alata*, a large-leafed plant often grown domestically. Though the plant is used as a tranquilizer both as external symbol and in a medicine ingested for that purpose, there is no evidence its "tranquilizing" effect is more than semantic, as its name, "calmant" (from *lemba*, "to calm") suggests. *Sisia-sisia*, on the other hand, identified as

Amomum alboviolaceum, is considered and used as à poison, as its name, "terror" (from *sisya*, "to terrify") suggests.

44. Part of this analysis was suggested by Fukiau.
45. Van Wing, *Etudes Bakongo*, pp. 435-436.
46. Emile Durkheim, *Rules of the Spciological Method*. New York: The Free Press, 1966, p. 80; Mary Douglas, *Purity and Danger*, New York: Praeger, 1966.
47. Bittremieux, *La société secrète des BaKhimba au Mayombe*, pp. 215-230.
48. *Lemba-lemba* is identified above in note 43; *lemba-ntoko* is *Ocimum basilicum* (Labiateae); "White" *kilembe-lembe*, Erigeron floribundus; "red" *kilembe-lembe*, Virectaria multiflora. This cure was "purchased" by Bilumbu of Kivunda from a Zombo in Angola.
49. Kusikila Yoswe, *Lufwa evo Kimongie?* (Death or Pestilence—Which?) Kumba: Academie Congolaise, 1966.
50. "Children" here refers not to age but to social relationship; they are persons whose fathers are members of the clan in question, but who, following the matrilineal (or avunculocal) principle, are themselves members of their mothers' clans, and probably reside with mother's brother or are under some degree of jurisdiction by him.
51. Jadin, "Aperçu de la situation du Congo en 1775," p. 372
52. Identified in various parts of Africa as *Erythophleum guineense*, this ordeal ingredient, the bark of the tree, contains substantial alkaloid erythrophleine with powerful digitalislike cardiac action which induces paralysis of the respiratory center, strong adrenalinelike blood pressure increase, emetic action, and other delliterious effects. (J. Watt and R. Breyer, *Poisonous and Medicinal Plants of East and South Africa*. London, 1962, pp. 602-605.)
53. J. P. Makanzu. *Zakama* (Trembling), mimeographed MS, Kinshasa, 1966, and my own field notes are the basis for this reconstruction of the Munkukusa rite.
54. *Ibid.*
55. *Ibid.*
56. This is a ritual act reminiscent of that recalled with the *nkondi* canine or anthropomorphic statue into which nails and iron wedges were driven by contestants in land feuds and disputes. *Nkondi* and his priest were believed to "control" the parties, binding them to their oath to desist from further fighting by mystical force.
57. This interpretation and other exegeses of verbal categories are based on my own field work and consultation in Karl Laman's *Dictionnaire KiKongo-Francais* Bruxelles: I.R.C.B., 1936.
58. Makanzu, *Zakama*, p. 11.
59. From my field notes, 1965.

5

African Mythology: A Key to Understanding African Religion

Kipng'eno Koech

African mythology is a living chronicle in the minds of human beings. The myth expresses the history, the culture, and the inner experience of the African himself. The myth portrays the wishes and the fears of the African man as he gropes to understand the unknown by dissecting and remolding it to fit his frame of reference. In the myth, the African's metaphysics are created and his beliefs constructed.

African mythology, as every other form of African conceptual pattern, emphasizes human interaction in life itself. Even when treating the concept of death, the myth transcends death (without using the word itself) and brings the worlds of the living and the dead together. According to most African cultures, people may communicate with their deceased loved ones either by means of a mediator or by acts of humility before them. In this way, the cultural phenomenon of the extended family is carried on to include the dead. This spiritual communication often occurs in myth as a means to uplift the living from the sorrows of their entanglements in the here and now.

To carry on this interaction between the living and the dead, a myth is created that it is possible for one to come back to life through reincarnation. This concept is confusing sometimes since there are arguments whether the dead reappear on earth through rebirth in their natural essence, or whether they are reincarnated in spirit through someone else. In either case, those who believe in reincarnation offer the reincarnated the same respect due the reincarnator.

So, living is intertwined with dying in a matrix of human fellowship. The living are persuaded to live a life of smooth human interaction so that they may be "called" back at death as a reward for their perfect lives among the living. A myth is developed to explain the fate of those who lived contrary to the cultural norms and therefore were not called back to life.

Perhaps the most universal myth is that of human creation. In the mythology of the Kipsigis, the tribe of this author, man was created by forces directed by the Great Worker. Working through the sun (Asis), He molded earth and water to create man. The myth goes on to explain how other creatures were made with water, air, and earth, and how most living things except man come from under water—making man's creation mysterious and superior.

Another Kipsigis myth treats the nature of the moon and sun's domain. The moon, having lesser power, was wrestled by the sun to the ground on the dark side. Because the sun was too hot, the moon melted and drifted away to the dark side to cool off, and since then it has never dared to call for a rematch. Again, one notes that myths involve living, which includes the element of struggle.

Thus, the African myth explains in the context of African cultures such great human concerns as death, creation, the evolution of living things, man's relationship to man, man's relationship to other living creatures and natural phenomena like day and night. Nonetheless, the purpose of the myth is more than explanatory. Let us here put the purposes of the myth in context.

(1) African mythology acts as a socializing agent. It is used to nourish and continue the traditions of the elders or ancestors. The morals, norms, conventions, customs, and manners are part of the myth.

(2) Education is another function of the myth—teaching people, especially youngsters, the meaning of the universe and those things which comprise it.

(3) The myth provides emotional and psychological easement by pointing toward the redeeming features in what appears to be a bad situation.

(4) The African myth is entertainment, and may become a part of drama, of art, and of skill. The African mythologist, or his students, seeks to employ all forms of theatrical skill and to put to use every faculty in his delivery. The tale is told using hands, feet, head, eyes, and even breathing (an emotion is evoked in the audience by changing breathing patterns). Like a good play, the myth evokes suspense, sorrow, sympathy, and most of all laughter—for death and laughter are intertwined.

It is one thing to talk about the African myth and another to experience one. An important myth to the Kipsigis is one developed to explain a particular dry season which caused many cows, goats, sheep, and wild animals to perish from lack of water and grass.

Many aspects of our culture and our belief system are woven into this myth of "Nagoro, the Sacrificed Girl." In reading it, one may discover ways in which his own family culture is linked with that of East Africa.

THE MYTH OF NAGORO, THE SACRIFICED GIRL

Once upon a time, when the world had come to life, when the tribe of Myot and the tribe of Masai lived together around the great salty lakes surrounded by the magnificent smoking [volcanic] mountains, the god of the rain was angry at the people of the land. The people were becoming rich, and were not practicing the traditions of the elders. They were drinking too much. They were not watching those women and elder men who were attacking the young children and taking them to the land of the underground [a reference to the slave trade]. The god had followed them and had seen how badly they were treating the disabled, tying them on trees and leaving them to the scavengers of the wild. Children did not respect their parents and the cattle were not well kept. The elders warned that a punishment from the Most High was imminent, and the people were to be ready to take the punishment.

It had been raining heavily at the night of the full moon, with furious thunder and lightning. The birds were silent; not even the brave lion roared, let alone the silly hyena who feels he must cry every night. There was a feeling that the world was coming to an end. Suddenly the rain stopped and the clouds were no longer seen and the moon was bright.

The following morning the elders gathered at the foot of the *simotwet* tree [fig tree]. The families of Myot and Masai were represented, and they sat in council to determine the meaning of the anger of the thunder and lightning. The omen of each of the elders showed bad fortune. For example, Ole Tiptip stumbled as he came to the *baraza* [council], Arap Korir saw the hawk sitting with its back facing him, and a snake crossed the path of Kipkeino. They advised the people to revive the customs of the land; but the country did not heed their calling. Normally, two or three moons would die after the rain stopped; this time six moons died but there was no rain.

After the moon of Kipsunde [December] had died, it was calculated that fifteen moons had died since the time of the last rain—the longest time anyone could remember hearing tell of. The dry season had brought death to uncountable hundreds of animals, domestic and wild alike. There was no water running in the rivers. The people had dug dams to preserve the water, but the dams dried up. The people obtained a little water from the sap of the trees and from beating up leaves and processing them. They began digging wells, but every time they found some water it would dry up quickly because of the number of people and animals drinking from it. The main source of water was from the bamboo trees (whose cavities collect rain water). The people were becoming desperate, and they urged their elders to meet again and plan a course of action to be taken to appease the god of rain, thunder, and lightning. The elders took a very long safari to the highest council of the land. There they met in council day and night for four days.

At the end of the four days, the elders called the people together. The head elder gave a report. "My fellow countrymen; honored mothers, and the bearers of the seed of existence of our peace-loving tribes; and you children which dot our land as the first fruits of our toils: listen to the council of the elders; heed the teachings and practice well the traditions of our forefathers; this is no time for play, but a time of serious thinking, for our existence is threatened and our land is faced with perilous times. Let us rid ourselves of evil doings; let every person ask pardon of Asis [the Great Light], the molder of us all, who has given us this land to inhabit, and to multiply in. Then at the break of day, let everyone dress in beautiful garments for the march to the place of prayer [Kapkoros]. The day before and the day after the march are to be days of taboo and of meditation on the traditions and customs of the land. We find wisdom in the words of Mugeni, the great thinker and predictor of events. 'No man can fight nature and live happily with himself. To find harmony one must sacrifice.' The word is 'sacrifice.' You know, you sharers of our sorrows, that we have sacrificed every kind of possession we have, and no rain has come. It is our practice to care for each other, each man for another. We pride ourselves on this; we do this to please ourselves and the molder of the earth. Is it then wise if we say even the sacrifice of men is part of the sacrifice? One of us, it seems, must be sacrificed to appease the heavens. Let us therefore look among our families and pick a girl who is willing to be given so that her sisters and brothers may live."

With that he concluded his speech. There was great silence and faces showed the awesomeness of the moment. Everybody was summoned to stand, face the east, and raise their hands in unison towards the east. Then each family went home.

Whenever there is a procession to Kapkoros, the place of worship, the next day, the taboo-night is observed. Silence reigns over the land. So it was on this occasion. The children canceled their planned nightly songs and dances. No lights were to be seen after dark and no night yelling calls from the *moran* [newly initiated young men]. The priest came out at midnight and directed his ear to the sounds coming to him. He observed that there were no human voices. He could hear the roaring of the roaming lion, the yelling of the greedy hyena, the singing of the brown bird, and the clacking of the flying bats as they snatched their prey. The priest was glad that his people had observed and kept well the laws of the ancestors which the Most High had blessed. He returned to his house to await the rising of the sun.

The bugle (made of buffalo horns) was sounded by the leading bugler exactly at the time when the elephants go to drink [about 4 a.m.]. Everybody got ready to go out to the altar in the eastern part of the house to await the rising of the sun. The children were washed and oiled; the older boys and girls went to the river to clean themselves, to decorate their faces and to polish their beads. The warriors decorated their shields and polished their swords and spears. They kept them ready for the moment they would march to the exalted place of the sacrifices. At dawn all the warriors left for their respective places to regroup and start the procession. The sun had risen, and the priest observed that it was the time for prayer by stretching his right hand toward the sun: the hand was parallel to the ground and his eyebrows were not raised when he looked at the sun.

The priest signaled the bugler, who immediately blew the prayer sound. At the hearing of the horn everybody raised his hands toward the sun, repeating the prayer in unison, the fathers leading.

Immediately following the morning prayer, the procession began. It was always the custom for the army to march down to the plains where they would drill and display maneuvering techniques to celebrate the occasion. But this time it was a solemn march. It was not all over yet: the ritual of rituals had not been performed. Instead the warriors marched to isolation, the women went to the house of the elder women, and the elders left for the tree of the council. The hardest had to be done.

The Chattering of the Women

As soon as Obot [Mother of] Kipkorir reached her house, she prepared the noon meal, which was a bread of finger millet and vegetables. She had very little milk, so she spared it for the baby. The mother briefed the older daughter, Chebet, in caring for the children, cleaning the house, and collecting the vegetables in the garden. She then left for the meeting place in her neighborhood.

Everybody had arrived and the women were talking. The head woman summoned the crowd to observe silence, and then she spoke.

THE HEAD WOMAN: No one wants to sacrifice her baby, but if the people see that this is the only way to survive we have no choice but to act quickly too. It is hard for me to think that I may be the one to sacrifice my baby. but, since I have never experienced any death in my present family, my stomach tells me that nothing bad will happen, but that we will get rain from above. The omen has been good: our feet have not stumbled, the observation of the birds by the elders has been in our favor, no snakes have bothered the travelers, and the prayers at Kapkoros went on without trouble. The smoke rose up and bore our prayers to the blue and our sacrifice was observed by the priest as good. What do you think now?

THE MIDWIFE: Nobody else sees the suffering like I do. I suffer from my own labors and I suffer the labors of others. The children look frail and helpless when they are born; they are pretty when they have begun to crawl, stand, and learn to talk. You know well that when I am ordered to stop life from entering the body of a child-to-be, the traditions of the land do not count it a crime because no life is taken from it, since it has none. But if we take the life of a grown-up girl, we are condemned by the traditions. In that case we have to justify ransom and declare the killer unclean until such time that he performs the ceremony of cleansing. If we think therefore we must sacrifice a human being, we must let somebody else do the killing.

ELDER WOMAN: Well spoken. If the Heavens want a sacrifice, they must perform the sacrifice. In that case, we cleanse ourselves of any responsibility.

THE PROPHET: I worked on my charms last night and my predictions, spoken as well by the elder, show nothing evil about to occur. I noted a cloud that moved in great strength; but when it reached the ground its power died, and when it rose again the noise was that of a lion with pain.

ELDER WOMAN: Well said. It is my privilege to attend to the problem of selecting a girl to be sacrificed. Let us line up the girls according to families and see whom you can pick. You remember that this is not the first time we have done this. Every year at harvest festivals, the women select a virgin girl whose brothers and sisters [are not dead]. Her parents must be good, must be loved by Asis, the Sun God, and must be blessed with cattle and other animals. They must not be known to curse, must always be soft spoken, tender to their children, and always sharing with their neighbors. The mother must be cooperative and fulfill her duties in communal farming and performing of tasks. The father must hold the respect of both young and old. He must be a provider and good father. Let us look around therefore and see which family meets our goal.

Everybody laughed when Obot Cheptanui mentioned the name Cherop; "She loves the boys too much," said one young woman. "Who doesn't?" said another, and everybody laughed again. Then, everybody looked at one another. They noted that the mother of the girl was not there. They immediately appointed someone to go and see whether they could find her. The report was that she was not at home. They then asked if anyone of the members of the family was there. There was a shy young woman in the corner. She was the sister-in-law to Cherop. She was asked what she thought about it. "Mother knew that Cherop might be sacrificed and so she did not want to come to this gathering but asked me to take the news to her."

Because the whole process was a difficult one, no one really wanted to be the one to say which girl was to be sacrificed. There was a big silence; everybody looked at one another; but from their eyes and their faces it was clear that Cherop was the girl.

ELDER WOMAN: Please pick another girl, and we will
choose from the two.

The name Chepkorir was given as a second choice. The families or relatives of the two girls were asked to leave the house, after which the selection went on. After concluding remarks, there was a unanimous decision that Cherop was the girl to be sacrificed. The sister-in-law confirmed that she was a virgin. The question was, who would carry the news to her parents?

Cherop's sacrifice had been somehow predicted or it was a surprising coincidence. The name Cherop means the "sacrificed one," or the "one that was dressed white with ostrich feathers." If it meant death, she had been doomed from the time of birth. So Cherop faced the unpredicted alone. But what had to be done must be done—nature had ordained it. Obot Talai was chosen to take the news to the parents of Cherop. When she heard the news, Obot Cherop was sad. "I cannot go against you, you can take her." She broke into tears and when she had revived she sent for Cherop. When Cherop entered the house, the mother began crying again.

CHEROP: What's wrong, Mother? Why are you crying?

OBOT CHEROP: Nothing, my daughter. You have been
chosen to be sacrificed.

CHEROP: And what is wrong with that? Langok was
sacrificed at the last harvest and she carried
the offering; why not me? I am just as good
as she, am I not?

OBOT CHEROP: I did not say otherwise. Yours will be a
different kind of sacrifice; you will be
sacrificed that others may live.

Cherop ran to tell her friends. She asked Langok to go with her to the cabin of the warriors to meet her boyfriend and break the news to him.

Cherop's Treacherous Journey

The day had been very hot and so Cherop and her friend Langok decided to travel at night to her sweetheart's cabin. They knew there was a full moon and the sky was clear. Normally, it is not advisable for girls to travel at night. They did not want to let the parents know because they would be stopped, for the journey might bring death to them.

As soon as the sun set, the girls began their journey. They would run some and trot some when they were tired. They would hide when they saw someone coming; if anyone saw two young girls traveling at night, they would be advised to discontinue their dangerous journey. The moon had not risen and it was beginning to get dark. They could not see the way properly. Every time they saw stumps Cherop and Langok thought they saw dangerous animals. Just before they reached the river, they heard the noises of running and screaming hyenas. The scavengers soon caught up with them. The girls knew that hyenas are cowards and they scared them away by throwing stones in that direction. Along with the noises of the hyenas they also heard the lion roaring at a distance. It seemed as if the lion were following them, and so they climbed a tree. The moon had now risen and they were able to observe anything approaching them.They noted that the lion was following their tracks. When it got to the tree they were on, it smelled around the tree and after looking up and scratching the tree for awhile it walked away, roaring as it did. After some time the lion roared again and they figured it was now one to two yells away (the distance in which, figuratively, two sounds can be heard if hinged together). They came down and began running toward the cabin.

Just as they thought they were approaching the camping place, they heard a sound of an approaching animal. It had been known that somewhere near the mountain of Menengai there was a man-eater. They were horrified because if it was one they had no chance of surviving, since a man-eater can jump so high that it can reach any height. Cherop screamed at the height of her voice and the animal jumped away shaking the whole place, yelling in that threatening voice of a man-eater. The mouth of the man-eater is red like fire, and the nose is long and the teeth so sharp that one bite can break any human bone. When the man-eater jumped away the girls ran as fast as their feet could carry them, screaming for help. No one answered, and when they reached an opening they noted that the camp at which Cherop's boyfriend had stayed was now abandoned. There was still a cabin standing but it was all torn up. The hyenas and other animals had broken into the cabin, making several holes. They ran in and tried to climb to the roof. Before they did, the man-eater was there. He was roaring and pulling down the rafters. Langok, who was a little bit braver than Cherop, told her to get a sharp stick and begin hitting the man-eater. She looked around and found the firemaker and began spinning it, using the grass that had fallen down to start the fire. It took the girl a few minutes to light the fire. When the fire burned brighter, the man-eater jumped down from the roof and began running around the hut. Langok put a burning log at the door and near every big opening. The man-eater did not leave, and was beginning to pull down the logs attached to the wall. Two other man-eaters arrived to add to the confusion. The girls had almost run out of breath when a lion roared at the top of the hill. Every animal stopped yelling. The hyenas, sounding as if they were grumbling, slipped into the thickets. The man-eaters ran anxiously and quietly around the hut. The fight ended in the river. There was a great quietness. Neither the lion nor the man-eaters ever came back. Langok suggested that they make fires surrounding the place where they were going to sit. They arranged it so that one of them slept while the other one watched.

When morning came, they observed that the cow dung was very recent. They decided that if they followed the trail of the cows, they would locate the warriors and the cows. They walked for the whole day and never saw anyone. They had brought some grain, which they ate. They were thirsty and tired. The trees had no fruit and they did not know how to hunt for honey. They had heard about how hunters sometimes sleep in caves at night when they fail to reach their destination. Night was approaching and they did not want to go through another ordeal. They went to the bank of the river and noted that there was an old salt-leak cave. It had been abandoned and the animals seemed to use it. There were some noticeable tracks of one animal—the footprints of a lion. The girls had no choice but to go in. They collected wood and piled it at the gate of the cave. They inspected the cave and found it safe. They did not look up just above the gate. A python had lain up there and was waiting to attack the two girls, but they were always a little bit too far from it. Before long the fire had risen quite high and it drove the large snake away. Cherop was the first to see it.

LANGOK: I told you that this trip was dangerous. Your boyfriend is not going to die. You should have waited until he came home. Now maybe you will miss both him and the thing you are so excited about. The python may not miss you.

CHEOP: If I die, then take my dress to him and tell him that I loved him that much, to take the risk of being eaten up by animals.

LANGOK: The python will live to tell it, not anyone of us.

Cherop's boyfriend Sigilai had made bells for their cattle. He had small bells for the young heifers and bulls and big bells for the older cattle. One which had the loudest sound he put on the leader of the cows. The night before, Cherop and Langok had not heard them. This time they told themselves that they were going to listen to everything that sounded like a bell. Sure enough, they faintly heard what sounded like a bell. Langok immediately tested the direction of the wind by picking up some dirt and spilling it to see which way it was blowing. Cherop was performing the ear test. She closed one ear and then the other, turned around and tested each time, making marks on the dry ground with her toes every time she noted the difference in the intensity of the sound. They noted that every time the wind stopped blowing they could hear the bell; they concluded that the sound was in the direction of the wind. After jogging for a while they observed the cowbird [a brown bird which picks ticks from the cow] flying above them. This was another sign that they were close to the cows, but how close they did not know.

Langok and Cherop embarked on their journey promising each other not to forget their goal. The sun had turned (late afternoon) and the thick shrub was making the path darker. Just as the sun was setting, they noted smoke at a distance, and they figured it would take them a short time to reach there. The bells were audible too. Cherop was quite excited because she was going to see her sweetheart for the first time in a long while. They waited by the kraal until it was dark and watched. Sigilai and his protégés led the cattle to the kraal. Sigilai went to his cabin, picked up his harp, and began to sing a lovesong he had written for Cherop. Langok and Cherop were safe in the kraal, and they listened outside the cabin of Sigilai. When everyone was asleep, Langok and Cherop opened the door and went inside Sigilai's cabin. Cherop picked up the harp and sang in a very low tone her own lovesong for Sigilai. She put the harp down. Sigilai raised his head; seeing that it was Cherop he rose, went and hugged her, and shook the hand of Langok. The other warriors were awakened by the sobbing Cherop as she leaned against Sigilai.

SIGILAI: How do you fare, my sweetheart? is everything all right.

CHEROP: [Sobbing loudly]: Yes.

SIGLILAI: How did you get here? Who showed you this place? You might have been eaten by the man-eaters.

CHEROP [Wiping her face with her bare hands]: I don't care.

SIGILAI: I do care. It's a wonder nature saved you.

They repeated the story to the young warriors, who were surprised that they could get into the kraal and the cabin without being detected. The other youngsters who were patrolling the area arrived from their shift and were also amazed that the girls could get in past their lines. The girls were given one of the sleeping compartments. When morning came, Sigilai decided to go home with the girls to hear the news. He did not like the word "sacrifice." Sigilai led the way, observing the ground for lurking animals or enemies but walking within sight of the girls. He was also carrying milk on his back in a basket-like container, to allow him to carry his spear and sword in his hands. The reached home safely.

With The Elders

A number of meetings were being held in several locations in different homes. Beer had been brewed for the purpose of discussing the nature of affairs. The home of Kipkalya, father of Cherop, was chosen for the neighbors of the shire of Tulo. In the evening middle-aged and older men left for Kipkalya's home. Each person sat alongside the wall with his long pipe reaching the pot at the center of the house. The pot contained beer and was refilled whenever it got empty.

The inlaws are not to use the left side of the house, so a chair was reserved for them in the other side of the house. Drinking lasted for the weekend. On the second day of the week [Sunday] Sigilai and the girls arrived. Sigilai was escorted to the right side of the house and there he was presented a pipe by an older neighbor. He had drunk for a few minutes when he was interrupted by Kipkalya. "Young man, my daughter seems to be looking only in one direction—your way. I don't really know whether you are brave enough and wise enough to win my daughter. We will see. These elders have decided to sacrifice her to the bird up above. I see you don't have wings. How do you think you can save her?" Everybody laughed, but Sigilai kept his silence, sipping the beer. The owner of the pipe snatched it from him, saying, "Answer the elder, young man, and no beer. Young men are not supposed to drink much."

Sigilai was so angry at the insult that he got out, took his spear, sword, and shield, and walked away. He persuaded his friends to embark on a safari hunt. Sigilai had to bring an elephant's ear and a lion's skin to show his insulter his bravery. He had to hold the tail of the lion while the other hunters chopped off its feet, or face the lion with a spike in his hand and thrust it into the lion's mouth when it attempted to bite. They traveled two days and two nights to the ra-

vine where the lions and the elephants roamed. The lions had detected the men. The female lions had crouched low to attack while
the males retreated and went around back to drive their prey for the
kill by the female lions. But the warriors did not run away at the roar
of the male lions; they attacked. This took the male lions by surprise
and they retreated to the dry river bed. Sigilai was at the back of one
of them—hurling his spear. The male lion was pierced at the thighs.
The fight began, the lion stood to fight. The other hunters had advanced forward, and the lionesses, catching the human scent, had
slipped away. It is known that lions do not attack men for prey, only
if they are in danger or fear that their young may be killed. The lion
man-eaters do attack men on any occasion.

Sigilai jumped back and forth trying to goad the lion into attacking. His three-dimensionally decorated shield would confuse the
eyes of any animal, including man. The movement of the shield and
the confusion of the colors made the lion so mad that he attacked the
shield rather than the man, exposing himself to the mercy of the
sword. Sigilai had approached the lion, and the lion, seeing the
danger, turned to run. Sigilai rushed and caught the tail of the lion.
The lion moved so fast that he was thrown away and landed on the
muddy bed. The lion was turned back by the others and before long
he was completely surrounded. He then fiercely attacked, tearing
the branches on his way and roaring all the time. Sigilai closed in on
the beast, this time to hold its tail and hang on. Another person offered the shield, and the lion bit it while he chopped its front teeth.
He did not succeed and once again the lion turned to attack Sigilai.
But he could not be reached, he was turning around with the lion.
Showing some signs of weakening, the lion rushed forward, caught
one of the hunters on the waist, and threw him to the ground, tearing his garment and hurting his knee on the rocks. While he was
down, he cut the throat of the lion and the beast succumbed. They
skinned it, took the skin, and left the flesh on the bank of the river.
The hyenas had flocked around the King. Even at his death they
feared to get near it. The vultures swooped down to devour the
King. The hyenas joined in, although they were frightened away by
every little sound they heard. The hunters rested for a while, then
started for a hunt of the elephants.

Elephant hunting is not as difficult as hunting small and dangerous game. The elephant can detect a person easily by using its
strong sense of smell and hearing. The secret is to approach the elephant, cut its ear, and show how brave and wise one is. The protege
of Sigilai first saw the elephant standing by the trees. After testing

the air, they were able to approach the animal from the direction of the wind. Sigilai had to climb the tree to reach the ear, but it was hard to do it without disturbing the animals. The best way is to approach the elephant, then scare it away; running close to the elephant one can cut its ear. That's exactly what Sigilai did.

The crew returned home with their spoil: the elephant's ear and the lion's fur. Kipkalya was seated outside his home when the young men arrived. Sigilai placed the spoil at his feet without saying a word and walked away. Kipkalya, apprehending the intensions of the young man, called him back.

KIPKALYA: You have expressed your physical courage and indeed proved yourself brave. It is not always physical bravery that counts. One must have the courage to face life as it is, to go through sorrows, and always to sacrifice oneself for the sake of others. It is also humility that exalts one and favors him against his friends. But remember, young man, everybody's bracelet is his own.

SIGILAI: What do you mean by that?

KIPKALYA: I mean that you die your own death.

SIGILAI: What are you referring to?

KIPKALYA: Cherop has been offered to be sacrificed, and she is yours free if you can save her from the claws of the big bird.

SIGILAI: I don't understand what you are saying. Cherop was saying the same thing. I came here to find out about it, and all you did was to insult me. Now I have proved that I am not a coward and you are still confusing me. Tell me, what is all this about?

KIPKALYA: Well, young man, I will tell you, only it won't go down the throat if you are really serious about this girl. The elders and all the world have decided to offer an alternative sacrifice to the god of rain—everthing else has failed to date. A human sacrifice is the only one which has not been tried. To make a long story short, Cherop was chosen. As parents we could not object since it is the mind of the people that said it. We have cried enough, her mother and me. It is your turn.

The Attempted Escape

Angrily Sigilai left the elder and went into seclusion. He decided to take the girl away until he heard that another girl had been sacrificed. He sent for Cherop and told her the news, and how the sacrifice would mean death for her. She was shocked, and made plans to leave with Sigilai the next day. Sigilai built a treehouse for them to live in. Cherop wondered how they would live. She had not been initiated and therefore could not be married, according to custom. Sigilai assured her that he intended to keep the traditions of the tribe. "I do not want them to have the excuse that our escape was eloping; no young man elopes with an uninitiated girl, no matter how much he loves her." He began to teach Cherop how to search for honey, how to use bows and arrows, and other skills they would need to survive.

One day, a leopard attacked Sigilai. He finally killed the beast, but sustained many wounds in the process. Some hunters heard the noise of the battle, but could not figure out what it was. When they got home, they heard the news of Cherop's being called to be sacrificed, and of her escape with Sigilai. They immediately associated this with the noises they had heard.

A group of young men were assigned for the search to bring the pair home, although the people understood the determination of the young man to defend his loved one. After a long search they came to the place where the path ended on the ground and continued up a tree. They decided it was a baboon nest and were going to abandon it. But one of them insisted they climb up the tree and, if it were a baboon nest, they would not lose anything.

They discovered it was Cherop and Sigilai's treehouse. Sigilai's wounds were bad, but he could move his hands easily. He threatened to shoot the young men with poison arrows. The group knew he meant his threats, and they left for discussion of how to deal with the situation. Finally they decided that some would move under the tree and cut it down while the others protected them with shields. Their plan succeeded and before long both Sigilai and Cherop took a soft ride to the ground. 'After long argument both agreed to go home.

The searchers took Sigilai to the hut of the warriors where they began treating his wounds. Because of the lack of proper treatment and the loss of blood, he was so wasted that they thought he would die. They killed a goat to shed blood for his cleansing—a custom which must be observed whenever a beast attacks anyone. In examining the entrails of the intestine they noted that it told of a bad omen—it was probable that Sigilai would die. People began to fear for his life, and word went out that he might not survive.

Some of the best medicine men were called in to treat and assess the seriousness of the sickness. One of those contacted was a man known for his skill in surgery and another one was an expert in treating wounds. It is believed that leopards always leave hair in the lungs of their prey, so a person who knew how to treat the inside of a man was also called. Everybody in the neighborhood sympathized. Women brought water, wood, and vegetables for the family of Sigilai. Some of Sigilai's symptoms gave signs of a relationship between his physical pain and some mental anguish. He appeared to be worrying about something and was not struggling to pull himself out of the sickness. His parents tried to conceal the fate of Cherop by suggesting that things may change. They wanted him to get well. But this was to no avail and so they tried something else. They were hoping for a supernatural intervention in the sickness. "Sickness is evil and if anyone knew where it came from a thorny fence would be constructed to bar it." This is a popular saying in the tribe. To save a person, symptoms must be treated. But to treat symptoms one must know the remedy and how to apply it. The prophets are the only ones who know, and so Sigilai's parents found it necessary to consult one of them.

Talai was a prophet, a wise woman endowed with the knowledge of the society. She knew the causes of most emotional and mental problems. To her, such problems are caused either by the spirits that troubled the ancestors (emotional people nurture and make emotional children) or by the victim's inability to solve problems and therefore seeking to escape from them, running all the time so that reality does not catch him (lunatics tend to be restless and removed from reality). Thus, a person troubled by either one of these problems may not respond well to physical treatment. Talai was different from those who bewitch people; they use pressure and the power of suggestion to make sick someone with whom they are angry or of whom they are jealous. Talai was wise enough to help people with these emotional illnesses, and she was a good woman who would cause no evil. So Sigilai's mother went to Talai's home.

TALAI: I am only a woman of humble upbringing. You came
                to me for advice? Let me hear your problem.
SIGILAI'S MOTHER: Yes, I have a problem. My son is sick.
TALAI: I see he is sick. My mind tells me that he is sick. Sit
                quietly, think what has happened. I will
                speak to supernatural powers. They will tell
                me what the trouble is.

Her voice was small and high-pitched. She gurgled and made funny noises in her throat and the room was dark. She jingled shells in her gourd and asked Sigilai's mother not to be frightened but to cooperate. She had put on the cloth of power—a rough, untreated hide of heifer, with decorations of cowrie shells.

SIGILAI'S MOTHER: Do you see any good omen?

TALAI: I do not deal with omens. That is for everybody to do. I am trying here to determine the trouble and prescribe some solution to it. I see two things fighting, maybe human beings, maybe animals.

SIGILAI'S MOTHER: Yes, it is my son and the leopard.

TALAI: The leopard? You have my sympathy! I get messages that someone is angry but not human beings—it is a wind, a flying wind, a rain, a god, or something like that. What did your son do?

SIGILAI'S MOTHER: Yes. he took a girl away who had been. chosen by the whole world to be sacrificed to appease the heavens to give us rain.

TALAI: Now I see the trouble. That is easy now. The blue sky has punished him and he will not get better until a cleansing and reconciling ceremony is done. You must go home now, find a young he-goat, kill it, shed the blood to the ground, and have an elder spit and breathe the word of mercy to him. Asis will be happy and grant pardon, because the forgiveness of men is the forgiveness of the Great One, since our laws are His laws. Sigilai himself must do his part, get up, walk to the altar, hit it with his walking staff everyday as a sign of repentence. He must also put a hide ring on his left middle finger. He must call his friends, abandon his past plan and publicly admit his foolishness. That will do it.

That did not do it. Sigilai continued to stay in bed. He did everything he was told, and although his wounds appeared to have improved considerably, he lay in bed and pretended to be still sick.

The Day of Sacrifice
Early in the morning of the day of the sacrifice, everybody left for their respective meeting trees and each shire assembled its people

ready to march up the hill overlooking the lake. The previous night, the trumpet had been blown to indicate that this was the day when everybody must go to the hill—except those who were unable to go for reason of sickness or those who had done wrong and had not undergone the rite of cleansing. Women had to approach the hill from the less rugged side. The armies had to march in single file and array themselves overlooking the lake on which the sacrifice was to take place. As usual, everyone was dressed in his best ornaments and clothes. Although a short prayer was going to be offered, women did not take any sacrifices since the only sacrifice was to be the girl to be given to the blue.

At home, they were dressing Cherop with white plumes of the ostrich. She had to be presented as the girl who is adorned white (chepta-kilel), with the best beadwork and laces. After she was ready, she was led to the front of the crowd where two young men stood behind her. Langok, her girlfriend, stood by her holding her trembling hand. The priest stepped forward, ordered everybody to turn and face east with outstretched arms, and offered a prayer.

After the priest finished the prayer he turned to the girl, took her hand, motioning to Langok her friend to step aside. She broke into tears and had to be helped to stand by two other girls. Cherop was serene; she had the heart of a lion although truly feminine. She raised her head to look at the priest; she looked at the crowd.

PRIEST: My countrymen, the children of our beloved tribes, the fruit of our toils: this is the day which has haunted our hearts, which everyone wished would not come. We had hoped that the Great One would not commit us to this hard act. But as men of one heart and understanding, we have to be realistic regarding the operation of nature. It is hard for me to imagine what is about to happen. But the courage of Cherop to offer her life so that the lives of her brothers and sisters might be spared speaks louder than words. I must say that we have enjoyed Cherop's presence. Children love her, old people love her, she loves everybody. She is the symbol of the best of our land. It is hard for me to give her as a sacrifice, but you have appointed me to stand between you and the powers that there are. [Holding the hand of Cherop they both turn toward the east; visibly touched, he says:] Look, O Great One, the Rising, the sacrifice we offer—may it please you. I now pronounce her Nagor—"the sacrificed."

As soon as the priest finished, he dropped the hands of Nagoro and gave a sign for her to be escorted a few steps in her lonely journey to the lake. When the young men stood by her, she turned, faced the crowd again, looked at her mother, embraced her, and touched the heads of her little brothers and sisters. Then she looked around to see if she could see Sigilai—her sweetheart. She had a feeling that he might force himself out of bed, but he wasn't there. She sighed and turned around and the march began. At fifty feet the young men turned and went back while she continued down the hill to the lake to meet her doom.

The question in everybody's mind was the nature of her death. Was she going to be tortured, or taken away, or killed outright? The spectators held their breaths as the lonely girl walked down majestically as if devoid of fear to give her life that her country might be saved. What a sacrifice! The mother of Nagoro wept audibly and so did a number of women. Everybody began shedding tears. But time was running out—the lonely figure was only a few feet from the lake. Clouds had gathered around the surrounding hills and there was already a moist wind. Suddenly there was lightning, followed by thundering—all at a distance, but there was no visible rain. Soon the whole place was full of horror. The ground began to quake and the tremor was so strong that there was visible movement of trees, and stones rolled down the hill. The two mountains nearby exploded; smoke began to issue from them and everybody began to fear. The priest summoned the people to keep away from heavy rock but they had to remain there until they saw what would happen.

Boom! The place resounded with a power like that of armaments clashing in war. There was a shout from a human being and a roar of a beast of unknown nature. A sword was seen glittering but then it was covered by a thick smoke which rose from the place. After a while, the smoke gave way, and a person who looked like a warrior was marching back and forth and around Nagoro. Nagoro's feathers were now scorched but she stood straight and firm. Someone in the crowd noted that the man was limping and suggested that it was Sigilai. Few people believed him.

Then the two persons, Sigilai—for it was he—and Nagoro, walked up the hill. Sigilai had struck the big bird with his sword, wounding it on one leg and the wing. He had defended his sweetheart. When he reached where the people were, he did not know what was going to happen. But then the clouds opened and the birds and flamingos came from it, swerving into the lake. They made formation in groups and gave a magnificent display. A heavy rain followed and the people had to walk home in the rain.

The Battle As Reported By Sigilai

"I pretended I was too sick because I wanted to challenge the creature alone. I knew I was going against the wishes of the people, and I didn't know what I was really after. I took my sword and my shield. I also took my bow and poisoned arrows. I had killed a leopard with it and I have killed many animals with it. This time I doubled the amount of poison.

"There were times when I doubted my own bravery, but Cherop meant much to me and to die was to gain because life without her would be difficult. I decided to die with her. I moved quickly, although my knee was stiff and a little painful. I didn't know where Cherop would be led to so I observed where the people were facing and decided the position of offering. The wind was beginning to blow hard. It was blowing hard against my shield, which now seemed to be as heavy as the grindstone. I noted the path of the wild animals and I figured that Cherop would trail that way. Then I crouched low as soon as I stepped on the dry sandbank and waited for the worst.

"Cherop came down and I saw her face, firm and unafraid, but sorrow seemed to have filled her heart. She immediately noticed my presence and without a word she turned and performed her routine of waving to the crowd, and I saw the crowd wave to her. That made me angry, and I felt as if my own anger would tear me to pieces. I had never loved a girl, but Cherop meant a lot to me, and I had come to defend her.

"Cherop did not say a word to me. She looked at me as if to say, why come to die with me? She moved closer to the bank of the lake where the salt blocks—the lake is salty—had dried like stones. I felt as if fire were going through me, and my heart was beating hard. I began moving back and forth in front of Cherop. I had drawn my sword and held my shield in my left hand. The arrow sheath was dangling down, and I could see the feathers of the poisoned arrows ready to pull out in case I needed them.

"I saw the dry, salty lake crack up because of the strong wind and the clouds were moving as if troubled by a mighty hurricane. First, there was lightning that was so strong that it blinded my eyes. It was then I saw the figure of the greatest bird I had ever imagined. I saw it come down and set one foot on the surrounding ground. The place rose up as when a bull sticks his horn on a hill and shovels it up. Fire came out of the bird and his smoke rose to heaven. I trembled. When my eyes could see again, I noted that Cherop was still standing close to me, her hands clutched together on her breast, but unmoved. That really shamed me. Here I was a brave man that had faced lions, snakes, man-eaters—everything—and I was scared to death, perhaps because I wanted to live. Life is grand!

"My attention was attracted to the beauty of Cherop's elegant feathers. I noted that she was more beautiful than I had thought. I was tempted to suggest an escape to her, but I knew we didn't have a chance to do so.

"Then, as I was looking at her, the lightning flashed across the sky—this time so close that I could see even the smallest sand. Before I was aware, Cherop's feathers were aflame. I hit her with the shield to try to extinguish the fire. Then I remembered that if you cover a burning fire with dust it will die. So I called Cherop to drop down so I could pour dust on her. She was immovable; so I picked her up and laid her down. Quickly, I used my shield to bury her under the sand. I managed to extinguish the fire. I noted that Cherop had not suffered any burns. So I waited again. Then the sky opened and I saw this monster bird coming. I got ready with my sword. The claws were extended as an angry hawk and its hooked beak was open and ready to tear the sacrifice apart. I brandished my sword, and, noticing this, it slowed down a little bit. Just as it got a few feet above us, I gave it a poisoned arrow and watched it pierce the feathers. I knew then it was like human beings and, although it was twice the size of an elephant, I knew the arrow would work. Still, we both might die before the beast was disabled. I quickly waved my sword and pushed Cherop under my feet. I struck the bird on the feet with the sword. The sword was twisted and the contact vibrated my hands. I decided to go for the soft parts of its body but the feathers were so thick that I could not reach its flesh. The claws caught me but I had crouched low and had lain on top of Cherop, rolling next to some stones. The claws of the bird reached us, but instead of us they picked a log that I had begun to clutch. Thinking that we were the log, the bird began to take off. I told Cherop to get into the grass; but she did not respond to my advice. I thought of covering her with the shield—leaving myself exposed to the claws of the monster.

"Perhaps what disabled me was the thundering which blocked my ears and scared me. But as I fought on I became more and more courageous. The claws of the bird had taken their toll and I was bleeding all over; but I had seen blood before. There was one thing I had not done. I wanted to throw sand into the eyes of the monster—I tried it and it worked! The bird could not see properly, and I had the advantage of dodging. As soon as it was able to see me, it made the greatest mistake, I thought, by bending toward me, trying to pick me up with its bill. I struck hard with my sword and sent the bird crumpling down with a dull thud into the dirt. The wings rested on me and I had a hard time finding my way through the feathers. When I got out, the bird had regained consciousness and was beginning to pull itself up and, amid great lightning and thunder, it took off. The wind stirred the sand and the whole place was a colossal whirlwind.

"Following the ascent, I saw the clouds falling down in torrents and breaking into pieces of hawk-size. As they reached halfway, they turned into the most beautiful birds I had ever seen. Then rain came and I walked to Cherop, held her hand and the first words she spoke were, 'Are you all right?' Then tears rolled in my painful eyes."

Sigilai married Cherop later and lived a happy life. They bore many children because the Most High honored the willingness of Cherop to die for others and the bravery of Sigilai to defend the one he loved even to death.

CONCLUSION

From this tale, one might see how the myth functions in African society and begin to understand how the myth relates to metaphysics in African cultures. The myth is in essence the African himself in history. The modern African, if he is to find his real identity and to grasp the remnant of his culture, must look for it in myth. The Western world brought us fear, doubt in our own selves, negative attitudes toward our frame of reference, and alienation from our conventions. The African myth tarried to preserve the last drop of African-ness. It is the encyclopedia engraved in the chambers of the African mind to be passed from generation to generation—at the fireside, at bedtime, and whenever the African seeks to reach other brothers and sisters in that vast continent. It becomes the catalyst in human relations—and it is in humanism that Africa is to remain the leader of the world.

6

Some Aspects of Religion and Art in Africa*

Roy Sieber

It is difficult to apply definitions of religion or art developed in our society to traditional Africa because of the way we tend to view, codify, and pigeonhole concepts. For example, Western society has recently rejected the concept of art as the handmaiden of religion, despite a long tradition of religious art. To assume that art must not or should not be at the service of religion—or, indeed, any shared social value system—would impose a most inaccurate restriction on the examination of the relationship of art to religion in traditional African societies.

The interaction of roles or categories that we consider mutually exclusive may be illustrated by a mask which I saw and collected in 1958 and which is now in the National Museum in Nigeria (Fig. 2). It is a most important mask type among the Igala of Northern Nigeria, examples of which are to be found in each politico-religious unit consisting of a village or group of associated villages. [1] The responsibility for the mask was in the hands of the chief. The mask is called Egu Orumamu. *Orumamu* means "most important," "chief"; *egu* means "mask," but also refers to a class of spirits. Only in context is it clear whether the Igala are speaking of a wooden object—the mask—or the spirit force which the mask symbolizes. Although the mask is presented as if it were the spirit it represents, the elders knew perfectly well that it was a piece of wood carved by a certain person at a known time. They knew the mechanics of its production and use and are not confused in the least. Thus at the level of the leaders there is a clearcut distinction between the object and what the object represents or sybolizes. They are clearly not involved in the "idolatry," which is to equate, confuse, or confound the object with what it represents. The more I look into it, the more I

*Portions of this paper are based on field research. I am grateful to the Foreign Area Fellowship Program for support for research in Nigeria in 1958 and to the African-American Universities Program, IndianaUniversity and the University of Ghana, for support for research in Ghana in 1964 and 1967.

am convinced that there never was any "idolatry" in Africa. Popular misreading or nonunderstanding may occur in Africa as it has in every society, but when we have evidence at the level of the philosophers of the society I can discern no real confusion and thus no idolatry.

This mask will appear officially and normally twice a year, at the beginning and at the end of the agricultural season—at the beginning in order to insure enough rains for a successful crop and at the end as a thanksgiving for the successful harvest. In other words, there is a basic level at which this mask is closely involved with human survival, for each family must grow enough food each year to sustain itself until the next harvest. No matter what else a man does in the way of specialization, there is still the hard-core need to grow enough food for one's own family. Thus Orumamu is involved at the basic level of human survival.

It must be emphasized that the mask is not the representative of a grain god, but rather represents collectively the spirits of the ancestors who intercede in the spirit world to insure the harvest.

It is generally believed in Africa that the body and the soul are separable, that the body is corruptible but the soul has relatively eternal or persisting life, and that the spirits of the ancestors continue to live in contact with human beings. Among the Igala they are viewed as a collective force in the spirit world which can be used by the living, a power source which can be "tapped." The ancestors, to phrase it another way, are lobbyists in the spirit world and get the things done that are needed to insure the security of the living—such things as assuring enough rain for a good harvest. The mask, through its association with the ancestors, symbolizes a security and a power whose locus is believed to lie in the spirit world. Through the ancestors who are collectively symbolized, the mask becomes an authority symbol in the medieval sense of *auctoritas*, the accumulated wisdom and authority of the group.

The role of the mask as authority symbol may be discerned in a number of ways in which the mask is used—ways that range over our categories of criminal and civil law, economics, and general peace-keeping. In the case of murder this mask will come out to supervise the apprehension and execution of the murderer. It does not play policeman or judge, but rather comes out to lend the weight of its authority to the proceedings. In a small, relatively circumscribed group the murderer (or the responsible family) would most often be quickly known. Then, dramatically, the mask would make its way to a particular household to demand that the household give up the murderer. The elders would have been exceeding their authority by going to the house, but by bringing the mask they bring an authority which is outside ordinary human acts. It is an exterior factor which is not involved with the accidental personality factors of individuals. The apprehension of the murderer has now become an act of semi-divine vengeance.

Should the family fail to give up the criminal, Orumamu can seal off the household from human society. Fields remain untended, no hunting takes place, women cannot go to market, no water can be fetched; above all, the family is excluded from society in all normal group interactions. It was reported that sequestering the family never failed to produce the criminal.

The market women are the backbone of Igala economics. When they have difficulties their final recourse is to the mask. It adjudicates their problems and, reaching a solution, sends its secondary masks out to collect overdue debts or punish offenders. Further, the mask was involved in basic peace-keeping, sometimes through a secondary mask which acts as a policeman. For example, in the dry season when the supply of water is low, the source may be muddied by small boys or arguments may arise among families because some people are not getting their fair share. In such circumstances the secondary mask polices the water source to be certain that the water stays clean and that there is a fair rationing. The whole pattern of peace-keeping, of the freedom of the society from criminals, of the sense of basic survival, is a part of the response of the people of the village to the mask. It is seen as a generalized symbol of stability, whatever particular role it plays at a given moment in time.

Now, what aspects of this mask may be described as social or as aesthetic or as religious? Does not such a question imply Western separation, alien to the Igala sense of the meaning of the mask? Should it not be seen as the interweaving of religious authority with social control in a form called "art"? Our tendency to separate religion, law (criminal or civil), economics, and agricultural success can therefore be misleading. We need to consider the mask in several dimensions, including the spiritual, in which the collectivity of the ancestors stands behind the physical object as the aesthetic form is read as a reinforcement of the value system the object symbolizes.

At an art exhibition when one sees masks and figures stripped of their attributes and removed from the context of ritual it is difficult to realize that there may be a philosophical system which underlies or pervades the objects. We must remember that what is significant in a mask is not simply the carved wooden face, nor the costume; we must look beyond these and even beyond the music, the dances, and the mythology. The wooden face that we tend to focus on as sculpture is only a small part of a much larger complex of meanings and acts.

From the example of Orumamu it is obvious that a "first-level" description of the mask by the Igala users would not include data we would consider either religious or aesthetic, but would seem to be totally practical or social. Yet a closer examination would allow us to discern the religious authority that the mask expresses and the aesthetic form that symbolizes, even represents, that authority to the Igala viewer.

Perhaps now we can examine more closely some of the definitions of art and religion as they would seem to pertain to traditional Africa. In the twentieth century, especially in the West, we have become adjusted to a museum-centered, connoisseur-oriented art that seems to be aimed at a small audience and to have little shared social purpose or meaning. It is evident, however, that historically in the West, as in the instance of the Orumamu mask, a work of art may be meaningful on several levels of association to a broad segment of the society that supports the object or event. Yet it is difficult to discern what art *is* in many societies, particularly those that do not share our sense of, or necessity for, verbalizing the aesthetic. It might be argued that if a society has no word for "art" (in our sense) then it has no art. Or it may be suggested that a rather open or loose definition might be proposed that would serve to let us explore the phenomena we loosely call "art." Let me try the latter.

If one were to try to communicate a mathematical formula, it could be written or printed in any form of script or type on any size piece of paper and it would not change. No matter how one presented it, with chalk on a blackboard or gold lettering on a piece of vellum, a mathematical formula is communicating the same idea at the same level. In a work of art this is not the case. The idea being communicated is of course crucial, but the mode or form of transmission of the idea is at least as important as the idea itself. Indeed, one might suggest that art could be defined as the combination or fusion of formal context and idea. From this stance it is obvious that significantly different sorts of communication take place in art and in mathematics. Art must be persuasive in terms of what we normally call the aesthetic, but persuasive about something else—the idea or symbol. The aesthetic is a tool by which the artist persuades us that an idea or a concept is meaningful. It is a way of saying something that cannot be said as effectively in any other manner. It is not embroidery or ornament; it is a way of making a meaningful statement. One level at which this exists in our society, sometimes quite effectively, is the editorial cartoon. The cartoonist makes a comment, political or otherwise, using his artistic tools to reinforce the point. However, his meaning is literal and his· most effective weapons are satire and exaggeration. Thus his greatest impact is ridicule and his effect is usually negative in sharp contrast to the positive thrust and meaning of most art.

We must be careful not to apply the religious values developed in one society to others. Brash as it seems, I would like to suggest a definition of religion that appears not to be particularistic, but rather is based on man's search for extrahuman (divine, supernatural, spiritual) assistance in achieving a sense of security. Religion may thus be defined in terms of a goal (security—in life and in death) and the process of reaching toward that goal (ritual, ceremony, worship, prayer).

Art in the service of religion, or the search for a more secure state, must then reinforce the particularized goals of a given society through the persuasive impact of symbolic or representative forms. Thus, in one sense, the Orumamu mask is a shared image, persuasively reinforcing conservative, traditional values, be those (in our jargon) legal, social, or religious. Art in such a context *is* tradition oriented, reinforcing fixed, shared values, conservative to the core, as are the values it reinforces and the spiritual authority it symbolizes. Orumamu lends a basic sense of security to the group, a sense that what it does and believes is fit, proper and right, that the world is a better place for it, and, indeed, that survival is insured. Thus art—like religion—may involve a positive interpretation, an optimistic reading of human life, human acts, and human futures.

Some cautions are in order. First, not all African masks have the density of meaning of Orumamu. Further, we must not expect of Africans a greater sense of systematization than we ask of ourselves. And systematization has been overdone. Griaule, the French anthropologist, seems to have overstructured the philosophical views of the Dogon. [2] The system he attributes to them is so beautifully organized and consistent that one wonders whether any human society could have developed it.

Also, we must be wary of the sources of information. In any society there are persons with varying degrees of understanding, of intelligence, and of the ability to abstract concepts and ideas. In some instances we do not know the role and status of the informants. It is possible that one individual may provide a seemingly coherent and reasonable account that in fact would not be accepted by the elders who constitute traditional authority.

Given these problems and cautions I would like to present a number of examples selected from the literature of African art and anthropology as well as from my field of experience in order to suggest some of the points where traditional African religions intersect with and are expressed or reinforced by traditional African arts. These range over most activities, especially those associated with times of crisis or transition, the so-called rites of passage, such as the move from childhood to adulthood.

In many African groups there is a major set of activities that formally introduces the child into adulthood, a structure or system that he enters as a child and leaves as adult. In other words, the whole of the adolescent pattern is focused in a series of activities which do not allow for the "lost adolescent" of our society. The ceremonies can take weeks, months, or years. Essentially what is involved is a series of events which are related to the achievement of sexual maturity and adult responsibility. These are cast in a framework of a semi-formalized education in the mythology, history, precepts, songs, "secrets"—in sum the lore that encompasses the accumulated tradition of the group. In addition, in some cases there may be a training as a specialist in a craft. Often there is a death and rebirth symbolism. According to George W. Harley, [3] the initiate of the Poro society in Liberia is "eaten" by a bush monster, "lives" in the bush monster's belly, and is regurgitated—"born"—as an adult. At least that is the story that is told to the women and uninitiated in the village. What in fact happens is that he is carried off to an encampment outside the village where he learns the responsibilities of adulthood, and, when he graduates from the "bush university," as it has been called, he comes back to the village "reborn" as an adult. When he was a child he was an "imitation," not yet a real human being. When he graduates he is a citizen. Masks are associated with this transition in the Poro and in other groups in Africa. Again the masks are the symbols of the spiritual forces that validate the acts and the precepts of the elders. Indeed, Harley tells of one mask that is so intensely meaningful that it may never be worn. It represents the spirit force which, transcending the more usual symbols, represents the ultimate force—the god spirit—that gives final approval or disapproval of the decisions reached by the elders. Thus Poro continues to be effective as a factor in adult society.

There is in Poro one mask type which represents the face of a woman, but which is worn by a man who is a major judge. There seems here to be a contradiction: a man dressed as a woman, who imitates a woman as he moves around, yet makes serious decisions about controversies in the village. How easy to suggest that here we have a sense of justice (masculine) tempered by mercy (female), to think that the mask is female because women are supposed to be "softer" than men. Yet without hard field evidence this—or any other interpretation—cannot be accepted.

Parallel to Poro is a woman's society which is responsible for the introduction of girls into adult responsibility, just as Poro is responsible for the introduction of boys into adult responsibility. It too has masks which represent the supervising force, the authority structure for the women's society which serves as the female balance to the male Poro.

Masks may also serve as the symbols of various sorts of cults associated with agricultural success (as with the Chiwara masks of the Bambara), purifying the village through the eradication of social evils such as disease (the Do masks of Western Ghana)(Fig. 3) or witchcraft (the Gelede of the Yoruba). Several cults among the Bambara are reported to serve cleansing functions. They are involved in efforts to eradicate social evils, such as cannibalism, adultery, and poisoning with the aid of supernatural forces. A mask is kept in a special hut in the middle of the village which can be entered only by members of the society. [4]

It is thus clear that African sculpture can serve as the visible expression of a spiritual force or authority that validates the basic beliefs of a society, that it can serve as well to reinforce acceptable social modes of conduct and can symbolize the spiritual authority that eradicates social evils. In this way a range of factors appear to have been dealt with from harvests to murder, from initiation to witchcraft. In these ways social goals are reinforced and social evils wiped out.

I should like to summarize one example of the intersection of art and religion as a "case study." For this I shall use the Dogon, mentioned earlier, who live in the rocky cliffs of the Bandigara escarpment. [5] They apparently came as refugees to escape the political and religious pressures of Islam sometime after the eleventh century. As we shall see, their oral tradition acknowledges this move.

According to the Dogon basic myth the Earth Mother gave birth to the animals and humans. She cohabitated with her firstborn, the jackal, and this incestuous act resulted in the first appearance of menstrual blood. She spread out her skirt, discolored by the menstrual blood, to dry on an ant hill, the symbol of her sex. [6]

At first there was no death in the sense of the separation of soul and body and the resultant corruption of the body. When a man grew old he could decide that his strength was lessening, his use diminishing, and initiate a transformation. By entering an anthill he would be transformed in a series of steps into a water spirit. In the first step he took the form of the python, which is associated with water.

After the Dogon moved to their present home, a woman out gathering foodstuffs one day stumbled upon a group of the earlier inhabitants, the Tellem or little red men who had been displaced by the Dogon. The Dogon woman observed these autochthons using masks and costumes and dancing. By coming upon them suddenly she startled and frightened them and they ran away, but they left behind a mask with its costume. She put on the mask and costume, returned to her village and frightened the men. They were terrified until they discovered that it was one of their women who had played this trick. The men took the mask and costume and began to play with it themselves. Because they did not know what to make of it they captured one of the little red men to find out what it was all about. He kept warning them that the mask and costume were dangerous objects and that they should talk to their chiefs and elders and seers, but they ignored his advice. One day while playing with the mask they came upon a python which was in fact an elder in the process of transformation. He saw what they were doing, foresaw danger, and harangued them in order to warn them. In doing so, however, he did something which should not have been done. No longer in human form, he had used human speech, and the result was that the process of transformation was halted—he could not move on to a spiritual form nor return to human form. The process of transformation was thus forever blocked and death came to the Dogon. The body of the python decayed and it was necessary to create a surrogate house for the soul of the first dead man. Thus the first ancestor "figure" of Dogon tradition is a mask about thirty feet long, a great flat structure, painted with spots, which represents the body of the python.

The Dogon seers realized that the real contamination lay in the stolen costume, for it consisted of a red skirt—the skirt of the Earth Mother contaminated by menstrual blood. Now that man could die—indeed must die—trouble developed, because the spirits of the dead began to clutter the villages. A way had to be found to send the spirits of the dead to a place of afterlife. Further, they found that the spirits of the dead were being plagued: hunters by the spirits of the animals they had killed, warriors by the spirits of the enemies they had killed. The Dogon had somehow to protect their ancestors from these forces, so in increasingly large numbers masks came into being that could be used to control the spirit forces and protect the ancestors.

Thus there appeared a whole *corps de ballet* of masked dancers among the Dogon. Each of the masks has its own myth of origin, its own group and solo dancers, and its own songs. Each of the masks exists as a unit within the larger structure of Dogon mythology.

There is, for example, one mask type that represents an antelope. The myth of its origin tells of an antelope that was destroying the crops. A pit trap was dug and the antelope fell into it. As the hunters left the village to kill the beast, a woman said, "Walu (the antelope) is a dangerous animal." Suddenly the Walu escaped from the pit and gored one of the hunters, wounding him fatally. Some of the hunters killed the animal and others took the dying hunter back to the village. Some time later the son of the hunter began to have bad dreams. He went to the seers and they told him that the spirit of the antelope that had killed his father was still worrying his father's spirit. They suggested a mask be made in the form of the antelope. In that way the spirit of the antelope which could injure the spirit of the hunter would be controlled by having been trapped in a mask.

The mask, at the moment of completion, is too powerful for a human being to wear. In the cliff overhangs there are rock paintings which represent the mask. One of these was renewed and the mask touched to it in order to bleed off some of the spiritual power so that the mask could be worn without danger to the dancer. [7]

When a man dies the formal burial lasts several days and on one of the days all the personal equipment of the dead, such as his food bowls, his bow and arrow, and his hoe, are broken because no living person may ever use them again. On the last day the entire group of masqueraders moves across the village like an army driving the spirit of the dead person out of the village and into the land of the dead.

Clearly then the religious beliefs of the Dogon that concern death and the afterlife intersect with mythology, masks, dances, music, and much more. There seems to be a system of thought wherein it is believed that each generation must atone for the appearance of death. To achieve that atonement, men must use masks and costumes. A red skirt—*the* red skirt of the myth—is an essential part of the costumes, and use of that skirt symbolically condemns the ueser to death. In short, each generation must atone for the death of the previous generation by using equipment which condemns it to death.

It was noted that the first mask was also the first ancestor figure for it represents the python, the physical form in which man first experienced death. Because all men have since met death in human form, all other ancestor figures are human in form. Apparently the container of the soul must be in the form in which the person existed when he died. When an important person dies, an ancestor figure representing him will be carved and then kept by the family in its ancestral shrine. Quite possibly for persons of lesser importance an earlier figure may be brought out and placed next to the body so that the soul can move into it.

It is necessary to realize that the condition of the soul in the spirit world is not a passive one; the ancestors are considered to be actively involved in helping meet the needs of their living descendants. The modes of contact may include shrines, sacrifices, and libations. At fixed points in time or at times of crisis the ancestors are approached and offerings or sacrifices made to entreat the soul to do something of practical advantage to the living. It is not necessarily to be taken for granted that the ancestor is either beneficient or committed. The potentiality is there because of the blood ties, but the actuality of commitment depends upon certain rituals which must be carried out by the living. Not all souls are of equal ritual importance; those of children or of adults whose lives were of little significance are not likely to be the focus of rituals. The souls of elders or chiefs are of greatest ritual importance because of their role in preserving the stability of large segments of the society.

Ancestor figures are a major aspect of African art. Yet quite often these representations are not of specific ancestors. Among the Kota (Fig. 4) and Fang (Fig. 5) of Gabon, for instance, images are fastened to containers holding the skeletal remains of ancestors. Symbolizing ancestors and serving as a focus for rituals, the images ward off evil forces which would contaminate the skeletal remains.

Incidentally, the style of the ancestor images of the Kota and Fang are remarkably different despite the nearness of their meanings and use. The Kota figures are reduced nearly to two-dimensional forms wherein sheets of metal are applied over a wooden core and the body abstracted to a lozenge-shaped opening. In contrast Fang figures are remarkable for their three-dimensional sculptural development.

In the instances thus far cited, the Dogon, Fang, Kota—and in many other groups—the focus of ancestor rituals is the family shrine. It should not be surprising, however, to discover that these societies are relatively decentralized and the extended family serves as a primary focus for social, political, and religious activities. Nor should it be surprising to discover that with the growth of more centralized political authority, attitudes toward the family ancestor may be transferred to the leader, the "ancestor" of the political unit. The living chief is more important than the family elders and, as ancestor, more important than any individual family ancestor. Over time an accumulation of dynastic ancestors may appear.

This paper is not the appropriate place for yet another controversy over the definition of divine kingship or its origins. Suffice it to say that one element of divine kingship that does appear in West Africa and that is appropriate to this paper is the concern with the soul of the leader. Concisely stated, the well-being of the kingdom is believed to be a direct reflection of the state of well-being of the soul of the king. There exist ritual structures to insure the purity and well-being of his kingdom. Thus it is possible to interpret the cult of the God-King and the cult of the dead kings as related to the more widespread belief in the ancestors. Indeed, there may be an historical sequence that may someday be better understood.

In any case, the arts have again been pressed into service. In some instances leadership has usurped the ancestor image, or taken over masking traditions that possibly developed in less centralized political systems. Further, utilitarian objects that become attached to leadership may become transformed into symbols of power.

Among the Kuba of Zaïre, figures of a particular sort are limited to representations of kings. In Kuba tradition there is a culture hero, Shamba, a king who brought marvelous things to the society. Among the traditions that he introduced were a game, called *mankala*, a cut-pile embroidery technique of raffia cloth making, and the concept of the king figure (Fig. 6).

We know of only one other area where the cut-pile cloth technique appears together with the type of funerary figure that shows the deceased seated cross-legged on a plinth. That area is along the west coast in the area of the mouth of the Zaïre (Congo). It seems probable that Shamba visited groups to the west of the Kuba and appropriated the figure type, limiting its use to leadership. Each king figure has a fixed set of elements, including such items as a particular cap, a sword, and a raffia belt. These are the three crucial symbols of kingship among the Kuba. In addition, the kings are individualized, not through portraiture in our sense—that is not through a physiognomic likeness—but through an attribute. For example, Shamba is to be identified by the *mankala* game board which is carved at the front of the plinth. These figures are in their own way as richly iconographic as medieval saint figures of the Western world. Each exhibits a fixed set of attributes: the cross-legged position that symbolizes death of an ancestor, the sword, hat, and belt that symbolize kingship, and the special attribute that serves to identify a particular king.

A number of old traditions of art in West Africa appear to have been dedicated to the commemoration of royal ancestors. There seems no question that the bronze and terracotta "portraits" of Ife were dedicated to royalty [8] and that they were in use as early as the twelfth century A.D. Similarly the bronzes of Benin, possibly as early as the sixteenth century, and known to Europe by the late seventeenth century, were dedicated to royal use. The use of bronze for figurative art was the prerogative of the chief. As one of the first responsibilities, each ruler or *oba* would set up a shrine dedicated to his immediate predecessor. He would assume as well responsibility for the upkeep of the shrines dedicated to all the earlier kings. On the altars were placed heads of cast bronze or brass. On each head was mounted an elephant's tusk with relief carvings, which, like the bronze plaques that decorated the façades of the courtyards, commemorated specific events during the reign of the honored king. One plaque, probably dating from the sixteenth century, shows the king riding on a horse, a power symbol, his arms supported on one side by his war chief and on the other by his heir-apparent. Two other figures hold up shields which protect him from the sun. In the background warrior figures possibly symbolize the armies. The king is placed in the center and is the largest figure—to emphasize his importance.

Finds from Igbo Ukwu in eastern Nigeria which date to the ninth century also seem related to leadership. A major excavation has revealed the tomb of a priest king. [9] The terra cottas from the Nok culture of northern Nigeria have been dated to about 200 B.C. These are the earliest examples of sculpture yet found south of the Sahara. Although they survive mostly as fragments, [10] one small complete example depicts a male figure so heavily loaded with jewelry that it must represent a person of high status. Possibly future excavations will reveal that the Nok terra cottas were an early instance of commemorative ancestral imagery, or even a royal art.

A much more recent example is that of the kingdom of the Ashanti, founded about 1700. Actually, it was a confederation of states, and was only the most recent, though perhaps the most powerful, of a whole series of kingdoms established by Twi-speaking peoples in the region of modern-day Ghana, the old Gold Coast. The first official visit from England to Kumasi, the capitol of Ashanti, took place in 1817. The visitor, Thomas E. Bowdich, was remarkable, for, although he observed the Ashanti during a relatively brief official visit, he understood and sympathized with them far better than most British officials did during the rest of the century. In the illustrations of his book [11] we can identify with assurance types of objects which are still in use or which existed until the recent past: war trumpets and war drums, stools, swords raised in salutation, linguist's staffs carried by the royal spokesman, the umbrella which shades the king, and fans for cooling the royal presence. In most books these symbols of royalty have been called "Ashanti." That is technically accurate, because they were used by the Ashanti; any implication that the Ashanti invented them, however, is not accurate. A great many of these symbols of power are much older than the Ashanti kingdom. The umbrella, for instance, is a Near Eastern device for shading the king or leader. The earliest reference I know for Africa is in a description by the Arab writer, Ibn Battuta, of the ruler of Mali in about 1340.

In the state of Akwapim, which remained independent of Ashanti, we find the chief appearing almost exactly as Bowdich describes. He is carried on a palanquin and gestures to his people in a seated dance. He brandishes a sword which is a symbol of royalty and wears a form of crown obviously based on European prototypes. [12] In front of him in the litter sits a small boy wearing a rather ornate helmet. The small boy is called the *okra*, which is the Twi word for soul. Each chief or king will identify, usually among his nephews or grandsons, a child who will symbolize the purity of the chief's soul. The helmet the child wears is a war trophy. The last attempt, in the late nineteenth century, by the Ashanti to capture the Akwapims and make them part of the Ashanti kingdom failed. During the battle a major Ashanti war chief was killed and it is his helmet that is worn as a symbol of the supremacy of the Akwapims.

Carried behind the king, usually with an umbrella of its own, is the royal stool, or throne. A typical Ashanti or Akan [13] stool is basically rectangular in form with a concave seat supported by four or five posts. It is part of the basic furniture of any traditional Akan village. Although it serves as a utilitarian object, the stool is also the house of the soul of its owner. It is treated in a fairly casual way on the popular level, yet one does not get up and walk away from his stool as we would get up and walk away from a chair. The stool should be tipped on its side or leaned against the wall at sharp angle to prevent any evil force from sitting on it and thereby contaminating the owner's soul. At the level of kingship this concept is obviously of much greater significance because of the importance of the purity of the soul of the king. The stool cannot even be carried in procession without being turned upside down.

Thus the meaning of an essentially utilitarian object becomes much more intensive when it is associated with leadership, so much so that the symbolic seating of the king on his stool is part of the ceremony of investment. In legal terminology in modern Ghana, the installation of a chief is an "enstoolment" and if he is removed from the throne he is "destooled." Thus, when it is associated with leadership, the connection of soul and stool becomes sharply intensified because the well-being of the entire kingdom is now at stake. Indeed, after he dies the stool of the chief will often be placed in an ancestral shrine much as an ancestor figure. It is then covered with a blackening substance, a mixture of blood and soot, in a ceremony which changes it from a white stool, a stool in use, to a blackened stool, an ancestral object. Once it is blackened nobody ever can sit on it. It has now totally lost its utilitarian context and becomes a symbolic object.

The Golden Stool is the major symbol of the Ashanti. It was invented by, or revealed to the first *asantehene* (king of Ashanti) about 1700. Each of the constituent groups of Ashanti nation had its own tradition, its own blackened stools symbolic of leadership and tradition. The king in his search for a symbol that was greater than these could not threaten traditional affiliations. The symbolic brilliance of the Golden Stool lay in the fact that it did not house the soul of a man; rather it was the repository for the collective soul of the Ashanti nation. This marvelous bit of political symbolism is reported to have descended from heaven to rest gently on the knees of the first *asantehene*. It exists still as a unifying symbol of the state, based on an extension of the concept of the royal soul—the divine king. Its meaning was sadly misunderstood by at least one British officer who insisted that he be allowed to sit on it, an act of sacrilege. He completely misread the importance and the symbolism of it and his suggestion was so fantastically offensive that it resulted in an impasse that led to one of the Ashanti wars.

There exists a particular group of priests who have the responsibility of maintaining the purity of the soul of the leader. They are described by Bowdich and may be seen today dressed in black and white *kente* cloths, their heads shaved and with chalk marks on heads, shoulders and arms. They wear a gold disk as a badge of their responsibility to cleanse and purify the king's soul.

Other symbols of leadership among the Akan may be less oriented toward religious beliefs and more toward militarism, such as war drums, war trumpets, and the swords that symbolize royal power. Swords of the so-called royal type now in Copenhagen and in Ulm are known to have been in Europe before the formation of the Ashanti state. Thus, just as the umbrella and the system of royal stools preceded the formation of the Ashanti, so did the sword as a symbol of royal might. In addition to these and to the linguist staffs, special sandals, cloths, chairs, fly whisks, and gold jewelry have become associated with chieftainship. Usually these have little religious association, but rather spring from associations of prestige and wealth. Yet at times special secondary symbols may appear on sword handles or atop linguist staffs. These are meant less to impress the public, which really sees from afar only the sword or staff that is the primary symbol, than to be aimed at the chief and his subordinates. Often their meanings depend on Twi parables relating to the proper attitude and behavior of leaders and, at times, have a religious base. For example, the symbol of an upraised hand with the index finger pointing upward refers to a Twi parable, *Without God*, and reinforces the firm belief that no man can succeed without the help of God.

Finally among the Akan there is a tradition of terra cotta funerary portraits that probably predates the seventeenth century; these have been described elsewhere. [14] They are noteworthy here because they indicate once again the use of imagery commemorating dead leaders (Fig. 7). Thus they would seem to be part of a long history of sub-Saharan funerary portraits that reflect beliefs concerning the souls of the royal dead.

In present-day Nigeria and Ghana we have evidence of old traditions of authority symbols associated with leadership. Concepts relating to the soul and to the ancestors are concentrated in the context of the "divine kingship." The idea of "soul" as it relates to leadership seems to be in Africa an extension of the concept of the soul at the level of the family ancestor. In both the concepts of the family ancestor and the dynastic ancestor the sense of security that stems from the beliefs seems to depend on a spiritual reinforcement of human values and the assurances of spiritual intercession that will secure the well-being of the family or group. Dynastic ancestors appear to have become associated with the military power of the nation and are commemorated in artistic objects that are in part based on symbols essentially militaristic and in part on the ritualization of the living king-as-god.

The arts of centralized societies tend to reinforce the basic structure of leadership through symbols which associate the security of the group with the well-being of the leader. In less centralized groups art forms often reinforce traditional values by symbolizing the spiritual forces that lend authority to the activities and decisions of the living. The same premise would seem to invest both; the responsibility for a secure life (and a secure death, in some cases) is firmly placed on a spiritual agency which is strong, trustworthy, and is or once was a living part of the society.

Seen in this light, a part of African religious thought—and there is no intention to argue that this suggestion exhausts the rich potential of the intellectual and religious life of traditional Africa—appears to be expressed in the artistic forms that symbolize and reinforce the search for a secure life. Thus, once again, the same premise would seem to explain the apparent inconsistency to a Westerner of the uses and meanings of Orumamu with its confusion of religious, economic, and legal associations; the use of masks in Poro both to educate the young and, through judgments, to achieve a more stable society; and, in the case of the Dogon, the logic of the cross-referencing, or cross-confirming of mask, myth, death, and the ancestor figure.

In sum, these brief notes on the associations of art and religion in traditional Africa are meant less to enlighten than to persuade the reader to set aside his prepackaged views and to search for the premises and the logic that every society builds for itself.

NOTES

1. I have earlier published some notes on this mask. See *Sculpture of Northern Nigeria.* New York: Museum of Primitive Art, 1961, and "Masks as Agents of Social Control," in *African Studies Bulletin,* vol. V, II, (May 1962), pp. 8-13, and reprinted in *Man in Adaptation, the Institutional Framework,* ed. Y.A. Cohen, 1971.
2. The essay on the Dogon in C. Daryll Ford, *African Worlds,* London: I.A.I., 1959, is an instance of this.
3. In "Masks as Agents of Social Control" and "Some Notes on the Poro," both *Papers of the Peabody Museum,* Harley describes masks, beliefs, and practices of the Poro Societies of Liberia.
4. See, for example, R. Goldwater, *Bambara Sculpture,* New York: Museum of Primitive Art, 1960, figures 7, 8, and 19-23.

5. The French anthropologist Marcel Griaule and his students have published extensive descriptions of the Dogon. This summary is based on a number of publications, notably: *Masques Dogon,* Paris: Institute d'Ethnologie, 2nd., 1958; *Folk Art of Black Africa,* Paris, 1950; and the essay in *African Worlds,* (see fn. 2). Pictures of Dogon masks can be seen in the *National Geographic,* CXXV, 3 (1969).
6. Menstrual blood is considered unclean and dangerous by many societies.
7. The process of making and painting the mask involves as well the containment of the spirit of the wood. Many of the masks have on the forehead a little metal pin which locks in the spirit of the wood, so that its spiritual force does not confound the issue.
8. See Frank Willett, *Ife in the History of West African Sculpture,* New York: Thames and Hudson 1967.
9. Described in Thurston Shaw, *Igbo Ukwu',* London: Faber and Faber, 1970.
10. Some are illustrated in Willett, *Ife in the History of West African Sculpture.*
11. *Mission from Cape Coast Castle to Ashantee,* London, 1819. Reprinted by Barnes and Noble, 1966.
12. A.A.Y. Kyerematen, *Panoply of Ghana,* London: Longmans contains descriptions of a great number of chiefly attributes, Fraser and H. Cole, University of Wisconsin Press, 1972.
13. The term Akan is used to refer to all Twi-speaking groups, whether or not they were part of the Ashanti empire.
14. See R. Sieber, "Kwahu Terra-cottas, Oral Traditions and Ghanaian History," in *African Art and Leadership*, eds. D. Fraser and H. Cole, Madison: University of Wisconsin Press, 1972, pp. 173-183.

7

God and the Gods in West Africa

Newell S. Booth, Jr.

In the past it has been widely assumed that Africans are "poly-theists"; more recently, evidence has been produced supporting the view that basically they are monotheists. Now, however, it is affirmed that both these views are alien to Africa and that in this whole discussion African deities have been "used as mercenaries in foreign battles." [1]

It is possible, of course, that what is true for one part of Africa is not accurate for another. Before confident generalizations can be made we must give careful attention to evidence for limited areas. In this discussion I propose to focus on the beliefs regarding one God and many gods among the Yoruba of southwestern Nigeria and their neighbors to the west, the Ewe, especially the Fon of Dahomey. [2] There are many similarities between these groups, due to a common basic heritage and/or contacts and mutual influences through the centuries.

The Yoruba are an important group in terms of numbers, historic significance, and contemporary influence. They and their neighbors provided, involuntarily, a considerable proportion of the Africans taken to the Americas; the area they inhabit, in fact, used to be known as the "slave coast." Yoruba and Fon traditions have been especially prominent in Afro-American religion; it has been said that "no African group has had greater influence on New World culture than the Yoruba." [3] The published material on the religion of the Yoruba and Fon is extensive and, especially in the case of the Yoruba, includes significant works by scholars who are themselves Yoruba.

It has been said that the traditional religion of the Yoruba is rapidly dying; undoubtedly the majority now profess either Islam or Christianity. According to the 1952 census, a little over 40% professed Islam and a little under 40% professed Christianity. [4] In 1972 I was told that 95% of the Yoruba professed either Islam or

Christianity. This, of course, was only an estimate, but it seems to represent a fairly general opinion. However, when I asked "What percentage practice the traditional religion?" the answer was again "95%"! This was another rough estimate, but it is widely agreed that while only a small minority of the Yoruba identify themselves exclusively with the traditional religion, a large majority still relate to it for some purposes. These people are nominally Muslim or Christian—and in many ways may be devout Muslims and Christians—but they see no reason to give up all traditional practices. Observers from other parts of the world have been surprised by the friendly three-way relationships among Yoruba Muslims, Christians, and traditional believers.

This tolerance for ambiguity may prepare us for the complexities of the traditional systems themselves. Certainly the beliefs of the Yoruba and the Fon regarding God and/or the gods cannot easily be reduced to one coherent account. Any attempt at an "organizational chart" in two dimensions (or even three dimensions!) oversimplifies and distorts the data. My purpose in this article is to present something of the diversity of Yoruba and Ewe belief regarding the divine and also to suggest how this diversity may be understood.

The Yoruba name for the "supreme God" is Olorun or Olodumare. Olorun appears to be the more common name at the present time but there is reason to think that this popularity is of relatively recent origin. The name clearly means "owner of the sky"; its very clarity may suggest that it is not very ancient. Its monotheistic implications make it acceptable to Islam and Christianity, religions which, as we have seen, have been growing rapidly among the Yoruba for the last 150 years. It should be noted that Olorun is not identified with the sky in a literal way but is understood as "associated with the world beyond," to which the sky is the "gate." [5]

The more mysterious "Olodumare" seems to be the older Yoruba name for God. A possible meaning is "one who has Odu, child of Ere." *Odu* can refer to the figures in the Ifa divination system, which will be discussed later, and also to "whatever is unusually large, as a large pot or container." [6] Olodumare does have an association with Ifa and is said to be the brother of Orunmilla, [7] the divination god, or even an alternative name for this god. [8]

Ere can mean "python" or "boa" and Olodumare may then mean "Olodu, child of the python." [9] According to one myth, Olodu was the child of "the large primeval boa" who acquired such "a reputation for prowess and goodness" that "earth could no longer contain him" so he moved to heaven where "he exceedingly increased in all good and divine qualities." [10] Thus Olodumare may be associated with the "cosmic serpent" Oshumare, of whom the rainbow is also a manifestation.

In general, it appears that Olodumare represents an older, less rationalized concept of God than does Olorun. He is a kind of cosmic power, manifesting himself in various ways in different contexts. For instance, as Olorun, he is identified with the sky, which is his "mat," and thus is the one " whose Being spreads over the whole extent of the earth, the owner of a mat that is never folded up." [11] From the sky his eyes see all things so that he is able to pronounce a final and absolute judgment. He is "the King who dwells above, who executes judgment in silence." [12]

At one time, Olodumare/Olorun and the sky which is his abode were nearer to earth than they are now, so near that one could reach up and touch the sky. Man did something that annoyed the Divine Being, such as using the sky for food or wiping his hands on it; as a result God and the sky separated themselves from the earth. Since that time Olodumare has controlled the world from a distance. The ultimate power is in his hands but, like a great king, he does not attend to the details of administration. These are intrusted to his agents, the lesser divinities, who represent him on earth. Olodumare has no regular cult of his own but he may be thought of as the ultimate recipient of worship offered to other divinities.

Although thus in some ways a rather distant being, the name "Olodumare" has

> always carried with it the idea of One with Whom man may enter into covenant or communion in any place and at any time, one who is supreme, superlatively great, incomparable and unsurpassable in majesty, excellent in attributes, stable, unchanging, constant, reliable. [13]

To the west of the Yoruba, among the Ewe peoples, the term "Mawu" is both a generic name for "god" and specific name of one God. For the Anlo-Ewe of eastern Ghana, Mawu is definitely the Supreme Being, understood as male. He is personal but never has been human; like the wind, he cannot be confined to any one place. In a sense he is omni-present, and yet he is also said to live in the distant sky. He is not worshipped directly and has no images, shrines or priests, yet prayer may be directed to him and it is assumed that in some sense the sacrifices made to the lesser deities ultimately reach him. [14]

Mawu has created all things out of formless clay. Not only does he create, he continues to watch over and provide for all his creation. Thus it is said that "God can never destroy his own child" and again "it is God who drives away the troublesome flies from the animal which has no tail." [15]

Among the eastern Ewe, especially the Fon, Mawu is not so clearly the one Supreme being. Mawu is the generic name for "god" but also the particular name of a female deity associated with the moon. Unlike Mawu further west, she has her own temples and priests. At Abomey she used to be represented by a wooden statue, "coloured the red of dawn, with large breasts and a crescent in one hand." [16] She is said to represent "coolness" and the wisdom associated with age. [17]

Closely related to this female Mawu is Lisa, who is variously described as her twin brother, husband, or son. He is associated with the sun and represents strength; [18] he is also represented by the chameleon. [19]

According to one account, Mawu is "a Janus-like figure, one side of its body being female, with eyes forming the moon, and bearing the name of Mawu. . . . The other portion is male, whose eyes are the sun, and whose name is Lisa." [20] Thus "Mawu" can mean the dual "Godhead" as a whole and also its female half. It is said that "Mawu-Lisa express together the unity of the world conceived in terms of duality." [21]

The concept of Mawu thus is not simply that of one particular deity but rather of ultimate power. Mawu is said to have created the world, although as creator she may be "called by other names." [22] If asked about the origin of Mawu, the answer might be that she was created by a pre-existent Mawu; "there may have been many Mawus." [23]

In parts of central Dahomey and Togo the original creator is said to have been Nana-Buku (Bruku, Buluku), who is represented as female or androgynous. She is referred to as a "sky-god" [24] but also as "the oldest of the water gods." [25] Several shrines in central Dahomey are places of her worship. [26] She may be said to be the parent of Mawu and Lisa, as in the following report:

> The world was created by one god, who is at the same time both male and female. . . Nana-Buluku. In time Nana-Buluku gave birth to twins, who were named Mawu and Lisa, and to whom eventually dominion over the realm thus created was ceded. [27]

Another name for the supreme God among the Ewe is Dada-Segbo. "Se" is often translated "soul"; thus "Segbo" may suggest

"Great Soul", or God as the source of human souls. It is suggested that he may be an "earlier god" than Mawu.[28]

The name of the Fon deity Lisa is almost certainly related to the Yoruba *orisha*, a word commonly used for the multitude of "lesser gods." The chief or "great" *orisha* of the Yoruba is Orishanla, who is said to have been the first creation of Olodumare or even his "image or symbol on earth." [29] Other names for him are Orishala, the "white divinity" or Obatala, "King of the white cloth." He is always clothed in white, the inside of his temple is white-washed and his priests wear white. As he is averse to blood, his favorite sacrifice is the bloodless snail. Orishanla/Orishala is the chief of the "white divinities" of whom there are said to be over fifty. [30] At times he seems to take on the role of the supreme God; "Orishanla may be an expression of Olodumare in respect of his role as an artificer." [31] It is even speculated that because he "is sometimes referred to as creator...it is possible that his cult was independent of or earlier than belief in Olorun, who usurped his position...." [32]

According to one account, Orishanla was entrusted by Olodumare with the task of creating the world and given some earth and a five-toed chicken. He threw the earth on the "watery waste" and set the chicken to work spreading it out. [33] The place from which this process started is the location of the present city of Ile-Ife.

There are a number of variations on this story. According to one of them, Orishanla, on his way to carry out the job of creation, was distracted by a party, became drunk on palm wine, and went to sleep. His younger brother, Oduduwa, took the earth and the chicken, proceeded to do the job, and then established himself as king at Ile-Ife. When Orishanla awoke he felt that his brother had improperly usurped his place and a battle ensued. Olodumare intervened and allowed Oduduwa to continue as king but gave to Orishanla the responsibility of creating men to populate the earth. Thus it may be said that while Oduduwa is creator of the world, Orishanla is creator of mankind. [34] The latter manifests his power especially through those who are in some way deformed: cripples, dwarfs, albinos. These are not "mistakes" but evidences of the activity of Orishanla and thus sacred to him. [35]

The story of the conflict between Orishanla and Oduduwa may represent an encounter between early inhabitants of the land, represented by Orishanla, and an invading group, represented by Oduduwa, who established the divine kingship at Ile-Ife. At any rate, descendants of Oduduwa then spread out, establishing their rule in the whole of Yoruba land. Some Yoruba still refer to themselves as "the sons of Oduduwa."

The relationships between Orishanla, Oduduwa, and the supreme deity are extremely complex and confusing. According to still another creation story, the task of creation was entrusted to Oduduwa in the first place rather than to Orishanla. [36] The matter is further complicated by the fact that Oduduwa is sometimes represented as a goddess, the wife of Orishanla/Obatala. Thus it may be said that "she is the chief female orisha, just as Obatala is the chief male orisha." [37] It is reported that Oduduwa is older than her husband, Obatala, that, in fact, she is "coeval with Olorun and not made by him as was her husband." [38] She may even be tne mother of Obatala [39] and is said to be "self-existent." [40] Oduduwa is also reported as being identified with the Creator, Olorun. [41] In a liturgy used in Ile-Ife, Oduduwa is referred to as Iye'male, "mother of the divinities" or "mother-divinity." [42]

Oduduwa may also be identified with the earth. According to one Yoruba view, the cosmos is to be compared to the two halves of a hollow, closed calabash, the lower part being the earth and the primeval waters, on which rests the habitable world. Obatala, identified with the sky, and Oduduwa, identified with the earth, are sometimes represented as the upper and lower halves of a calabash which can never be separated. Thus it may even be said that Obatala and Oduduwa "represent one androgynous deity." [43]

One theory is that Oduduwa was originally a goddess, perhaps called by a different name, who "became male" in some contexts by a process of identification with a priest-king who was her worshipper. [44] The original goddess may perhaps be identified with Yemowo ("Mother Mowo") who is worshipped at Ile-Ife as the wife of Obatala/Orishala. [45] According to one myth it was Yemowo and Orishala who together created the world. [46]

Another name given to this "Earth-Mother" is Onile (Earth-owner) or simply Ile. According to Morton-Williams:

> She is conceptually the counterpart of the Sky God, since Earth and Sky are coeval; and she is asserted by those Yoruba who worship her to have existed before the other gods, the orisha. In her rites she is addressed as Iya, Mother. [47]

This "Earth-Mother" has close associations with the ancestors and the dead generally, who are thought of, for some purposes, as living in the earth. Aiye (the world) "rests on her"; "she supports people during their time in the world and. . . receives them when they die."[48] She has a cult, the Ogboni, which traditionally was "the major governmental organ for preserving law and order, checking excesses in kings and keeping the citizens law-abiding. . . [49] Members of the Ogboni cult consider themselves to be in a special sense the "sons of Oduduwa," suggesting again that Oduduwa has been to some extent merged with the Earth-goddess.

If this sky-earth, male-female relationship reminds us of Mawu and Lisa of the Fon, there is probably good reason. Yemowo (Ye-Mowo), whose qualities seem to have been taken over by Oduduwa, may originally be the same as Mawu. [50] It is interesting to note that Oduduwa, like Mawu, appears in some areas as female and in others as male. Lisa and Orishala can also be identified. It is widely agreed that "Lisa" and "Orisha" are originally the same word and, as we have seen, Orishala/Orishanla is the "orisha *par excellence.*" Lisa shares certain important characteristics with Orishala, especially the fondness for white objects:

> His worshippers and priests wear white clothes, albinos are sacred to him, no blood or oil may be poured on his altar, bloodless white snails and white kola nuts are his favorite offerings, and a whitened calabash is kept in his temple or in the priests' house. [51]

Thus far we have been speaking of the concept of "ultimate" or creative power. It is clear that among both the Yoruba and the Fon there are alternative ways of conceiving this power. Olorun, Olodumare, Orishanla/Obatala, and Oduduwa all represent the original power of the universe. They are not simply "different names for the same god," yet they overlap, interpenetrate, and are for some purposes interchangeable. The same is true of Mawu, Lisa, Nana-Buku, and Dada-Segbo. It appears that basically the Yoruba and Fon believe in one ultimate power, yet this power is complex, associated with the phenomena of sky, earth, and sea, with the establishment of kingship on earth, and with relationships between male and female.

The English words "divinity" and "deity" may be helpful here as they can refer to "that which has the quality of being divine" in a comprehensive sense and also to a particular divine being. Olodumare and Mawu can be thought of as "divinity" or "deity" in both these senses.

The various myths which personalize "divinity" may be contradictory in a logical sense but in fact they represent the divine power in different contexts. In part this complexity may be due to the mixing of originally distinct systems but it is also probably due to the Yoruba and Fon way of thinking; the "elaboration of composite data strikes the inquirer as one of the most original characteristics of Fon thought." [52]

It has been suggested that the Yoruba and other West African groups think of God both as Creator and as ancestor; he transcends the world and humanity, acting upon them from without, but he also is immanent, acting within and through nature and man. [53]   There may even be a "pantheistic" element in African thought, an idea of a universal unity of Being, manifested in the variety of the human and natural worlds. [54]

This immanent aspect of the Divine is personalized in the "lesser divinities." We have already noted that among the Yoruba these are generally known as *orisha*; this word may originally mean "head-source." [55]   In the narrower sense *orisha* applies specifically to the "white divinities" who are associates of Orishala/Orishanla.[56] In a broad sense it refers to a mltitude of divinities; traditionally such numbers as 401 or 1700 are used, suggesting an indefinitely large number. They are associated with persons, places, functional concerns, and even diseases, and appear to have increased in number over the years. In some cases several names may refer to what is basically one deity. Another term used more or less interchangeably with *orisha* is *imale*; this appears to have a more mysterious, dreadful, or awe-inspiring connotation, and may originally have referred to spirits especially associated with the earth. [57] Among the Fon *vodun* is the term used for the lesser divinities while among the Anlo *tro* (pl. *trowo*) is used. *Vodun*, which has been carried over in the "voodoo" of the Caribbean, may have the original sense of "separate" or "sacred." [58]

Olorun or Olodumare is not normally thought of as an *orisha*, although it is reported that he is "sometimes termed 'The Orisha' as containing all the orisha within himself." [59]   Mawu as a specific deity may be spoken of by the Fon as a *vodun* but the Anlo apparently do not speak of him as a *tro*.

An *orisha* or *vodun* is thought to "live" in the spiritual realm, but is also associated with particular places. It is said that the Fon "will point to a particular spot where a large jar is imbedded and will say that the *Vodu* is there." [60] One informant put it this way:

> The vodu itself is in the ground... The vodu has a jar next to it, but the vodu is not in the jar which is in the cult house. It is the power, the 'force' that goes about in the temple.... [61]

The physical image of the divinity at times is referred to by the Yoruba as the *orisha*. This may be taken as meaning that the image is inhabited by the *orisha* on certain occasions for certain purposes, although ultimately "the home of the divinity is in heaven." [62] That the image is not finally to be identified with the divinity is indicated by the fact that the former can be replaced when it has worn out. In other words, these people are not "idolators."

The process of installing a *vodun* in his shrine may be spoken of as "making the *vodun*." [63] The existence of the divinity thus depends on its being recognized and worshipped by man; it is by prayer and sacrifice that men "give power to the *vodu*." [64] There is also a Yoruba saying that "Where there is no man there is no divinity." [65] In the *orisha* and *vodun* divinity is "brought down" to the human level; thus in a sense they are "man-made."

Each divinity has his own particular worshippers, "called" by the god and initiated into his cult through ceremonies which usually involve a symbolic "death and resurrection." Those so possessed are the "wives" of the orisha or vodun, regardless of sex. Each deity has his/her own appropriate music, dance, offerings, tabus, and specific functions to perform in relationship to human needs and problems. All, however, seem to be involved in the basic concerns of fertility and health.

Cult groups associated with the worship of particular divinities probably developed originally from kinship groupings, and it is still true that "many deities are identified with a particular clan in which all members, male and female, are worshippers by virtue of birth into it." [66] Worshippers of a divinity may be called his "children." Perhaps some deities were originally ancestral figures who once lived on earth "but instead of dying...became gods." [67] Certain deities were at first associated with particular towns, from which their worship spread to other areas. People became worshippers of deities not only through inheritance but also as a result of certain needs which became manifest through disease or other difficulties.

The lesser deities are of various kinds. Two of them, Orunmilla/Fa and Eshu/Legba, have a special relationship with the Supreme God, serving as "a pair of divine mediators." [68] Although frequently spoken of as *orisha* or *vodun*, they actually have a somewhat more "universal" quality in their concern for relating the other deities to each other and to mankind.

Orunmilla is the Yoruba god of divination and thus of foreknowledge, destiny, and wisdom; he is the "word" or "writing" of God. [69] Other Deities, including Olodumare himself, are said to turn to him for counsel; [70] Lucas states that Olodumare may even be identified with Orunmilla and also that Orunmilla is "by far the most important and the most popular deity in Yoruba land." [71]

The system of divination itself is called Ifa; sometimes this name
is also used for the deity. The Fon have borrowed the system from
the Yoruba; they call it Fa. The divinity associated with the system
is also known as Fa; in some circumstances he may be equated with
Mawu. [72]

The priests of Orunmilla are also the practitioners of divination;
they have the title *babalawo*, "father of mysteries."

> The Babalawo constitutes a focal point in the traditional Yoruba
> religion, channeling sacrifices and worshippers into different
> cults.... He helps his client deal with the wide range of
> personalized and impersonal forces in which the Yoruba believe,
> and to achieve the individual destinies assigned to them at birth. [73]

Among the Ewe practitioners of Fa are known as *bokono*. They
are said to form the best organized and most knowledgeable
"magico-religious institutions" of the country and to officiate frequently at the worship of other deities. [74]

The basic purpose of Ifa is "to determine the correct sacrifice
necessary to secure a favorable resolution of the problem confronting the client...." [75] Whenever a deity wants a particular sacrifice
to be performed, the message is sent through Ifa. A person's life
destiny may also be determined by means of Ifa.

One method employed, in brief, is for the *babalawo* to transfer
quickly sixteen palm nuts from one hand to the other. If one nut is
left behind a *double* mark is made in the powdery substance placed
on the divining tray. If two are left a *single* mark is made. If none are
left or more than two, the "throw" does not count. The process is repeated eight times, with the result of two series of four marks each,
such as:

$$
\begin{array}{cc}
1 & 11 \\
11 & 11 \\
1 & 1 \\
1 & 11 \\
\end{array}
$$

There are sixteen primary figures or *odu*, representing the combinations possible with four marks. Each figure may be combined
with the same figure or any of the others to make a total of 256 possibilities. For each of these there are a number of verses, which also
may be known as *odu*. They usually describe a problem involving
some mythological figure, a sacrifice that was made, the outcome,
and the application. [76] A competent *babalawo* should know several
verses for each of the 256 *odu*. Thus when a particular *odu* has
resulted from the process of divination, the diviner will recite the

verses until the client selects one that appears to suit the problem. There are a number of variations and complications of the procedure but this is the basic outline.

The verses associated with the 256 *odu* have been called the Yoruba "unwritten scripture." Certainly they provide considerable information regarding the deities and their activities, much of it ancient. How many verses there are altogether is uncertain; Bascom states that 4000 is probably a conservative estimate. [77]   No one diviner would know them all.

As Orunmilla or Fa represents the element of order and predict- ability in the divine, so Eshu/Elegba of the Yoruba and Legba of the Ewe represent the element of uncertainty or spontaneity. Among the Fon, Legba is said to be the youngest child of Mawu-Lisa; this may be thought to account for this capricious qualities. He is the agent and messenger of the other deities, who has no realm of his own but "plays the delicate and dramatic role of intermediary be- tween the different vodun, between the vodun and men, (and) between men." [78]   Eshu/Legba may sometimes be thought of not simply as one being but as a group of deities.

Eshu has his own cult and worshippers but those belonging to other deities also worship him; it is said that one is able to approach the other deities only with Eshu's help. Thus every sacrifice must include an offering to him. [79]   Legba, unlike Eshu, is said to have no separate cult; his worship is universal. [80]

Eshu/Legba is very tricky and unpredictable, "the personification of accident." [81]   He causes quarrels among the gods as well as among men but also may suggest how to avoid trouble; thus he can be "tricky" in helpful as well as destructive ways. He is "the indul- gent child of heaven; he whose greatness is manifested all over the place; the hurrying sudden one; he who breaks into fragments and cannot be gathered together!" [82]   Often he is represented as "over-sexed," willing and able to sleep with all women.

It is said that Legba was responsible for the fact that Mawu is not as close to earth as he once was. Because Mawu reprimanded Legba for misbehaving, the latter suggested to a woman that she throw her dirty dishwater up at the sky, which at that time was only about two meters from earth. This annoyed Mawu so much that he moved away; Legba remained on earth and is to be found everywhere. [83]

Eshu/Legba is often equated with the Devil or Satan but this would appear to be a mistake unless Satan is understood, as in the prologue to the book of Job, as a kind of "heavenly inspector." He is not positively evil so much as unpredictable, with a "shadow" quality, one who thinks and does what is not otherwise acceptable. In spite of his tricky and sometimes negative character, it is said that in Dahomey the dominant attitude toward Legba is one of affection rather than of fear.[84]

Eshu is closely associated with Orunmilla, both positively and negatively. His face normally appears as part of the carved decoration of the divination tray. Unless otherwise specified, the sacrifices called for by Ifa are offered at his shrine; a small part is for him, as a "bribe," "to insure that he will carry the rest to Olorun..."[85] On the other hand, Eshu is able to upset the plans and predictions of Orunmilla if he so chooses, thus introducing an element of uncertainty into man's destiny.

Another deity, who is not a "divine mediator" as are Orunmilla and Eshu, but shows something of their universal quality, is Ogun of the Yoruba and Gun (or Gu) of the Ewe. He is the god of iron and of those whose occupations are related to the use of iron: hunters, farmers, warriors, smiths and, in the modern situation, chauffeurs and mechanics. Among the Fon it is said that "Gu himself is not iron, but that property of iron which gives it the power to cut."[86]   He is also the pioneer god who goes before others to clear the way; "Ogun, the possessor of two machetes: with one he prepares the farm and with the other he clears the road."[87]   Offerings must be made to him in connection with any sacrifice because he is responsible for the knife that is used.[88]   For similar reasons, apparently, he is associated with circumcision and other operations. Because of his relationship to machinery, Ogun is one god who seems to be more than holding his own in modern society.

Ogun is also associated with justice; oaths are taken in his name over pieces of iron; anyone breaking such an oath must expect to be hurt or killed by iron in some form. In general, Ogun is a rather fierce and unbending deity:

> Where does one meet him?
> One meets him in the place of battle
> One meets him in the place of wrangling;
> One meets him in the place where torrents of blood
> Fills with longing as a cup of water does the thirst.[89]

Ogun is sometimes said to be the eldest son of Oduduwa. Among the Fon, Gun is the child of Mawu and Lisa and is closely associated with them in the "sky pantheon."[90]

Alongside the gods mentioned above, we find somewhat more "independent" deities who in turn have their own associates or pantheons. One of these is Shopona of the Yoruba, Shapata of the Ewe. According to Herskovits, Shapata is the "eldest son" of Mawu-Lisa, who was sent to rule the earth. He is not, however, as closely associated with Mawu-Lisa as are Gun and Legba, but seems to be in some sense an independent source of power. Actually he is not simply one god but the "generic name for a group of deities." [91] According to one account, Mawu and Lisa first gave birth to male and female twins, from whom the "earth gods" are descended; [92] Shapata appears to be the name used when these gods are thought of collectively as one being.

Shopana/Shapata is sometimes said to be the "earth-god" but his concern is not so much with earth as a source of fertility as with earth as the locus of disease and death. He is often referred to as the "smallpox deity;" this is the result of identifying him with the most obvious sign of his wrath. He is associated not only with smallpox but with all fevers, boils, and rashes. [93] He is a "hot" deity, especially present in hot, dry weather.

When a person dies of smallpox the usual term for death is not used; it is said that "The King has taken him." In such cases there must not be any mourning but instead an expression of gratitude for what the king has done; otherwise his anger will increase. [94] Special funeral rites are carried out by the priests of Shopona/Shapata; presumably the body is disposed of in a way that will minimize the chance of spreading the disease. However, the priests have sometimes been suspected of intentionally causing the disease; because of this the cult of Shopona was outlawed in Nigeria in 1917. [95]

Shopona's shrine is often *outside* the town, either because of his fierceness or because as "King of the earth" he cannot be too close to a human king. [96] Whether this is due to his jealousy of human rule or the human king's jealousy of him may not be entirely clear.

Another semi-independent deity, with his own associates, is the one who manifests himself in thunder and lightening. Among the Yoruba he is generally known as Shango, who is said to have been an ancient king of Oyo and the grandson of Oduduwa. According to one account he was a violent and cruel king who was so hated by his subjects that he finally went out into the forest and hanged himself. However, when someone said that he had hanged himself, Shango became very angry and sent down lightning from heaven to destroy the one who had insulted him. According to another account, the official one told by his priests, Shango really ascended into heaven and was then falsely accused of hanging himself. In either case, it is important to refer to Shango as "The king who did not hang himself" in order to avoid his wrath.

It appears that Shango has taken over to some extent the characteristics and functions of a more ancient "thunder god," Jakuta, the "one who hurls stones." [97]   Some have suggested that Jukuta was an early "Supreme God"; [98] unlike Shango, he does not seem to have ever been a human being. He is an expression of the "wrath" of God against various forms of immorality, such as lying and adultery. This same concern has come to be associated with the figure of Shango. [99]

It is not surprising that thunder is seen by the Yoruba as a manifestation of the divine wrath as the area is noted for its violent storms: in fact, it is said to be "the second region in the world for lightning frequency." [100]   "The resounding booms, the sudden deafening sound of the thunder claps; the blinding, dazzling, criss-crossing, end to end flashes of the lightning" all contribute to the sense of divine presence in the storm. [101] The following song is reported as addressed to Shango:

> O Shango, thou art the master!
> Thou takest in thy hand the fiery stones,
> To punish the guilty!
> To satisfy thy anger!
> Everything they strike is destroyed.
> The fire eats up the forest,
> The trees are broken down,
> And all things living are slain. [102]

The priests of Shango have responsibility for the burial of anyone killed by lightning. They may also inspect property struck by lightning in order "to find the thunderbolt." [103]   Shango's symbol is the double axe; representations of Shango with this axe rising above his head are common among the Yoruba.

In the political sense it may be true to say that "Shango is the great national divinity of the Yoruba", [104]   although not in the ultimate religious sense. He is a rather "nationalistic," almost "imperialistic," god, who is given a great deal of attention. The Alafin (King) of Oyo, who claims to be a descendent of Shango, is traditionally crowned in his shrine.

Shango is associated with the goddess Oya, who is the River Niger, as well as the strong, damaging wind that brings no rain. She is fierce, wears a beard, and is supposed to be terrible to look at, although she can also be attractive. [105]

Among the Ewe the thunder god is So, Sogbo, or Hevieso, who is sometimes represented as "a ram painted red: lightning is coming from his mouth and two axes ending in curves like lightning stand by his side." [106]   Sogbo is said to be "an androgynous being, living in the sky, who produced a number of children." [107]   Among the Anlo, Yevhe is an alternative name for this god or for the group of gods associated with him. [108]

> Yevhe seems, on the whole, to be considered by the Anlo as a creation or a divine emanation, not localized, offering a number of aspects which themselves decompose into multiple facets of which each sanctuary is the artificial receptacle.... [109]

Although frequently called the "thunder-pantheon" these gods might better be thought of as forming an "atmosphere-pantheon" or a "water-pantheon":

> There is a constant emphasis on water, whether as in sea, the rivers, the lagoon or the rain. Although the cult distinguishes between what is above and what is below, the two spheres are united in the perpetual cycle of the waters. [110]

Sogbo, also considered by some as an alternative name for Mawu, resides in the sky, while her son Agbe is responsible for the sea. It is said that "Agbe of the Thunder-pantheon corresponds to Lisa in the sky group of gods." [111]   On the other hand, among the Anlo, So is male and has a wife, Avleketi. [112]

Among the Fon each of the three main pantheons, sky (Mawu-Lisa), earth-smallpox (Shapata), and water-thunder (Sogbo), has certain common characteristics. Each one, according to some accounts, is headed by deities who are either androgynous or a pair of male and female twins; in each there is a youngest god who is mischievous and unpredictable, corresponding to Legba. [113]   This parallelism suggests that the three "pantheons" may be alternative ways of organizing the divine realm, perhaps originally associated with different, though related, groups of people who later coalesced. The sky pantheon has come to have a certain precedence, with the heads of the other two pantheons sometimes thought of as children of Mawu and Lisa.

Both the "earth-gods" and the "thunder-gods" can be seen as personifications of "the supernatural forces that mete out justice to evil doers." [114]   The "wrath of God" is symbolized as smallpox and thunder, respectively. It might also be noted that among the Yoruba, Shopona and Shango, the pantheon heads, are both referred to as "king."

We have already observed the close connection between the "thunder-gods" and water, including the fact that Oya, the wife of Shango, is associated with the river Niger. A number of other deities are sometimes spoken of as "water-gods." It has already been mentioned that Nana-Buku, considered by some Ewe to be the original creator, is also said to be the "the oldest of the water-gods."[115] The Yoruba Yemoja, "mother of all rivers,"[116] is the daughter of Obatala and Oduduwa. She married her brother, god of the dry land, and had a son. The son desired his mother and finally succeeded in commiting incest with her. She fled from his continued pursuit but finally fell in exhaustion, burst open, and produced streams of water and fourteen deities, including Olokun, god of the sea; three river goddesses; the great deities, Shango, Shopona, and Ogun; and the gods or goddesses of agriculture, wealth, and hunting. [117]

A concept which is important to the Fon, but very difficult to fit into an orderly account, is that of Dan, the cosmic serpent who manifests himself in the rainbow. He may be referred to as a *vodun* and has his own cult but his characteristics are somewhat different from those of other *vodun*. He is a "semi-personal power...present at the side of the creator, acting at once as instrument and as conscious assistant in the work of ordering the world." [118] While it may be popularly held that Dan was created by Mawu, the more informed opinion appears to be that he is "coexistent with Mawu" and was created by whoever was the original creator. [119]

Dan is manifested in the rainbow under the name Ayido Hwedo. It is suggested that the cult associated with this deity was originally a separate system of belief which has been incorporated into the Fon system or that Ayido Hwedo pervades all the pantheons as "the personification of those deities who lived before man existed." [120] He may, however, have a special association with the "thunder pantheon."

Dan is both male and female, one being with a dual nature; [121] frequently he is represented as a snake swallowing his own tail. It is said that he "revolves around the earth and causes the movements of the heavenly bodies." [122] Thus he represents life-force, continuity, uninterrupted motion; he "incarnates the quality of dynamics in life...movement, flexibility, sinuousness, fortune." [123] Dan also stands for the distant, forgotten ancestors. [124] His qualities are not totally positive, however. One informant is quoted as saying, "We have no love for him. He gives and takes away." [125]

The Yoruba cosmic rainbow-serpent, Oshumare, does not seem to be as important as Dan; perhaps this is because at an early time he was practically merged into the figure of Olodumare, as mentioned above.

Many of the deities we have dealt with have clear connections with significant powers in the natural environment. According to Verger, "the worship given to the orisha is addressed, in principle, to the forces of nature." [126] From a somewhat different perspective, Ojo suggests that "the multiplicity of Yoruba gods is a logical consequence of their keen recognition of the numerous elements in their physical and biological environment" and the problems associated with them. [127] The *orisha* are not simply "nature-gods", however; they are also related to heroic human figures associated with Yoruba origins. In some, such as Shango, there is a fairly obvious merging of the natural and the human elements in the "Thunder-god" who was also a king. Kingship in general is closely associated with the divinities. A king may sometimes even be spoken of as an *orisha*, meaning that "he derives his authority to rule from the divinities and ultimately from the Deity, and that he is a visible, concrete symbol of the theocratic government of the world." [128] There are said to be 201 divinities in the palace of Oni (king) of Ife, the Oni himself being the 201st. [129] The king is thus the earthly representative of the divine order. The Fon rulers, unlike those of the Yoruba, did not claim a divine origin, but they did come to be closely associated with divine powers. [130]

We have observed only a part of the complexity of the concept of divinity among the Yoruba and the Ewe; there are many more deities and ambiguous relationships among deities. This complexity is accounted for in part by the fact that the *orisha* and *vodun* are "functional deities" having to do with superhuman powers that are in some sense available to man. The concept of the divine is closely associated with the natural environment and with human relationships. The *orisha* and *vodun* can be thought of as ways of conceiving and coming to terms with such practical concerns as weather, disease, fertility, kinship, and government.

It is also apparent that there has been much borrowing, both within these groups and from outside sources. New deities have come into existence while old ones have faded away, merged with others, or changed their name or sex. Certainly the religious concepts of these peoples are not static or rigid; there is a willingness, perhaps an eagerness, to use alternative approaches. Yet there seems to be a common underlying perspective in which the divine is understood as available to man.

It has been recognized by several observers that African thought is basically man-centered; this suggests that we will misunderstand the Yoruba and Fon concept of divinity unless we look at it from the human point of view, in terms of man's needs. Man not only has concrete needs in terms of his environment and society, however; he needs to affirm "ultimate reality," the "other" which is beyond both man and nature.

Perhaps we can be assisted here by Tillich's paradoxical phrase, "the God above God." [131]   God cannot be thought of apart from specific manifestations, functions, or symbols; neither can he be identified with these. Thus Mawu may be "the Ultimate" and also a particular female deity associated with the moon. There may, in fact, be "many Mawus"; this possibility recognizes that any particular "god" is transcended by "God." There is always a "Mawu beyond Mawu" who can never be grasped or tied down.

"God," according to Tillich, is "the name for that which concerns man ultimately." But there is a tension here: "on the one hand, it is impossible to be concerned about something which cannot be encountered concretely...on the other hand, ultimate concern must transcend every preliminary finite and concrete concern." Such a "conflict between the concreteness and the ultimacy of the religious concern is actual wherever God is experienced...." [132]   Certainly this is true of the Yoruba and the Fon. The "divinities," the *orisha* and the *vodun*, can be described in Tillich's terms as "images of human nature or subhuman powers raised to a superhuman realm."[133] In a sense they may be considered as "projections" of human needs. But a projection is always a projection on something which "is not itself a projection," [134]   in this case on the ultimate, the "God beyond God."

We began with the question of "polytheism" and "monotheism." Tillich points out that:

> The concreteness of man's ultimate concern drives him toward polytheistic structures; the reaction of the absolute element against these drives him toward monotheistic structures.... [135]

There can never be an absolute polytheism or an absolute monotheism, for concepts of the divine must include both concreteness and ultimacy. The Yoruba and Fon tend towards an emphasis on concreteness, on the divine as available to man. The *orisha* and *vodun* are basically functional, "divinity" in the service of man. That they are in a sense "man-made" or "projections" is recognized by their worshippers. Yet there is also recognition of an ultimate which transcends man, expressed in the "Supreme God," Olodumare or Mawu. Even here there are elements of concreteness but the tendency is to emphasize the ultimacy. When the focus is placed on this God, it is appropriate to speak in terms of "monotheism."

But this "monotheistic" concept of God tends to be unstable. On the one hand it may take on such a burden of concreteness that "God" ceases to be ultimate. Perhaps earlier "Supreme Gods" have thus been reduced to "divinities." There is then need for a God that is "more ultimate," "another Mawu." On the other hand, insofar as God is ultimate, he is unavailable for practical needs and thus tends to be irrelevant to life. This is the truth in the commonly expressed view that in Africa the Supreme God is "otiose."

Christianity and Islam provide new ways of dealing with this problem, putting much more emphasis on the "Supreme God." This may leave people with the sense that concrete problems are not adequately cared for; thus we find Christians and Muslims still relating to the traditional religion for certain purposes.

Whether the Yoruba and the Fon—and other peoples—are "monotheists" or "polytheists" depends largely on which aspects of their beliefs are emphasized. They have not escaped the tension between the ultimate and the concrete. They differ from others and among themselves in their specific attempts to deal with the tension; that which is most characteristic of them, in fact, may be their willingness to try a variety of alternative approaches. The tension itself, however, they share with other religious people.

NOTES

1. Okot p'Bitek, *African Religions in Western Scholarship.* Kampala: East African Literature Bureau, 1970. p. 102.
2. "Aja" is sometimes used as an alternative for "Ewe." The western Ewe, including the Anlo are sometimes called the "Ewe proper." (Manoukian, Madeline, *The Ewe-Speaking People of Togoland and the Gold Coast.* London: International African Institute, 1952, p. 11.) The Fon are an eastern Ewe group which was dominant in the Kingdom of Dahomey. The name is sometimes written Fo; there are other words in the language which can be found written either with or without a final "n." I have used the "n" except in quotations where it has been omitted. In any case, the sound is a nasal, somewhat resembling the French final "n."
3. William Bascom, *The Yoruba of Southwestern Nigeria.* New York: Holt, Rinehart and Winston, 1969. p. 1.
4. *Ibid.*, p. 2.
5. G. F. Afolabi Ojo, *Yoruba Culture: A Geographical Analysis.* London: University of Ife and University of London Press, 1966. p. 183.

6. Samuel Johnson, *The History of the Yoruba.* London: Routledge & Kegan Paul, 1921. p. 143.
7. William Bascom, *Ifa Divination.* Bloomington: Indiana University Press, 1969. p. 104.
8. J. Olumide Lucas, *The Religion of the Yorubas.* Lagos: C.M.S. Bookshop, 1948. p. 74.
9. Bascom, *Ifa Divination,* p. 325.
10. Idowu, *Olodumare,* p. 35.
11. *Ibid.,* p. 40.
12. *Ibid.,* p. 42.
13. *Ibid.,* p. 36.
14. Christian R. Gaba, "The Idea of a Supreme Being Among the Anlo People of Ghana," *Journal of Religion in Africa,* Leiden: E. J. Brill, 1969. Vol. II, fas. 1, 64-78 passim. Another author, however, states that among the Anlo "Mawu" has become a general term for a large number of secondary deities so that when the Supreme God is referred to one must say "Mawu Ga," "ga" meaning great or powerful. See Albert de Surgy, *Contribution à l'étude des cultes en pays Keta.* Paris: Group de Chercheurs Africanistes, n.d. p. 28.
15. Gaba, "The Idea of a Supreme Being," pp. 69, 75.
16. Geoffrey Parrinder, *West African Religion,* 2nd ed. London: The Epworth Press, 1961, p. 18.
17. Melville J. Herskovits, *Dahomey: An Ancient West African Kingdom.* New York: J. J. Augustin, 1938. Vol. II, p. 103.
18. *Ibid.,* p. 103.
19. Among the Anlo it is said that "Lisa" is "a rare word" for "chameleon" and is occasionally used as a "praise name" for the Supreme Being. See Gaba, "The Idea of a Supreme Being," p. 74f.
20. Herskovits, *Dahomey,* p. 129.
21. W. J. Argyle, *The Fon of Dahomey.* Oxford: The Clarendon Press, 1966. p. 177.
22. Herskovits, *Dahomey,* p. 131.
23. *Ibid.,* p. 290.
24. Parrinder, *West African Religion,* p. 29.
25. Pierre Verger, *Notes sur le culte des orisa et vodun.* Dakar: IFAN, 1957, p. 24.
26. Parrinder, *West African Religion,* p. 29.
27. Herskovits, *Dahomey,* p. 101.
28. Parrinder, *West African Religion,* p. 19.
29. Idowu, *Olodumare,* p. 71.
30. Bascom, *Ifa Divination,* p. 104.
31. Harry Sawyerr, *God: Ancestor or Creator.* London: Longman, 1970, p. 56.

32. Geoffrey Parrinder, "The Idea of God Among the Yoruba and Ewe Peoples" in Edwin W. Smith (ed.), *African Ideas of God.* London: Edinburgh House Press, 1950, p. 228.
33. Idowu, *Olodumare*, p. 19.
34. Bascom, *The Yoruba*, p. 80f.
35. Idowu, *Olodumare*, p. 71f.
36. Peter Morton-Williams, "An Outline of the Cosmology and Cult Organization of the Oyo Yoruba," *Africa*, London: Oxford University Press, vol. XXXIV, No. 3, July 1964. p. 243.
37. Lucas, *The Religion of the Yorubas*, p. 93.
38. A. B. Ellis, *The Yoruba-Speaking Peoples of the Slave Coast of West Africa*, orig. pub. 1894; reprinted Ooterhout, Netherlands: Anthropological Publications. 1966, p. 41.
39. Parrinder, *West African Religion*, p. 27.
40. Parrinder, "The Idea of God." p. 226.
41. P. Amaury Talbot, *The Peoples of Southern Nigeria.* London: Oxford University Press, 1926, vol. II, p. 31.
42. Idowu, *Olodumare*, p. 27.
43. Ellis, *The Yoruba-Speaking Peoples,* p. 41.
44. Idowu, *Olodumare*, p. 27.
45. Verger, *Notes*, p. 449; Lucas, *Religion of the Yorubas*, p. 96.
46. R. E. Dennett, *Nigerian Studies*, orig. pub. 1910, reprinted London: Frank Cass & Co., 1968. p. 18.
47. Morton-Williams, "An Outline," p. 245.
48. *Ibid.*, p. 248.
49. Idowu, *Olodumare*, p. 28.
50. Verger, *Notes,* p. 449; Morton-Williams, "An Outline," p. 250, ftnt. 2.
51. Parrinder, *West African Religion,* p. 28.
52. P. Mercier, "The Fon of Dahomey" in Daryll Forde (ed.), *African Worlds*, London: Oxford University Press, 1954, p. 216.
53. Sawyerr, *God*, p. 56.
54. Geoffrey Parrinder, "Monotheism and Pantheism in Africa," *Journal of Religion in Africa.* Leiden: E. J. Brill, 1970, vol. III, fas. 2. pp., 82, 86, 87.
55. Idowu, *Olodumare,* p. 60.
56. Bascom, *The Yoruba*, p. 82.
57. Idowu, *Olodumare*, p. 61f.
58. Parrinder, *West African Religion*, p. 35. It is reported that Yehwe and *hun* are used in other Ewe areas. (Robert Sastre, "'Les Vodu' dans la vie culturelle, sociale et politique du sud-Dahomey," *Cahiers des religions Africaines*, Kinshasa, vol. 4 July 1970, p. 178.
59. Talbot, *The Peoples of Southern Nigeria*, vol. 2, p. 29.
60. Herskovits, *Dahomey*, p. 169.

61. *Ibid.*, p. 172.
62. Idowu, *Olodumare*, p. 66.
63. Herskovits, *Dahomey*, p. 172.
64. Idowu, *Olodumare*, p. 63.
65. E. Maupoil, *La Géomancie a l'ancienne Côte des Esclaves*, Paris: Ins. d'Ethnologie, 1961. p. 57. Quoted in Sastre, "Les Vodu," p. 186.
66. Bascom, *The Yoruba*, p. 71.
67. *Ibid.*
68. Morton-Williams, "An Outline," p. 248.
69. Bascom, *Ifa Divination*, p. 109.
70. Idowu, *Olodumare*, p. 77.
71. Lucas, *Religion of the Yorubas*, pp. 74, 71.
72. Herskovits, *Dahomey*, p. 97.
73. Bascom, *Ifa Divination*, p. 12.
74. Surgy, *Contribution*, pp. 38, 47.
75. Bascom, *Ifa Divination*, p. 60.
76. *Ibid.*, p. 101.
77. *Ibid.*, p. 121.
78. Honorat Aguessey, "La divinité lêgba et la dynamique du panthéon Vodoun au Dan-home," *Cahiers des religions africaines*," Kinshasa, vol. 4, Jan., 1970, p. 93.
79. Verger, *Notes*, p. 110.
80. Herskovits, *Dahomey*, p. 229.
81. *Ibid.*, p. 222.
82. Idowu, *Olodumare*, p. 85.
83. Herskovits, *Dahomey*, p. 224.
84. *Ibid.*, p. 223.
85. Bascom, *Ifa Divination*, p. 60.
86. Herskovits, *Dahomey*, p. 106.
87. Idowu, *Olodumare*, p. 86.
88. Verger, *Notes*, p. 141.
89. Idowu, *Olodumare*, p. 89.
90. Herskovits, *Dahomey*, p. 105.
91. *Ibid.*, p. 139.
92. *Ibid.*, p. 129f.
93. Idowu, *Olodumare*, p. 96f.
94. *Ibid.*, p. 97.
95. Ojo, *Yoruba Culture*, p. 190.
96. Idowu, *Olodumare*, p. 101.
97. *Ibid.*, p. 93.
98. Dennett, *Nigerian Studies*, p. 97.
99. Idowu, *Olodumare*, p. 93.
100. Ojo, *Yoruba Culture*, p. 171.

101. *Ibid.*, p. 172.
102. Stephen S. Farrow, *Facts, Fancies and Fetich.* orig. pub. 1926, reprinted New York: Negro Universities Press, 1969, p. 50.
103. Idowu, *Olodumare*, p. 92.
104. Parrinder, "Ideas of God," p. 229.
105. Idowu, *Olodumare*, p. 91.
106. Parrinder, *West African Religion,* p. 31.
107. Argylle, *The Fon*, p. 181.
108. Surgy, *Contribution*, p. 103.
109. *Ibid.*, p. 106.
110. Argylle, *The Fon*, p. 182.
111. Herskovits, *Dahomey*, p. 151.
112. Surgy, *Contribution*, p. 103.
113. Argylle, *The Fon*, p. 199.
114. Herskovits, *Dahomey*, p. 166.
115. Verger, *Notes,* p. 24.
116. Geoffrey Parrinder, *Religion in an African City.* London: Oxford University Press, 1953; reprinted, New York: Negro Universities Press, 1972, p. 29.
117. Farrow, *Facts, Fancies and Fetich*, p. 46.
118. Mercier, "The Fon," p. 217.
119. *Ibid.*, p. 220.
120. Argylle, *The Fon*, p. 177. Herskovits, *Dahomey*, p. 291.
121. Verger, *Notes*, p. 233.
122. Argylle, *The Fon*, p. 178.
123. Herskovits, *Dahomey*, p. 255.
124. Verger, *Notes,* p. 233.
125. Herskovits, *Dahomey*, p. 255.
126. Verger, *Notes,* p. 29.
127. Ojo, *Yoruba Culture*, p. 184.
128. Idowu, *Olodumare*, p. 61.
129. *Ibid.*, p. 67.
130. Mercer, "The Fon," p. 231.
131. Paul Tillich, *The Courage to Be.* New Haven: Yale University Press, 1952, p. 182.
132. Paul Tillich, *Systematic Theology,* vol. I. Chicago: University of Chicago Press, 1951, p. 211.
133. *Ibid.*, p. 212.
134. *Ibid.*
135. *Ibid.*, p. 221.

1) A Kilumbu (prophet-diviner), Baluba. Photographed in Kamina, Zaïre, by N. Booth, 1972.

2) Egu Orumamu. Chief mask of the Igala. H-23", wood. Carved about 1941. Photographed in Ikeja, Nigeria by R. Sieber, 1958.

3) Do. Purification mask of the Aowin. Photographed in Dadiaso, Ghana, by R. Sieber in 1967.

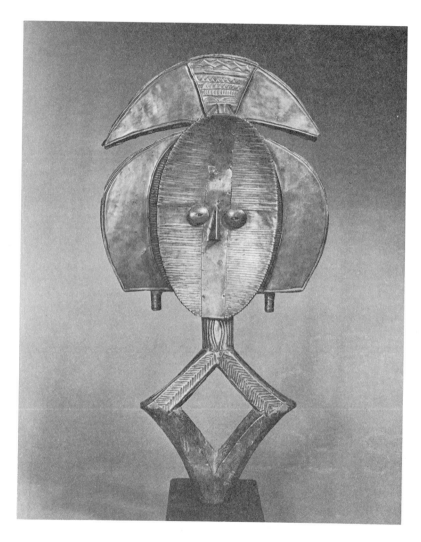

4) Reliquary figure, Bakota, Gabon. H-21½", wood and brass. Courtesy of the Indiana University Art Musuem.

5) Reliquary figure, Fang, Gabon. H-24", wood. Courtesy of the Indiana University Art Museum.

6) Bom Bosh, 96th King of the Bakuba, Zaïre. Courtesy of the Brooklyn Museum.

7) Funerary terra cotta of the royal high priest of Bruku. Photographed in Kwahu-Tofo, Ghana, by R. Sieber, 1964.

8) Possession by *preto velho*, Brazil. Photographed by F. Sturm, 1971.

9) His Excellency Mr. Diangienda, son of the prophet Kimbangu, leader of the Church of Jesus Christ on Earth through Simon Kimbangu. Photographed in Kinshasa, Zaïre, by N. Booth, 1972.

10) Mosque, Bagamoyo, Tanzania. Photographed by N. Booth, 1969.

8

African Religion in the Americas: The "Islands in Between"

Leonard Barrett

GENERAL STATEMENT

Paul Blanchard, in one of his inspired moments, referred to the Islands of Caribbean as "God's gems." This description is uniquely fitting because it captures all the changing hues of the thousands of islands that lie between the two large American continents. Here the deep blue waters of the Caribbean meet white beaches and beyond them evergreen mountains rise high into white clouds, giving one the feeling of being in paradise. To the early inhabitants, these islands were the "Land of Springs" (Jamaica) and the "Land of Mountains" (Haiti).

Although these islands still retain their gemlike beauty, their history, beginning with the discovery by the white man in the fifteenth century, is a history of sad intrigue, human suffering, lawlessness, and immoral profit.

At the center of the historical drama of the Caribbean Islands is the African, who at the hands of Portugal, Spain, England, France, Holland, and Denmark, was carried across the Atlantic as human cargo destined to work and die in the most inhuman conditions of slavery imaginable for well over 300 years. No precise figures are available on the number of Africans who came to the various islands, but a conservative estimate would put the overall figure at over three million.

The early slave trade dealt mainly in Africans from the highly developed kingdoms of the Kongo, the Gold Coast, Dahomey, and Nigeria. It was much later that slaves from the interior and from farther south on the continent began to appear. The early slaves were a cross-section of the African population; consequently, they brought with them a variety of culture forms which was soon to enrich the Caribbean. Contrary to the often repeated myth that the

Africans arrived in the New World devoid of culture, it is now generally accepted that the African slaves were the true culture-bearers, freedom-fighters, and artists of the Caribbean. [1]
The history of West Africa before the entrance of the Europeans provides ample proof that, in the fifteenth century, West Africa had already passed through several centuries of cultural development and had reached a stage comparable to the most developed countries of Europe of that period. Indeed, she had progressed far beyond most of her future oppressors. Richard Wright in his book *Uncle Tom's Children* [2] describes Africa's complex culture which included iron smelting as well as the use of brass, ivory, quartz, and granite. Her sculpture in clay, bronze, and wood is still a marvel to Western civilization. Her music, dance, and folklore have captivated the West and in many places displaced all other cultural forms of this *genre.* She mined silver and gold and utilized them with such artistry that in places like Brazil the Africans were sought after to work these metals. Africa's legal system was so highly developed before the white man came that in places like Ghana the indigenous legal system was never superceded by British laws. The medical knowledge of the traditional doctors of Africa has to be fully explored. But most important is the religious system of Africa. There is no other land in which religion has so permeated the life of its people. St. Paul's statement to the Corinthians, quoting one of the poets of Greece, suitably applies to the Africans, for in their religion they live and move and have their being (Acts 17 : 28). For all these reasons the slaves who came to the New World should not be thought of as culturally deficient but rather as people from a highly developed culture carrying with them a multitude of skills that enabled them to leave an indelible mark on the New World.
It was African traditional religion, the motivating force of all African peoples, that was first to find expression in their land of bondage. The slave master was able to claim the body of the slave, but the world view of the African was nurtured in his soul and this soul was impregnable. This very impregnability was to find expression later in the "spiritual": "Jordan river, chilly and cold, chills the body, *not the soul."* The Africans' resistance to spiritual indoctrination is so important a factor that it demands further attention.
All people see the world through the filter of their particular consciousness, a consciousness grounded in tradition. Because of this all people carry with them a heritage of patterned behavior. It is from this perspective that all men see their world and act in or react

to it in their day-to-day lives. To the Africans the world was both dynamic and pragmatic.

The African world view is dynamic. The universe is a vast system consisting of God, the Supreme Power who created it, spirits and powers who rule over every aspect of this creation, and, at the center, man. Everything below man, all lower biological life, was created for man, and the inanimate things serve him also. The whole system is alive because it is energized by a spiritual force emanating from the Supreme Being. This force is allotted hierarchically. Flowing from the Supreme Being, it descends to man and through man to all things lower on the scale of life. Man's very being depends upon maintaining a harmonious relationship between himself, his God, and the nature that surrounds him. As long as the vital force which emanates from God is operative throughout the system and in proper proportion, the universe is considered to be in ritual equilibrium. This dynamic concept of the universe is generally referred to by older writers as "animism," which is not a bad term if used properly—that is, if used to indicate the organic unity of the world wherein all the parts work together yet are dependent on one life source.

But the African is not a mystic. He does not conceive of the world as a place in which to *contemplate* life. He sees his world as an arena for activity. Life for him is a *pragmatic reality*. Gods and spirits are the sources of his being and all things below him are the agencies of his life. To live strongly, then, is his most engaging concern. His prayers are petitions for long life, health, and prosperity; the strengthening of his family, his clan, and his tribe is his great concern because through them he too lives.

This same preoccupation with life force is also manifested in rituals. The gods are the guardians of life, and if they fail they are reprimanded. The ancestors, whom we will discuss later, are the guardians of posterity, and men are heavily dependent on them in all aspects of life. They are appealed to for success in birth, marriage, business, and many other activities.

The pragmatism in the African world view finds its greatest expression in African folklore and proverbs. The main theme of the folktales is the will to survive in adverse conditions. Here we find the ever-recurring theme of the weak against the strong, and here the stress is on cunning, craftiness, and speed. These folktales gained new significance in the slavery of the New World. And that same pragmatic quality permeates the African proverbs, which contain all the reflective wisdom of the African peoples. In them we find instructions for the preservation of life, leading a moral life, living cautiously, loving God, and holding respect for the aged as well as the wisdom of gratitude and the beauty of temperance. We may conclude, then, that the world view of Africa is above all life affirming.

It is with this world view that our forefathers came to the New World. By them the foundation of African culture was laid for all their black descendants. This world view found expression in the spirituals, music, dance, and the general life style of later generations who came to be known as Afro-Americans.

We will now turn to the Africans in the Caribbean, their period of slavery and the way they adapted to these inhuman conditions, how they Africanized the New World through their traditional religion, and how through this world view they survived their oppression. It is the thesis of this paper that the survival of the Africans in the New World was only possible because of this zest for life which expressed itself mainly in religious terms, and that the Old World environment still remains the unconscious force behind all the combinations and permutations of Afro-Caribbean life to the present day.

CARIBBEAN SLAVERY: DOMINATION AND RESISTANCE

The presence of Africans in the New World became necessary because of the failure of European planters to make a profit using the labor of Indians and white indentured servants. By their very nature the Indians of the Caribbean were unsuitable for sedentary work such as was demanded on European-run plantations. Forced to do such work, they either moved away from the field into the rugged mountain interiors of the islands, or died of the diseases introduced among them by the Europeans. By the middle of the seventeenth century, most of the Indians of the Caribbean had been annihilated either by massacre or by disease. The system of indentured servants was then introduced, but this type of labor was too expensive and temporary to realize the kind of profit demanded by the planters. A new source of labor had to be sought and the lot fell to the Africans.

The leader in bringing slaves to the Caribbean was Spain. By the time the English and the French gained a foothold in the area, slavery was over 100 years old. At the beginning of the seventeenth century almost all the important islands of the Caribbean held vast plantations destined to become very lucrative pieces of real estate. Of course the price for all this was paid in the suffering of the many Africans who were brought to these regions as slaves.

The introduction of the Africans in the Caribbean was the beginning of a new day for plantation history. Not only were the Africans better workers on the plantations, but their physical condition was uniquely adapted to the brutal climate of the region. The Spaniards soon began to call them "the geniuses of the tropics" because of their ability to withstand the onslaught of malarial disease. This was due, incidentally, to the presence of the *sickle cell*, developed in Africa over many generations.

Such a change of fortune for the planters transformed their outlook. The dream of sudden riches with the chance of returning to Europe to live in splendor made planters into demons. The profit motive demanded that they drive the slaves to the last inch of their capacity even at the expense of the slaves' lives, as the Minutes of Evidence of 1790-1791 indicated: "The object of the overseers was to work the slaves out and trust for supplies from Africa." [3] Slavery had lost every vestige of humanity and the reign of terror had begun. The power of the master over the life of the slave was absolute. The slaves were chattels, no different from any other piece of real estate. As such they had no legal or moral rights but were completely subject to the whims of the master, who saw them as nothing more than beasts of burden. The vast number of African slaves in the Caribbean (they outnumbered the whites fifteen to one) meant that such complete minority domination had to be maintained by violence. It is essential to understand this aspect of Caribbean life in order to appreciate the reaction of the slaves in later days. Every form of violence known in history was used against the slaves and all passed under the guise of maintaining law and order. The aim actually was to amass the greatest amount of wealth in th ⁻hortest period of time, with the least amount of risk involved.

It is a well-known maxim in human history that all forms of domination encounter some resistance. This maxim has been well documented in the slave literature of the Caribbean. The myth that the slaves were satisfied and obedient children to white domination is a European fabrication, far from the facts of slave life. It did not take long for the slaves to assert themselves against European domination and inhumanity. In fact, all the evidence clearly shows that the Africans resisted oppression every inch of the way from Africa to the Caribbean and continued to do so right up to the abolition of slavery.

In the Caribbean, slavery resistance took two main forms. First, there was passive resistance and, second, violence. Resistance in the first sense took various forms, running all the way from a simple refusal to work to complaints of suffering from an undiagnosable disease, procrastination on the job, or doing the job so badly that it became unprofitable for the master. Another form of passive resistance was withdrawal from the plantation into the forest. Such "runaways" started the first communities of Maroons. Examples of Maroon communities can be found in Jamaica up to the present day. Of course, the extreme form of passive resistance was suicide, and, even though extreme, many of the slaves poisoned themselves and their children with potions known and readily available to them.

The second form of resistance was violence, and this occurred both on the individual and the collective level. Despite the fact that the laws forbade the slaves to even imagine the death of the master, many slaves did much more than just imagine it. Poison was often used for this too. The flora of the Caribbean provided the Africans with an abundance of herbs which were well known to them from Africa. They knew the properties of each herb first hand, and with their knowledge the unsuspecting master was easy prey. On this subject we have the testimony of Sir Spencer St. John, the British Ambassador to Haiti in the nineteenth century. His attitudes to the black race were certainly not praiseworthy, but this makes his observation even more to the point here. Of the Africans' herbal knowledge, he observed,

> And if it be doubted, that the individuals, without even common sense, can understand so thoroughly the properties of herbs and their combinations, so as to be able to apply them to the injury of their fellow-creatures, I can say that tradition is a great book, and that they receive these instructions as a sacred deposit from one generation to another, with further advantage that in the hills and mountains of this island grow in abundance similar herbs to those which in Africa they employ in their incantations. [4]

Sir Spencer went on to relate that he knew of many victims who retired to their beds in sound mind to awaken as idiots and remain in that state despite the aid of science.

The most significant form of resistance was collective violence. Three aspects of this type of violence stand out. First, rebellion was continuous. We have already obseved that the slaves actively fought their situation from Africa to the shores of the Caribbean. After reaching the Caribbean, not one year passed between the sixteenth and the nineteenth centuries without a rebellion or the threat of one. Second, these rebellions were not simply riots, but in many cases large-scale uprisings that involved thousands of slaves. The end result was usually the massacre of hundreds of slaves and planters. Examples of such crises are the Maroon war of 1735-1740, the 1760 Rebellion, and the Sam Sharpe Rebellion of 1831, all of which took place in Jamaica alone. When we turn to Haiti, the history of rebellion is even more full. The third point of special interest about those rebellions lies in the fact that their effect on the plantation system was so destructive that the whole system soon became nonproductive. It is now commonly believed by Caribbean scholars that the primary factor in the abolition of slavery was not the "humanitarian movement," but the debilitating effect of slave rebellions. The classical example of violent resistance comes from Haiti, where under the leadership of the slaves Boukman, Toussaint, Dessalines, and Christophe, the Haitian slaves proved decisively that they not only loved freedom but were prepared to die for it. It was here that the Africans proved their mettle against the elite soldiers of Napoleon and finally wrested the island from its slave-masters. Very few Europeans have been bold enough to write on the heroism of Caribbean slaves. That entire story is yet to be unfolded.

AFRICANIZING THE CARIBBEAN

Like the Hebrews in exile, the early Africans found the Caribbean a "strange land." Here they were separated from family, clan, and tribe but most of all from Guinea—a word which in Haiti became synonymous with Africa—and so from the protection of the Gods and the ancestors. To the Africans this was a psychic shock that could only be handled when explained as the result of witchcraft. Their collective *force-vitale* had been totally overcome by the sorcery of the white man. Sorcery or not, the entire word view of the Africans was shattered and there was, at first, no *hope*, no means in sight through which they could reassemble the pieces of their lives. Anthony F. C. Wallace's concept of the "cultural mazeway" provides a helpful way of viewing the African stituation in the Caribbean. According to Wallace, [5] every person in a society maintains a mental image of that society and its culture. His conception of the total social complex, involving his own person and the objects of his environment, both human and nonhuman, provides a mazeway of experience through which he moves; and this movement must be free and unimpeded in order for him to function in that society. Once this mazeway is mastered by the individual, he functions unconsciously as a member of that society. However, should his mazeway become blocked, he must seek alternative paths through life, paths that make it possible for him to continue to function in his culture. Otherwise extreme stress will develop. If the mazeway becomes blocked for a number of persons, sooner or later the entire society will suffer from the stress. Cultural distortion will result and, if satisfying alternatives cannot be found, the death of the culture may be the end result. Africans in bondage to the slaver suffered what we will call mazeway disintegration. Slavery threatened the total African personality. The slave was forbidden his language, his religion, his traditional family life, and in the end his humanity. It is therefore something of a miracle that anything of African religion survived to provide occasion for a paper of the sort I am writing.

The survival of Africa in the Caribbean must be attributed to the miraculous appearance of those African religious specialists whom the European writers and the slave masters called "witch doctor." Writing of the slaves in Jamaica, Herbert DeLisser observed:

> Both witches and wizards, priests and priestesses were brought to Jamaica in the days of slave trade, and the slaves recognized the distinction between the former and the latter. Even the masters saw that the two classes were not identical and so they called the latter myal and myal women; i.e., the people who cured those whom the obeah men had injured.[6]

In the above quotation DeLisser informs us that both the legitimate priests and priestessess of African traditional relgion and the sorcerers (the workers of witchcraft) came to the Caribbean in the days of slavery. He further explains that the function of the legitimate specialists was that of curing those whom the *obeah* men (sorcerers) had injured. Here we have "tangled" evidence that the Africanization of the New World had begun. But even more enlightening is the appearance of the phrase "*obeah* men," which demands some further discussion in relation to the slave society as a whole.

It now appears quite clear from the records that rather early in the period of Caribbean slavery there occurred a fusion of the various African tribes and the new groups centered around the religious specialists. It also appears that much of the religious practice during slavery was directed against the supposed sorcery of the white man. It was expedient and prudent for the slave to seek out that tribe whose witchcraft powers were considered most potent. To this base particularly successful and potent rites from other tribes were added. Thus, in Jamaica and in fact in all the British colonies, the word *obeah* (a select form of African witchcraft) became associated with the whole community. It is also clear that the tribe with the most potent witchcraft became the dominant leaders in the slave community.

The word *obeah* is a shortened form of the Ashanti word *obaye*, and he who practiced *obaye* is called an *obayifo*. [7] The word can be broken down as follows: *oba*, meaning "a child," *yi*, meaning "to take," and the suffix *fo*, meaning "he who." The full meaning of the word *obayifo* is then read as "he who takes a child away." This suggests the rite that an initiated sorcerer must perform to become a full-fledged practitioner. The appearance of the word also authenticates the dominance of the Ashanti people in Jamaica and in many other Caribbean islands, and further supports the thesis that the greatest freedom fighters in the British Colonies were none other than the Ashantis.

A similar sort of situation is found in Haiti. Here again we see the survival technique of many tribes fusing around shared ground of traditional religion. It has been recently suggested that at least 115 tribal groups were represented on the island of Haiti, [8] but the name of the religion is *vodun*, a word derived from Dahomey. The leader is a *houngan*, a word from the Congo; the leader of the Haitian rebellion was none other than the Houngan Boukman. And the witchcraft is called *ouanga*, also a Congo word; to this day, the strongest witchcraft in Haiti is still considered that of the Congo variety.

One of the foremost authorities on Haiti, when writing about the Haitian revolution, said of their leaders:

> The belief in their invulnerability was not at all the result of calculation, but was a true state of mind, a sort of autosuggestion which explains very well the chronic heroism of certain leaders of the revolution in Saint Dominque and the war of Independence of 1802-3. [9]

This "invulnerability" was the work of the *houngan* who empowered the warriors with magical medicine, medicine to make them invulnerable to bullets.

Madiou, the first Haitian historian, spoke of *vodun* as "a savage survival" and called it sorcery. [10] Both Dorsanvil and Madiou were mulattoes and had no love for the masses, but their assessments are still relevant to our thesis. We must conclude, then, that the legitimate priests and priestesses and the illegitimate sorcerers who came to the Caribbean later joined forces and pooled their psychic and spiritual powers to free their people from the inhumanity of slavery. It was they who comforted the sorrowing ones; it was they who buried their dead and "sent them off to Guinea"; it was they who led the dance. The dance was the only "recreation" on the plantations, but these African religious men knew the difference between the sacred dance and recreation. It was they who mixed the bullet-liquefying potion for the heroes in the slave rebellions and sealed the mouths of the slaves with oaths. They also prescribed the poison against their oppressors, and set the *obeah* for both their oppressors and those of their own race who betrayed their secret plottings. This was indeed ritual regression, but the legitimate priests saw this as a necessary evil under a situation of total mazeway distortion. What the African priests and sorcerers were doing here was adapting their inherited pragmatism to a new world situation.

Witchcraft, however, is inimical to African society. It is an anti-equilibrium device and, if continued, it could have destroyed society. It has been observed that in Africa, whenever the power of witchcraft becomes pervasive, a witchcraft-cleansing cult emerges to rid society of its menace. Members of such a cult must have been what DeLisser referred to as "*myalmen*" and "*myal women.*" This cult seems to have emerged soon after the 1760 rebellion in which witchcraft was let loose in an unprecedented way. Edward Long, a historian and a member of the planter class, whose book was published in 1774 wrote,

> Not long since [the war of 1760], some of these execrable wretches in Jamaica introduced what they called the Myal-dance, and established a kind of society, into which they invited all they could. The lure hung out was, that every Negro initiated into Myal society, would be invulnerable by [sic] the white man.[11]

Here, Long missed the true meaning of the Myal society. In truth and in fact, what was happening here was nothing less than the emergence of the traditional religion of Africa. For the first time Africans began to practice their rites in public. The legitimate priests were now beginning to assert themselves and to organize what was later to become the Cumina cult.

The word "Cumina" is a combination of two Ashanti words: *Akom*, "to be possessed," and *ana* "an ancestor." Cumina, then, was an ancestral-remembrance cult, and myalism came to be identified with the possession-inducing dance that formed part of it. J. H. Buchner, a Moravian missionary writing in 1854, left us a description of the Myal society which seems quite accurate:

> As soon as darkness of evening set in, they assembled in crowds in open pastures, most frequently under large cotton trees, which they worshipped, and counted holy; after sacrificing some fowls, the leader began extempore song, in a wild strain, which was answered in chorus; the dance followed, grew wilder and wilder, until they were in a state of excitement bordering on madness. Some would perform incredible revolutions while in this state,

until, nearly exhausted, they fell senseless to the ground, when every word they uttered was received as a divine revelation. At other times, Obeah was discovered, or a "shadow" was caught; a little coffin being prepared in which it was to be enclosed and buried.[12]

This is by far the most objective description of myalism that the present author has discovered; in fact, it fits perfectly with many of my own observations.

It is necessary to highlight a few of the points quoted above; the pastoral setting under a cotton tree is just the kind of setting popular among the slaves at this period, and the cotton tree is holy to the Africans. This holds to some extent today although the tree has lost its "sacred" quality for modern Jamaicans and this has been replaced by the common fear of ghosts harbored in the trees. Animals are still sacrificed in the Cumina cult in Jamaica and in *vodun* in Haiti. The extemporaneous song with choral response that is found in the Caribbean is a reflection of the typical statement-response singing of Africa which has come down to us in the Negro spirituals. Also the dance which was known as *myal*, or spirit possession, is beautifully described by Buchner. The revelatory quality of words of those under possession is still felt in Jamaican folk religion. Myalism, the frenzied dance of Cumina, broke out periodically. It appeared at Emancipation in 1834, and again in 1860 during what is known as the Great Revival, when it disrupted the missionary efforts and established what is now known as Pukkumina, a syncretic form of Cumina and Christianity.

The Africanization of the Caribbean was accomplished as the result of many factors. First, the numerical strength of the slaves over the masters made communication between the slaves easier. A strong slave community was developed around their religious leaders and their religious festivals. The vast numbers of the slaves gave them a feeling of majority, over against the white minority who secluded themselves from the slaves. This lack of interaction between slaves and masters inhibited the acculturation process in the Caribbean; such blending actually occurred much faster in the United States.

A second factor crucial to the Africanization was the attitude of the Christian Church to the slaves. The Church in the British slave colonies denied the Africans religious instructions for well over 200 years. Not only did they deny them Christian teachings, they also sought, through every legal means, to rid the Africans of their traditional religion. Their laws against dancing, drumming, and slave gatherings are enshrined in the slave records. In the Latin slave system some attempts were made to Christianize the Africans—at least they received technical baptism and were to be present for the sacraments—but this was done without enthusiasm and, at the expense of the planters, because the priests demanded payment for their services. An example of the kind of Christianity for form's sake the slaves received in the Latin system is recorded for us in Ralph Korngold's book *Citizen Toussaint*:

> A hundred or so negroes freshly arrived from Africa would be herded into a church. Whips cracked and they were ordered to kneel. A priest and his acolytes appeared before the altar and Mass was said. Then the Priest followed by the acolytes carrying a basin of holy water, walked slowly down the aisle and with vigorous swings of the Aspergillam scattered the water over the heads of the crowd, chanting in Latin. The whips cracked again, the slaves rose from their knees and emerged into the sunlight, converts to Christianity. [13]

This was the extent of the Africans' introduction to the religion of "civilization." In this way *vodun* and Christianity were united, with Christianity remaining no more than a gloss over the essentially African slave culture. It has often been said that *vodun* is an African religion with a veneer of Catholicism, and there can be no denial of this because even those elements of Catholicism which the slaves did absorb were completely Africanized.

AFRICAN RELIGION IN THE CARIBBEAN

In our previous discussion we saw that the Africans who entered the Caribbean were thrown into a state of "mazeway disorganization." We also saw that as a result of this situation they were forced to reorganize themselves and unite around their traditional religious leaders who held the group together against the common enemy. We suggested also that they conceived this disorganized condition as the work of the white man's witchcraft and that both sorcerers and so-called medicine men of Africa collaborated to meet the threat of slavery. It was in this way that the Africans began to adapt to their New World environment by invoking the gods of Africa to help them in their fight for survival. The gods on whom they called were mainly the gods of war—Shango, Ogun, and others like them. We have further suggested that the Africans were working within their philosophy of pragmatic realism in utilizing witchcraft to maintain their *force-vitale* against an enemy who threatened their existence. In this distinct though peripheral element of their culture, they found the resource to stand up against the slavers and resist both overtly and covertly the devastation of the life of an African in slavery in the Caribbean.

Our discussion now turns to a short review of some of the African religions transported to the Caribbean. I want to show their historical development and then attempt a comparative summary of those ritual elements common to all of them. First, we turn to Jamaica where we will discuss Cumina-Pukkumina; second to Haiti and *vodun*; and third to Trinidad and Shango. These three examples will serve as case studies for all the islands. The Shango cult in Trinidad and that in Cuba are similar in most ritual elements. Haitian *vodun* and that found in Martinique and Guadaloupe are also similar in ritual and belief. It is not the purpose of this paper to indulge in details but rather to give an overview of African religious retention in the Caribbean.

Cumina-Pukkumina in Jamaica

In the previous discussion we mentioned that the word "Cumina" is a corruption of the Akan words *akom-ana,* meaning "to be possessed by an ancestor." No record of this word was discovered in Jamaican literature until 1938, when Zora Hurston's book *Voodoo Gods* appeared. Hurston was told by informants that the word Cumina meant "the power" and that it was associated with the dead. [14] In the 1950s Donald Hogg and Joseph G. Moore discovered that the cult was still alive in the eastern part of Jamaica. We may safely assume that Cumina as a family ritual was the first African religious expression among the large body of Akan peoples in Jamaica. As such the meetings were most likely held among the Maroons who inhabited the hills of Jamaica. Later they were taken up by the plantation slaves in the vicinity of Maroon settlements. Soon after the 1760 Rebellion what we know today as Cumina emerged as a Myal society taking its name from the possession dance which accompanied it. According to Moore, membership in Cumina was inherited, but in some circumstances the rule was altered and people of other tribes could become members provided they were acceptable to the ancestral community. Membership was determined matrilineally; the spirits who possess the members are the spirits of their mothers' clan. The matrilineal association is further proof of the Akan origin of the cult.

Cumina ceremonies generally take place at night and are performed for various purposes: memorializing the dead, placating the ancestors in the name of someone seriously ill, and celebrating the birth of a child. A Cumina festival may take place during the Christian holidays, especially at Christmas, and it is the opinion of this writer that the popular festival called "Jonkunu" (and known by various other spellings) originated from a Cumina adaptation of the yam festival common to most West African peoples. [15]

The drum is very important in Cumina. Two drums are necessary but as many as six drums can be used along with the African trumpet, the triangle, and other instruments for beating out rhythm. Cumina festivals are accompanied by the sacrifice of fowls or goats. The blood is mixed with rum, which is a necessity in Cumina, and the meat is cooked and eaten during the festival. The dance leading to possession is the peak of the festival. The woman, "queen," leads the dance and is generally someone who is known to be experienced in spirit possession. Anyone is likely to be possessed, but possession is more frequent in the family which summoned the festival.

We may conclude then that Cumina is the matrix in which many Africanisms were nurtured in Jamaica. In the beginning it was a secret society that supplied the impetus and framework for the psychic struggle against slavery. About the middle of the eighteenth century it emerged as the Myal society; it grew until the middle of the nineteenth century, when it merged with Afro-Christian cultism and became known as Pukkumina.

Pukkumina, the present form of African traditional religion in Jamaica, emerged in 1860 during what is known as the Great Revival. [16] In that year a great wave of evangelical emotion swept the island of Jamaica. Many historians attribute this religious outburst to the efforts of Christian missionaries, especially the Moravians, the American Baptists (under the leadership of the slave George Liele), the Methodists, and others, who had begun to preach Christianity to the slaves. But this seems unlikely, since the efforts of the missionaries which covered the period from 1734 to 1860 were mostly fruitless and the "awakening" in 1860 broke out without much warning. To the missionaries, this was the work of God made manifest, the result of their efforts, and for a while the churches began to prosper under the great influx of new converts. But the Christians soon realized that the new converts did not follow their "rules" of spiritual behavior. The result was that what was once construed as Christian movement soon showed its true nature; within a short time the Christian churches were left empty and the Pukkumina cult was born.

This Africanizing process is not surprising when one considers the nature of missionary religion at this period. First of all, the churches were under the leadership of European missionaries who had no real sensitivity to the experience of the slaves. One of the ministers who was a contemporary of the famous Revival called the religious enthusiasm of the new converts "wild extravagance and almost blasphemous fanaticism"; [17] and another (obviously considering an isolated incident) was quite pleased that after the first wave of "intense excitement" the evening service was conducted "with perfect quietness and decorum." [18] What the missionaries wanted was nothing short of de-Africanizing the Blacks, making them into carbon copies of themselves. All of the emotional expressions that are part and parcel of the African soul were to be held down. At first, the Africans saw the church as their only hope and, in fact, some of the churchmen did fight for emancipation. But their introduction to missionary Christianity appeared to them to be another form of slavery; slavery of the mind and soul.

Pukkumina centered around native charismatic leaders, most of whom had some knowledge of the Christian Bible, although they were more influenced by myalism. With their knowledge of the Bible, their charismatic fervor, and their African heritage, they attracted members recently converted and organized their own religious cult. In a short while numerous groups known as "bands" or "societies" were formed all over the island. The heads of bands were called "papa," or "mother" if women. They were also called shepherds and shepherdesses. The band was organized hierarchically. At the head was the charismatic leader, who was all powerful. Below him were sub-shepherds and sub-shepherdesses with varying functions. It is not uncommon today to find such names as "wheeling shepherd," who leads the dance; "warrior shepherd," whose work it is to see that order is kept in the meetings, "spying shepherd," whose work is to see the different kinds of spirits functioning in the meeting and to dispatch unwelcome spirits, and so on.

Central to a Pukkumina cult is the drum-accompanied dance. Unlike Cumina drums, which are played by drummers sitting astride them on the ground, the Pukkumina drums are played slung on the arm of a standing drummer. The dance generally takes place in the clearing of the cult compound called a "yard." Members form a circle around a flagpole which designates the center of power called the holy seal. The movement around the pole is counterclockwise and performed with the aid of the drums; the movement gradually gains momentum until possession takes place. Those possessed may prophesy or speak in a spiritual language or a form of glosso-lalia.

One of the major functions of Pukkumina is curing, and to this end there is generally a balmyard attached to the compound. Here herbal remedies are dispensed for various kinds of psychosomatic illnesses. The major function of balming consists in bathing the patient in a herbal concoction, the recipe for which is claimed to have been revealed to the healer by the spirits. Some medicine is given to the patient in liquid form or as raw herbs to be boiled and taken internally. No one is able to measure the effectiveness of these cures, but, judging from the popularity of the balmists, one can only conclude that these healers are perceived by their patients to be effective. Their usefulness in the health service of Jamaica can be assessed only when it is realized that a trained physician is inaccessible in many parts of the island.

The Pukkumina cult claims almost fifteen per cent of the Jamaican population and is comparable only to *vodun* in Haiti, where ninety-seven per cent of the people claim to be believers. There are other names for those Afro-Caribbean religions in Jamaica; they are sometimes called Revival and Revival Zion, but the author has seen fit to use Pukkumina for all of them since this word evokes the African roots of the religion more directly.

Haitian Vodun

The word Voodoo (*vodun*) never fails to spark excitement in the minds of people the world over. The word brings to mind all kinds of dark superstitions, blood sacrifice, and sexual orgies. So many books have been written around these themes by the seekers after instant literary popularity that any research that does not follow this genre is suspect. Despite this obvious distortion of the folk religion of Haiti, however, a serious study of *vodun* will prove that it is the religion of the greatest relevance to the mass of Haitian people. Alfred Metraux calls *vodun* a conglomeration of beliefs and rites of African origin that, having been mixed with Catholic practices, functions for the Haitian peasants to provide a remedy for ills, satisfaction for needs; and hope for survival. *Vodun* has had a noble history in Haiti. It is now commonly believed that it was a *vodun* priest who started the war of liberation which finally wrested freedom from France. The three leaders of Haiti in the early days of the Black republic, Toussaint, Dessalines, and Christophe, were well acguainted with powers of *vodun*, and the recently deceased

President Francois Duvalier was a student of *vodun* history.

James G. Leyburn suggested four stages of development in the history of *vodun*. [19] First was the period of gestation in the new environment which covers the years between 1730 and 1790. This was a period of a steady increase in the importation of slaves, the largest number of these coming from Dahomey. Second, Leyburn notes the period between 1790 and 1800, when the numerous African tribes fused under the banner of *vodun* and invoked the Gods of Africa in their quest for freedom. The third period, between 1800 and 1815, saw the suppression of *vodun* by the Black rulers who greatly feared its power, although Christophe is said to have had some faith in it. The last period falls between 1815 and 1850, when, despite its suppression, *vodun* quietly diffused among the people and settled into its present form.

The word "*vodun*" is derived from Ewe and refers to the lesser deities of the Dahomean pantheon. The word, however, is misleading because the Haitian religion is not ruled over by Dahomean spirits alone. *Vodun* in Haiti stands for the gods and spirits of all the major peoples of Africa who make up the Haitian nation. At a *vodun* service one will hear the voice of the priest calling to Atibon Legba, Dambella, and Agwe, who are gods of Dahomey, and in the same breath he will call for Shango or Ogun, gods of Nigeria, followed by the gods of the Congo. *Vodun* then is a divine confederation honed on African pragmaticism. It is another example of the flexibility that enabled the Africans to survive.

There are two main *vodun* pantheons, Rada and Petro. The Rada divinities consist of Legba, Damballa, Aizan, Agwe, and Erzulie and include the Nigerian Shango and Ogun, to name only a few. The Petro divinities are Bosu Trois Cornes, Simbi d'leau, Guede, Mait Gran Bois, Mait Calfour, and a host of others. The folklore of the Haitians says that the Rada gods are benevolent, while the Petro ones are malevolent. It was the Petro variety of *vodun* that inspired the revolution, and this is how they acquired their malevolent nature. It is clear, therefore, that this type of malevolence must not be interpreted as evil but rather as warlike. The Western concept of good and evil does not fit in African thought.

The most important gods of *vodun* are Legba, Guede, and Damballa. Legba is the first to be invoked in a ceremony. Like his counterpart in the Dahomean pantheon he is the go-between carrying man's messages to the gods and vice versa. He is the guardian of gates and barriers, the protector of doors and crossroads. No gods will enter nor possess a devotee unless Legba is invoked. Damballa

Wedo is the god of supreme *mystère*, whose symbol is the serpent. Thus, the sign of the serpent is the coat-of-arms for the *vodun*. So strong is his influence in Haiti that the sign of the serpent can even be seen in the architecture of the land. The graceful Yanvalo dance which depicts the flowing movement of the serpent Damballa is performed in the *vodun* service. In fact, Haiti could easily be called the land of Damballa. The word is the combination of the names of two African provinces, Adangwe and Allada.

In Haitian *vodun* all the gods are called *loas*, or "powers." It is said that there are over 300 of them, most of whom have abstract stylistic representations called *vever*. The *vevers* are intricate drawings executed on the floor of the *vodun* temple just before the entrance into the service of the specific *loa* in whose honor the service is being held. The *vevers* have inspired a marvelous art form in Haiti and are greatly sought after by tourists. A systematic study of these caballistic signs is long overdue.

At the center of *vodun* is a priest called the *houngan*, who is both feared and respected. His female counterpart is called a *mambo* and has the same authority as the *houngan*. These leaders are people of knowledge, the carriers of the tradition of the people. They know the names, attributes, and special tastes of the gods and must be able to conduct the rites appropriate for the various ceremonies each desires. Only after long and tedious training are they given the *asson*, or rattle, which is the symbol of priesthood. A good *vodun* leader is priest, healer, adviser, and teacher. He is respected not only by his followers but by the community at large.   Below the *houngan* is the *hunsi*, an assistant in the service. Below the *hunsi* is the *hungenikon* or the leader of songs, who plays a very exciting role in the service. Next come the drummers, three of whom must be present for a *vodun* ceremony. Last, but not least, the *vodunsis* or the members, who may have formal or loose connections with the cult. The highest group of *vodunsis* are the *canzos*, those who have undergone initiation. All the different groups together form a *société* which conducts ceremonies in a *houmfort* or temple.

Having given only a bare outline of the *vodun* religion, it might be helpful to conclude this section with an eye-witness report of the author's visit to a ceremony. In this way the reader may be able to better appreciate the complexity of the Haitian religion.

In the fall of 1971, while doing research in Haiti, I tried in vain to see an authentic *vodun* ceremony; each of the visits planned was of the tourist variety. Then unexpectedly, on the evening of November 21, I was invited by a leading Haitian scholar to see a ceremony which turned out to be the real thing. We arrived at the southern outskirts of the city of Port-au-Prince at 7 P.M. and were led to a *houmfort* behind a large middle-class dwelling. The *houmfort* was a substantial extension of the house itself, with a floor space about forty feet wide and sixty feet long. At the end of the hall facing north was a gallery with rows of seats made of concrete slabs; access to this gallery was through a door close by. We entered the *houmfort* by the door facing east which led to several rows of chairs provided for important guests. At the entrance of the eastern door was a small refreshment bar where one could buy beer and soda. Immediately behind the bar was a staircase leading up one flight to a room in which food (roasted mutton and rice) was served to visitors at a small price. In front of the room was a balcony on which stood a large woman about fifty-six years old—graceful and commanding. She was the *mambo*. From this balcony she directed the early part of the ceremony until her entrance was necessary. At the center of the *houmfort* was a large concrete column known as the *poteau-mitan* around which the figure of two life-size snakes were entwined heads down and meeting at the middle of the column. The three drummers were already seated to the right side of the *houmfort* as we entered and, for a while, they adjusted their drums in the same way the players of an orchestra would tune their instruments before a concert.

About thirty minutes after our entrance a large audience was gathered and an air of expectancy was over us. At 7:30 P.M., a shrill whistle sounded, and a man appeared at the northern entrance with a white cock in his hand. He moved in a crouching dance across the floor and disappeared with the rooster into one of the two rooms behind the audience. Immediately following his departure the singers marched in step to the drumbeats and took their places to the south of the *houmfort*. The *hungenikon* or song leader chanted a tune answered by the chorus and the ceremony was under way. As the singing took on volume and the chorus began to move to the rhythm of the drums, the rooster-man and the woman appeared with their ritual items and placed them at *poteau-mitan*. First the *asson*, the symbol of the *mambo's* power, was brought in, then a bottle of liquor, some candles of various colors, an enamel basin of water, a whip, and finally two candles which were placed in an open space under the *poteau-mitan*.

The ritual items now in place, the assistant priest (the *hunsi*) took the whip in his right hand and the bottle of liquor in his left, faced the north entrance and cracked the whip nine times. This was also done at the east entrance and then in front of the *poteau-mitan*. He next poured libations at the base of the three drums. Filling his mouth with the liquor he sprayed it at the two entrances, then to the four cardinal points after which he was joined by the woman and they performed a ritual salutation crossing both hands in front of their faces in the form of a cross. First they saluted the drums and the *poteau-mitan*. During this time the singers chanted the well-known song:

> Papa Legba ouvri barrie pour moin ago-e
> Papa Legba ouvri chemin pour li ago-e, etc.

> Papa Legba, open the barrier for me, pay heed,
> Papa Legba, open the road for him, pay heed, etc.

The preliminaries now ended, the chorus phased in the dancing. This chorus was largely composed of women, most of them below thirty-five years of age. Although some were as old as sixty-five or more, their movements were as nimble as those of teenagers.

After a brief lull in the singing, during which the chorus continually greeted each other without breaking the momentum of the ceremony, the leader "pitched" into a new song with a faster tempo. All of us in the audience felt that a new dimension of the service had now begun. The woman who performed in the first part of the ceremony reappeared with farina flour in her left hand, saluted the *poteau-mitan* as a Catholic priest would do before the altar, proceeded to within three feet of the drums, and began to draw one of the intricate *vever* on the floor. This ceremony was held in honor of Guede, the god of death and sexual potency, this being the season of All Souls according to the Catholic calendar. A drawing of the *vever* in my notebook was later checked out against the Guede *vever* in Maya Deren's book, and parts of it were identical; there were, however, several other sections to this elaborate drawing that did not match and would need further explanation. The drawing of the *vever* marked the halfway point of the ceremony. The *vever* suggested that Guede had now approved the service and his entrance was assured. From here on the spirit would take over under the leadership of the *mambo*.

Soon after the execution of the *vever*, the *mambo* appeared, escorted by two assistants who led the earlier parts of the ceremony. The atmosphere of the ceremony again changed dramatically; there was a heightened tension all over the *houmfort* because it is only under the leadership of the *mambo* that the *loa* appears. She took hold of the *asson*, saluted the drums, the *poteau-mitan* and then greeted other *vodun* priests and priestesses who were present. (It was later explained to the author that this particular ceremony was a united one.) Each visiting leader was given the *asson* and each in turn performed a short ritual of salutation similar to that of the presiding *mambo*. At the end of each salutation by the visiting leaders, a peculiar handshake took place between the visitor and the *mambo*. The handshake started with the left hand, then the right—each with a sudden release and flipping of the fingers, as if each had experienced an electric shock from the other.

The drum tempo and the singing was now at fever pitch. The audience was sitting on the edge of their seats and those standing were on tiptoes. Something was about to happen. The first appearance of possession was in the *mambo* herself. Technically, this is not supposed to happen, because it is she who controls the service. Possession came while she was performing a ritual around the *poteau-mitan*. Unexpectedly, she received a sudden jolt which left her limp and falling backwards; but just when she was about to lose footing her assistant sprang into action, caught her in his stride, swung her around while her legs were dragging on the ground almost lifeless. She was a corpulent woman, and a fall could have been serious. The drums changed rhythm and worked her back into consciousness. This experience lasted for about two minutes—but she was no sooner back at her role when another shock spun her around, again the agile assistant saved her from the hard concrete floor. This time the shock lasted for a longer period and she only recovered after an extended dance to a special rhythm of the drums, all the time propped up in the arms of her assistant. After this dramatic episode, the *mambo* left, accompanied by her assistants and two of the *vodunsis*, all of whom were under possession.

After a short while, which appeared to have been an intermission, the audience was directed to rise. The four participants reappeared; the assistant came first wheeling a machete above his head (the symbol of Ogun), the two *vodunsis* were each draped with a flag. On one of the flags was the word Guede. (The author was unable to identify the second.) The prevailing colors of the leading participants were red and black—the colors of Guede.

During this part of the ceremony, the gods came down. The drums played evocative polyrhythmic tunes in a dialogue with the spirits. Suddenly the *mambo* began looking around as if she expected heavenly visitors and almost at once the participants began to wheel and fall in all directions, completely oblivious of the audience or the concrete below them. Some plunged forward headlong and were only saved from injury by the agility and strength of those who were not possessed. But despite this apparent commotion there was not any sense of the chaotic; this was a serious matter. Guede, the god of death, was present. The possessed regained consciousness after a few minutes and continued dancing or just moved around in a daze shaking hands. They seemed full of indescribable happiness.

Then the drumbeats slackened the pace, and the two flags were given to the *mambo* who gave them to her assistant who draped them in the shape of a "v," the two emblems at the ends of the flags meeting at a central point. He extended the points of the flags to the audience; many moved forward, knelt, and kissed the emblems. This was done not only by the visiting cult leaders but by the rank-and-file of the audience as well. Evidently this ritual was perceived to have healing qualities, since many of the people kissing the emblems appeared to have attended the ceremony for reasons of health. The author could get no real explanation of this ritual from those who invited him. They either did not know or did not want to tell what they knew. After the ritual a libation was poured on the ground, and those who had kissed the emblems of the flags bent over the spot touching the libation with their left hand and with the same hand touched each other on the forehead. After this, the *mambo* and her assistants processed to the ritual dressing room. This part of the ceremony seemed to be the high point of the evening. It was accompanied with much pathos, tension, and drama. Afterwards, the audience seemed more relaxed and more free.

After a ten-minute lull in the ceremony filled only by drumming, the assistant appeared once more at the door of the ritual room and announced, "Guede!" The crowd rose and the *mambo* appeared, this time dressed in black slacks, red blouse, a black hat, and with a pistol in her pocket; her face was heavily smeared with white powder, signifying death. The assistants all carried mock weapons of war, and were dressed in eighteenth-century French military uniforms. One leader, a woman, conducted a drilling ceremony and led a charge against the *mambo*, who drew her pistol and fired at them; all fell to the ground. This, I was informed, was a reenactment of the Haitian revolution, in which the *vodun* god of death, Guede, played an important part.

The mock battle completed, the meeting switched to a rather comical vein which pleased the younger element of the audience. In this last part of the ceremony the other function of Guede took over. Guede is not only the God of death, but the God of the erotic, the phallic deity. Such a sudden turn in the ceremony, from a highly mystical experience, to one of exaggerated pelvic movements and sexual suggestiveness, could give the casual visitor a distorted picture of *vodun*. Maya Deren referred to Guede as "Corpse and Phallus, King and Clown" and said of him: "As Lord of Eroticism, he embarrasses men with his lascivious sensual gestures; but as God of the Grave he terrifies them with the evidence of the absolutely insensate...." [20] A great deal of this part of the ceremony was lost to the author. There was much dialogue between the *mambo* and the participants with bursts of hilarious laughter from the audience—but all of it in Creole. The final portion of the ceremony ended with a short dance of rapid gyration. Afterwards there was a feast. In all the ceremony took seven hours.

A truly meaningful analysis of *vodun* in Haiti would demand much more study. It would be necessary to see many different kinds of ceremonies under the leadership of many *houngans* who are devotees of many different *loa*. The ceremony discussed above was in honor of Guede with the theme of death and resurrection in which we observed again the pragmatism of the African mind. Guede is the God of death and must be feared, but he is also the God of sexuality and life and must be enjoyed. To the Haitians he serves as a terrifying reminder of the tomb which is the inevitable resting place of all men; yet he is also the generator of life itself. In this service joy and sorrow mingled; the secular and sacred were united. The experience of possession by Guede acted as a taste of death, but immediately afterwards life sprang forth. As in Africa, death is not to be primarily a time of sorrow, it is also a time to rejoice—dancing, singing, and feasting were all parts of this one experience called Guede or death. When someone dies it is a time to recall the exploits of the ancestors and this was done in the service by reenacting the Haitian revolution.

One would like to delve more deeply into the *vodun* gods: Damballa seemed to have a central place even in this service where Guede was the god being specifically honored. Ogun's influence also was evidenced by the machete and the pistol; he is the god of iron and firearms. Legba was the first to be invoked (as he always is) for without him the other *loa* would not appear. We need to know more of the significance of alcoholic spirits in *vodun*; they also have an important role in African religion. We need to analyze more carefully the symbolic meaning of colors, for example, of the red and black which dominated the ceremony discussed above. And most of all we need to better understand the importance of the

drums and the various rhythms used for each section of *vodun* ceremonies. A *vodun* ceremony is so complex that the visitor on first
seeing a service is unable to take in all the simultaneous operations.
It is like an opera with the conductor, the orchestra, the actors, the
setting, and the audience continually moving and changing. A
vodun ceremony is an experience of total involvement for audience
and actors; all are engaged in a religious experience. In truth, there
can be no spectators.

Shango in Trinidad

The present author has never been to Trinidad, consequently this
section of the paper will be based on the research done by other
scholars, especially the work of J. D. Elder, [21] a native of Trinidad,
Melville J. Herskovits, [22] and George Eaton Simpson. [23] With the
exception of the work of J. D. Elder, much of what has been done on
Shango in Trinidad is vague and contradictory. Here only the bare
outline of the religion will be evoked to further our thesis about
Caribbean religion in general.

Slavery in Trinidad appears to have been much less severe than
slavery in other parts of the Caribbean. The number of slaves from
the Spanish period to 1797, when Trinidad was acquired by the
British, never exceeded 20,000. However, there seems to have been
a sufficient number of Yoruba slaves to dominate the population and
stamp their culture mold on the other peoples. L.A.A. de Verteuil,
writing of Trinidad in 1858, laid great stress on the important place
of the "Yarrabas" in the slave society:

> Newly imported Africans are, generally speaking, industrious, but
> avaricious, passionate, prejudiced, suspicious, and many of them
> still adhering to heathenish practices. The Yarribas or Yarrabas
> deserve particular notice. . . . They are laborious, usually working
> for day wages on estates, but preferring job labour . . . in fact the
> whole Yarraba race of the colony may be said to form a sort of
> social league for mutual support and protection. [24]

So in all of Trinidad one tribe seems to have dominated the slave
community with its cultural patterns and its religion; this pattern
repeats itself throughout the Caribbean. We may note the specific
emphasis on the social league, in the above quotation, which we believe to be none other than the Egungun, a secret society of the
Yoruba.

Shango, in Yoruba conception the manifestation of the "Wrath of
Olodumare," is the god most feared among the common people of

Trinidad. Shango manifests himself in lightning and thunder and is still worshipped widely in Yorubaland where he has an organized priesthood and a cult. Originally, he was a king, more specifically, the fourth king of Oyo. Legends about him relate that he was either killed in battle or ascended to heaven. Whichever way, he has long been a god to the Yoruba.

Shango in Trinidad, like Santeria in Cuba and *vodun* in Haiti, is the generic name for a confederation of African divinities worshipped collectively by the common people. Like *vodun*, it is lightly infused with Catholicism; the gods of Africa have their counterpart in the Catholic Saints. In Cuba, this same combination of traditional African religion and Catholicism is called "Santeria" or "the saints." Under the name Shango are found these gods: Shango and his wife Oya; the trickster deity Eshu, another name for the Dahomean Legba; Oshun and Erinle, who are river deities; Shakpana, related to Yoruba Shopona, god of epidemics; and Abatala, one of the powerful god-kings of Nigeria. All these gods are called *orishas* by the Shango cultists, a word which simply means "powers." Along with these unmistakenly Yoruba divinities are names of divinities of the Dahomean pantheon, Legba being the most obvious. Other divinities carry either the names of recent family ancestors or corrupted names of divinities from other areas of Africa. [25]

An especially interesting aspect of Shango is the form of witchcraft which the adherents practice. This is none other than the *obeah* of which we have already spoken. Again our observation is borne out that the African cults were very flexible and pragmatic. Thus we have Yoruba deities at the center of Shango, but the witchcraft of the Akan peoples, who appear to have been in the minority, was perceived as strongest.

J. D. Elder observed that the major elements which welded together the Africans in Trinidad were:

1). Identical ethnic origin and identity with Africa
2). A common slave background in their history
3). Common recognition of African *orishas*, deities, and "powers" of a pantheon interested in the welfare of the livings
4). An ethos in which "Africa" and its culture-heroes serve to inspire morality, a sense of identity in the world, and cultural pride
5). Intermarriage among the *nations* with powerful taboos about non-African exogamy [26]

In Trinidad the word "nations" is used to refer to all the collective festivities of the African population. Thus we have the festival of the nations and the drum of the nations, all of which suggests that the people were conscious of the integration that took place in their development. The Shango cult, then, is a conscious, organized attempt of African peoples in exile to reformulate in one whole certain aspects remembered from their culture. In Trinidad as elsewhere in the Caribbean the mazeway was reorganized in religious terms.

AFRICAN RELIGIOUS RETENTION IN THE CARIBBEAN: A COMPARATIVE SUMMARY

Anyone who visits the Caribbean will not fail to observe what appear to be two distinct societies existing side by side. At the top of the social scale are the European-oriented elites. This group mainly consists of the mulattoes, the descendants of masters and slaves, who have not come to occupy the positions of slave masters but have imitated their behavior in many ways. Along with the elite are the educated Blacks whose training and upbringing have elevated them in society; they have come to be known as the "Afro-Saxons." Many of these sons of Africa have traditionally rejected any connection with an African heritage.

Below this small but dominant elite is the mass of peasant folk who have traditionally identified themselves with Africa and who are the backbone of the society. It is they who give flavor to every aspect of Caribbean life. They are the people whose pride in their African origin is accompanied with no apologies. Speaking of this latest group of people, Herskovits said:

> African elements are observable in language, folklore, family life and kinship, property, marketing, medicine, magic and religion, exchange-labour, economic organizations.... In music, dress, dancing, and domestic life, the African contribution is unmistakable. [27]

Let us analyze a few of these contributions.

Language

Throughout the Caribbean languages spoken today, there are literally thousands of African words that have been retained. The unofficial language of the Caribbean is Creole, an important linguistic emergence in the Caribbean, a product of the meeting of

Europe and Africa. This new language creation, with its engaging rhythm and great capacity for creative expressions, is just now catching the interest of students of language. It is, however, in the area of religion that we find the most African-language retentions. Many of the names of the African gods were transported to the Caribbean in their original form. The names for African religious specialists and for their professions have also survived the transplantation. Under possession, the Caribbean cultists speak an unknown tongue, which they claim to be the language of Guinea. And finally, names are generally the day-names of Africa. This custom is gradually dying out, but in the island of Jamaica it is still quite common to find people whose names are Cudjoe, Cuffie, Kwaku, Quasie or Kwamie—all day-names of the Akan peoples. The same hold true for the people of Haiti, where we meet personal day-names in French.

Folklore

In the area of folk tradition we are on solid ground in claiming that African folklore has dominated all the New World regions from North to South America. In support of this claim, we need only to refer to the animal stories of Brer Rabbit, Anansi the Spider, the Tortoise, and the famous Uncle Remus stories. In the area of proverbs, Africa again reigns supreme. Examples from Jamaica will be sufficient for our limited space. Thus from the Ashanti we have the following:

1). "It is the Supreme Being who pounds *fufu* [mush] for the one without arms," appeared in Jamaica as: "When cow lose him tail, God Almighty brush fly."
   (In both of these, the providence of God is evident.)

2). "When a fowl drinks water, it first shows it to the Supreme Being," appears in Jamaica as: "When fowl drink water him say 'tank God,' when man drink water him say nutten," or, "Chicken member God when him drink water."

3). "The hen's foot does not kill her chicken," appeared in Jamaica as: "Fowl tread upon him chicken, but him no tread too hard," or, "Hen neber mash him checken too hot."

4). "When a great number of mice dig a hole, it does not become deep," appeared in Jamaica as: "Too much rat nebber dig good hole."

5). "All animals sweat, but the hair on them causes us not to notice it," appeared in Jamaica as: "Darg sweat, but long hair cober i'."

6). "When too many people look after a cow, hunger kills it,"

appeared in Jamaica as: "Too much busha, darg Crawney."
7). "Wood already touched with fire is not hard to set alight,"
appeared in Jamaica as: "Ole fire stick no hard fe light." [28]
This is a small sample, and taken only from Jamaica. There are literally thousands of these proverbs yet to be collected. All Jamaicans use them as their ancestors did in Africa. In Haiti and the other islands we find the same oral tradition. J. J. Audin collected and published 1,011 proverbs from Haiti, which, we are told, forms only a sample of the enormous body of proverbs existent in that island. They are used by elders to instruct youth in prudence and morals, or to spice up an address in politics and religion.

Marketing

The African market system has received very little attention from Western scholars because few know the African concept of marketing. The African market was not only a place of selling and buying produce; it was also a social organization *par excellence*. It was a microcosm of the entire society. The atmosphere of African markets was festive, part religious festival and part carnival. The African markets served as political forums, as communication centers, as trysting places, as places for meeting old friends, as arenas for the performance of religious rituals, and as a host of other things. It is interesting to note that this market organization was brought into the Caribbean with all its African flavor, and the markets remain African to this day. Anyone who has visited West African markets cannot fail to see that almost every aspect of this social organization is retained in the contemporary Caribbean market.

Medicine

We must refrain from repeating ourselves in detailing the African system of curing in the Caribbean. We have already mentioned that the Africans found in their lands of exile an abundance of herbal medicines which were well known to them in Africa. It was therefore easy for the African specialist to continue his practice in the islands. His work has recently come to the attention of modern scientists who are now busy testing some of the age-old herbs for their own use. Not only are they experimenting on these herbs, but they are also studying the techniques of African healing. The technique is the key to their success but will prove the hardest to imitate since it presupposes a special conception of the world. The magico-religious perception of the world is a prerequisite for the proper use of African medicine. For the African specialist, herbs in themselves do not cure, the incantation of power is needed; this is the key to the success of the medicine man. The power of the medicine must be aroused by incantation; therefore, healing in the African view of things is both herbal and ritual. The African healer is not only a doctor, he is a psychiatrist and a pastor. The Western-trained doctor is still at a disadvantage in the Caribbean because much of the illness he confronts is of the psychosomatic variety due to the extreme stress of marginal living conditions. The average peasant in the Caribbean thinks of the professional doctor as ill prepared to deal with his condition because his social position makes him so far removed from them. The scarcity of trained doctors in the islands and the peoples' faith in the knowledge of the Afro-Caribbean medicine man makes it easy to project a long and prosperous future for the African specialists.

Music and Dancing

The music of Africa was probably the major source by which the Africanization of the Caribbean was accomplished. Africans cannot live without music. Music is the soul rhythm of the African people, and so it was not long after their arrival that we find the white masters in distress over these most disturbing sounds of Africa. The many laws against drumming, blowing of horns, and beating of boards and dancing suggest to us that the whole Caribbean had broken out into one mass African orchestra.

The drum was and still is the king of African musical instruments, and every variety of this instrument can be found in the Caribbean. From the majestic *assoctor* drum of Haiti, the *tambour* of *vodun*, the *dunno* of Shango, and the *akete* of Cumina, drums have been calling the gods of Africa to possess their devotees, sending messages across the hills in times of rebellion or merely pounding out African rhythms to the New World.

The dance is also an expression of the African *force-vitale*. The Caribbean Black dances in sorrow and in joy. African religion in the Caribbean began as a dance. So we hear of the *vodun* dance or the Cumina dance that the masters saw as a simple amusement, having no idea that the dance was the channel through which the African immersed himself in the very force of being. In the dance he became one with the powers of divinity and the ancestors; in the dance he became immortal. Thus the dance became the instrument of rebellion and revolution.

The African dance forms soon replaced all other forms of the dance in the New World. The beat of Africa became the foundation of the shuffle, the foxtrot, the mento, the calypso, the meringue, the rhumba, the blues, jazz, rock and roll, and present day "soul."[29] Thus we can see that out of the African traditional religion has come the rhythm that has influenced not only the New World, but the fatherland of the slave masters as well. In this sense, the statement "Europe ruled but Africa reigned" is most fitting for the Caribbean.

CONCLUSION

If we were to search for an African folk figure to use as a symbol of the slaves in Caribbean slavery, we could do no better than the tortoise. When matched against the size, strength, and agility of the other citizens of the forest, the tortoise is a poor candidate in every respect; yet despite his handicaps he generally comes out the winner. His doggedness against all odds, his calculating cunning, and his ability to survive under adverse conditions makes him a match for any, even in the most difficult circumstances. No wonder, as a folk figure, he continues to live in the hearts and minds of Africans.

We have seen that soon after the Africans entered the Caribbean a wholesale reinterpretation of their new environment took place. They gradually introduced their African pantheon into every nook and corner of the Caribbean and soon their gods, spirits, and powers permeated the new land. Every tree, every herb, and every stone became imbued with the dynamic powers of Africa, thus setting the stage for a new growth of African life and customs in the New World.

Out of what seemed to be a total disintegration of traditional life, the Africans regrouped themselves around their most cherished institution: their religion, and with the help of their *orishas* and ancestors they created a modified African society which has lasted over three hundred years. The dynamic of this transported society remains the basis of the Caribbean ethos to this day.

The Christian religion of the masters was no match for the deeply felt "soul religion" of the slaves. From the very start the slaves saw that the religion of the masters was a mere "form," devoid of reality, so it was easy for them to adopt this form as a disguise allowing them to continue practicing their more sophisticated and satisfying African rituals.

This is not to say that some Africans did not become genuine Christians. There were many Black Christians in the Caribbean whose grasp of the true meaning of Christianity was superior to that of their masters. But these were the exceptions to the rule. The majority of the slaves were true to their African world view and (like their masters) paid only lip service to Christianity. The Caribbean still remains one of the most fruitful laboratories for the study of African retentions, from their pure forms to the more modified ones, to those that are reinterpreted and now almost forgotten.

Finally, we cannot conclude this short paper on African retentions in the Caribbean without noting that it is out of the Caribbean that the spirit of African renaissance emerged during the last decades of the nineteenth century. The present return to "things African" came out of the *Zeitgeist* of the African which was nurtured in the soul of such men as Dr. Jean Price-Mars, the father of Indigenism in Haiti.[30] It was Price-Mars who called the Haitian people back to an awareness of their folklore and their African past. He made them realize that their cultural roots were not in the French culture which once threatened their destruction but in their African past, from which they drew their inspiration to fight against oppression. A similar movement known as "Negrismo" [31] came from Cuba. But the movement which caught the imagination of Africans the world over was Negritude. [32] It had its origin in Martinique and was fathered by the immortal poet Aimé Césaire. It was the spirit of Negritude that inspired such men as Léopold Sédar Senghor, the present president of the Republic of Senegal, to strip himself of the veneer of French culture and return to an African sense of himself. Negritude was an attempt to redeem the African past and to revive the dynamic and pragmatic philosophy of Africa which had been destroyed by the deadening influence of Europe. Out of this returning, a new African personality was born. Space will not allow us to write at length on the Jamaican prophet of Africanism, Marcus Garvey, the founder of the Back to Africa movement. Let it suffice to mention that, in the first decade of this century, he organized the United Negro Improvement Association both in the Caribbean and in the United States and gathered a following of over two million people dedicated to the reclamation of Africa from colonialism. His motto—"One God, One Faith, One Destiny—Africa for the Africans at Home and Abroad!"—is still the inspiration of Black movements in our day. His influence is still being felt in such movements as the Black Muslims of America but even more at the present time in the rapidly growing and influential Jamaican cult of Ras Tafari, which proclaims a coming return to Africa.

In no other area of the world has the African been more dynamic or more influential in keeping the ethos of the motherland alive than in the Caribbean. Out of these small islands have come the culture-bearers, freedom-fighters, artists, and apostles of Africa in America.

NOTES

1. For an interesting discussion of these three contributions see Frank Bayard's chapter "The Black Latin American Impact on Western Culture," in *The Negro Impact on Western Civilization*, edited by Joseph S. Roucek and Thomas Kiernan. New York, Philosophical Library, Inc., 1970, pp. 287-336.
2. Richard Wright, *Uncle Tom's Children*. New York-London: Harper, 1938, p. 13.
3. Orlando Patterson, *The Sociology of Slavery, etc.* (quoting from Minutes of Evidences of 1790-1791). London: MacCibbon and Kee, publishers, 1967, p. 44.
4. Sir Spencer St. John, *Haiti or the Black Republic.* London: Smith, Elder and Company, 1884, p. 216.
5. Anthony F. C. Wallace, "Revitalization Movements," *The American Anthropologist*, LVIII, (April 1956), p. 266.
6. H. G. DeLisser, *Twentieth Century Jamaica.* Kingston, Jamaica; The Jamaica Times, Ltd., 1913, p. 108.
7. Rev. J. G. Christaller, *Dictionary of the Asante and Fante Language (called Twi)*, second edition. Basil: the Evangelical Missionary Society, 1933.
8. Robert Rotberg, *Haiti: The Politics of Squalor.* Boston: Houghton Mifflin Company, 1971, p. 34.
9. Dr. J.C. Dorsainvil, *Vodou et Névrose.* Port-au-Prince: Imprimerie "La presse", 1931, pp. 33-34.
10. Thomas Madiou, *Histoire d'Haiti.* Port-au-Prince: Impr. de J. Courtois, 1848, vol. III, p. 33.
11. Edward Long, *History of Jamaica*, vol. 11. London: T. Lowndes, 1774, p. 416.
12. J. H. Buchner, *The Moravians in Jamaica.* London: 1885, pp. 139-140.
13. Ralph Korngold, *Citizen Toussaint.* New York: MacMillan Press, 1943, p. 33.
14. Zora Neale Hurston, *Voodoo Gods.* London: J. Dent & Sons, 1939, pp. 56-60.
15. For a good study of Jonkunu see Sylvia Winters' "Johnson in Jamaica," *Jamaica Journal: Quarterly of the Institute of Jamaica*, vol. IV, No. 2 (June 1970). See also Orlando Patterson, *op. cit.* pp. 245-246. Evidences of this festival seem to have been widespread in the English Colonies of the United States on the Eastern coast of the Carolinas.
16. For a discussion of Pukkumina in Jamaica see George Eaton Simpson, "Jamaica Revivalist Cults," *Jamaica, Social and Economic Studies*, No. 4 (1956), pp. 321-442. Also Donald Hogg, "Jamaican Religion: A Study in Variation," unpublished Ph.D. dissertation, Yale University, 1954. The

most authentic analysis of the cult is done by the former Minister of Finance for Jamaica, Edward Seaga, entitled "Cults in Jamaica," *Jamaica Journal: Quarterly of Jamaica*, III, 2 (June 1969).

17. William James Gardner, *History of Jamaica from its Discovery by Christopher Columbus to the Present Time.* London: E. Stock, 1873, p. 464.
18. *Ibid.*
19. James G. Leyburn, *The Haitian People.* New Haven-London: Yale University Press, 1966, pp. 131-165.
20. Maya Deren, *Divine Horsemen: The Voodoo Gods of Haiti.* New York: Chelsea House, 1970, p. 104.
21. J. D. Elder, "The Yoruba Ancestor Cult in Gasparillo," *Caribbean Quarterly*, X, 3 (September 1970.) pp. 5-20.
22. Melville J. and Francis Herskovits, *Trinidad Village.* New York: Alfred Knopf, 1947.
23. George Eaton Simpson, *The Shango Cult in Trinidad.* Puerto Rico: the Institute of Caribbean Studies, 1965.
24. L. A. A. deVerteuil, *Trinidad: Its Geography, Natural Resources, Present Condition and Prospects.* London: Ward, Lock and Company, 1958, p. 175.
25. For an authentic study of Yoruba religion, see E. Bolaji Idowu, *Olodumare: God in Yoruba Belief.* London: Longmans, Green and Company, 1966.
26. See Elder, "The Yoruba Ancestor Cult," p. 15.
27. See Melville J. Herskovits, *The New World Negro: Selected Papers in Afro-American Studies.* Indiana University Press, 1966, p. 53, *et passim.*
28. John Joseph Williams, *Psychic Phenomena of Jamaica.* New York: Dial Press, 1934, pp. 44-47.
29. For an interesting study of the influence of African dance form on the New World, see Janheinz Jahn, *Muntu: The New African Culture.* New York: Grove Press, 1961, pp. 61-95.
30. The classic study of *indigenismo* is found in Jean Price-Mars, *Ainsi Parla l'oncle...Essais d'ethnographie.* Port-au-Prince, 1928. This book is long out of print and has now become a collector's item.
31. The most important writer on African culture in Cuba was Orlando Ortiz.
32. The literature is too large to list here.

9

Afro-Brazilian Cults

Fred Gillette Sturm

A little over fifteen years ago Parrinder could speak of the 'twilight of the gods' of the traditional Yoruba pantheon. There can be little doubt indeed that within the present century there has been a considerable drift away from the ancestral cults. The old patterns of belief and ritual no longer have any significant formal following, and it is only among the older generation that one finds any enthusiasm for the traditional *orisas,* as opposed to Christianity or Islam.

...The fate of the Yoruba traditional cults is fairly predictable. It is extremely doubtful whether, *as a formal entity,* these will survive much longer than the present generation or so. The present proportion of the population in Ile-Ife who still adhere to these cults is less than five percent and these are largely drawn from the older people who have not been touched by the advance of education and urbanization.[1]

Traditional patterns of belief and ritual may be moribund in the ancient centers of Yoruba society, but they are very much alive and operative in the modern cities of Brazil. Constituting the basic ingredient within the varieties of religious syncretism known as Afro-Brazilian cults, Yoruba beliefs and practices have experienced a widespread acceptance on the part of a broad spectrum of Brazilian society which cuts sharply across racial and socio-economic class lines.

It is in Brazil, perhaps, more than any other part of the Americas, that African influence has played its profoundest role in the formation of modern culture. The African presence is discernible throughout the total fabric of Brazilian society, and it is especially evident in the religious dimension of Brazilian life. Part of the reason for this phenomenon is the high percentage of African descendants in the population, [2] but more important was the open attitude of the Portuguese, as opposed to that of the Spanish and English, at the time of colonization, toward miscegenation, and the

relaxed nature of Portuguese Catholicism which was easily receptive to religious syncretism. [3]

Over thirty distinct societies have been identified as the sources
of Brazil's African slave population. The first slaves came from the
"Malagueta Coast" or "Portuguese Guinea," that strip of coastal
land stretching from Senegal to Sierra Leone. These were the partially Islamized Fulas and Mandingas, [4] who were settled on the
newly established sugar plantations of northeastern Brazil in Bahia
and Pernambuco. Later, toward the end of the sixteenth century,
and throughout the seventeenth century, the Portuguese secured
most of their slaves from various Bantu-speaking societies of Angola
and the Congo, with a few from the "contra-coast" of Mozambique.
The names used to refer to these peoples relate as much to the
coastal cities where they were obtained as to linguistic or tribal designations. [5] These people were distributed extensively in Brazil as
the colonial settlements expanded down the coast as far as Rio de
Janeiro. During the eighteenth century the Portuguese obtained
their slaves from the coastal regions along the Gulf of Guinea, [6] and
from the interior of the western Sudan. [7]

By this time the Portuguese colonists had established a policy of
societal mixture as far as geographical distribution of enslaved
peoples was concerned, in an effort to discourage resistance and
revolt. The policy was not entirely successful and the colonial period
was marked by a succession of slave revolts which continued into
the post-independence period of the nineteenth century. The revolts
were led much of the time by the Islamic blacks, especially the independent Hausa who, from the vantage point of their Muslim culture, looked disdainfully at their enslavers. As revolts were put
down, the numbers of Muslim slaves declined drastically, so that
there remains only a minimal Islamic element in Afro-Brazilian culture today. Eventually the colonial policy worked, resulting in intermarriage and considerable loss of distinct societal identity. Two
general patterns of Afro-Brazilian culture emerged. In the Rio-Sao
Paulo area Bantu-speaking peoples from Angola tended to predominate, while in Bahia and the northeast the Yoruba and Ewe became culturally dominant. In the latter half of this century increasing mobility of population and improved media of communication
have given rise to a situation in which Yoruba language and customs
provide the mainspring for Afro-Brazilian culture with strong Bantu
elements still evident.

The development of religious life in Brazilian society has been
complex and is characterized by much syncretism. This is true with

the Afro-Brazilian communities themselves. By the middle of the nineteenth century it was clear that Yoruba beliefs and practices had become widely dispersed, the principal *orixás* [8] being mentioned and consulted within communities which were not basically Yoruba demographically or linguistically. At the same time the Bantu emphasis on consultation with ancestral spirits was influencing Yoruba-Brazilian cultic practice. The clearest example of this is the inclusion of the spirits of *pretos velhos* [9] alongside the Yoruba *orixás* in the ranks of spiritual forces capable of possessing the spirit mediums.

A second form of religious syncretism involved various Amerindian societies and the Afro-Brazilian communities. The Tupí-Guaraní peoples of southern Brazil practiced a form of ancestral spirit possession in which the heroic chiefs and warriors of the past returned to provide guidance and assistance for the living. This bore striking resemblance to the ancestral spirit possession practiced by the Bantu. The utilization of medicinal herbs was another close Tupí-Guaraní/Bantu resemblance which led to an Afro-Amerindian religious synthesis in the Rio-São Paulo region. Spirits of *caboclos* [10] were added to those of the *pretos velhos* in the emerging Afro-Brazilian "pantheon." The religious life of Amerindian peoples in northern Brazil and the Amazon valley tended to center around the primal forces of nature which are confronted in the daily struggle for existence. The *pajé*, or shaman, invoked the spirits of mysterious forces which have come to be known by the Portuguese word *encantados*, [11] especially for purposes of healing. The resemblance to a large number of Yoruba *orixás* which represent natural forces (thunder, storm, rivers, waterfalls, etc.) made possible a different Afro-Amerindian syncretism in the north and northeast.

The close relationship which obtained in the Brazilian northeast during the colonial period between the plantation owner and his family and the slaves of the plantation, along with the relatively open nature of Portuguese Catholicism, especially as it was practiced in colonial plantation society, provided the context within which an Afro-Catholicism developed easily. The Yoruba concept of the high god *Olorun*, who does not interfere directly in natural events and human history but works through a host of intermediaries, the *orixás*, was easily identified with the idea of the Christian creator who works primarily through his Son, Jesus Christ, and can be approached through the mediation of the Virgin Mary and a host of saints, many of whom have specific functions as patron saints of various classes of people. Hence Jesus is seen as the Christian equivalent of *Oxalá* (a shortened version of *Orixalá*, the chief or "great" *orixá*); the Virgin is identified with *Iemanjá*, the *orixá* of the ocean; and the major saints are correlated with other important *orixás*. Catholic devotion to, and invocation of, particular saints was viewed by Afro-Brazilians of Yoruba descent as constituting the same activity as invocation of the *orixás*. In both instances the spirit is called upon for consultation and assistance, and frequently an amulet, image, or idol is involved. The difference—and here Yoruba practice proved more powerful and effective—is that the spirit of the *orixá* becomes physically present through the person of a medium.

During the nineteenth century, after having declared independence from Portuguese rule, Brazilians looked to France for cultural innovations and inspiration. Brazil proved to be receptive soil for several French movements in literature and the arts, political theory and religion. One of these was Allan Kardec's "spiritism." The importance of mediumship and spirit possession in Afro-Brazilian cults helps to account for the ease with which Kardecism was transplanted to Brazilian soil. In popular parlance today the word *espiritismo* refers to both the Kardecistic movement and the Afro-Brazilian cults as if they represented the same general religious phenomenon. Afro-Brazilian religious leadership conceives the Kardec movement as a latter-day European discovery of the basic principles underlying African-based religious practice. Kardec leadership, on the contrary, is unhappy with the identification of the two movements in the popular mind. In their eyes Afro-Brazilian cultic phenomena constitute spiritism on a very primitive and unscientific level.

Syncretistic tendencies have continued in the decades following the Second World War as the intellectual leadership within the Afro-Brazilian cultic communities has become aware of Asian religious traditions and non-Christian elements in European cultural history. This has resulted in a number of attempts to incorporate concepts, symbols, and practices from such diverse sources as the Cabala, Kundalini yoga, and astrology. [12]

The result of such complex syncretization is a plethora of types of Afro-Brazilian cults, varying one from another in terms of the traditions which have been included, and the relative importance of each in the particular mix. Before the middle of this century it has been true as a general rule that the Yoruba tradition has been the predominant factor in cults of the Northeast, especially in Bahia; that

Bantu practices have dominated the Rio de Janeiro cults; that São Paulo cults have emphasized the Catholic element; and that Amerindian elements have been dominant in the Amazon valley. As population mobility increases these geographical and regional characterizations are becoming less and less accurate. The popular names given to Afro-Brazilian cults from region to region do not therefore indicate the kind of synthesis characteristic of the area. In some instances they are derived from the drums used to accompany the dances central to the ritual. This is true of the Bahian *Candomblé,* [13] of *Batuque,* [14] and *Tambor.* [15] Other names for the cults stem from the central participants in the ritual. Such is the case with the *Macumba* of Rio de Janeiro, [16] and with *Pajelança.* [17] It may be the case with the São Paulo term *Umbanda* as well. [18] Amerindian words are sometimes used: *Babaçue,* [19] *Catimbo,* [20] and *Pará.* [21] In the case of *Xangô* [22] the name is obviously derived from the *orixa* who was the "king of Oyo" and became the spirit of thunder and lightning. There are some names whose derivation seems lost, as is the case with *Cabula,* popular in the state of Espírito Santo. Some students of Afro-Brazilian cults have made the mistake of dealing with these names as if they delineated separate "denominations" or distinctive "movements." This is not the case. It should be evident from the derivations that these differing designations are largely accidental. Of course it is true that the use of an Amerindian name would indicate a stronger Amerindian element than would be the case in some region where a Bantu word were used. This is becoming less true, however, as the groups exert increasing influence upon each other. *Umbanda* is fast becoming the generic term for the entire range of Afro-Brazilian religious phenomena.

In recent years there have been efforts to organize the cults into federations on city, state, regional and national levels. One of the motives has been the need to create a united front for dealing effectively with repeated repression and persecution on the part of police officials encouraged by certain elements within the Roman Catholic Church. Alfredo Costa Moura, president of the Umbandist Federation of the State of São Paulo, in founding the organization in 1953 succeeded in reaching a *modus vivendi* with Catholic authorities and civil officials. This was done by emphasizing the Catholic elements of Umbanda on the one hand, and by instituting certain regulations governing cultic behavior on the other. [23] A second motive for establishing a superstructure is the effort to restore and conserve a "pure" African cult. José Ribeiro de Souza has been at the forefront of this movement. He was one of the founders of the Institute of Afro-Brazilian Studies in Rio de Janeiro during the mid-1940s, and continues to serve as Professor of Sudanese Languages. In his published work he has attempted to identify the various African societies and trace the unique contributions each has made to the syncretistic Afro-Brazilian cult movements. Several of his books contain appendices in which appear lexicons of Portuguese and the Yoruba, Ewe, and Kikongo languages. The most ambitious attempt at providing an ecumenical movement was the incorporation in 1955 of the National Union of Afro-Brazilian Cults, and the establishment of the Supreme Afro-Brazilian Sacerdotal Council called for by Article 9 of its statutes. The latter body, headed by Byron Torres and Wladimir Cardoso de Freitas, has undertaken to oversee and organize the "centres, *tendas* and *terreiros* of Brazilian rituals having African, Amerindian and Asiatic origin," to submit the leaders of such centers to a standard religious examination, awarding those who pass such an examination with the "Diploma of Priesthood," to represent the movement before civil authorities whenever necessary, and to take measures insuring the inner peace of the movement. [24]

Basic to all Afro-Brazilian cults is the task of putting the living human community into direct touch with a source of superhuman power: either fundamental natural and historical forces, or spirits of those who have died. The purpose of the spirit confrontation, which is central to the ritual, is the promotion of healing, the overcoming of obstacles, and the strengthening of body and mind through the transmission of power, along with the offering of guidance for the solution of problems through consultative dialogue. The contact is effected through human intermediaries chosen by the spirits involved to serve as vehicles for incarnation and manifestation. The mediums are prepared for their role by a process of rigorous training, discipline, and initiation.

The use of Yoruba terminology for naming the natural forces is becoming universal. It would be difficult to provide an accurate rendering into English of the generic term *orixá*. It would be incorrect to refer to *Xangô* as "god" of thunder, or to *Iemanjá* as "goddess" of the sea. Since the Yoruba *orixás* have been identified with Catholic saints since colonial times, the Brazilian has utilized the word *santo*. However, one does not refer to "St. Ogun." It is either "*orixá* Ogun" or "St. George." The medium is called a "son" (or "daughter") of the saint—but is possessed, not by the saint, but by the *orixá*.

Although more than one hundred Yoruba *orixás* have been identified in contemporary Brazilian usage, there are a limited number which enjoy universal popularity and are conceded to be the most powerful. The correlation of these with Catholic saints varies from locale to locale, although a tendency toward greater uniformity is discernible. There is wide variation as well in the identification with specific *orixás* of fetishes, color symbolism, appropriate food and beverage, and feast days, but here, too, a drift toward a uniformity seems to be occurring.

Oxalá is the principal *orixá*, representing creative and procreative forces, and always identified with Christ Jesus. There is, however, a growing tendency to use the word to refer to God the Creator. The Yoruba designation *Olorun* is seldom encountered, although *Zambi* is frequently used, and some authors do seem to use *Zambi* and *Oxalá* interchangeably. [25] White is the color assigned to *Oxalá* throughout the country, and there is universal agreement that Friday is dedicated to him, a possible survival of African Islam. [26]

Ogun is associated with iron, and with the tools manufactured from that metal. This has led to a dual representation of the forces of war and strife on the one hand, and agriculture and land fertility on the other. He is usually identified with St. George, and is the *orixá* most often invoked for protection from enemies and all danger.

Xangô, the legendary ancestor of Yoruba kings, originally represented thunder and lightning. Through a process of associations he has been interpreted as that force which makes for justice and wisdom, for prosperity and peace. Because several of the Yoruba legends about the life of *Xangô* involve periods of wandering or exile in the forest, it is not surprising that he has been identified with both St. Jerome and St. John the Baptist.

Oxossi is the patron saint of hunters. It is perhaps because a bow and arrows are his traditional symbol that he has often been identified with the very popular St. Sebastian. The hunt is a forest activity, and by association he has become interpreted as the force of medicinal plants, an attribute which he shares with *Ossae*, whose symbol—a seven-branched tree topped with a bird in a cup—is frequently encountered.

The most important of the feminine *orixás* is *Iemanjá*. She controls salt waters and is often pictured as tall, slender, and blue-robed, coming forth out of the sea. Usually identified with Our Lady of the Conception, she represents maternal forces.

Another very popular feminine *orixá* is *Oxun,* ruler of springs and brooks, and the representative of romantic love, marriage, and hu-

man fertility. She is variously identified with St. Catherine and
several of the manifestations of the Virgin Mary, Our Lady of the
Manifestation (Patroness of Brazil), Our Lady of Glory, et al.

Omolú, or *Obaluaé,* is the force of contagious diseases, especially
the dreaded smallpox, and as a result is linked with the power of
death as well. Usually identified with St. Lazarus, his favor is sought
to overcome illness and guarantee health. [27] Disease and death are
more feared, perhaps, than any other natural forces, so that it is not
strange that he is surrounded by an aura of almost complete negativity in the minds of those who approach him. [28]

The *orixás* represent the forces encountered by humans in the environment, whether natural (storm, sea, disease, et al.) or social
(war, economic activity, et al.). Only a few have played a human role
in mythical history (*Xangô,* the king-turned-*orixá,* and *Iansã,* his
wife, are outstanding examples). Although there is sexual differ-
entiation, this is sometimes blurred; *Xangô,* for example, is
sometimes identified with St. Barbara! Although the forces which
they originally represented are highly particularized (thunder and
lightning, smallpox, salt water), through the process of association
they become much more generalized, often betraying the social
transition of the people from a forest-dwelling, hunting stage to that
of settled agriculture and urbanization, and in latter days to mod-
ernization. The religious syncretism characteristic of Afro-Brazilian
cults is clearly evident in the identification of each *orixá* with one or
more of the Catholic saints. Further evidence of the complicated
pattern of syncretism appears when Ewe and Kikongo names are
used alternatively with the Yoruba. There are some Amerindian designations also, but the situation here is one of highly complicated
cross-fertilization. [29]

Exú is technically not an *orixá* but plays a crucial role in *orixá*-
human encounters. [30] He is the messenger who prepares the way
for successful communication. He is also the "trickster," that amoral
being whose pranks can result in human disaster. The tendency,
therefore, has been to think of him as a predominantly evil force
rather than amoral, and he is identified in the popular mind with the
devil. Satanic horns and tail are sometimes used in representations
of *Exú,* with the trident as his symbol. Recently the word *exú* has
become a generic name referring to a variety of forces generally associated with negativity. As many as fifty-eight are identified,
although I suspect that some have been created to fit precon-
ceived schemata. [31] Among those most often mentioned in practice
are *Exú da Meia Noite* (the Midnight *Exú*), *Exú Tranca Ruas* (the

Roadblock *Exú*), and *Exú Tirirí* (the *Exú* of the Bird *Tyrannus melancholicus*). There are several feminine principals as well; *Exú Pomba-gira* is the most popular. Such proliferation is found also among the *orixás* themselves [32] and is not unlike the phenomenon found within popular Catholicism where the Virgin Mary manifests herself in several forms: Our Lady of the Manifestation, Our Lady of Guadalupe, Our Lady of Fatima, Our Lady of the Immaculate Conception, Our Lady of Glory, etc. A "satanic" cult dedicated to the practice of "black magic" is under constant attack. Referred to as "Quimbanda" it relies heavily on the operative power of the legions of *Exú*. The victim of Quimbanda practice is often forced to do something he would not do under normal circumstances, or finds himself incapable of the full exercise of a faculty. Therefore an unrequited lover may request the favor of *Exú Pomba-Gira* to break up a successful marriage and cause one of the partners to fall in love with him.

In addition to *orixás* and *exú*(s), Afro-Brazilian cults work actively with ancestral spirits. The *preto velho* represents for Brazilian Blacks an important link with African origins, and provides a sense of historical continuity within the worshipping community. [33] The terms of address are familial: *Pai* (Father) and *Mãe* (Mother), and less frequently *Tio* (Uncle) and *Tia* (Aunt). Indeed, the *pretos velhos* are often referred to as *espíritos familiares* (familial spirits) and *espíritos da casa* (spirits of the house). (Fig. 8) Smoking a clay pipe, and speaking a broken Portuguese characteristic of the early slave community, interspersed with words of West African or Bantu origin, the spirit of the *preto velho* provides sound advice in a kindly and solicitous fashion. He will provide information about the welfare of deceased or distant friends and relatives as well—doubtless the result of Kardecistic influence in cultic practice. The second line of ancestral spirits, the Amerindian *caboclos*, appear in marked contrast to the *pretos velhos*. Although many of them hold important societal positions during their lifetimes, they are viewed as coming from a much more primitive level of culture, often referred to as "spirits of the woods." In place of the relaxed air of the old Black, there is an atmosphere of Prussian authority when a *caboclo* is present. A cigar replaces the clay pipe, and the speech is interspersed with words from Guaraní or some other Amerindian tongue. Despite these differences the functions of *Caboclo Urubatão* and *Cabocla Jurema* are essentially the same as those of *Pai Arruda and Mãe Maria Conga*.

The influence of Kardecistic spiritism has introduced the

"descent" of "inferior spirits"—Blacks and Amerindians who were not community leaders in the past. Interpreted in Kardec terms, these are spirits in process of development who can disrupt regular worship, but who constitute an opportunity for the living to be of service to members of previous generations.

This vast company of spiritual entities—*orixás, exús, pretos velhos,* and *caboclos*—is often organized into "lines" and "phalanxes." In general the schemes call for seven principal lines of spirits, each one of which commands seven phalanxes. Five of the seven lines are almost universally seen as being commanded by the same *orixás; Oxalá, Iemanjá, Ogun, Xangô,* and *Oxossi.* The most popular leaders of a sixth line are the *Ibeji,* the Yoruba twin-force. They are referred to more often as *Iori,* are identified with Saints Cosmas and Damian, and are known affectionately as "the children." The seventh line, traditionally led by *Omolú,* has become increasingly reserved for the spirits of the *pretos velhos,* led by St. Cyprian.

The large number and wide diversity of "spiritual entities" involved in Afro-Brazilian cults are well represented in the following passages from a typical opening prayer:

> Merciful and just Father, give permission to the Superior Spirits of Light, to Angels, Saints, *Orixás* and Chiefs of Phalanxes and their commanders, to the *Caboclos* and *Pretos Belhos,* spirits of the sea, of rivers, springs waterfalls, to all the pure or purifying spirits, that they may cast over this *terriero* their salutary radiations, their regenerative fluids, for the benefit of those who come here in search of alleviation, assistance and healing for their moral and physical pains, for their earthly miseries....
>
> Spirits of Light, give to the mediums [34] your force so that they can transmit it to the brethren who have come to receive it. May the energies of the Universe, under the action of the Spirits of Light, Guides, Protectors, Guardian Angels, be released in enlightened, beneficent and strong form in this place, purifying it, illuminating it, casting out the evil elements of Space and of the Earth and of this *Tenda* and *Terreiros.* Superior Spirits, defend this *Terreiro,* hindering the approach of evil and disturbing spirits...[35]

A typical center, [36] whether in a separate building in the outskirts of a village, or occupying an apartment in a highrise building located in a downtown urban center, provides space for at least three areas. The *peji* is the sanctuary including the altar, usually three-tiered, upon which are placed symbols of the *orixás* and the Catholic saints identified with them, along with dishes containing the food and beverages appropriate for offering to each *orixá,* and other cultic objects and instruments. This usually serves as the "little room," the place of temporary residence for aspirants to mediumship during their period of initiation. The large room in which spirit possession and consultation occurs is divided between the area for spectators to be placed, and that where the actual cultic events occur. The latter includes a corner for locating the drums and other musical instruments.

The people affiliated with such a center fall into several categories. The "son's of faith" are those who are regular in attendance and support. In addition to this relatively close-knit group is a large number of individuals who come to the public services in moments of personal crisis for consultation and assistance. These "seekers" have often exhausted other available resources and come to the *terreiro* as a last resort.

From the ranks of the faithful are selected the *ogans*, "lay" men and women who perform specialized functions necessary for the smooth operation of the cult. These include men of means and community standing who concern themselves with questions of budget and property, public relations, and legal matters. There are the drummers who must know the varieties of instruments and the wide spectrum of rhythmic beats used in the services. Percussion music accompanies the singing and dancing which are essential to cultic practice. Each *orixá* responds to a particular beat, and many are the *toadas* or *pontos cantados* (songs or chants) which are appropriate for either summoning its presence or for accompanying its descent within the community. The position of the drummers is one of high specialization demanding great skill. There are several offices related to the preparation of sacrifice. The *Mão de faca* [37] is responsible for the preparation of sacrificial animals. This requires knowledge of which animals are appropriate for offering to each *orixá*, including size, color, and sex, as well as of the proper procedure for killing and cutting the animal in each instance. The *iaba*, or *iabasse*, prepares the cooked food appropriate for offering to each of the *orixás*. The recipes and procedures to be followed are African in origin [38] with occasional Brazilian modifications. The *Mão de Ofá* is an expert in the selection of herbs and their correct processing for the preparation of the various types of *amaci* or baths of purification. Responsible for the care of the *axês*, or sacred objects, is the *ialaxê*. There are functionaries, the *ekédes* or *cambonos de terreiro*, who assist in the services by providing drinks for the *orixás* and lighting the pipes of *pretos velhos* and performing similar services when spirit possession is taking place. The *Cambono da*

Rua is responsible for taking *despachos* to their proper destination—a cemetery, a crossroads, or a river bank. The *despacho* is a package containing specific items requested by a spirit and ordered placed in a specific location to achieve desired ends.

Presiding over the entire life and activity of a *terreiro* is either a *babalorixá* or an *ialorixá*. Although these Yoruba words are widely used to designate the office, the Portuguese terms *pai do santo* (father of the saint) and *mãe do santo* (mother of the saint) are frequently encountered. This is the spiritual authority *par excellence* within the community of the faithful, responsible alone for the selection and training of all officials, and the final arbiter of all intracommunity disputes. There is only one distinction between the offices of father of the saint and mother of the saint: that method of divination called *jôgo do Ife* is reserved to male use only. There may be an assistant—"the little father or mother"—and there is usually a "spiritual director" or *pejí-gan* who organizes and conducts the order of the actual service, insuring smoothness and ritual correctness in outward form.

The most important members of the cult community are the mediums themselves—the "sons" (*abaô*) and "daughters" (*iaô*) "of the saint." It is through their bodies and voices that the spiritual entities—*orixás, pretos velhos*, *caboclos*—descend to the level of human existence and for a short while become incarnate and dwell among us. Theirs is the sacred responsibility of serving as the instruments through which the divine power of *orixás* is transmitted to men, and the wisdom of ancestral spirits brought to bear on the problems of contemporary life. They do not volunteer for the office but are chosen by the spiritual entities for the task. The selection is made known through a variety of means, ranging from dreams to abnormal occurrences. Actually, every human being is protected by one of the spirits known, insofar as this specific function is concerned, as the individual's "guardian angel." It is assumed when someone is selected for mediumship that the spirit involved is the same as that person's protector. This is not always the case. To ascertain whether it is or not, as well as to validate the "call" itself, the chief of the *terreiro* (i.e., the "father" or "mother of the saint") utilizes one of the accepted methods of divination. The technique most often used today is the *jôgo-dos-búzios* [39] in which conch shells are moved and interpreted in a manner which bears a striking resemblance to the Chinese *I Ching*. When the authenticity of the call has been revealed the candidate is officially told who his *orixá de cabeça* (*orixá* of the head) is. He then purchases the ceremonial clothing and other objects necessary for the lengthy process of initiation. Initiatory rites and procedures vary from center to center and region to region. I shall confine myself to a description of the stages of initiation which are traditional within the centers of greatest Yoruba influence. [40]

The day for beginning the novitiate is selected by further divination. An herb bath is prepared by the *mão-de-ofá* and given, preferably out-of-doors, at 3:00 A.M. The street clothing is removed and new clothing suitable for the period of initiation donned. The novitiate has now begun and the candidate takes up residence in the "little room" of the *terreiro*. The daily regimen includes a bath of purification at daybreak, ceremonies at 6:00 A.M., noon, 6:00 P.M., and midnight, and an intensive program of education. The candidate must learn the songs and dances appropriate to each of the *orixás*, and master the drumbeats as well. He must learn the details of each of the special rites and ceremonies. Knowledge of herbs, food, and animal sacrifice is required. The procedures for offering food and beverage to the *orixás* is included. Language study involves facility in the use of Yoruba along with enough basic knowledge of other languages to serve cultic purposes. The art of divination is taught. After a fortnight or two have passed a ceremony is held in the large room during which the candidate is for the first time possessed by his *orixa*. He is now called *abaô* or *iaô*. Immediately he is taken to the "little room" and submits to a shaving of the head. After a ceremonial washing with water, the appropriate animal is sacrificed and a baptism of blood follows, the blood poured over the shaven and washed head and allowed to flow down the body. Several hours later he is washed and then the body is painted: face, arms, chest—a procedure which is supposed to symbolize the cutting of skin which took place at this point in the initiation rites in precolonial days on African soil.

A period of rigid discipline follows which can last anywhere from fifteen to one hundred and twenty days, the exact length of time determined by the chief of the *terreiro* in consultation with the *orixá* by means of divination. The candidate cannot leave the *terreiro*, nor can he receive visitors. Certain foods are proscribed, as is sexual intercourse. Speech is also prohibited, or at least kept at a bare minimum. At the end of this period the ceremony of *ôrunkó* is held. This is the special "day of giving the name" and is popular with the faithful who attend in large numbers. Once again the novice is possessed and then shouts out the special name by which the *orixá* is to

be known when acting and speaking through this particular *cavalo.*[41]
Once again we are in the presence of an *orixa* known by several
different names, and the insistence upon the possibility of the same
force manifesting itself under a variety of modes, while also
acknowledging the adaptation of manifestations to the peculiarities
of specific mediums. At daybreak, after the proclamation of the
name, the candidate's clothing is washed and purified, and the
time of rigid discipline is past. The Sunday following is one of
celebration and merriment. It begins with a "public auction" during
which the son or daughter of the saint is sold to the highest bidder
amid much singing, clapping, and beating of drums. There follows
the *quitanda,* a mock fair. The initiate "sells" produce at an inflated
price, while the "public" attempts to rob him. Under possession of
an inferior spirit the initiate staves off the thieves, and there is
reported to be much laughter and *camaraderie.* He returns to the
little room until the next Friday and then makes a pilgrimage in
company with officials and members of the *terreiro* to a Catholic
Church. In Salvador, Bahia, this has been the Church of Bonfim, the
manifestation of Christ as Our Lord of Bonfim being the most
popular identification with *Oxalá.* The initiatory period is at an end.
The "son" or "daughter" has been "made" and returns home. For
three months longer, however, he wears a slave pendant around his
neck before it is placed at the foot of the representation of his *orixa*
on the altar in the *terreiro.* A party marks the first anniversary of his
initiation. After seven years have passed there is a ceremony
through which he is given senior status and can then assume higher
positions of responsibility. In effect this means the ability to become
the chief of the *terreiro* or to form a new *terreiro.* But the responsibilities of mediumship or "priesthood" are heavy from the outset.
The new son or daughter of the saint is obliged to be present at the
terreiro assisting in public ceremonies and many of the private rites.

   Public sessions vary in liturgical form and content, not only from
center to center and region to region, but also within a given center
in accordance with specific purposes and celebrations. Basically
they follow these general steps:

   1). An offering is made to *Exú* to guarantee that the avenues of
communication are open, and that no disturbing forces be permitted
to interfere with the work of the evening.

   2). First the altar, then the mediums, and finally the persons who
are present within the large room to attend the service are purified
with incense. This is known as the act of *defumação.*

   3). A chant (*ponto cantado*) to *Ogun* follows to insure the strength and safety of the circle. Sons of the saint are lined on one side, daughters on the other, both lines facing the altar.

4). The opening prayer (*preçe de abertura dos trabalhos*) is intoned, consisting of a general invocation of all spirits of light.

5). Greetings (*saudações*) follow—to the protector spirit of the *terreiro*, to the leaders of the community, to the drums, to the altar—in form of chant and song.

6). The "work" itself then begins. This consists of the invocation of a particular "line" of spirits, the proper drumbeat sounding, the sons and daughters dancing and singing until one or more experiences the descent (*baixar*) of the spirit. A sudden change in the entire bodily movement occurs as the vibrations of the incarnate spirit become manifest in the person of the medium. This extends to gestures, voice, and speech patterns. The spirit demands the reason for invocation. It is at this point that persons who desire to receive the force or power of the spirit, or to consult with the spirit, are permitted to come forward one by one and either receive the vibrations through bodily contact with the medium or carry on conversation through an interpreter. When this is done the spirit is thanked, again through chant or song, and then encouraged to leave the body of the medium. A second "line" is then called, and the same process occurs in relation to a different spirit force or power. The experience of serving as intermediary for a spirit is an intense one, usually involving much physical exertion. Often the spirit has to be encouraged to leave the body of the medium without doing violence to the person involved.

7). The sons and daughters are purified at the conclusion of the "works."

8). A closing prayer (*preçe de encerramento*) expresses appreciation to the spirits which had descended and graciously offered assistance in the service.

Public services of this kind are liturgical acts through which the spiritual forces of nature and the great crowd of witnesses who surround us from our historic past become incarnate and are made available for the immediate benefit of those individuals who desire their assistance. There are other ceremonies which have a more cosmic and communal significance. They follow the regular cycle of the sacred year. An excellent example is the Rite of the Waters of *Oxalá*. This marks the opening of the "African year" and represents a time of renewal. It begins on the eve of the first Friday in September and continues for three Sundays. In terms of the seasonal calendar it is a rite of spring. In the course of the lengthy ritual there is a purgation of the entire community of the faithful. Thursday night is dedicated to the act of *bôrí*, offering appropriate food and drink to the principal *orixás* by the sons and daughters of the saint. When Friday dawns the symbolic instruments representative of *Oxalá* are removed from their place on the altar. A solemn proession takes them to a place of temporary exile, the *baluê*. Three "processions of the waters" follow. The chief of the *terreiro* and the children of the saint carry liturgical jars to a nearby spring (or source of pure water) and then return to pour the water over the "seat" of *Oxalá*. The processions take place in silence, and the jars are left at the *baluê* at the end of the third journey. The first Sunday is the day for celebrating the Festival of *Oxalá*. The festivities occur in the *terreiro* in the presence of *Oxalá* and the other principal *orixás*. Served at this occasion are two dishes: *adiê* (chicken cooked with onions and lemons) and *ebbó* (boiled white corn), and the beverage *aluá* (made of rice flour or pineapple husks fermented with sugar). Since the color of *Oxalá* is white, only food and drink which is "white" can be offered to him or consumed in his honor. On the second Sunday the symbols of *Oxalá* are returned from the *baluê* to their rightful place on the altar. The third Sunday is the Day of *Pilão* (pestle-and-mortar), in which the community of the faithful submits to a process of purification through an act of symbolic flagellation. *Oxalá* descends upon the body of a son or daughter of the saint, arms himself with a switch, and whips those who are present as punishment for the sins of the past year. The food served at this occasion is mashed yam (or an arum root of some sort). The "Waters of *Oxalá*" is not open to the public at large, but is intended to be a corporate act of penitence and cleansing by the children of faith.

There are other rituals of a more private and individual nature. The *Fechamento do Corpo* (Closing of the Body) is typical. The purpose of the *fechamento* is to protect the body from all attacks, ranging from animal and snake bites through assaults by enemies to "spells" cast by practitioners of black magic. The candidate for *fechamento* dresses in white and is barefooted. He abstains from food and sexual relations for a twenty-four-hour period prior to the ceremony. The day chosen is the Friday closest to the full moon. The hour is either 6:00 P.M. or midnight. A song of entrance praises the patron saint or protector of the house. The *ponto riscado*, a symbol representing the presence of the saint, is drawn at the entrance of the house. [42] A glass of salt water is placed upon it, and a song of invocation (*ponto cantado* or *toada*) follows. The same is repeated at the four sides of the room: *pontos riscados* representing *Iemanjá*,

Ogun, Oxossi and *Xangô* are drawn and *pontos cantados* sung to them. *Defumaçaõ,* or incensing of the entrance, the four corners, and the candidate, follows. The candidate then stands in the middle of the room with his arms outstretched. The chief of the *terreiro* addresses a prayer of supplication to *Ogun,* or St. George. [43] He takes a ceremonial dagger and touches the following points of the candidate's body with it: forehead, nape of neck, back, chest, elbows, palms, knees, feet. A second prayer is directed to *Ogun.* [44] The power of *Ogun* is transmitted to the candidate through the vibrations which emanate from the hands of the chief as they touch the body. Once again the candidate is incensed. A second *ponto riscado* of *Iemanjá* is drawn and a *toada* chanted to her. After a closing prayer the *pontos riscados* are erased, the glass of salt water is emptied, and the first part of the ritual is ended. One week later the ritual is repeated for the sake of confirmation. This time the candidate lies on the floor with arms and legs spread apart. Candles are lighted and placed at his head, and at each of his hands and feet. After prayer and *defumaçaõ* he rises. The chief of the *terreiro,* with back to the candidate, takes the dagger in hand and plunges it backwards in a series of motions describing the outline of the candidate's body. If the dagger fails to touch any point of the body, the *fechamento* is complete and secure. The candidate is safe from external threats and dangers.

Following the lead of the Christian churches on the one hand, and the Kardecistic spiritist centers on the other, the Afro-Brazilian cults have entered upon programs of social outreach ranging from medical assistance and provision for orphans and the elderly to community service activities. They publish daily and weekly newspapers, and even support candidates for public office in local, state, and national elections. There are no adequate statistics of "membership" or "adherents." A religious census would be difficult to take in which the significance of Afro-Brazilian religious movements could be stated quantitatively. This is in part due to the ease with which crossing of religious lines occurs. Many Catholics and Protestants become involved in the life of *terreiros,* not only as "seekers," but often as "children of faith" as well. Despite the lack of adequate census figures it does seem evident that the Afro-Brazilian cultic movement is thriving and expanding. [45] Long ago it ceased to be an *Afro*-Brazilian phenomenon, or to appeal primarily to members of the lowest socioeconomic stratum. Professionals and intellectuals have been attracted to the movement, and there are centers in which non-Blacks predominate as far as numbers of active participants are concerned. Along with this wider appeal there has come a tendency to "de-Africanize" the movement. Many of the intellectual leaders have stressed pre-African origins and a universal appeal. The suggestion is that Umbanda represents a continuation of the original divine revelation to man, communicated to sub-Saharan African societies and then to Brazilian soil. In keeping with this claim for universality has been the inclusion among the seven lines of spirits of the "Line of the Orient" consisting of representative spirits from Asian religious traditions. References are made to *pretos velhos* of "all races"! Sophistication in symbolism and in music is taking place. Still, in the literature and ritual of the most sophisticated and universally minded circles of the movement, the names of the traditional Yoruba *orixás* continue to be heard and invoked: *Oxalá, Ogun, Xangô, Iemanjá*, and the rest. Exerting diminishing influence in Nigerian Society, they play an ever-increasing role in the lives of contemporary Brazilians, proving to be relevant in a modernized culture which is fast on its way to becoming economically developed and politically powerful.

Saravá Umbanda! Saravá Oxalá! [46]

NOTES

1. J. K. Parratt, "Religious Change in Yoruba Society-A Test Case," in *Journal of Religion in Africa*, II, 2(1969), pp. 111, 127. The Parrinder reference is to *Religion in an African City,* London: Oxford University Press, 1953. Some observers might not agree with such an extreme statement of the decline of traditional Yoruba religion.
2. The latest census figures: 10.96 per cent Black; 25.54 per cent mulatto.
3. For the fullest discussion of these characteristics of the Portuguese as they affected the development of Brazilian culture see the work of Gilberto Freyre, especially *Casa Grande e Senzala* (English translation, *The Masters and The Slaves,* by Samuel Putnam, published by Alfred A. Knopf).
4. Portuguese designations are used throughout.
5. Benguela, Cambinda, Cacanje, Muxicongo, Rebolo.
6. Nago (Yoruba), Gege (Ewe), Fanti, Ashanti, Gá, Txi.
7. Hausa, Kanúri, Tapa, Grúnci, and once again Fula and Mandinga.
8. Portuguese orthography is used: "x" represents the sound "sh." Thus orisa or orisha is written *orixá*, and *Shango* becomes *Xangô.*
9. Literally "Old Blacks," i. e., the spirits of slaves, usually born in

Africa and brought to Brazil. These "elders" of the black communities replaced the great chiefs of the heroic past who possessed the *kilumbu* in pre-slavery African times.

10. The word was used at first to refer to the indigenous peoples of Brazil. It has come to mean in popular parlance halfbreed Amerindian-Europeans, and also anyone who lives in the rural areas of the interior. Religiously it refers to the great Amerindian leaders of the past who become available through the intercession of a medium for assistance and consultation.

11. Literally "enchanted," i.e., the "mysterious" forces of the animal and inanimate worlds.

12. An example of highly complex syncretistic system-building is found in *Umbanda de Todos Nós; A Lei Revelada*, by W. W de Matta e Silva. Rio de Janeiro and Sao Paulo: Livraria Freitas Bastos, S.A., 1960.

13. From *candombe*, a popular slave dance during colonial times named after the kind of drum used as accompaniment.

14. The term used both in Amazonas and in Rio Grande do Sul, with a variation, "Batucajá," in Bahia, which is derived from "atabaque," a kind of drum.

15. The designation of cults in Maranhão, which also refers to a type of drum.

16. *Ma-cumba*: "the elders"; earlier, any of the dancers who became possessed by spirits; perhaps at one time that dancer who specialized in possession by the "trickster" *Exú*.

17. Term used in Amazonas, Pará, and Piauí, referring to the *pajé*, or Amerindian shaman.

18. A heated controversy rages over the derivation of this word. Heli Chatelain published a book in 1894 entitled *Folktales of Angola* in which he suggested that it is related to *quimbanda*, the designation at that time of the "grand priest" of the Bantu centers in Rio. It referred also to Bantu-based rituals as well as to the place where such ritual took place. Since then the word *quimbanda* has come to refer to "black magic" as opposed to *umbanda*, which is "white magic." Many Umbandistas, therefore, tend to object rather strenuously to Chatelain's derivation.

19. Used in Amazonas.

20. A Northeastern designation derived from the word meaning "pipe," which is smoked by the shaman.

21. This is used in Rio Grande do Sul and is probably of Tupí origin. The suggestion has been made, however, that it is a variant pronunciation of "Bara," a term used to designate the trickster *Exú* in the south. It might even be a geographical designation referring to the origin of those who brought the

cult to the southernmost region of the country, viz., the northern state of Para in the Amazon valley.

22. The name widely used in Northeastern Brazil to designate Afro-Brazilian cults.

23. Such as: the prohibition of the use of alcoholic beverages, poisonous plants, and knives in the rituals; placing a curfew at 9:00 P.M. on the use of drums at public ceremonies; placing a curfew at 9:00 P.M. on the participation of minors under sixteen at the rituals.

24. The official documents of the Union and its council, including the Umbandist and Afro-Brazilian Sacerdotal Code, are published in the book *Os Orixás e a Lei de Umbanda*, by Byron T. de Freitas and Wladimir C. de Freitas, Rio de Janeiro: Editora Eco, n.d.—1965?, pp. 77-118.

25. An interesting example of this is given by Alfredo Costa Moura. In the prayers, which he composed for the opening and closing of Ubanda services and which have been widely distributed, Zambi is the name by which the high God is addressed, seven times in the opening prayer and nine times in the closing prayer. In a personal letter to me, however, no reference is made to Zambi, but he does indicate his intention to devote his life to the cause "until *Oxalá*-God calls me," accomplishing everything "to the extent that *Oxala*-God permits." There are four references to "*Oxalá*-God" in the letter, as well as an explicit identification of *Oxalá* with "God or His Son Jesus Christ." Compare this with a more explicit use of the names interchangeably found in a song prescribed for use when a visiting dignitary requests permission to enter into the sanctuary area and participate in a service. The visitor ends his sung request: "*Dá licenca, Babá*" ("Give permission, Father"), and the "Father" (director of the host center) responds by singing: "*A terra não é minha, é de Zambi e Oxalá. Todo filho de Umbanda pode saravá Gongá.*" ("The place is not mine, it belongs to *Zambi* and *Oxalá*. Every child of Umbanda can greet this sacred assembly.") In Laudemir Pessoa, *Ritual de Terreiro Umbandista* Rio de Janeiro: Editora Eco, 1970?, p. 105. *Zambi* (*Zambe, Nzambi*) is a widespread name for God among the Bantu of the Congo and Angola regions.

26. Edison Carneiro considers this an example of Catholic influence. See his *Candombés da Bahia* 3rd ed., Rio de Janeiro: Conquista, 1961, p. 109.

27. In the words of Carneiro: "He is a very popular *orixá*—the physician of the blacks." (*Ibid.*, p. 78.)

28. José Maria Bittencourt, president of the Tenda Pai Jacob in Curitiba, Paraná, ranks him as one of the leading demonic

forces. (*No Reino dos Exús* [Rio de Janeiro; Editora Eco, 1970], pp. 29f., 58ff., 83ff., *et passim*.)

29. Carneiro describes it succinctly: "The *Caboclo encantados* are the same Yoruba and Ewe gods, already modified by the influence of blacks from Angola and the Congo and, more recently, by Spiritualist influence" (*op. cit.*, p. 86).

30. He is also known by his Ewe name, Legba, or in Amerindian tradition as *Martím Pescador* ("Fisher Martin," a bird).

31. Cf. Bittencourt: "According to some authors, the Major State of His Highness Lucifer is composed of 45 or 47 or 49 or 54 elements, with which I am in complete agreement. But, if my Umbandist friends and my Quimbandist and Quiumbandist cousins will examine and test my Organogram, you will see that the number which I present is greater than the other authors, or rather 58.... The major state of His Highness Lucifer is composed of 6 ministers and 2 auxiliaries who transmit the orders to the Lines.... The Realm of *Exús* is composed of 7 Lines, each Line of 7 Phalanxes...." (*op. cit.*, pp. 83f.)

32. Cf. José Ribeiro de Souza: "*Ogun* is one, but he has 7 names because the numbers are associated with him." (*Cerimonias da Umbanda e do Candomblé*. Rio de Janeiro: Editora Eco, 1970?, p. 134.)

33. In addition to the spirits of African-born slaves there are several spirits which represent national or tribal origins: Rei Congo (the "King of the Congo"), Pai Bengüela, Pai Cabinda, Pai Guiné, Pai José d'Angola.

34. The introduction of the word "medium" is doubtless due to the influence of Kardec spiritism.

35. *Catecismo de Umbanda* São Paulo: Círculo Internacional de Umbanda, n/d , pp. 44f.

36. There are many designations for the centers. The most widely used are *terreiro* (literally, "terrace," plaza, marketplace) and and *tenda* (literally, "tent," booth, shop).

37. Literally, "hand of the knife." The Yoruba designation: *Oxogun*. At times this word means "he who kills quadrupeds," and "*Alô-Oxogun*" is used to refer to "he who kills bipeds"[fowl].

38. E.g., "...all and every food of the saint is prepared in pans of clay, and cooked over a fire of wood or coal, never in pans of aluminum, and never on a gas or kerosene stove." (José Ribeiro de Souza. *Comidas de Santo e Oferendas*. Rio de Janeiro: Editora Eco, 4th éd., n.d., p. 9.)

39. Literally "shell game." The method is described in William

Russell Bascom, *Ifa divination: communication between gods and men in West Africa.* Bloomington: Indiana University Press, 1969.

40. For fuller descriptions: Edison Carneiro. *op. cit.,* pp. 113-118; and José Ribeiro de Souza, *Candomblé no Brasil: Feitichismo Religioso Afro-Ameríndio.* Rio de Janeiro: Editôra Espiritualista, 2nd ed., 1957, pp. 73-82.

41. Literally, "horse." Several images are used to refer to the relation between medium and spirit. The spirit "rides" the medium, or is "seated on the head" of the medium.

42. It is usually drawn with chalk as part of a ceremony, although the signs do appear sewn on articles of clothing and in artwork. In the latter case they are merely symbols for the spirits, but when actually drawn during a ritual they take on the nature of symbolic presence. There has been a decided evolution in the symbolism. Many of the signs in their modern form   reveal the complex syncretism which characterizes the movement. There have been attempts to standardize the symbolism and to develop a logical rationale for it, but these have not proved successful as yet.

43. E.g., "Who goes there? It is St. George, come to kill the dragon. Who sent him? God, owner and builder of all things, sent him and gave him power to conquer. Overcome the dragon, O glorious St. George, overcome my enemies with your sacred sword and your white horse. May all the evil cast against me by my visible and invisible brethren be trampled under foot, and all works of magic be cut off before they reach me. Do thou serve me as a shield, my glorious St. George. Amen. All hail St. George! All hail his phalanx! All hail St. Sebastian!" (Sílvio Pereira Maciel, *Alquimia de Umbanda.* Rio de Janeiro: Centro Espiritualista Fraternidade, 1951, pp. 90f.)

44. E.g., "I shall walk clothed and armed with the armour of St. George so that my enemies having feet cannot reach me, having hands cannot grasp me; having eyes cannot discern me, and cannot even think of doing evil to me. Firearms cannot reach my body; knives and lances will break without touching my body; cords and ropes will break without binding my body....Oh! glorious St. George, in the name of the phalanx of the divine Holy Spirit, extend your shield and your powerful weapons."(José Ribeiro de Souza, *Candomblé no Brasil.* Rio de Janeiro: Editôra Espiritualista, 2nd ed., p. 38.)

45. "A university professor in Rio de Janeiro has warned that the Catholic Church in Brazil is losing many of its members to fast-growing African cults. Basing his analysis on a recently

completed three-year study of the cults, Father Valdeli Carvalho da Costa said that although 90 per cent of the 93 million Brazilians are nominally Catholics, many practice both Catholicism and cultism." (*The Christian Century*, March 1, 1972, p. 244.)

46. The traditional "All Hail!"

10

African Religions and the Quest for Afro-American Heritage

Charles S. Brown and Yvonne R. Chappelle

BLACK INTEREST IN AFRICA

A significant group of Blackamericans [1] is presently engaged in a "quest" involving both *discovery* and *re-creation* of their identity. The quest turns on two axes: (1) the meaning of being Black in America; and (2) the African component of *blackness*.

This is not the first time the former question has been raised. Indeed, there has been a significantly long history of attention to this question by Black individuals and groups which has been generally ignored largely because it has not conformed to socially and culturally legitimated modes of stating the problem of Black existence in America, [2] nor was it regarded by many Blacks as a desirable concern in their efforts to improve their lot in American society. [3] Thus, contemporary Black interest in Africa results from the convergence of the emergent "Black consciousness" of the late nineteen-sixties with the continuing concerns of an existent group of African nationalists among Blackamericans.

What is new is the fact that the contemporary movement has probably a larger following among Black intellectuals, in particular, and the Black middle class in general, than has been true at any other time in the history of this concern. The extent of participation has also been influenced, undoubtedly, by the rise of African independence from colonial control in the second half of the twentieth century.

African religions are significant for this quest, in that religion contains core elements of culture and personality. Religious life focuses on the *meanings* and *meaning-apprehending* qualities of human experience; it also expresses the *integrity* of human identity. In this respect, the rise of African independence takes on added significance as the fundamental factor in the new "respectability" enjoyed by African religions as carriers of the past.

Blackamericans engaged in the quest described above view African religious life as providing important cues to their own cultural heritage as well as the heritage of contemporary Africans. They understand that portion of their cultural heritage to be marred by the discontinuities involved in the American experience, but they also regard it as *subliminally* present in their feelings, perceptions, and attitudes. [4] The concern of those engaged in the quest is not limited to *recovery of the past*. It also includes *interpretation of the present* and *creation of the future*. Thus, the forms and content of African religions are of interest in the quest because of their contribution to present choices, in addition to their potential role of explaining the past.

This "interest" is engaged in unabashedly by its most committed practitioners, among whom the authors would include themselves. On the one hand, it is a fundamental consideration in the development of authentic "Black consciousness." Africa is clearly the *motherland* of Americans who know themselves, and are known, by the color designation "black." This has much to do with the fact that Africa is the *primordial "spiritual home"* of American Blacks as well as the geographic location of their ethnic origin.

Ultimately, the "roots" of blackness are to be found in Africa. It is in this sense that the quest acquires profound existential significance for Blackamerican identity. Indeed, C. Shelby Rooks suggests that the image "of an African Diaspora, based on the Biblical story of the Babylonian Exile and the Final Jewish Diaspora," is a more accurate, and a more useful, image in "the quest for Black selfhood" than the prevailing Exodus image. [5] Referring to the implications this has for Black theology, he writes: "Black theology in these days must construct or utilize a new image that lifts up the African roots of Blackamericans, an image that recognizes an extended sojourn in an alien culture, and that fixes the collective eye on a future unconnected with physical possession of this land or assimilation of its culture." [6]

However, more than the identity of Blackamericans is at stake. To the extent that Americans of African descent have been *actors* in the American experience, that experience itself has an African component. [7] This means that inquiry into the Africanness of American Blacks is *essential* to a more complete understanding of the American experience—a consideration that needs increased attention in the discussion of ethnic and national identities that is presently underway in America. As Shelby Rooks indicates, Black-americans constitute *a particular group of Africans,* different from the present inhabitants of the continent yet related to them by unique historical and cultural bonds that make these Americans participants in the identity "African." Thus, the influence of Africa on America through the presence of this group of "Africans in exile" is a seldom asked question that increasingly demands answers.

For these reasons, the authors are convinced that the commitment implied in the interest described above makes it no less credible—or more suspect—than any other "interest" in the investigation of African culture. It introduces important and, at points, essential questions into the investigation. It also has the advantage of being *an explicit cultural interest.* By contrast, some kinds of interest in the study of religions mask cultural commitments that shape the findings even though the study is carried out under the rubric of "objectivity" and "value free" research.

Granted the importance of *scientific integrity* in the study of religion, it does not necessarily follow that those who have no participant interest in a religious tradition are more accurate interpreters of it than those who have a participant interest. The integral relation of facts and meanings in the data of religion contributes to the authenticity of both approaches in the study of religion. Neither approach is self-validating; nor is either, solely by definition, invalid. Both commitment and detachment have a long history of contribution to the understanding of religious life. The issue is the validity of the aims, methodology, and findings of such studies, and their uses in interpreting and molding religious life in Africa and America.

Thus Blackamericans involved in the quest described above boldly combine the effort to gain knowledge of African religion with concerns flowing from a prior *motivating interest* in issues of identity and commitment. In so doing, they assume freedom to invest the meanings discovered there with meanings appropriate to their own situation and experience, since their interest in African religion has to do with understanding their blackness rather than a concern to explore "exotic" or "primitive" cultures.

METHODOLOGICAL AND CULTURAL CONSIDERATIONS

Methodological issues involved in the quest for Afro-American heritage have been well stated by Roger Bastide, who treats the question of "African survivals" versus total obliteration of the African heritage as a matter requiring careful determination. [8] Previous choices pivoted around acceptance or rejection of the methodological presuppositions of Melville Herskovits, [9] E. Franklin Frazier, [10] or others [11] whose theories, Bastide suggests, are probably rooted in ideological considerations and the disciplinary approaches of the theorists. By contrast, he recommends more careful attention to the social and historical context of the phenomena being interpreted:

> The mistake, as it seems to me, that all these theories make is that of being over-systematic, of attempting to explain what I consider a highly complex and variegated group of cultural features by some one single factor—whether this be collective memory, social disintegration induced by slavery, or the economic conditions prevailing in America. One gets the feeling that in such cases the choice is dictated (more or less consciously) by ideological considerations (e.g. negritude or national integration), rather than by any desire to work out an interpretation that fits all the facts. . . . My own personal feeling is that all these factors have had, or continue to have, some influence—but that some weigh more heavily than others, depending on the social context in which they occur. The most important thing is not to confuse cultural characteristics which bear a superficial resemblance to one another, but in fact are fundamentally opposed. [12]

Implementation of this approach involves an important reversal of the order of investigation of African and Afro-American cultural patterns. Noting the difficulty in tracing the specific ethnic origins of imported Africans, some of whom "have left no surviving trace of their native cultures," Bastide suggests that "the best method of investigating Afro-American social groups is not to start in Africa, and see how much of what we find there survives across the Atlantic, but rather to study Afro-American cultural patterns as they exist today, and then work gradually back from them towards Africa." [13]

On this basis, Bastide distinguishes between three types of culture: (1) *African*, in which older African traditions are faithfully preserved; (2) *Afro-American*, in which mutually supportive traditions of two cultures are fused, as in religious syncretism; and (3) *Negro*, cultural patterns, devoid of African survivals, that have been *created in response to environmental pressures*. Despite clear evidence of African influences in lowerclass religion and one of their major folkloric traditions, [14] the greater part of the social and cultural life of Blackamericans belongs to the "Negro" type of culture identified by Bastide. This situation defines the limitations as well as the possibilities in the quest for Afro-American heritage.

These limitations and possibilities are expressed in Bastide's concept of "Negro culture." On the one hand, in agreement with Frazier, Bastide views Negro culture as lacking valid African cultural elements. [15] On the other hand, in opposition to Frazier, Bastide maintains that Negro cultures differ from the dominant white cultures with which they are associated:

> Thus, side by side with African culture—though a certain amount of interpenetration does take place between them—we find an original Negro culture, with its own laws, which are quite different from those governing a white society. A superficial theory of acculturation cannot take this distinction into account, since for its advocates anything not African has to be white, and whatever does not derive from ancestral tradition is assumed to be borrowed from the customs of the master-race. This kind of thinking ignores the part played by adaptation, the influence which economic infrastructures can have on the creation of social superstructures, and, indeed, the whole basic process by which civilizations are formed—the mental or motor response to a highly variable range of factual situations.[16]

Further, and more important to the topic under consideration, Bastide finds that individual and group "mental patterns" provide the most important link between African and Negro cultures. In this respect, Negro cultures, as responses to a new environment, have been "filtered through a mentality which, in many if not all respects (e.g., the passion for brotherhood associations or acts of collective communion) is still shaped by the old traditions of African culture." [17]

This line of inquiry, suggested rather than developed by Bastide, is an important consideration in the quest for Afro-American heritage in the United States. Frazier and others are quite right in their contention that, in terms of institutions, Blackamerican social life is an American rather than an African phenomenon. However, continuity with African backgrounds is not to be found in institutional forms alone. The most frequent, and the most subtle, form of their expression is the perceptual orientation that informed the adaptation to American society. In this process, African cultural traditions have both *undergone transformation* and *survived* in the American context. Thus, John Lovell describes Blackamerican spirituals as African folk songs in which the basic African element was not eroded by slavery. On the contrary, he writes,

> the evidence points to the conclusion that the ruggedness of American slavery developed the African element in new and

unexpected ways. The songs, African in root and branch, were charged with new life and new color by the challenges and chemistry of an utterly brutal slave experience. The fact that they were African is attested by President Senghor of Senegal, by Nicholas George Julius Ballanta Taylor, and by other Africans. These incontestable witnesses have affirmed that the identical melodies and the sentiments of many songs have been heard for centuries and can still be heard in the outlying districts of Africa.[18]

The basis for this line of interpretation of African influence is an understanding of persons as "carriers-of-culture." Thus, Bastide writes,

The slave ships carried not only men, women and children, but also their gods, beliefs, and traditional folklore. They maintained a stubborn resistance against their white oppressors, who were determined to tear them loose, by force if need be, from their own cultural patterns, and acclimatise them to those of the west.[19]

and Charles Long points out that

The persistence of elements of what some anthropologists have called 'soft culture' means that given even the systematic breakdown of African cultural forms in the history of North American slavery, the slaves did not confront America with a religious tabula rasa. If not the content of culture, a characteristic mode of orienting and perceiving reality has probably persisted.[20]

Admittedly, institutional forms are the most accurate "carriers" in this sense, but, lacking opportunity for continuity in institutional expression of culture traditions, the resulting discontinuity includes the given cultural orientation of the persons who are required to adjust to a new situation. Their adjustment, then, is always, in some sense, an *adaptation* of the new requirements to the old way of life. And, even when the adjustment is forced, mechanisms of *selectivity* operate to add an adaptive dimension. The point at stake in the present discussion is to *emphasize* the fact that adaptation has occurred alongside adjustment in order to correct previous understandings which excluded consideration of perceptual aspects of African influence. The nature and boundaries of such influence can only be determined when its relevance to the consideration of African backgrounds is acknowledged.

An additional methodological problem has to do with the fact that, as Long puts it, Africa is a *religious image* as well as a historical reality in the experience of Blackamericans.[21] Indeed, the quest for Afro-American heritage is fueled more by imaginal capacity to participate in African identity than by the persistence of African modes of perceiving reality. The latter are in fact discovered and enhanced by persons who have been motivated by the former.

Discontinuities intrinsic to the American experience have, for the most part, severed the direct connection between Afro-American institutions and their African cultural origins. Unlike Americans of European descent, who, when necessary, have been able to recover and reproduce previously abandoned cultural institutions, Black-americans participate in African heritage through a process of *recreation.* African identity on the continent and in America is multi-form and dynamic. This fact has much to do with the impact of Africa as a historical realtiy on the quest and the interpenetration between that reality and the imaginal character of Blackamerican participation in African identity.

Historically, Africa is a more diverse place of origin than the shape of the quest suggests. Black Africa is made up of a number of societies. In this sense, the origins to be found there are multi-ethnic as far as language, culture, and social organizations are concerned. However, there is also a broad cultural unity among the West African societies from whence the majority of Black slaves in America came. Thus, based on the findings of C. Darryl Forde and Joseph Greenberg, Long cites an underlying cultural unity of language *and* religious forms among West African societies and the common situation of slaves in America as potential bases for the persistence of an "African style" among Americans of African descent. [22]

Moreover, the American experience itself had the effect of forging a unique *unity of ethnic identity* among slaves and free Blacks. Tribal differences crumbled under the myriad pressures to create a *single class* and ethnic group out of the different African peoples brought to America for the purpose of enslavement. Thus, the American experience created a new group of "Africans," conscious of themselves as originating from a single land mass which they soon perceived as a geographical and cultural unity.

This perception of Africa as a cultural unit remains a central ingredient of the quest for existential, practical, and religious reasons. Existentially, Blackamericans have experienced this oneness of identification with Africa in their own constitution as a people, despite varying origins and *profound* internal and external tensions. Practically, the particular ethnic heritages of the majority of Blackamericans are irrecoverable [23] and, even if discovered, do not solve the problem of their common fate. Religiously, Africa, understood as the land of origins, has been invested with important symbolic meaning in a variety of Blackamerican religious movements. [24]

To affirm this mode of identification with Africa should not be taken to suggest an unambiguous commitment to African identity among Blackamericans. All of the particular, distinguishing, identities—*Black, slave, African*—have been treated as barriers to assimilation of Blackamericans into the American mainstream. Subconsciously, among white Americans, Blacks could qualify as persons only if they could be regarded as "non-threatening," or *nothing-other-than-white*. Pressure to prove that Blackamericans were no different than (and no threat to) the white majority required Blacks to separate themselves from all non-white (and anti-white) identities.

Thus, Africa, as an "image" in the mind of whites, [25] as the source of the problematic skin color black, and as a subject continent, has stood "over-against" Blacks in their struggle for survival and security in America. In this sense, the quest for Afro-American heritage represents a reintegration of the personal and cultural history of Balckamericans. It also represents one in a series of efforts to come to terms with the opposition, as well as the opportunities, intrinsic to the identification *Black*. As Long indicates, Black response to this situation—even under conditions of slavery—was both *adaptive* and *creative*:

> The slave had to come to terms with the opaqueness of his condition and at the same time oppose it. He had to experience the truth of his negativity and at the same time transform and create *an-other* reality. Given the limitations imposed upon him, he created on the level of his religious consciousness. Not only did this transformation produce new cultural forms, but its significance must be understood from the point of view of the creativity of the transforming process itself. [26]

The contemporary quest for Afro-American heritage is such an adaptive-creative venture. It involves the appropriation of Black identity through affirmation of its African origins, the effort to identify the role of African origins in shaping the religious consciousness of Blackamericans, and inquiry into the implications of African identity for the theological, normative, and constructive (political, social, and ecclesiastical) tasks facing Blackamericans. It also has important implications for Africa as well as America. These implications may be positive or negative depending on the extent to which the venture comes to terms with Africa, in terms of Africa itself, and does not confuse images generated by apologetic interests with African reality. [27]

IN PURSUIT OF THE INTEREST

For the Blackamerican who approaches the study of Africa with a partisan "interest," the undertaking is fraught with difficulty; for one thing, published information is scarce. The American scholar has always been discouraged from studying Africa because of the long-held prejudice that there was nothing of value to be gained from such investigation. African studies has become a "legitimate" subject of study only since World War II, when the more insightful scholars began to see the inexorable march toward independence of the colonies of the world, and to understand the significance of this development in the light of the United Nations, the cold war and geo-politics.

Another factor contributing to the paucity in America of meaningful scholarship on Africa is the fact that America has had no colonies in Africa, and little presence on the continent. Although American missionaries settled throughout Africa, information generated by their presence seems to have been primarily for the use of other missionaries headed for that continent. The curiosity about Africa that was nurtured in Europe by the fact of colonization was not so present in America. Moreover, information current in Europe rarely crossed the Atlantic because of our own ethnocentrism and isolationism.

A more serious problem for the "interested" Black scholar is the matter of putting the facts into perspective. What has been the case is that, even when the information was available, it was usually distorted, misinterpreted, and negative. Indeed, how could it have been otherwise when the whole rationalization for the African slave trade, and later for the colonization of Africa, was based upon the supposed high purpose of "civilizing those child-like people." African societies were examined and judged on the basis of the cultural perspectives of Western observers, and they were found to be illogical from these foreign frames of reference. No attempt was made to discover the inherent perspectives which determined the character of these societies, so as to enable a valid assessment of the logic of African cultures.

As recently as 1945, Possoz could say in his introduction to Father Tempels' book, *Bantu Philosophy,* that

> Up to the present ethnographers have denied all abstract thought to tribal peoples. The civilized Christian European was exalted, the savage and pagan primitive man was denigrated.[28]

Even today, it is difficult for the Western-born observer of Africa to overcome labels like "primitive," "childish," "pagan," "animistic," and "savage" in examining African culture.

Nowhere are the tragic results of this misguided scholarship more evident than in the study of African religions. Here, Western myths about Africa are inextricably interwoven with Western understandings of Christianity and its opposite, paganism or heathenism. These myths include the notions that:

1. "Pagan" religions are primitive and inferior.

2. Nothing in traditional African religions, culture, or history has contributed to the development of Christianity.

3. In order to be saved, the African must reject traditional religious values and practices *in toto*, and adopt whole cloth the values and practices of Christianity (i.e., of the Christian sect seeking to convert him.)

4. The primitive African mind is a *tabula rasa* on which may be imprinted in assembly-line fashion the Western ontological system.

5. As Africans became Christianized through slavery or through colonial annexation, they "lost" their traditional African religious values and characteristics.

6. Differences between African Christian sects (on the continent or in the diaspora) and their Western counterparts may for the most part be explained as imperfect imitations by the Africans of Christianity as they observe it. [29]

Permit us to postulate, however, a series of new myths to be based on new evidence and on new interpretations of the old evidence. The authors believe that:

1. African traditional religions are based on sophisticated cosmological notions, consistently applied.

2. African traditional religions have contributed to Christianity at every stage of its evolution.

3. African converts to Christianity often are able to accept Christianity because they find it possible to accommodate important aspects of traditional beliefs with aspects of Christian doctrine.

4. Some of the differences between African Christian churches (wherever they exist) and their Western counterparts may be explained as survivals of African traditional beliefs and customs.

In order that these new myths might prevail, certainly one must begin to reexamine the evidence already available. Let us take, for example, an observation from the autobiography of Olandah Equiano, also known as Gustavus Vassa, the African. Writing in 1789, Equiano observed that he had always been struck by "the strong analogy which...appears to prevail in the manners and customs of my countrymen and those of the Jews, before they reached the land of promise, and particularly the patriarchs while they were yet in that. pastoral state which is described in Genesis—an analogy, which alone would induce me to think that the one people had sprung from the other." [30]

Equiano, an Ibo, had been kidnapped and sold into slavery at the age of eleven. He spent most of his life in bondage to sea captains of the West Indies and of North America. His travels with them enabled him to know a good deal of the world. He was a keen observer, and had read extensively during his free time at sea. Thus, this similarity he saw between the Ibo and the Hebrew cultures had been tested and tried by him before he made it known. Equiano went to great pains in his autobiography to support this theory. He cited the work of the leading theologians of the day, whose conclusions also suggested a link between the two peoples. However, his principal basis for the opinion is the strong resemblance between the cultures.

Like the Israelites in their primitive state, our government was conducted by our chiefs or judges, our wise men and elders; and the head of a family with us enjoyed a similar authority over his household, with that which is ascribed to Abraham and the other patriarchs. The law of retaliation obtained almost universally with us as with them....We had our circumcision..., we had our burnt offerings, our washings, our purifications, and on the same occasions as they did. [31]

Equiano's observations made it clear that there exist within African cultures practices and beliefs which Western man has sought to understand, and has even admired and venerated—when they were found characteristic of Hebrew culture. Yet, Western scholars have been on the whole unable or unwilling to get past the derogatory labels, and to seek equal understanding of African societies. These scholars have rarely interpreted observations about Africa in ways which would acknowledge that the traditional African is a complicated and sophisticated human being whose world view, while different from that of his neighbors to the North and West, is nonetheless consistent, logical, and worthy of respect.

There is also a lesson to be learned from the conclusion drawn by Equiano on the basis of his observations. A product of his times, the African slave looked at the evidence and determined that the Ibo were of Hebrew origin. Yet, this same set of facts could be explained by a variety of other theses. For example, the Ibo and Hebrew tribes may have had a similar pattern of evolution purely by coincidence. Or, they may each have been influenced by a third society. It could also be that the Hebrews are of Ibo origin, rather than the other way around. Thus there are several different interpretations possible for the same body of facts; the interpretation one chooses is largely influenced by the perspective from which one proceeds. The important point is that if Africa is to be interpreted with honesty and with integrity, it is essential that the interpreters take seriously *African* perspectives. As Father Tempels put it:

> Folklore alone and superficial descriptions of strange customs cannot enable us to discover and understand primitive man.... If in fact, primitive peoples have a concrete conception of being and of universe, this "ontology" of theirs will give a special character, a local colour, to their beliefs and religious practices, to their mores, to their language, to their institutions and customs, to their psychological reactions and, more generally, to their whole behavior. [32]

Information about African peoples and cultures that seeks to take into account the perspectives from which they have evolved is only now beginning to be generally available in the Western world. New insights into the body of recorded fact are now possible. It is also possible to begin to evaluate the myths about Africa which have been thrust upon us.

For the "interested" scholar of African religions who is immersed in the historical misinterpretations which prevail in the West, there is a need to pursue avenues of study which dispel these misinterpretations, which restore dignity to our understanding of Africa, and which help to link the African in diaspora to his heritage. The authors propose, in this regard, vigorous efforts to:

1. Analyze points of similarity and of differences between African traditional beliefs and Christian doctrine;

2. Seek out historical, anthropological, and other evidence tending to link African cultures to Judaism and to Christianity;

3. Examine similarities between indigenous Christian churches in Africa and Black churches elsewhere in the world; and

4. Look for practices within Black churches outside of Africa which appear to reflect African traditions.

The results of these studies must be fairly presented by individuals with a clear sense of the human dignity of all mankind, and with a concomitant ability to respect and to value ideas different from their own. This is the only hope for putting Africa into perspective.

We have suggested one point at which the study of African traditional religion contributes to the quest for the Afro-American heritage: the similarities between the traditional beliefs and practices and those of Biblical religion. This provides a basis upon which Afro-Americans can claim Christianity as their own, not simply as the result of outside influence. Becoming Christian, whether in Africa or the diaspora, does not necessarily mean an abandonment of African roots. In fact, it may well be that Biblical religion has closer affin'. ies with the African tradition than with the classical tradition of the West, that an African ontology provides a more appropriate context for Christianity than does a Greek ontology.

NOTES

1. This term is adapted from its use by C. Eric Lincoln in a paper on "The Black Church and the Black Community" presented to the Theological Colloquium of the National Committee of Black Churchmen at Interdenominational Theological Center in Atlanta, Georgia during the Spring of 1970.
2. E. U. Essien-Udom, *Black Nationalism: A Search for Identity in America.* Chicago: The University of Chicago Press, 1962, Chapter II, "The Nationalist Tradition"; also John H. Bracey, Jr., August Meier and Elliot Rudwick, eds., *Black Nationalism in America.* Indianapolis: The Bobbs-Merill Company, Inc., 1970.
3. Essien-Udom, *Black Nationalism*, pp. 1-4.
4. Charles H. Long, "Perspectives for a Study of Afro-American Religion in the United States," *History of Religions*, vol. XI, No. 1 (August, 1971), p. 57; also W.E.B. DuBois' comments on "The Gift of the Spirit" in *The Gift of Black Folk.* Boston, Mass.: The Stratford Co., 1924, p. 320.
5. C. Shelby Rooks, "Toward the Promised Land," The 1972 Scott Lectures, Texas Christian University, February 15-17, 1972, pp. 7-14.
6. *Ibid.*, p. 10.
7. DuBois, *The Gift of Black Folk*, p. 320.
8. Roger Bastide, *African Civilisations in the New World*, trans. Peter Green. New York: Harper and Row, 1971.
9. *The Myth of the Negro Past*, 2nd ed., rev. Boston: Beacon Press, 1958 .
10. *The Negro in the United States.* New York: The Macmillan Co., 1949, pp. 3-21.
11. Bastide, *African Civilizations,* pp. 33-36.
12. *Ibid.*, p. 37.
13. *Ibid.*, p. 8.
14. *Ibid.*, pp. 164-165, and p. 174 respectively.

15. *Ibid.*, pp. 24, 43, 194-210.
16. *Ibid.*, p. 208.
17. *Ibid.*, p. 210.
18. John Lovell, Jr., *Black Song: The Forge and the Flame*. New York: The Macmillan Co., 1972, p. 136.
19. Bastide, *African Civilisations*, p. 23.
20. Long, "Perspectives," p. 57.
21. *Ibid.*, pp. 56-58.
22. *Ibid.*
23. An important exception to this statement is Alex Haley's experience in tracing a fragment of oral history in his own family to precise African origins, including contact with contemporary African members of the family. Alex Haley, *Roots*, New York: Doubleday & Co., 1974.
24. Long, "Perspectives," pp. 56-58.
25. Philip D. Curtin, *The Image of Africa*. Madison: The University of Wisconsin Press, 1964.
26. Long, "Perspectives," p. 59.
27. Bastide, *African Civilisations*, pp. 214f and 217-223.
28. Placide Tempels, *Bantu Philosophny*. Paris: Presence Africaine, 1959, p. 14.
29. For an early attempt by a Black scholar at a refutation of some of these myths, see William Leo Hansberry, "Indigenous African Religions," in *Africa from the Point of View of American Negro Scholars*. Paris: Presence Africaine, 1958.
30. As quoted in Richard Barksdale and Kenneth Kinnamon, *Black Writers of America: A Comprehensive Anthology*. New York: The Macmillan Company, 1972, pp. 13-14.
31. *Ibid.*, p. 14.
32. Tempels, *Bantu Philosophy*, p. 23.

11

Traditional Christianity as an African Religion

Calvin Rieber

In studying the religion of Africa, it is customary to see the tribal religions and Islam as traditional to Africa while considering Christianity as a European import not indigenous to Africa. Consequently Black Americans who are seeking to recover their roots are likely to reject Christianity while being open to either the tribal religions or Islam. This response is quite understandable in view of the way whites have so often taken Christianity as their possession and used it to maintain their suppression of other races. Other facts should not be forgotten, however. Christianity, like Islam, originally came to Africa from the Middle East and it had become the predominant religion of North Africa before the rise of Islam. More important for our purposes is the generally ignored but impressive history of Black involvement in the propagation of Christianity in sub-Saharan Africa. This essay seeks to affirm that Christianity is an African religion by showing how much its introduction into tropical Africa was carried out by Blacks who led in the establishment of churches related to western denominations but of distinctive African character. The equally valid claims of Christianity to be an African religion by right of its early North African and Ethiopian existence or by right of the existence of large numbers of independent African churches not related to the traditional Western denominations are widely treated elsewhere.

EVANGELIZATION BY COLONIZATION

Although Christianity entered Africa in the first century after Christ, according to our present knowledge it did not have a strong influence south of the Sahara until the beginning of the Protestant missionary era. During the earlier age of exploration the Portuguese touched the west coast near the end of the fifteenth century and the Jesuits began working there. Later the Dutch and English centers in the seventeenth and eighteenth centuries also had chaplains who ministered to Africans. [1]

These efforts were offset by the bad examples of Europeans and they were also forbidden when it became clear that the conversion of Africans hindered the slave trade. [2] It was only with the British awakening to the evil of slave trade that widespread efforts were begun on behalf of Africa. These efforts took three main directions: 1) The establishment of colonies of freed slaves; 2) the halting of the slave trade; 3) missionary endeavors in Africa. All three of these resulted in large participation of Blacks in establishing Christianity in west Africa.

As a result of the evangelical revival in the eighteenth century, a group from England known as the Clapham sect became deeply involved in the issue of slavery. One of its members, Granville Sharp, secured in 1772 a judgment that ruled the holding of slaves as contrary to the law of England. This meant that henceforth all slaves in England were free men. [3] This created a new problem, for Blacks were cast adrift by their former masters to become destitute. The problem was increased after American independence by Blacks who had fought on the British side. In addition to relieving this problem, the establishment in Sierra Leone of a "civilized colony" where free men cultivated the soil and opened schools that "native children" also could attend was seen as a witness against the slave trade and for a free Africa. [4]

The original party of 411 "Black poor" from around London arrived in Sierra Leone in 1787 but were depleted to 130 survivors within a year. In 1792 they were joined by over 1,200 Blacks who had served the British in the American Revolution and had settled in Nova Scotia. Unhappy with the climate, they were glad to return to Africa. In 1800 a group known as "Maroons" also arrived. They had revolted against the British in Jamaica and, after an offer of equable peace terms, were tricked into leaving their stronghold, then captured and removed to Nova Scotia. [5]

These settlers brought with them the faith they had acquired in their exile as naturally as the Pilgrims brought their faith to America or as the American pioneers carried theirs across the plains. They organized their churches under their own pastors and witnessed to those who came to the colony after them. Even at this point they did not bring an unadapted European Christianity; the Christian faith had become their own and they lived and proclaimed it as such. The likeness of their situation to that of the Pilgrims is made vivid in a report of the Nova Scotian settlers arriving in Sierra Leone at a bad time of the year with many having died of fever on the way. As they disembarked and marched singing into the forest, the Bible was carried at the front with their preachers leading the way. Immediately they proceeded into a service of worship. [6]

Frederick Bultman, a German missionary of the Church Missionary Society, affirmed the effectiveness of one of these preachers, the Reverend Joseph Jewell, when he wrote of him, "he has been ... the instrument of converting hundreds and inducing thousands ... to receive baptism at his hands. " [7]

When in 1807 the British Parliament passed a law making the slave trade illegal within the British Empire, and an Order in Council established a Vice Admiralty Court for handling cases of captured slaves, a new group was added to the population, and the number of people rose from 2,000 in 1807 to about 45,000 in 1850, chiefly liberated slaves. [8] These recaptives of mid-passage set free in Sierra Leone found in Christianity a new religion that met their needs. It took no account of their diverse origins and addressed them as individuals of value. The accent on personal conversion and responsibility appealed to those cut off from their tribal customs, and the form of Christianity proclaimed by the Nova Scotians provided warmth and group experience while granting opportunities for leadership by laymen seeking a place in the new society. [9]

Although American colonization efforts centered in the area which became Liberia, its pioneer expedition went to Sierra Leone and was led and financed by an American Black. Paul Cuffe, a Massachusetts merchant and shipowner, whose father had come from Africa as a slave and earned his freedom, took thirty-eight persons to Sierra Leone as colonists in 1815 and paid $4,000 of their expenses. [10]

The American Colonization Society, which became the chief manifestation of American concern, revealed the very mixed motives that led to support of Negro migration to Africa. While there were those who genuinely believed that Blacks desired and would be helped by a return to Africa, even these were influenced by the unwillingness to grant equality to freed Blacks. Others were afraid of the incitement to freedom created by the presence of those already free. They wanted Blacks out of the way to whatever place. Still others saw colonization as a profitable business enterprise. Because of these factors and a complete failure to communicate with Blacks in order to learn their desires, the efforts of the society did not gain great Black support. [11]

Nevertheless, enough Blacks did go to make possible the

establishment of colonies in Liberia. In 1820 the first party of eighty-eight began a succession of colonists which led to a total population of American origin of 2,281 in 1838. As these people carried with them their Christian faith, churches were formed, reflecting the variety of denominations from which they had come in the United States. Baptists and Methodists had the largest numbers, with Presbyterians and Episcopalians also present. While some white missionaries were sent from time to time, because of climate-produced illness there never was significant personal or financial continuity of support. The churches of the colonists were begun and continued by Blacks, and the strength of their efforts is indicated by the officially Christian complexion of the City of Monrovia and the government leadership of Liberia to this day.

There were many strong leaders but none more impressive than Lott Carey, one of two ministers who went with the party in 1821. To go to Liberia he gave up a pastorate of nearly 800 members, a home worth $1,500, and a salary of $1,000. By 1825 he had a church in Liberia with a building and more than sixty members. He became a leader of the whole Black community and led in dealings with the white-imposed leadership of the Colonization Society. It was reported of him that he was "active in church work, interested in school affairs, instructed the recaptured African, aiding the care of the sick." [12]

The hope that the colonists would become the evangelists of the African tribes was never completely fulfilled for reasons that are understood by any who observe the encystment of colonies everywhere in the world. Nevertheless a Liberian Baptist Missionary Society was formed in 1826, and in 1827 it had forty-five members who had paid a dollar each for membership. This society was directly involved in the formation of at least one school and church. [13]

The major expansion of Christianity by the colonists beyond their own number and the recaptured Africans came in a different way from Sierra Leone. Among the liberated Africans there were numbers who were originally from the Egba, Yoruba, Kanuri, Hausa, Nupe, and Igbo peoples of Nigeria, a few of whom returned home. The Niger Expedition of 1841 was expected to pave the way for the return of many more who would then create evangelizing and "civilizing" centers. Even though this expedition failed, an emigration began to Abeokuta and other places in Yoruba Country. in 1851 estimates set the numbers of emigrants at Abeokuta as 3,000. [14]

The emigrants wished missionaries and both the English Methodists and the Church Missionary Society (C.M.S.) responded.

Thomas Birch Freeman accompanied by William de Graft went to Badagari in 1842 from Cape Coast and, finding that most returnees had gone on to Abeokuta, followed them there. Freeman was of mixed blood and de Graft was African. De Graft stayed at Badagari when Freeman returned to Cape Coast, began regular services and opened a day school, attended mostly by children of emigrants. [15] In 1844 the Church Missionary Society sent an African agent to Abeokuta who was followed by the Reverend H. Townsend and the Reverend Samuel Crowther, who was also an African. In 1846 a church and three temporary chapels were begun and twenty-eight persons were under membership instruction within the year. Crowther's own mother was one of the first to be baptized. [16] The returnees formed a particular social class with Western knowledge but they had returned because they wanted to belong to the people of their birth. Thus they did not become as separate as those in Sierra Leone and Liberia, and those who remained Christian were influenced by traditional ways. Thus they became the nucleus of an African Church that included eventually many more natives of the area than returnees.

After the Yorubas began to return to their land, Igbos also went back to the Niger area. In smaller numbers other emigrants returned to Nigeria from the West Indies and Brazil. [17] The Christians among those also became nuclei of the church in other parts of Nigeria. Among the emigrants from Brazil to Lagos was one Antonia who had been brought up in a seminary in Bahia. In Lagos he built a little chapel and there every Sunday tried to recreate the ceremonies he had known at Bahia, thus approaching observance of the mass. On Saturday he gathered his flock to say the Rosary. He baptized new-born babies, blessed marriages, and ministered to the dying![18]

In Ghana also the presence of colonists assisted the establishment of the church. One effort reflects the intertwining of relationships between areas and missions. T. F. Buxton, one of those who counted on the African evangelization of Africa, suggested that the West Indies would supply colonist-witnesses. Acting on this suggestion, the Basel Mission leadership in Akropong sent two missionaries and an African Christian, George Thompson, to the West Indies in 1842. Thompson had originally come to the Basel Mission in Liberia and was educated in Germany. In Jamaica they gathered a group of twenty-four colonists including the Black adopted daughter of a former governor's wife, Catherine Mulgrave, who had been educated in the Moravian girl's school and married George Thompson. The party, with financial assistance from Buxton's African Civilization Society, arrived in Christiansborg in 1843 and then proceeded to Akropong. [19]

This brief account cannot recreate the full history of the return migration to Africa nor adequately weigh the amount of that influence. Yet it does make clear that this migration was one factor in the evangelization of Africa. Its strength was sufficient for British and American antislavery groups to hope it would be a primary method of evangelizing and "civilizing" Africa. Consequently from the beginning of the modern period of evangelization Christianity was being shaped in Africa by the way Blacks had apprehended it, even though this was not always approved by white missionaries.

AFRICAN PARTICIPATION IN THE ESTABLISHMENT OF MISSIONARY CHURCHES

One of the chief arguments used for support of colonization was that Africans can best evangelize Africa. This belief, supported by the European's difficulty in surviving malaria, provided a large place for Blacks in the early days of missions in Africa. This place was filled with honor by some outstanding Black leaders until the European scramble for Africa. At times the first missionary representatives were Blacks, and at other times missions were kept alive by Black leadership when no white was on the field. When Black and white served together there was a much greater sense of equality than prevailed in the later period. Something of the size of this Black influence may appear from a brief survey of various areas and missions.

Ghana has the longest history in this regard through the influence of Pietism on the Danish and Dutch trading companies. Because of Pietism these trading companies were influenced to provide chaplains for their stations who would also be concerned for the local people. [20] The first African to receive Protestant ordination was a former slave, Jacobus Elisa Johannes Capitain. He was taken to Holland and educated at the University of Leyden where he achieved distinction and popularity. Ordained a minister of the Dutch Reformed church, he went back to the Gold Coast to become a Chaplain there of the Dutch West Indies Company in 1742. He opened a school and began production of Christian literature in the vernacular by translating the Apostle's Creed into Fanti. The spirit of the time is suggested by the fact that when he wished to marry an

African the authorities in Amsterdam objected because she was un-
baptized; a European woman was given in marriage instead. His
service as a chaplain was filled with difficulties, however, and his
life was short.

The first African priest of the Church of England also came from
the Gold Coast. Philip Quaque was born there in 1741 and was ordained in 1766 after education in England. He was appointed
"Missionary, School Master and Catechist to Negroes on the Gold
Coast." The English trading company which allowed his presence
considered him a chaplain and he lived with the European staff at
the fort. He conducted the baptism and marriages of Europeans,
baptized mulatto and black children, and set up a school in 1766.
Like Capitain, however, he found the duties of chaplain to the
Europeans burdensome. [21]

The school tradition faltered after Quaque, but when the African
Company ended in 1821 and the Gold Coast Forts became the Gold
Coast Settlements there came a new burst of life. The governor of
Sierra Leone saw the need to establish a school for young Africans at
Cape Coast Castle. The African in charge, Joseph Smith, was a devout Christian and included Bible reading in the curriculum. One of
the young men, William de Graft, became a Christian and established a society for Bible study. Eventually the Wesleyan
Methodists responded to the needs of the Gold Coast with the appointment of Thomas Birch Freeman, the son of a Negro father and
English mother. We have observed how de Graft and Freeman
worked together with the emigrants in Nigeria. This was only one
example of their collaboration and of the contribution of Freeman,
who had full standing as a Methodist Missionary. Freeman had
volunteered for service on the Gold Coast when reports came of the
death of the first missionaries sent there. He became known for his
tact and courtesy and had wide influence. Under criticism for his
handling of finances he resigned from missionary service to become
civil commandant at Accra and adviser in tribal negotiations. Later
he returned again to church employment, won large numbers of
converts, and served as an elder statesman in the guidance of
Methodist affairs.

In addition to leaders like Freeman, whose contribution was acknowledged by the missions, a careful study by Debrunner discloses
a heroic list of African associates who assisted missionary expansion
in Ghana. So completely was the work in African hands in this early
period that before 1874 Debrunner considers it to have been a
"black man's religion." [22]

Sierra Leone and the Church Missionary Society provided the best-known African in early missionary evangelization, Samuel Crowther, whose life story summarizes the hopes and disappointments of this time. [23] He was taken as a slave at about age fifteen but the slave ship was captured by the British Navy, and Crowther was freed in Sierra Leone. After baptism into Christianity, he was taken to England as a youth with promise. Later he became the first student of Fourah Bay, the pioneering college of West Africa in Freetown. He went along with the Niger expedition and was ordained and sent to Nigeria to lead in establishing the church there.

Henry Venn, the farsighted secretary of the Church Missionary Society, wanted a truly African church, and as a result of his influence, and despite the opposition of others, Crowther was made a bishop in 1864. In appealing to the missionaries to support Crowther, Venn wrote:

"I do not hesitate to say that in all my large experiences I never met with more missionary wisdom, nor—I write advisedly—more of the spirit of Christ than in him. Here I felt to him as much drawing and knitting of soul as to my own brother. Be you a brother to Bishop Crowther you will be abundantly repaid. God destines him for a great work. I should rejoice to be a helper however humble to him." [24]

Under Venn the whole Yoruba country and interior Nigeria were in Crowther's hands, while missionaries were in charge of the coastal work. Even Crowther's opponents were won over temporarily and the arrangement worked as long as Venn led the C.M.S.

In Nigeria the American Southern Baptist Mission also owed its survival to black leadership. The mission was founded in 1855 by T. J. Bowen, but when he had to leave the field for reasons of health, J.M. Harden, an American Black, kept the mission alive. When no funds were available because of the Civil War, Harden started the first brick manufacturing plant in Nigeria. After his death Harden's wife continued the work. Baptists testified that the church in Lagos was largely sustained by this "intelligent, pious, generous woman." [25]

In Sierra Leone J. Augustus Cole, representing a class in Freetown, asked the General Conference of the American Wesleyan Methodist church in 1887 for a pastor. Cole, who was described as "a man of unusual ability," was himself ordained and went back as a pastor. When A.W. Hall was sent to found a mission he found the church Cole led having 256 members, and following English Wesleyan usage. [26]

The history of the United Brethren church (now a part of the United Methodist church) provides a similar testimony to the work of

Black missionaries. Early in the history of the mission founded in 1854, J. A. Williams came from the Countess of Huntingdon Connexion to be its first African employee. S. G. Ziegler, long-time board secretary of the United Brethren Mission, wrote of him, "When no missionary was on the field, he held it together." In 1870 a Black couple from the Third United Brethren Church in Dayton, Ohio, Mr. and Mrs. Joseph Gomer, was sent to the field. Soon afterward J. A. Evans, a Black ordained in the Michigan Conference, was sent and later Daniel Johnson Wilberforce, an African educated in the Dayton public schools who also had a year in the United Brethren Theological Seminary, returned to serve the mission in Sierra Leone. The service of Mr. and Mrs. Joseph Gomer was especially noteworthy with twenty-two years on the field, during which they often were the only missionaries to keep the work alive.

The work of the Countess of Huntingdon Connexion in Sierra Leone was almost entirely in African hands until 1899. It had begun with Black leadership converted originally by Black missionaries of the Connexion in Nova Scotia. The home conference in Britain only established an active relationship with Sierra Leone in 1853. When the local district lost two strong leaders in a short time, the conference sent out a European, but this tenure was short and there was no other European appointment until 1899 when the African superintendent died. [27]

Liberia was the first scene of most American missionary work in Africa, and here again an indispensable part was played early by Black leadership. The American Board sent its first missionary in 1833 accompanied by a Black freedman. [28] Just three years later the same society sent a Black printer along with a white couple to Angola.

In 1854 the Disciples of Christ sent as its first missionary a talented Christian former slave whom the church freed by purchase from his master. [29] When the Women's Board of the same denomination later began its own work in Liberia, it was the son of slave parents who led this effort by founding a school in Schaeffelin. When he was drowned in an accident his widow carried on the work alone until reinforcements were provided. [30]

The Methodist Episcopal church sent Blacks along with whites in 1835 and by 1854 the staff in Liberia was completely Black. [31] Hence it was natural that the first bishop appointed to Liberia in 1859 was a Black, Francis Burns, and he was succeeded in 1875 by another Black. [32]

The Presbyterian church in the U.S. had fifty-eight Black missionaries out of 144 on its rolls between 1837 and 1887 in Liberia and West Africa. Harr has calculated the overall average length of service to have been six years, with the Black average 6.7 years and that of the whites 5.5 years. Comparing the ten of each color who had the longest service the Blacks averaged 20.7 years while the whites average was 18.8. [33] Thus it was clear that at that period Blacks were somewhat more able than whites to survive and minister in West Africa.

The American Protestant Episcopal church began its mission to Africa with the employment of Blacks in 1836. [34] In 1876 of its twenty-six missionaries twenty-one were black. [35]

These figures are obviously incomplete. A more complete record would require search of the records of all societies working in Africa. This would require care, since the use by Blacks of European names to replace those stolen from them adds difficulty. But even such search would not produce completeness. The unconscious prejudice in histories of white societies has often hidden the large contribution of Blacks. Moreover, the distinction between missionaries and local workers tended to neglect the large place of the African pastors, teachers and evangelists. This balance is being redressed in the newer histories of the churches in each country. Thus John Taylor observed in his study of the church in Buganda that the unusual expansion of the young church in the 1890s was the work of African evangelists stirred by the revival in 1893. He wrote, "within one year of the beginning of the revival 260 new evangelists were at work occupying eighty-five stations. . . . The number of catechumens in the African church had risen from 170 to 1500. [36]

This specific reference caused Steven Mackie to observe correctly, "To an extent far larger than is realized, or is represented in mission histories, the work of evangelism in parts of Africa. . . was due to indigenous first-generation Christians rather than to foreign missionaries." [37]

INDEPENDENCY IN TRADITIONAL CHRISTIANITY

The foregoing sketch of the large participation of Blacks in the founding of Christian churches in Africa has drawn most of its examples from the period prior to 1870. This is not caused by a concern only for beginnings, but is rather the reflection of an unhappy reality.

After about 1870 there came a change in European relations with

Africa which affected these relations in the church as well as elsewhere. The reasons for the change may be attributed variously according to one's weighing of economic, political, or social influences. The facts are clear. In the period of the scramble for Africa and the mastery of health hazards for Europeans in tropical lands, whites increasingly took top positions and placed a ceiling on those available to Africans. [38]   As a result Blacks were not welcome as missionaries and were denied entrance into colonies unless vouched for and under the direction of whites.

Within the missionary societies men like Henry Venn were replaced by lesser statesmen and the balance was thus tipped against African leadership. At times, as in the notorious treatment of Bishop Crowther, Africans were attacked without justice or mercy in the effort to assert European control. At other times the takeover was achieved by less heavy-handed methods through the increase of white personnel. So Taylor reports from Buganda:

> For the first fourteen years of the church's life there had never been more than a handful of missionaries in Buganda, with virtually no power to impose their will. The destiny of the church lay, humanly speaking, in the hands of the church council and other Christians in positions of secular leadership. But by 1904 there were 79 missionaries of the C.M.S. in Uganda, 83 of the White Fathers Mission and 35 ot the Mill Hill Fathers; and though they might make no overt use of it, they were supported by the authority of the Colonial Government. They enjoyed an almost limitless freedom to make, and carry out their own schemes. [39]

Even so, during the pre-1900 period African leadership in Buganda was still so strong that equality continued to exist. [40]

Although leadership was taken over by whites, the takeover was not so complete in church as in state. The church became a training ground for African leadership because in any church structure there was considerable independence in the local church. Hence the Nigerian historian Ayandele quotes as relevant to Nigeria the affirmation of Booker T. Washington, "there is no other place in which the Negro race can to better advantage begin to learn the lessons of self direction and self control than in the Negro church." [41]   Actually the first struggles for independence began in the traditional churches. At times there was nothing to do but make a complete break with the European or American Missionary Society. In other cases after a period of strain continuity with the West was maintained on an altered basis.

Although this article limits itself to those churches that

maintained continuity with the West, it is important to avoid exclusion of the independent churches from "traditional Christianity." Apart from Christian religious organizations in Africa there are others inspired by Islamic or Hebraic influences as well as by African traditions and beliefs. However, many independent churches came into being only because they emphasized important Christian truth neglected by European missionaries or because they valued their independence too highly to accept colonial missionary status. [42] That these belong in the Christian mainstream is indicated by the recent welcome of the Kimbanguists into the World Council of Churches.

Here we must note only the efforts by Africans to maintain control of their churches. In missionary analysis the autonomous church is that which is self-supporting, self-propagating, and self-governing. The willingness of Africans to support their own churches is sufficiently indicated by the numbers and growth of the independent churches and by the churches of the Black colonists of Sierra Leone and Liberia. Their early willingness both to support their churches and to assist further work is also suggested by the available information. In Lagos, Nigeria, as early as 1869 Christians began to relieve the mission of the support of schools. After the attack by the pagan party in 1867 caused the withdrawal of missionaries, the work for seven years was entirely in the hands of African clergy and catechists. When Townsend returned in 1874 he found that several more townships had been occupied by Christian teachers, the Gospel had been spread into new areas, and there was no perceptible decrease in the number of African Christians. By 1906, in the Yoruba Mission of the C.M.S., there were 13,240 adult members, 12,423 children of Christian parents, forty-eight Africans ordained, and four raised to the episcopate. [43]

In Buganda in April 1894 the church in the capital raised a fund for maintenance of teachers and catechists to be sent out. On Easter Sunday the people brought a large offering and some fifteen to twenty persons were sent out supported entirely by this church. In another town a missionary within two years was assisted by fifty teachers entirely supported by a local church. [44]

In Ghana one hears of such witness as:

> In 1891, the Reverend Nicolas Timothy Clerk, another West Indian of the second generation who had been trained in Basel, established a mission station at Worawora in Buem. These two new mission stations (at Buem and Adele) run entirely by Africans had a great impact on the small Guang and so-called Togo remnant people in the area. [45]

The Anglican church in Sierra Leone, with its early Creole beginnings and the sympathetic Henry Venn leading the Church Missionary Society, was best able to achieve and maintain its autonomy.
It was Venn's policy that "a native pastorate" should be established
which would gradually take over churches and provide missionaries
for other pioneer situations. In 1869 a native pastorate was established with nine parishes under African pastors transferred to it. [46]
By 1878 the last congregation dependent on C.M.S. funds was
transferred to the native pastorate and the Society retained responsibility only for institutions of higher education. By 1897 the
Sierra Leone church had missions on the Bullom Shore and among
the Sherbro as the beginning of the Mende Missions. By 1907 the
church was raising £1,000 a year for the Mende Missions. [47]

In spite of such indications of growth there were criticisms of the
Sierra Leone Church by persons skeptical of Venn's whole
approach. The opposition, however, was more effective in Nigeria
where the shorter history, more problems, and the aggressive efforts to downgrade Crowther led to sharp clashes between Africans
who wished to retain control of their churches and Europeans who
felt their overrule essential.

Conflict began in Lagos when in 1873 Africans formed a "Society
for the Promotion of Religion and Education in Lagos." They felt
that C.M.S. educational policies were designed to avoid forming a
native pastorate there like that which existed in Sierra Leone. So
they estimated that the C.M.S. was spending £310 in Lagos and determined to contribute £500 a year for the maintenance of churches
and schools. They were so intent on this effort that they raised £98 at
the inaugural meeting. The Africans regarded this as "a thing
ordained by God and beginning of an African Church Missionary
Society."

European missionaries saw it as a conspiracy to drive them out of
Lagos. They attempted to eliminate the danger by threatening to
dismiss subordinates who supported the movement and by appealing to the churches to act separately. Although this brought some
pastors and churches into line, it resulted in the transfer to Lagos of
James Johnson, the preeminent nationalist of the church in this
period. Consequently C.M.S. leadership recognized the strength of
the movement that threatened to exclude Europeans and sought
conciliation by the introduction of the Sierra Leone native pastorate
plan as the best option. [48]

James Johnson was an impressive and holy man with a large
vision. He saw an African Christianity which would incorporate

suitable aspects of African religion, adopt its own language, hymns and liturgy, and create a Christian nation. He considered the native pastorate as an acceptable means to that goal. His nationalist hopes troubled both missionaries and the C.M.S., no longer led by Venn.

Nevertheless, the native pastorate was established and grew. By 1889 all the churches in Lagos but one had been absorbed into it, and already in 1882 it had become a missionary body with stations outside of Lagos.

Some other missions seemed to profit from the C.M.S. experience. The Wesleyan Mission conceded to the Lagos circuit, organized in 1878, all authority in managing its affairs, including the payment of salaries. Self-government was complete by 1880. Also by 1880 the Scottish Presbyterians among the Efik had a committee which controlled all finances.[49]

The American Southern Baptists had to learn in their own way. Even though the mission had been kept alive by Blacks from 1863 to 1874 and the missionary sent in 1875 was sympathetic to African aspirations, W. J. David still felt that Africans must accept the leadership of white men; on the other hand, M. L. Stone had carried on too frequently and ably on his own as an African church leader to accept such a secondary role. When David sought to restrict Stone's opportunities, violated Baptist constitutional procedures, and dismissed those who opposed him, most members separated from the church in Lagos and became the Native Baptist Church in 1888. All the strongest members joined the Native Baptists and only a handful remained with the mission. Efforts to conciliate were not fully effective, but Baptist missionaries were withdrawn from Lagos until after 1914, when the independent Lagos churches again returned to mission fellowship with much greater strength than the mission organization. [50]

The sharpest conflicts arose in the C.M.S. Niger pastorate. At Venn's urging Samuel Crowther had been consecrated bishop in 1864 with his work centered along the Niger. The area was large and the difficulties were great. Crowther may have been too gentle with the failures of his clergy, but the real problem was a change of attitude in which Europeans considered only themselves fit to rule and to evangelize. Consequently aggressive new white missionaries were brought into the area and direct attacks were made on Crowther's administration. The effect was to enforce dismissal of the African missionaries, and to push Bishop Crowther to support the formation of a Delta pastorate of similar character to the independent Anglican pastorates in Sierra Leone and Lagos.

Although the Europeans who sought control had their way in eliminating African leadership from the Niger pastorate and in preventing the formation of a Delta pastorate under an African bishop succeeding Crowther, events affirmed the correctness and strength of the African position. In the Niger pastorate, of the fifteen ordained Africans who worked on the Niger between 1880 and 1890, only one remained in the C.M.S. employ in 1895. Yet in the end only one agent died uncleared while all the others were reemployed in either Sierra Leone or the Delta. Meanwhile, of the eight Europeans who came to the Niger in 1891, by 1894 only one remained. [51]   In the efforts to form the Delta pastorate Africans proved their willingness and ability to raise funds to achieve independence as well as a willingness to compromise and to trust the C.M.S. and its missionaries if there was the slightest evidence of their cooperation with the African desire for autonomy in church life. [52]

The strength of the African church was confirmed even in its defeat. The entire struggle between Africans and missions between 1870 and 1900 demonstrated the African claim that Christianity in Africa belonged to them and that they were willing to pay the price to possess their inheritance. The European desire to rule only delayed the possession which has now been realized in the in the mission-founded churches.

THE AFRICANIZATION OF CHRISTIANITY

In addition to affirming its claim to Christianity by Black colonization, participation in missionary evangelism, and struggling for autonomy in the mission-founded churches, Africa has also shaped to its own life the Christian message brought to it. It is widely acknowledged that the independent churches grew up all over Africa in response to the desire for a church where Africans may feel at home. This desire also shaped the worship, beliefs, and practices of the traditional churches to make these churches distinctly African. [53]

First, African Christians are more aware than many other Christians of the unseen world. This manifests itself especially in attitudes toward the dead. Thus Africans have preferred to bury their dead closer to them and at times in their own villages. Such practices created disputes with missionaries, who not only were disturbed by possible sanitary factors but also came from a different background, one in which there is an effort to keep the dead well separated from the living.

When Africans are allowed their way new practices result. A remote village in Liberia has the grave of a highly-respected chief in the center of the village marked by a horizontal cross. In Ghana a funeral procession is headed by a choir and minister for a service according to Christian rites. This may be followed by African rites in the evening and "wake-keeping" when the mourners sit up all night singing Christian hymns. Next morning libations are poured for the dead, and on the following Sunday a service of thanksgiving is held in the quiet order of the European tradition. Newspapers regularly announce both the libation and the service of thanksgiving in one advertisement without any sense of conflict.

In Sierra Leone, with its Creole Christian tradition, the newspaper advertisement is the approved way of acknowledging the memory of the deceased. On the anniversary of the death such an advertisement will recall the departure and testify to the abiding memory of the family. The family may also gather and invite others to share in a meal of remembrance. It is interesting that in Dayton, Ohio, the paid funeral announcements of Blacks much more frequently carry a picture of the deceased than those of whites.

Another aspect of the awareness of the unseen is shown in belief in divine guidance through dreams and visions. Bengt Sundkler in *The Christian Ministry in Africa* [54] has shown the importance of this special guidance in the call of men to the ministry. In addition to citing numerous specific examples, he has reported the insistence by the principal of a leading East African theological seminary that most of his candidates had been called through dreams. [55]

Second, the churches of Africa are seeking more adequate ways of worship than those given them from Europe or America. Although the independent churches have gone farther in this, mission-founded churches provide their own evidence. In Ghana there has been the rise of singing bands for singing indigenous hymns. There also developed the practice of having a leader read a Bible passage with the congregation joining in the chorus. In a Methodist church in Zaïre, after the sermon its message was restated in song by a leader, with appropriate responses from the congregation. [56] In other places in Africa there have been experiments in adaptation of services for marriage, confirmation, and birth. In some places there have been regular thanksgiving services for individual blessings. When the national father of Sierra Leone was saved from harm in an accident that frightened the country, thanksgiving services were held across the nation. In Freetown the major United Methodist church worship included formal prayers from both the Methodist and Anglican traditions along with the congregation joining in a gospel chorus during prayer and even at fitting times in the sermon.

In Ibadan, Nigeria, the church related to the American Southern Baptist tradition has had evening "native airs" services in which the choir sings hymns to African tunes. At this service the processional is marked by an African dance step, and the choir is accompanied by drums and other African instruments, as well as by organ. In Northern Nigeria Christians follow a similar pattern for Christmas caroling with a serenade to nearby villages of dancing and singing to a Christian refrain accompanied by drum. Elsewhere there is a growing use of African musical instruments in Christian worship. Also, African art forms are employed in the decoration of church buildings.

 Third, the church in Africa has also shown a greater interest in the Old Testament than most European churches. There are great similarities between the Old Testament and African life in social structure and in such obvious matters as polygamy. The African attitude toward the world in its reality, unity, and goodness is much more Hebraic than Greek. A significant parallel was found especially in the Creole experience of being enslaved and set free to become leaders of a new civilization. The testimony of a Freetown Creole speaks to this feeling. In the story of his boyhood, R. W. Cole writes:

> . . .There is a strong Old Testament strand among my people.
> The first in West Africa to embrace Christianity en masse with a strong tradition of having been delivered by God rather like the children of Israel under Moses, the Krios of Sierra Leone have for two centuries nursed proudly their connection with Britain. The very name of their capital Freetown, they have been taught was a sign of the purpose which through God's inspiration had found expression in the 18th century. . . . So when their first born child turned out to be a son my parents gratefully promised him to God. [57]

In the coming of independence new Biblical heroes came to prominent mention, and in discussing the relevance of the Old Testament an African chaplain of a University College warned of the dangers and urged that the message of the prophets must be set against a Biblical sense of destiny. This word is especially relevant since the African is also easily attracted to viewing sin as ritual impurity rather than ethical unrighteousness. Here again the Old Testament provides guidance from its similar experience.

Current efforts to establish an African Christian theology are being made by both Protestant and Catholic scholars. [58]   An adequate account of their work would take us beyond the appropriate limits of this essay, but in general it can be said that it involves a serious attempt to relate the Biblical witness to African life, without necessarily going by way of the Hellenistic, European, and American interpretations of this witness.

The evidence here presented should be enough to support the argument that the church in Africa, which was founded largely by Blacks and nourished by the sacrifices of other Blacks, has manifested a distinctive African character even in the mission-related churches that constitute "traditional Christianity" in Africa.

NOTES

1. Geoffrey Parrinder, *Religion in Africa*. Baltimore, Md.: Penguin Books, 1969, pp. 120, 123, 124.
2. C. P. Groves, *The Planting of Christianity in Africa*, 4 vols. London: Lutterworth Press, 1948-1955, vol. I, p. 158.
3. *Ibid.*, p. 183.
4. *Ibid.*, p. 186.
5. Arthur T. Porter, *Creoledom*. London: Oxford University Press, 1963, p. 11.
6. Christopher Fyfe, *Sierra Leone Inheritance* London: Oxford University Press, 1964, p. 119.
7. *Ibid.*, p. 147.
8. Porter, *Creoledom* p. 36.
9. Fyfe, *Sierra Leone Inheritance* p. 24; Porter, *Creoledom* pp. 78-88.
10. J. W. Cason, *The Growth of Christianity in the Liberian Environment*. University Microfilms, 1962, p. 102.
11. P. J. Staudenraus, *The African Colonization Movement*, New York: Columbia University Press, 1961, pp. 32, 204, 249-250; Cason, pp. 94-102.
12. Groves, *The Planting of Christianity*, vol. I, p. 294. See also Staudenraus, *The African Colonization Movement*, pp. 92-96; cason, pp. 94-102.
13. Cason, *The Growth of Christianity*, p. 102.
14. J. F. A. Ajayi, *Christian Missions in Nigeria*, 1848-1891 London: Longmans, 1965, p. 80.
15. *Ibid.*, pp. 32-33.
16. *The Yoruba Mission*. London: Church Missionary Society, 1906, pp. 32, 24.
17. Ajayi, *Christian Missions in Nigeria*, pp. 44-50.
18. *Ibid.*, p. 51. A biographical note by Father Holley in *Les Missions Catholique*, p. 26, May 1881.
19. Hans W. Debrunner, *A History of Christianity in Ghana*. Accra, Ghana: Waterville Publishing Co., 1967, pp. 107-109.

20. Groves, *The Planting of Christianity*, vol. I, pp. 151, 152; for other African Christians of this period (on the Gold Coast) see also Debrunner, pp. 60-83.
21. Margaret Priestley, "Philip Quaque of Cape Coast," in Philip D. Curtin, *Africa Remembered*. Madison: University of Wisconsin Press, 1968, pp. 99-139.
22. Debrunner, *A History of Christianity*, p. 163; see also pp. 103-173.
23. Along with the biography *The Black Bishop*, by Jesse Page, one needs to see the works of modern Nigerians such as J. F. A. Ajayi and E. A. Ayandele, *The Missionary Impact on Modern Nigeria*. London: Longmans, 1966.
24. Ajayi, *Christian Missions in Nigeria*, pp. 195, 196.
25. Groves, *The Planting of Christianity*, vol. II, pp. 70-72
26. George H. and Mary Lane Clarke, *American Wesleyan Methodist Mission of Sierra Leone*, West African Wesleyan Methodist Publishing Association: n.d., pp. 40-42.
27. Groves, *The Planting of Christianity*, vol. I, p. 207; vol. p. 219; vol. III, pp. 210-211.
28. Wilbur C. Harr, *The Negro as an American Protestant Missionary in Africa*. Chicago: University of Chicago, Microfilm, p. 15.
29. Groves, *The Planting of Christianity*, vol. II, p. 222.
30. *Ibid*.
31. Harr, *The Negro as an American Protestant Missionary*, p. 24.
32. Groves, *The Planting of Christianity*, vol. II, p. 222.
33. Harr, *The Negro as an American Protestant Missionary*, pp. 119-123.
34. Groves, *The Planting of Christianity*, vol. I, p. 297.
35. Harr, *The Negro as an American Protestant Missionary*, p. 22.
36. John V. Taylor, *The Growth of the Church in Buganda*. London: S.C.M. Press, 1958, p. 64.
37. Steven Mackie, *Can Churches Be Compared?* Geneva: World Council of Churches, 1970, p. 71.
38. Porter, *Creoledom*, pp. 62-67; R.W. Cole, *Kossoh Town Boy*. Cambridge: Cambridge University Press, 1960, p. 14; Harr, pp. 58, 94.
39. Taylor, *The Growth of the Church*, p. 73.
40. *Ibidi.*, p. 73.
41. Ayandele, *The Missionary Impact*, p. 203.

44. Taylor, *The Growth of the Church*, pp. 75, 76.
45. Debrunner, *A History of Christianity*, p. 217-218.
46. Groves, *The Planting of Christianity*, vol. II, pp. 217-218.
47. Groves, *The Planting of Christianity*, vol. III, pp. 209-210.
48. Ayandele, *The Missionary Impact*, pp. 184-186.

49. *Ibid.*, p. 192.
50. J. B. Webster. *The African Churches Among the Yoruba, 1888-1922,* Oxford: Clarendon Press, 1964, pp. 46-62.
51. Webster, *The African Churches,* pp. 15, 17.
52. For details on the whole sordid story see Ajcyi, *Christian Missions in Nigeria,* pp. 233-273; Ayandele, *The Missionary Impact,* pp. 194-238; Webster, *The African Churches, pp.* 1-41.
51. Webster, pp. 15, 17.
52. For details on the whole sordid story see Ajoyi, pp. 233-273; Ayandele, pp. 194-238; Webster, pp. 1-41.
53. This portion of the paper is based on observations of the author during a sabbatical leave in West Africa, 1962-1963, supported by observations of others. A more detailed exposition of these views is found in his "Distinctive Marks of the Church in Africa," *United Theological Seminary Bulletin,* LXIII,
54. Bengt Sundkler, *The Christian Ministry in Africa.* London: S.C.M. Press, 1962, pp. 9-30.
55. *Ibid.*, p. 22.
56. Personal communication from Dr. Newell Booth.
57. Cole, *Kossoh Town Boy,* p. 12.
58. E.g., see K. Dickson (ed.), *Biblical Religion and African Beliefs.* London: Lutterworth, 1970; William H. Crane, "Indigenization in the African Church," *International Review of Missions,* LIII (October 1964), pp. 408-422; E. B. Idowu, *Towards an Indigenous Church.* London: Oxford University Press, 1965; Harry Sawyer, *Creative Evangelism.* London: Lutterworth, 1968.

12

Kimbanguism: Authentically African, Authentically Christian

George B. Thomas*

Kimbanguism is an African religion—authentically African and authentically Christian. From the religious consciousness of the African personality and life, this independent Christian movement of the African church has burst forth as an expression of African Christianity and as an emerging world religion in the twentieth century. Kimbanguism, as a significant vanguard of African Christianity, has disengaged colonialism, persecution, and oppression and engaged liberation, struggle, and hope. Kimbanguism is expressive of the personality of African religious life and of a consciousness of being a part of the world Christian commitment and movement—not as a mission, but with a mission.

We will describe Kimbanguism as an authentically African Christianity in eight essential ways:

1). Existentially, because it accepts the meaning and relevance of the prior religious consciousness in the African experience;

2). In origin and leadership, because it suffers the birth pains of a movement initiated by a Congolese black prophet-martyr of the twentieth century;

3). In membership and history, because it is a genuinely Christian self-affirming African religious movement in development;

4). In its genuine African Christian life style of personal self-discipline and organizational self-determination;

5). In its expression of joyfulness in the spirit of freedom in spite of suffering, while maintaining creativity in witness;

6). In its qualities of trustfulness, integrity and openness and its spirit of nonviolence and cooperation;

7). In its brotherly compassion, its sensitivity, and its responsiveness to the whole range of human needs;

8). In its spiritual seriousness, its commitment and consecration to the revelation, in the African present, of the Spirit that was in the person of Jesus.

*This article, in slightly different form was published previously by I.D.O.C., March 13, 1971.

In all these ways, through the person and witness of Simon Kimbangu and Kimbanguism, Christ has now been clearly manifested
in direct revelation in the African religious experience and the Spirit
of Christ made authentically African.

First, Kimbanguism is genuinely African in the existential sense
because Simon Kimbangu, the black prophet, founder, and martyr
of the African Christian Church called "The Church of Jesus Christ
on Earth through the Prophet Simon Kimbangu" was an African,
originating among the BaKongo, who sought to exemplify the life
style of Christ through his personality and within the African community.

In the Ngombe region of the Lower Congo, before the prophet was
born, the name Kimbangu, as all African names, was both symbolic
and significant. In the natural African religious consciousness, the
life cycle is held central and precious. Names given at the birth
stage express black people's deepest aspirations and prayers for a
good and whole life. During any period of stress, when the event of
birth is unduly prolonged or threatened to be aborted, the women
express their prayers in song. The BaKongo women sang to the
good spirits and beyond to the Supreme God to grant mercy for the
life of the child. The name Kimbangu was an invocation of this
traditional African religious consciousness: "he who reveals is he
who is hidden."[1]

During a dreadful period, when an epidemic claimed the lives of
many babies, the prophet was born in the family of Tata Kuyela and
Mama Luezi in 1889. Tata Kuyela named him Kimbangu because
God spared him - he escaped death. The prophet was born in the
land where the spirits of the living dead and the rhythm of the life
cycle are linked in a continuity of humanity from time immemorial;
thus, Kimbangu was born in the will of black prophecy and history.
When his mother died a little later, he was reared by his aunt,
"Maman" Kinzembo, whose wise counsel placed him upon the path
destiny had charted for him.

In the early years of Kimbangu's development, a missionary
named Cameron of the English Baptist church, working in the
Lower Congo, was rebuffed by the inhabitants of the region. But
Maman Kinzembo helped Cameron andlater, when she related
more closely to his work, she brought Kimbangu within the influence of the mission. Soon, Kimbangu's keen religious genius and
perception began creatively fusing the richness of the African
spiritual sensitivity with the new revelations from the teachings and
the Spirit of Christ. Kimbangu "grew in stature and favor with God"

and in fulfillment of black religious phophecy and history. He studied four years at the mission in Ngombe-Lutete. Later, he married Muilu Marie and three sons were born: Charles Kisolokele, Salomon Dialungana, and Joseph Diangienda.

When the prophet was twenty-six years old, he was baptized at the mission and received the name "Simon." Perhaps this was another prophetic sign about one who would become a cornerstone of African Christianity. As a man of deep devotion and spiritual insight who had read the Scriptures carefully, he became a zealous teacher in his village and nearby villages where he gave meditations and expositions. Kimbangu's religious consciousness eagerly sought to realize a direct transposition of the life style of Christ into the witness and works of the African personality and community, but not as a traditional religious leader.[2] Nevertheless, in this work, God called Simon Kimbangu, and in 1918 he heard a voice saying to him: "I am the Christ; my servants are faithless; I have chosen you to witness and to convert your brothers."[3]

Perhaps he was frightened by the call, for he refused to obey. He insisted that he was not as wise and trained as the pastors and priests.[4] However, the call persisted night after night. Since Nkamba, his home town, was for him now a "fearful place," he sought to escape his call as some twentieth-century Jacob or Jonah. He first fled to Thysville with a friend, Mfinangani, who later became one of his secretaries. Failing to find work, he returned to the village, but there was no escape from the voice. Muilu Marie often heard him speaking in restless and disturbed dreams. Two years passed; deeply distressed and in search of peace he fled a second time, in 1920, going to Leopoldville (now Kinshasa). He lived with Tata Ngumbi and Tata Ntalaketo-Senkele. The latter secured work for him in the Oil Companies of the Belgian Congo. He was never paid. Owanga Jean states that this was because he refused the call, that every month an unknown person signed under his name in the register of salaries. After three months in Leopoldville, he decided to return to the village and farming. Again, God revealed to the prophet in a premonition that he would have power to do things such as Christ had made manifest on earth. He would also face evil and suffer terribly. He would be jailed, exiled, and sent far away, but God would be with him.

On April 6, 1921, the prophet could hold out no longer.[5] He was sought after to heal a woman in the Ngombe-Kinsuka village. Although he tried to resist the divine compulsion, he went, entered the home of Nkiantoudo, and put his hands upon her in the name of

Christ. Nkiantondo was healed and terrified; this was a strange and shocking event. Kimbangu was accused of sorcery. The prophet had to convince all that God's power was responsible. He healed others. Nevertheless, in part feared, in part taunted, he was called a magician, sorcerer, fetishist, and healer. He did do strange things. It is said that he raised the dead by the power and name of Christ. The God of Christ through Kimbangu was now alive in a new spiritual way, resurrected in the form of blackness, renewed African humanity. Because of the person of the chosen prophet, African religion had gained an authenticating center of Christianity, African Christianity.

Secondly, in the birth pains of Kimbanguism the revelation of Jesus Christ, in the power, will, and works of God, directly encountered the African religious experience. This was a decisive Christian event of God's initiative and revelation in a unilateral motion, "perpendicularly from above."

Consequently, an innumerable following came, the sick as well as the inquisitive.[6] Nkamba emerged as God's "New City" on earth. At Nkamba there was evangelization, the witness of the Word of God, in services of preaching, in praying and many deeds of healing. Needing help, the prophet gathered about him disciples. These were they who would be his sacrificial helpers; those willing to face death with him. Some of these were Mandombe Mikala, Ndangi Pierre, Mukoko Jean, and Mbonga Theresa, of whom the first two are still alive, accordikng to Owango Jean. These were the first of the faithful chosen to assist in the leadership of the movement, especially in healing and preaching. Kimbangu's fame spread rapidly; crowds came to him from throughout the Congo and neighboring countries. Though healing many and performing many other miracles, he refused pay.[7] These were unparalleled events; God's presence in the works of Christ was now manifest in the African religious consciousness and community.[8] At the same time, these events were threatening to the established Western Christian traditions and institutions, the Roman Catholic and Protestant mission work, as well as to the Belgian colonial power; all were angrily aggravated. But it was uniquely at this point that faith and experience merged, underscoring that an authentic Christian faith had come into African life to be an authentic African experience.

As distrust and suspicion increased, the European colonialists grew in apprehensiveness toward any kind of indigenous activity. The Catholics at first accused the Protestants of encouraging Kimbangu to empty their churches and of inciting the people by encouraging studies and discussions of the Bible. Simon had begun to justify their anxiety now by influencing thousands and thousands. Soon the Baptist and Salvation Army centers were being emptied and the people of Christian faith were found worshiping at the Bethel of Nkamba. The established Christian churches began, from this point, to endorse and to encourage the persecution of the prophet, his disciples and his movement. A certain Pastor Jennings of the Baptist Mission was sent to Nkamba to investigate these strange happenings. After investigation, he commented with a statement parallel to that of the Roman soldier at the crucifixion of Jesus Christ:

> For the first time I see great evidence of the presence of Christ in the Congo, but the sheep must not lead their shepherd. It is possible that you possess this power from God, but the merit belongs to us, the deacons. [9]

Once again the frozen traditionalists failed to face with openness and flexibility the new and creative thrusts of God's revelation in the African experience. Pentecost was now at Nkamba, Africa, explosively breaking out beyond the parochial bounds of government or mission control and determination.

Inevitably a plot was laid. Insinuations and charges were conveniently arranged and Kimbangu was now accused as one responsible for "incitement to disorder... incitement to refuse work... incitement to non-payment of taxes... incitement to chase the Belgians from the Congo... xenophobia." [10] The local administrator went to seize the prophet because of the accusations. However, seeing that the activities were uniquely religious, he hesitated to use the military; but, under pressure from "the rulers of this world," [11] he dispatched troops from Thysville to Nkamba. Nevertheless, the prophet's hour had not come and he passed through their midst and went into the more remote and inaccessible areas of the country. The sick searched him out as he traveled in the Nbanza-Sanda regions. The holy village was destroyed and ruthless persecution and suppression were set in motion, to drive out, to stamp out, and to exterminate the movement in its totality. These events were not new, but they still contain that paradox of God's mysterious working in spite of and beyond the destructive schemes of men. New Christian martyrs joined the ranks of the faithful, and the prophecy of an earlier Church Father of North Africa was being fulfilled anew: "The blood of the martyrs is the seed of the Church." [12]

For a very few months Kimbangu taught the Bansodisi, his special helpers, his "twelve," using the wilderness as their "Upper

Room." They were taught the importance of the scriptures, of reading and learning from the Word. They were taught the meaning of suffering, praying, fasting, and trusting in the Spirit of God to give the power to heal, to help, and endure all hardness. They were taught not to resist evil with evil, but to maintain a spirit of non-violence. The African spirit is one which aspires for consistency—word with works, faith with practice, trust with loyalty, prayer with power. Kimbangu himself symbolized the incarnation in the Black experience, with a ministry of healing and hope to the hopeless and love for the despised and the persecuted. He sought to prepare them for all things.

Finally, when he felt his time had come, exposing himself at Nkamba, he faced the hour of trial, his Gethsemene. On September 12, 1921, he was arrested [13] and a military tribunal, presided over by a Commander de Rossi, pronounced on October 3, 1921, his condemnation to death. In addition, he was given 120 lashes and other cruel and inhuman treatment. [14] Through the intervention of the Reverends H. Rose Phillips and J. A. Clark and the decision of King Albert of Belgium, his punishment was determined as permanent detention. So, at the age of thirty, the prophet was sent to a maximum security prison in Elizabethville (Lubumbashi).

He had demanded of his accusers, "Why are Africans not permitted to have their own God, prophet, and Bible as whites?" Owango Jean indicated also that his followers asked what he would leave as a sign for those who were not arrested. He left his followers the message: "Your only weapon is the Gospel. I leave you nothing else. Continue to attend church. Christ will conquer." [15]

The Kimbanguist church would emerge after almost forty years of persecution. The believers and followers would attend the traditional churches, but their loyalty and faithfulness would remain with the movement of Simon Kimbangu. In prophecy, he had given them the strategy of survival and liberation: to be a people in the midst of people, a body of believers in the midst of believers. In part, Kimbanguism went underground, in the forests and the bush, even in the "catacombs" of the Protestant and Catholic institutions, there to be *the* church in the midst of the churches, in spite of the churches. The witness of this "church incognito" was heard by the late William H. Crane in 1952, while a missionary of the Presbyterian Church working in Kasai, when he overheard an African Christian say to another in a conversation after the service at the mission station:

Before he died the prophet Simon Kimbangu enjoined us to

observe these vows as well as the teachings of the Book of God
until such time as the black man in Congo will be free to worship
God in his own way. [16]

Third, in membership and history Kimbanguism is a basically
African religious movement. After the Prophet Kimbangu was imprisoned, his oldest son, Charles Kisolokole was sent to Boma to a
Catholic mission to study. His "maman" and two brothers were permitted to return to the village. All of those who were arrested with
the prophet were deported to the Upper Congo, hundreds of miles
away. Even in the isolation and confinement of the concentration
camps they continued to practice their faith. At the same time, it
was impossible to root out the Kimbanguists who remained, some of
whom were domestic workers and laborers, while others were employed in the government, in mission schools, and in institutions.
The movement, rather than being uprooted and destroyed, sank
deeper roots and proliferated. The intensity and breadth of the
movement went beyond the comprehension and control of the
colonialists. By 1924, according to official records, the Kimbanguist
church movement continued at an accelerated pace of development,
even under persecution and oppression. "The official reports of 1924
indicate that in the region of Thysville two-thirds of the population
are under the immediate influence of the Kimbanguists and out of
the control of the administration and the missions." [17]   Both the
government and the church were astounded because they had felt
that their strategy of isolating the prophet and other known leaders
and members would destroy the movement. But they could not
know the great strength and resources in the depths of the black
religious consciousness, the force of which was now being conducted through Kimbanguism. [18]

Kimbanguism as a religious movement exemplified a fervent
spirit and life style similar to the early Christian movement. The
people of the lower Congo had already had a believing and practicing faith in a God-Creator before the coming of the Europeans,
actually from time immemorial. Violent reactions had already occurred in the Congo, after the coming of Diago Cao in 1487, fore-
runner of Vasco de Gama. These reactions were against the style
and spirit of European colonial Christianity. The Mwani Congo, the
sovereign ruler and his cabinet and government during the fifteenth
century, received the Portuguese Christians with friendship and
charity. The peoples of the Lower Congo were in a feudal-tribal
stage of development parallel to that of Europe and had the initial
respect of the King of Portugal and the Pope at Rome. Africans as a

religious people were open to the new message of European Christianity. However, firearms, slavery, and deceit, by 1665, had reduced the old Kingdom of the Lower Congo to a slave market for the Western world. At this point, Western Christianity identified the meek and mild Jesus as Savior of black souls for Africans, and as source of imperial power and domination for the white man in his mission of "civilizing" Africans for non-African purposes. Later the Western Christian nations fought over the spoils of exploration and exploitation of Stanley and de Brazza, and finally decided to split up the African pie among themselves. In a conference at Berlin, the Congo went to the King of Belgium, Leopold II, with American blessings. The Catholic Belgians designated the various sectors within the country for missionizing purposes, with, of course, the advantages belonging to the official state religion. In the course of time, the Congo was missionized by at least twenty-seven different religious groups anxious to save Congolese souls. At the same time government and business interests would save the Congolese soil. Historical Western Christianity bore all of the trappings of colonialism which could not ultimately cope with the strength of the religious consciousness of African peoples, including the direct revelation and emergence of African Christianity—for example, Kimbanguism, as a Christian religion with an African personality and agenda.

Failing to stop or destroy the movement through violent techniques, legal measures were imposed again and again to ferret out the Kimbanguists. Kimbanguism was outlawed in all Congolese territories. Neither in the churches nor in the concentration camps in exile could anyone any longer publicly practice an independent form of Christianity. Arrests were made everywhere of those rumored to be, or those suspected of being, implicated with Kimbanguism. By 1937, after the passage of the new law, over 38,000 families were deported to camps in places such as Lowa, Ponthierville, Bafusenda in the Oriental Province, Luisa, Bekese, Katako-Kombe, Kole, Lodja, Lomela in the Kasai, and Oshue, Bilingo, in Bandundu. Nevertheless, the believers practiced Kimbanguism more skillfully. Centuries of oral tradition had made Africans masters of transmitting culture from generation to generation.

The Prophet Kimbangu, while in prison, had anointed his youngest son, Joseph Diangienda, as his successor in the "apostolic service" of Kimbanguism. After thirty years in prison, on October 12, 1951, in a prison hospital, the prophet of God's church gave his spirit to the spirits of the land of his fathers and into the hands of his Lord and God.

As indicated before, the Kimbanguists continued to attend services in the churches of the mission as well as seek the best possible education in the schools. By 1956, five years after the death of Simon Kimbangu, the word was given: "Those who still believe in the miracles of Simon Kimbangu as the works of Christ are asked, if they are not cowards, to leave the churches."[19]   The churches again were emptied of many Africans (students and teachers, deacons and pastors) who had decided that the time had come to consolidate themselves openly and to confront boldly the colonialists. The church, Kimbanguist, was coming out of the catacombs of the Protestant and Catholic mission institutions. At this time, the movement declared and defined its personality and the name as "The Church of Jesus Christ on Earth through the Prophet Simon Kimbangu."

The unanimous choice of a leader was Joseph Diangienda, who had left work in administration to lead the people (Figure 9). Thus the people of the movement endorsed the prophet's choice and His Eminence, Joseph Diangienda, became the spiritual head, beginning a full and open ministry of leadership, giving himself the task of building up the organization and work of the Kimbanguist members.

In 1956, another young man, Lucien Luntadila, who had been a Catholic novice, was dismissed from the convent and had entered government service, chanced on a copy of *The Declaration of the Rights of Man*, forgotten on an official's desk. The Belgians had signed the *Declaration* with the United Nations but did not intend to publish the fact. Lucien Luntadila, having read especially Articles 18 and 19 on liberty, conscience, religion, and opinion, copied them and had them printed. They were made available to Joseph Diangienda. Luntadila was dismissed from government service but was taken on in the Kimbanguist movement as the general secretary. The document had a revolutionary impace and created a completely different social atmosphere. A new leverage for gaining the freedom of expression which belonged to them had come by the publication of the colonial power's commitment to freedom and humanitarianism in world affairs. Recognizing the threat and strength of this seemingly indestructible brand of African Christianity, other methods were devised to reassert pressure and oppression. Kimbanguist children in the schools and their sick in the hospitals were harassed and humiliated and socially ostracized. The sick were ridiculed and sent away with such advice as to go be healed by "the miracle-workers."[20]

The confrontations continued to escalate to parallel the oppression. In 1957, the Belgians had to deal with a variety of public manifestations led by the religious movement of Kimbanguism. Such manifestations had omninous undertones of political self-consciousness, although the Kimbanguist movement maintained its clearly religious objectives. Young people secured trucks and, with bold placards, paraded through the streets. Literature was printed and distributed extolling liberty, amnesty for the imprisoned believers, both near and far. Concerted efforts were vigorously taken to make contact with other peoples and nations and governments, including those in Belgium. They sought religious liberty and freedom from the persistent punitive persecution which they had already endured through the years. The United Nations was asked to intervene. A letter was sent June 10, 1957, to M. Buesseret, the Belgian Minister of the Colony, stating: "The union of indigenous people declares that there are 800,000 regularly affiliated Kimbanguists. It calls attention to the fact that 37,000 heads of families have been imprisoned since 1921 and that only 2,500 (original) followers remain."[21] This is tantamount to an accusation of genocide.

Finally the ultimatum was given by His Eminence Joseph Diangienda: either they would be emancipated or exterminated; their enemies would have to deal with them *en masse*. The leaders and people went as a group to the largest stadium in Leopoldville, Boudouin Stadium, for the showdown, to give the authorities "the opportunity to exterminate them all since there was no place for them in the country."[22] The Belgians capitulated and set up a conditional freedom for six months with the following stipulation or face-saving rationalization: "to determine whether these meetings are not pretext for revolutionary activities."[23]

So it was that by December 24, 1959, there were no more public prohibitions and public persecutions of the Kimbanguists on the part of the European colonialists. These events as well as others were carrying the country to the door of independence. In January 1960 the Kimbanguist church schools were officially created. At the same time, during this month, at the Round Table in Belgium, the National Constitution (*Loi Fundamentale*) was being shaped. On June 30, the Congo became independent and in December 1960 the Kimbanguist church was officially recognized by the Congolese government.

The Kimbanguist church continued as an African Christian movement. The church opposed suggestions of becoming a state religion, resisting a marriage of religion and politics in the constitution, and voiced expressions of conscience against compulsory military service. During the early days of independence, when so much confusion was erupting, His Eminence went into many situations with words and works of peace and reconciliation, in the spirit of nonviolence. The church refused to condone the politics of repressive police actions and armies. In 1964, at one church in Stanleyville, now Kinsangani, the people remained on their knees in the midst of bombings, strafings and conflict during the Congolese people's Civil War. Of the 170 in the service, none were wounded. Kimbanguists of all tribes were always without arms and gained the profound respect of the police as they sought to live in the spirit of Christ, above the ephemeral, political, and temporal temptations, pressures, and priorities.

Fourth, Kimbanguism has developed a genuine African Christian life style in terms of personal self-discipline and organizational self-determination.

One of the most impressive features of the Kimbanguists, as indicated by white Americans and Europeans such as William Crane and Jean Lasserre, is the emphasis on simplicity in dress, in conversation, and in conduct, as well as in eating and drinking habits. The wholesome life style of the Kimbanguists may well be a strong indication of a creative blend of the African and Christian life style in personality and community.

As a Christian African movement, Kimbanguism, African in organization as well as in leadership and membership, was not an anti-white movement nor only a negative reaction to white religious, political, or social intimidations and exploitations. The movement had been rejected and alienated by the white colonial power structure, nonreligious and religious, because they could not dignify the African personality in relationship to institutional power and potential autonomy. In order to understand the genius and authenticity of the Kimbanguist movement we must view it as a movement, initiated by African people, which can only be deeply perceived and interpreted by and from the African perspective.

As early as March 11 and June 12, 1958, the general secretary, Lucien Luntadila, had defined and presented in written form the constitutional base of the Kimbanguist church, incorporating the name of the founder and prophet Simon Kimbangu. He had stated that the prophet and witness of Christ was a native of Nkamba in the Central Congo Province. The church was born, "revealed," though hidden for many years, being driven underground by persecutions from 1921 until independence. It was constituted in 1958 as "The Church of Jesus Christ on Earth through the The Prophet Simon

Kimbangu," founded on the Word of God and the Spirit of God and in the life and spirit of its African personality.

The theological base of the church rests on the firm doctrines of God, the Father; Jesus Christ, the Son; the Holy Spirit; the witness of fulfillment of the power of God and the revelation in the Old and New Testaments. Kimbangu was a witness as a prophet in whom the Spirit of God was made manifest and who opened the revelation of Christ through the African religious experience in fresh ways.

Kimbanguism is well organized on an African model and system. Here briefly is an outline of the organizational structure of the church.

1). The Spiritual Head is His Eminence Joseph Diangienda, the youngest son of the prophet and founder. He gives overall direction to the Church.

2). The spiritual counselors, those who surround the Spiritual Head and who were the apostles in the movement with the founder.

3). The General Assembly of the World Council, the delegates who meet every two years, representing some three million members in some ten countries in Africa.

4). The international secretary, who coordinates the General Assembly of the World Council.

5). College of Counselors, who work in each country with the aid of a synod, including provincial leaders and national officers.

6). The secretary general, who works with national and legal representatives of the respective countries as well as with the International Secretary.

7). Provincial counselors, who are the liaison between the secretary general and the work within the provinces.

8). Provincial secretary, who coordinates the work of the provinces.

9). Regional counselors, who coordinate the work of the local church in the light of the general church movement.

10). Regional secretary, who relates the work of the local church in the light of the general church movement.

11). Sectional secretary, who coordinates the work between territory and the local church.

12). Under-secretary, who assists the sectional secretary.

13). Assembly, the members in their gathering as Kimbanguist congregations.

14). Catechumens and sympathizers—the affiliates and friends
of the movement. [24]

In all aspects, the genuine Christ-like life style is held central and
necessary for all to practice in personal self-discipline and in social
and personal terms. "...everybody, whether he be head of the
Church or the simplest catechist, remains very modest." [25]

The fifth aspect of Kimbanguism is the affirmation of joyfulness
in terms of the spirit of freedom and creativity in witness.

The exuberance and spiritual enthusiasm of the believers is a
manifestation of the work of the Holy Spirit. There is joy, the beati-
tude of happiness, vibrating in the mood and feeling tones of
worship—manifested in the rhythmic movement, in singing and expressions of praise and adoration, in greetings and fellowship. From
these positive attitudes, the spiritual objectives of Kimbanguism are
infused with a joyful undertaking to:

1). spread the gospel of Jesus Christ, the message of liberation.
2). teach the Word from the Holy Spirit, loving good and ab-
horing evil.
3). practice truth and divine justice, from a heart of moral
purity.
4). do all to promote progress and peace.
5). exemplify charity and fellowship with all, without distinction.
6). express reconciliation by the love of God.
7). evangelize those who have not heard that they are children
of God.
8). avoid political alliances and engage spiritual relationships
with all people. [26]

William Crane felt that this work was the work of the Holy Spirit
which would not be fully understood by external rational scrutiny
alone. Having spent two weeks with the Kimbanguists to examine
some of the theological and religious beliefs and practices, he
stated,

> ...[the] theological definition of the church must remain
> open-ended for the Holy Spirit is at work in the world raising up
> ecclesial communities like the Kimbanguists, who are consciously
> living 'salvation history' and not just reading about it and
> abstracting theologies from reflecting on it. [27]

Another Western scholar, David Barrett, has defined a new interpretation of the direction of Western scholarship in dealing with the
Christian movement and with religion in Africa:

> Independency and movements within the churches now begin to
> be seen not primarily as a negative reaction to mission, but in the
> more positive sense understood by the participants themselves as
> movements of renewal, attempting to create a genuinely
> indigenous Christianity on African soil. In view of this, continuing
> expansion of schism and renewal across the continent takes on
> very considrable significance.[28]

The work of the Holy Spirit is truly renewing the Church. African
music gives an aliveness to the faith that beats like the heartbeat of
joy, flowing into and through the whole life of human behavior. The
drums, flutes, guitars, and other instruments as well as body movements inspire light feelings in singing and religious dancing. The
European life style is utterly foreign as an authentic expression of
religious sentiment and feeling tones. The highly rational structures
rigidly compartmentalize beliefs from behavior; the British "cool"
chills religion; the Catholic preoccupation with the crucifix as an intrinsic end produces mourning for a crucified Christ. The Belgian's
vocation as an efficient colonial administrator reinforced structured
inequality for perpetual domination of Africans, regarding the
Congolese as children. Europeans could never grasp that affirmation of joyfulness which was like an unquenchable thirst for freedom
of expression in all of life, in spite of oppression, humiliation, and
suffering. Music and movement strongly expressed the struggle
and creativity of the African spirit to survive, to endure, and to realize liberation.

Faith, in the Kimbanguist style, is the affirmation of happiness,
"that your joy might be full," beyond the persecution, distress,
nakedness, and sword, which they had borne for forty years. Kimbanguism looked beyond the cool of the British, the ceremony of
ritualism in foreign languages and the pomp and arrogance of religious colonialism, to find profoundly in the Christ-faith a deeper
recognition and empathy, a deeper feeling of joy, peace, and love
that affirm life. The blend of the African spirit of life with the
Christian life style came in a way that could not be expressed in the
colonial church. The Kimbanguists creatively transposed the spirit
of joy into the worship experience, not in gaudy or sensational ways
but to inspire fellowship and community togetherness. Such a feeling tone is real and contagious, inviting any and all of open spirit
and heart to share in the freedom of liberation of joyful and happy

spirits. Martin described what it did for her as she traveled in the Congo:

> When we were traveling, congregations stayed until 3 and 4 A.M. to receive us with tremendous joy and brought forward gifts and sang and played so that we ourselves forgot all our fatigue and would rejoice with them. [29]

The quality of trustfulness in terms of the integrity of openness and the spirit of nonviolence and cooperation describes a sixth component of Kimbanguism.

Although Kimbangu was a member of the BaKongo tribe, he refused to countenance tribalism as a rigid and divisive sociological construct in which to define his movement. Within a new construct, a new synthesis was strengthened between his African humanity and the Spirit of Christ. In both there were the experiences of profound suffering. In both the African life style of communal sharing and the Christian life style of "bear ye one another's burdens," positive and powerful symbiotic mergings maturing in African Christianity took place in Kimbanguism. There were implicitly the strong elements of trust and cooperation—in the temperament of African people as well as in the nature of a Christ-like religion. The profoundly genuine feeling about the sacredness of life in the religious spirit of Africa was deeply congruent to the Christian life style.

The painful forty years of persecution was a long period of purification. Suffering, alienation and humiliation not only serve to purify the faith of the believers, but there came also a quality of strength in the faith of the faithful that paradoxically promoted the rapid expansion of the movement among other African peoples. Because Kimbanguism is existentially African, its flexibility, adaptability, and spirit of inclusiveness accentuated its growth and development. At the same time, under persecution, the meaning of oppression in the light of endurance and liberation is understood as being for righteousness' sake. For them trust, nonviolence, and openness are more than theoretical statements of possibilities; they are experiences of "salvation history."

The Kimbanguists were the poor, afflicted, meek. They hungered after righteousness. They were merciful and pure in intentions. They were peacemakers and were reviled and had all manner of false accusations leveled against them. These and other experiences reason cannot contain or explain, feel or reveal. The Christ-church of the Kimbanguist was the church of the scattered peoples whose history is a precious witness and revelation and whose faith and faithfulness may not be denied. It is from this kind of history and struggle, through these kinds of trials and tribulations, that the church of Christ emerged as authentically African. A church which can affirm a quality of trustfulness, maintaining the integrity of openness and the spirit of nonviolence, has something the world desperately needs. In gentleness and modesty, there is in the Kimbanguist style of African Christianity a freshness in the hope of the humanization of man. In the twentieth century humanity has been dampened anew with the dews of the Redeeming Christ through the gentle flock of the Kimbanguists.

The following quotations reflect upon the theme of trust, openness, nonviolence, and cooperation. In the statutes of the church, we read that "the church cultivates every religious practice which favors respect and concord between men and nations, the essential foundation of harmony and true peace in the world." [30]   His Eminence Joseph Diangienda illustrates the spiritual philosophy when he states that church members

> ...should fulfill all their civic obligations as they are imposed in the laws in effect in the countries in which they live.
>
> [The church] desires the building up of a new humanism in the world which will be able to bring men together whatever their race, tribe, ethnic background, color or social class....
>
> [She] considers it not only opportune but necessary that the Declaration of the Rights of Man be applied in every nation, especially in those matters which concern fundamental liberties....
>
> She considers it true that from the time that all religions converge on the same object—the service of God in the interests of men—nothing will keep all those religions based on the teaching of Christ from adopting parallel paths....
>
> She condemns the use of force for the settling of problems which divide men.
>
> She rejects every political system which deprives citizens of the enjoyment of their fundamental freedoms: freedom of expression, of worship, of religion, of the press, of opinion, of movement.[31]

Brotherly compassion, sensitivity and responsiveness to the whole range of human needs is a seventh characteristic of Kimbanguism.

When John the Baptist sent his followers to inquire of Jesus if he were "the one" (Messiah) or should they look for another, Jesus simply replied, "...tell John what you hear and see." It was enough.

Those who have gone to the Congo have seen with their own eyes and have heard with their own ears and felt in their own hearts the authentic life of the Kimbanguist church. Some of those who went especially to observe and make some critical evaluations were: Jean Lasserre, *Voyage au Congo*, François Choffat, *Perspectives de Collaboration*, M. L. Martin, *Prophetism in the Congo*, William Crane, "The Kimbanguist Church and the Search for Authentic Catholicity." All of them, in one capacity or another, for whatever reason they went, were profoundly impressed by the demonstration of brotherly compassion (*kitwandi*) as expressed in the ethical life of the church, a church that put love into deeds. "They are educated in the spirit of Kimbanguism, that is, in full respect for life and faith in nonviolence." [32]

When the children of the church were forced out of school, the leaders called their own teachers out to teach the children, without pay. They set up their own schools. Actually, it was not until 1963 that a sound program of subsidizing teachers was developed to benefit the Kimbanguists. In the same manner, when the sick were refused admittance to the hospitals or humiliated and driven away from public service institutions, the church called out the faithful who were trained nurses and opened dispensaries. Teachers, nurses, and other technical leaders gave voluntary service in situations of need, and at times the need was critical: "a total of 15,153 students was sent away from the Protestant and Catholic mission schools." [33]

Between 1965 and 1966, the students in Kinshasa alone numbered 14,803, with a total of 1,433 teachers. The church also had organized sports, scouts, theatrical groups, etc. (The Kimbanguists remained open and brotherly with all religious elements, including the Protestants and the Catholics.) Various kinds of programs were developed to meet the many needs of the whole community and to foster the development of the whole person—work with young delinquents, work in rural life developments, programs oriented around social needs, worship, schools, dispensaries, workshops, cooperatives, youth clubs, furniture making, stores, women's group activities, and theological education.

Finally, the eighth contribution of Kimbanguism is its spiritual seriousness and commitment to the revelation of Christ in the African presence.

Salvation history is the life, message, and event of God's progressive revelation in the present. The historical extension of the incarnation as the living reality of Christianity was now clearly made manifest in the person of Simon Kimbangu in the first half of the twentieth century and in the Kimbanguist church movement in the latter half of the twentieth century. God's activity in presence and power enters unilaterally and authentically the African personality through the experience of Christ-consciousness. In Kimbanguism, there is a striking parallel to the Christ-like life style of unmerited suffering for righteousness' sake. There is, in a real and deep sense, communion with God's will and union with God's Spirit. The fuller meaning of the life and death of the African prophet will increase in theological relevance in the present as well as in the immediate past experience of the "living dead," providing a fresh theological perception of the fellowship of witnesses presently surrounding and enjoining the contemporary world Christian consciousness.

The spirit that was in the Prophet Simon Kimbangu was the Spirit of God, the Spirit of Truth, the Holy Spirit, the Christ-promise of the grace of God now fulfilling, now anointing the African religious experience. His was an African religious experience, authentically Christian. The prophet gave himself unconditionally to be instrumental in conducting the power of God's loving presence into human thought and feeling and into the total life situation. His gift, then, was salvation in healing, in faith, in love, and in the whole, wholesome, and holy life.

Martin, as a part of a study committee sent to study Kimbanguism, after carefully sharing in the life of the people and church, summarized her study in a series of impressions. (These impressions are true to my observations while in the Congo, 1960-1963, and during visits in Kinshasa, even though my visit was during troubled times.) Martin states,

> After careful study I have come to the conclusion that the Kimbanguist Church is genuinely a Christian church, representing the Christian life of a type described by Luke in the Book of Acts.[34]

Her impressions were given under seven models:

> 1. The spiritual sensitivity of the head of the movement, his Eminence, Joseph Diangienda.
> 2. The intertribal and interracial character of the church.
> 3. The outreach of the church to all fields of human endeavor.
> 4. The simplicity, even in a highly organized and unified system.
> 5. The joy in worship, in greetings, in singing and dancing.
> 6. The spirit of generosity and dedication.
> 7. The emphasis on sanctification: a "life of goodness must be the fruit of good news."[35]

Although some sacramental rites, as stressed in the theological life of Western Christian tradition, such as the Lord's Supper and water baptism do not hold the importance they have in the West, this does not invalidate the Christian experience. In their early history, when the Kimbanguists were refused admittance to the tables of the mission Christian churches because of punitive or narrow policies, or chose to absent themselves because of the strict "Nazarite vows" which many took, the sacramental life was more precious in terms of being living examples of the symbols rather than as the manipulators of objects.

There are, however, some objects recognized as reverently significant—the cross as the symbol of the living Christ, the star as a symbol of the ascending power of hope. The holy water of Nkamba is for faith-healing. But the most important sacramental force, as we have stated, is the Holy Spirit. Any who practice the faith in the company of the Kimbanguists must show the fruit of being cleansed, regenerated, and renewed by the force of the Holy Spirit. This baptism of the fire of Pentecost is stronger than the waters of Jordan. [36]

When the Executive Committee of the World Council of Churches was locked in serious deliberations regarding the admittance of the Kimbanguist church into the World Council, Jean Bokeleale, on the Executive Council, sharply criticized the Western-oriented traditionalists of the Christian faith, stating: "If a Western missionary introduces a new church to Africa, it is automatically considered to be a church, but if an African starts a new church it is taxed with being a sect." [37]

Oddly enough it was a speech from Metropolitan Nikodim of the Russian Orthodox Church that brought the Kimbanguist church into the World Fellowship. As Crane says,

> The clinching speech in favor came from Metropolitan Nikodim of the Russian Orthodox Church. The final vote was overwhelmingly for admission, with only three votes against and three abstentions. [38]

Whereas there is a strong dualism in the Western Christian mentality which draws a sharp distinction between the sacred and secular and negates the wholesome life by focusing on a sterile concept of the holy life, the African consciousness and life style seek to express a living faith that moves with equal force through all channels of thought, feeling and behavior. In this way, life itself is altogether a growing, enriching and sacramental experience. The most authentic definition for the Christian church is to be found essentially in the Christian life, which life must undergird doctrine as well as ceremony. No amount of abstract speculation in doctrine nor "churchianity" can authenticate the Christian life. Kimbanguism is an experience-centered faith and a faith-centered experience—authentically Christian, authentically African.

Kimbanguism is expressive of the personality of African religious life and of a consciousness of being a part of the world Christian movement, which is embarked upon a glorious and yet-to-be completed mission.

NOTES:

1. François Choffat, "Notes sur la Kimbanguisme," *Cahiers de la Reconciliation*, Mai-Juin, 5-6, Paris, p. 4.
2. R. P. Van Wing, "Le Kimbanguisme vu par un temoin," *Zaire, Revue Congolaise*, XII, 6 (1958). Georges Balandier, "Messianismes et Nationalismes en Afrique Noir," *Cahiers Internationaux de Sociologie*, XIV, 1953, p. 50. A journalist attending his trial in September 1921 wrote that he was 28. (*L'Avenir Colonial Belge*, 8 Mai, 1921). Because of his achievements, it was suggested that he was 40 years old.
3. Owanga Jean, Cabinet du Chef Spirituel, "Notes et Résumé historique de Kimbanguisme," Kinshasa, 1970, p. 2. M. J. Martin, "Prophetism in the Congo," *Ministry Theological Review to Africa* (reprint), v. VIII, 4, Oct. 1968.
4. There are several versions. One is "'Voici un bon livre! Tu dois l'étudier et prêcher.' 'Non,' respond Simon. 'Je ne suis ni un prêcheur ni un professeur. Je ne puis faire cela.'" This account was given by Budimbu, a Black man speaking to P.J. Lebridgo, M.D., giving an account of a conversation which he had with Kimbangu. Efraim Anderssen, *Messianic Popular Movements in the Lower Congo*, p. 50. An account is also in the *International Review of Missions*, 1922, p. 27 ff.
5. *Ibid.*, given in Jules Chome, *La Passion de Simon Kimbangu*, 2nd ed., Bruxelles, *Les Amis de Présence Africaine*, 1959, p. 10.
6. Van Wing, "Le Kimbanguisme vu par un temoin," p. 568; also *L'Avenir Belge*, 8 mai 1921, indicated that thousands came saying "journalière plus de cinq milles indigènes...." Also in the *Tshimbayeke, Le Bulletin du Cercle Colonial, Luxembourgeis*, June, 1953; "meeting monstres où il y a jusque dix mille auditeurs," also recorded by Chome, *ibid.*, p. 104. In a Catholic reference, Ephenedes Romaine, *Afrique Fraternal, des Missions Catholiques*: "Il faut avoir veçu ici pour faire une idée du vent de folie qui secoue alors le pays. Les travaux étaient suspendus, partout à tout instant sur les routes conduisant chez les prophètes on recontrait des bandes de pèlerins qui passaient en chantant trainant avec eux viellards qui passaient eux et enfants, portant leurs malades à guerir et leurs morts à ressusciter, logeant à la belle étoile et bravant le froid, la pluie et la faim [p. 110]."

7. *La Vois du Redempteur*, Décembre 1921, p. 381.
8. R. P. Leon Mingauw, *Fifty Years in Lower Congo, 1889-1949.* Louvain: Imprimerie, 1949. Some were sent and some remained; but, between March and August 1921, an unbelievable force of God's activity took place through the prophet. R. P. Braeckman, *Le Kimbanguisme: 3ème semaine de missiologie* (Louvain), p. 159, "Il se choisit douze apôtres à qui il imposa les mains cette consecration 'La lusambula' leur conferait le pourvoir d'ensêigner et de guerir, mais non celui de consacrer eux-mêmes d'autres disciples." (Owanga, *Notes*, p. 3.)
9. Choffat, "Notes," p. 5.
10. *Ibid.*, p. 7.
11. Chome, *La Passion de Simon Kimbangu*, p. 107.
12. Frequently used quotation from church history.
13. *L'Avenir colonial Belge*, 2 Octobre 1921 (according to Anderson), "Je suis Simon Kimbangu." (Soldiers beat him fiercely. Thousands had been sent away. Others sought to defend, but he admonished them to refrain from violence. The soldiers killed women and children and others.) Martin, "Prophetism in the Congo," p. 8. Chome, "La Passion de Simon Kimbangu," p. 81: "Simon Kimbangu résigné attend dans sa prison charge de lourdes chaines, le cou entravé par la cravate nationale."
14. Some quotations strike a familiar cord with that of events which took place with Jesus as seen in the following comment. "Et la 'Mission des Noirs' redigée après la condemnation de Kimbangu, ferà mention de cette trahison, 'Celui que Dieu avait envoyé comme Sauveur des Noirs a été livré aux autorités....'" (*L'Avenir Belge*, 2 Octobre 1921.)
15. Diangienda, Joseph, "Notes," p. 7.
16. William H. Crane, "The Kimbanguist Church and the Search for Authentic Catholicity," *The Christian Century*, June 4, 1970.
17. Choffat, "Notes," p. 8.
18. Chome, "La Passion de Simon Kimbangu," p. 98. "La repression du mouvement religieux a amené...l'éveil d'une sorte de nationalisme." "...la libération religieuse prefigure la liberation politique de dégager les noirs de toutes inferiorités que revela ou créa colonisation" [p. 138].
19. Choffat, "Notes," p. 9.
20. *Ibid.*, p. 10.
21. *Ibid.*, p. 11.
22. *Ibid.*
23. *Ibid.*
24. Constitution de l'Eglise du Christ sur la Terre (unpublished notes).

25. *Ibid.*
26. Lucien Luntadila, *Base de l'Eglise du Christ sur la Terre,* 12 Juin (unpublished notes).
27. W. Crane, "The Kimbanguist Church," part II.
28. David Barrett, *Schism and Renewal in Africa.* London: Oxford University Press, 1968, p. 1.
29. Martin, "Prophetism in the Congo," p. 5.
30. Jean Lasserre, "Eglise Nonviolent des Kimbanguistes," *Cahier Reconciliation*, Article 4 des statuts, p. 31.
31. Diangienda, Joseph, "Eglise et Politique," *Cahier de la Reconciliation*, pp. 40-42.
32. Choffat, "Notes," p. 10.
33. *Ibid.*
34. Martin, "Prophetism in the Congo," p. 12.
35. *Ibid.*, pp. 3-6.
36. The practice of Holy Communion was initiated at the time of the fiftieth anniversary celebrations in 1971.
37. Crane, "The Kimbanguist Church."
38. *Ibid.*

13

Islam in Africa

Newell S. Booth, Jr.

Islam is an African as well as an Asian religion; in fact, its birth-place in Arabia is geographically closer to northeastern Africa than to most of Asia. If it were not for the great geological fault which forms the Red Sea, the Arabian desert would be the eastern part of the Sahara. Similar conditions of life are present on the two shores of this sea and crossings for trade, conquest, and settlement had been taking place for centuries before the rise of Islam. Thus it was not surprising that when Muhammad, facing persecution in Mecca, wished to find a place of safety for some of his followers, he thought of Ethiopia. The early Muslim contact with Africa is also evident in the tradition that the first to act as *muadhdhin*, calling the faithful to prayer, was Bilal, an African slave.

In its rapid early expansion Islam moved westward into Africa as well as eastward into Asia; by 708 the Muslim armies had reached the Atlantic shores of Morocco. The Berber inhabitants of the Maghreb (western North Africa) gradually became Muslims; some also were wholly or partially Arabized in culture and language. It was primarily these Berbers, crossing the desert as traders and, in some cases, as raiders or conquerors, who first carried Islam to sub-Saharan West Africa, known in Arabic as *bilad-as-sudan*, "The land of the Blacks."

Today the name "Sudan" refers to a political unit that includes only the eastern part of the area covered in the original and larger meaning of the term. For our purposes we can distinguish the western Sudan, which includes the areas drained by the Senegal and the Upper Niger rivers; the central Sudan, east of the Niger bend, with a focus in the area of Lake Chad; and the eastern or "Nilotic" Sudan.

On the east coast we can distinguish the northern area, some-times known as the African "horn," today dominated by Ethiopia and

Somalia, and a southern area, long known to the Arabs as the "land of Zanj," corresponding essentially to what are now the coastal regions of Kenya and Tanzania.

One might have supposed that Islam would first move into sub-Saharan Africa along the route of the Nile; in fact, this was not at all the case. The first Muslim contacts were trading posts established along the shores of the Indian ocean and along the southern "shores" of the Sahara. The sea in the east and the desert in the west had somewhat analogous functions in the origins of African Islam. In both east and west contacts developing as a result of trade were the major factor in the earliest phase of Islamic expansion in sub-Saharan or Black Africa.

The evidence available indicates that the first Black Africans to adopt Islam in significant numbers were the people of Takrur, living on the banks of the Senegal River. The Arab historian al-Bakri, writing in 1067, tells of a king who became Muslim some time before his death in 1040 and who "enforced the religion upon his subjects." [1] It should be noted that this took place in the westernmost part of Africa, far from the Middle Eastern birthplace of Islam.

After crossing the Sahara along the caravan routes established by Berber merchants, primarily in what is now Mauritania, Islam spread toward the east, along the southern edge of the desert. There were, of course, contacts at the southern terminals of caravan routes further to the east, which resulted in the conversion of a few rulers. The general direction of the more substantial Muslim influence south of the Sahara, however, was from west to east.

The ancient kingdom—or, perhaps, series of kingdoms—known to the outside world by the title of the king, "Ghana," had existed since about the fourth century of the Christian era. In 1067, according to al-Bakri, the capital was composed of twin cities, one a Muslim trading center, inhabited largely by foreigners, the other a royal town, where the traditional religion still prevailed. [2] The *Murabitun*, Muslim warriors from Morocco, attacked and largely destroyed the city in 1076. It appears to have been *after* the fall of the Kingdom that the Soninke people who had been at its core adopted Islam. It is likely that the disruption at that time encouraged them to seek a new religious foundation for their communal relationships.

Further to the east, on the Upper Niger, a kingdom of Mali was in

existence by the tenth century. Al-Bakri appears to say that the king
living in his time was the first to have become a Muslim, and gives
an interesting account of his conversion. The land was suffering
from drought and traditional sacrifices were to no avail. A traveling
Muslim persuaded the king that if he accepted Islam the people's
suffering would be relieved. The traveler taught him the basic ritual
obligations and on a Friday had him wash and put on new clothes
before spending the night in prayer. At dawn the rains came. The
king then had his "idols" destroyed and the court became Muslim,
although the common people continued in their traditional religion.[3]

One ruler of Mali, Mansa (King) Musa, became a legend in the
Arab world as a result of his pilgrimage in 1324-1325. He distributed
so much gold in Egypt that its value is said to have been depressed;
he also accumulated such debts that some of his creditors followed
him home in order to collect!

When Ibn Battuta, the Arab traveler, visited Mali in 1352-1353,
he found Muslim ritual widely observed in the capital but was
shocked at the continued observance of traditional customs incompatible with Islam. The local Muslims, however, apparently saw
no incongruity in the situation. Although the rituals were popular,
observance of Muslim law was minimal; Islam made its appeal as a
source of power more than as a pattern for life. Outside the governmental and commercial centers Islam had little influence at all.

One important early center was Timbuktu, which may have been
founded by Saharan Berbers (Tuaregs) sometime around 1100. It is
said to have been always a Muslim city.[4] After 1300 it became a
leading trading post or "port" at the point where the Niger River
makes its northern curve through the edge of the desert. It never
was a large center of population but was important as an intellectual
as well as a commercial crossroads, a collection point for ideas and
goods in transit between north and south.

Gao or Kawkaw, on the Niger bend east of Timbuktu, had apparently been a trading post at least since the ninth century and was
frequented by Muslim traders from the north. One source indicates
that by 985 the local ruler was a Muslim.[5] A tombstone from the
year 1101, inscribed in Arabic, is the earliest known physical
evidence of Islam in the Sudan area.[6]

There is frequent uncertainty regarding the date of the "conversion" of rulers, due in part to the fact that it is not entirely clear
just what is meant by "conversion." As has been the case in more
recent times, a ruler may have adopted an Islamic identity for the
purposes of commercial and foreign relations while maintaining a

traditional identity for rituals relating to the land, the agricultural cycle, and the ancestors.

This is well illustrated by the case of the conqueror, Sunni Ali (reigned 1464-1492), under whom the Songhai Empire rose to prominence. Sunni Ali's attitude toward Islam apparently was ambivalent. He conformed outwardly to certain Muslim requirements, such as prayer and fasting, but also persecuted the *ulama* (Muslim scholars) of Timbuktu. His authority was based to a large extent on the traditional "magical" powers of the Songhai kings. According to tradition, his father "passed on to him the 'master-word' by virtue of which all other divinities became subservient to him." [7] It would appear that Sunni Ali, like many other African rulers, saw in Islam a source of power that he wished to tap along with the traditional sources, but he did not welcome domination by Muslim scholars. He wanted Islam on his own terms or perhaps on traditional Songhai terms, adopting those elements which were consistent with tradition. [8]

Sunni Ali's son apparently did not even make a show of being a Muslim, which may have been a reason for his failure to keep control of the empire. He was replaced by Muhammad Ture, a general whose family was from the west, of Soninke or Tokolor origin. As an outsider and the founder of the new Askiya dynasty, Muhammad Ture had little claim on the traditional powers of the Songhai rulers; thus it is not surprising that under him the religious validation of authority shifted significantly toward Islam. The fact that his family was from an area where Islam had become more fully established may also be significant.

Soon after securing power, Muhammad Ture went on the pilgrimage to Mecca, where the Sharif designated him as *khalifa* (deputy) for the "land of Takrur." [9] This title, added to the mysterious power associated with those who had made the pilgrimage, provided a new, more distinctively Islamic, basis of authority. The traditional Sudanic "divine king" was thus replaced by the Muslim "pilgrim-king." [10] This change should not be exaggerated; just as the traditional king found added power through some identification with Islam, so the Muslim ruler found it advisable to follow a number of traditional practices. The difference was that, while the former incorporated Islam into the traditional pattern, the latter incorporated the traditional into Islam. One could say that the state itself had now become officially Islamic with Islamic symbols of investiture: the tunic, turban, and sword given by the sharif of Mecca. [11] There were also indigenous symbols, however, and the majority of the people were left undisturbed in their practice of the traditional religion.

Muhammad Ture engaged in one *jihad* (holy war) against the "pagan" Mossi to the south of the Niger bend. In accord with the requirements for such a struggle he sent a message to the Mossi ruler, inviting him to accept Islam. This ruler, after consulting his ancestors, declined. Muhammad Ture invaded the country in 1498 with some temporary success but then withdrew, and the Mossi gained the reputation of being resistant to Islam.

Muhammad Ture's only important successor, Askiya Dawud (reigned 1549-1583), had close ties with the *ulama*, but even he found it necessary to engage in traditional ceremonies that were abhorent to them. When one of the *ulama* questioned the king about this, wondering if he were "mad, corrupt or possessed," he replied,

> I am not mad myself, but I rule over mad, impious and arrogant folk. It is for this reason that I play the mad man myself and pretend to be possessed by a demon in order to frighten them and prevent them from harming the Muslims. [12]

Under the Askiya dynasty Islam had made significant advances as the religion of the state but did not have much effect on the people of the villages, although certain aspects of it appealed to them as new and exotic sources of magical power. In such urban centers as Jenne and Timbuktu "a brilliant traditional Moslem culture" had been established with "an elite of theologians, lawyers, writers, astronomers, and mathematicians." [13]

When the Songhai empire was destroyed in 1591 by a Moroccan army, centralized government and town life were seriously disrupted. As these were precisely the foci of Muslim strength, Islam was also weakened. It continued to be the religion of the urban centers but lost its position as the basis of indigenous political organization. The fact that the Moroccan *pashas* (governors) were Muslim did not help; in fact, it probably hurt Islam because they were regarded as unwelcome aliens.

One of the most important Islamic groups in modern sub-Saharan Africa is composed of the Hausa-speaking peoples of what is now northern Nigeria and the Republic of Niger. The first significant Islamic influence among them, however, was later than in the great empires of the west. In fact, this influence appears to have come from the west, although the area is usually considered to be in the "central Sudan."

A group from Mali, presumably traders, is said to have first brought Islam to Kano in the latter part of the fourteenth century [14]; about this time the rulers of Kano and Katsina adopted Islam, at least for purposes of commercial relations. As in other cases, one of the major appeals of Islam was the power it made available through ritual prayer. An early account tells how in Kano, during the fourteenth century, pagans were defiling the mosque; but, after the small group of Muslims prayed all night, the "leader of the pagans was struck blind that very day." [15] It was only after more direct contact was developed with scholars from centers of Islamic learning in the late fifteenth and early sixteenth centuries that there is evidence of a substantial Muslim presence, even in the towns. The most notable of these scholars was Al-Maghili, an orthodox Maliki scholar from Tlemçen (in western Algeria), who visited Kano and other centers in the late fifteenth century. As he was a leader in the Qadariyya order of Sufis, his influence was significant in the development of mystical as well as legal Islam.

Further east, in the Lake Chad region, we finally reach an area where the first Islamic influence was not from the west, but directly across the desert from Egypt. The ruler of the Kingdom of Kanem probably was converted about 1085; his son opened and desecrated the "sacred box," thus repudiating the traditional basis of royal authority. It was no doubt in order to strengthen the new Islamic basis of authority that he made two pilgrimages to Mecca; he is said to have drowned in the Red Sea attempting a third. [16]

In the fourteenth century the ruling family moved from Kanem, northeast of Lake Chad, to Bornu, southwest of the Lake, and in the late sixteenth century the kingdom reached a high point, under Mai (king) Idris Alouma. Islam became more than simply the royal cult; there was an effort to apply the *shari'a* (Islamic law) to at least some aspects of daily life.

In general the seventeenth century was a time of recession for Islam in the western and central Sudan, "marked by the eclipse of Islamic universalism and the ascendance of local religions." [17] However, there was considerable expansion southward through the influence of Muslim traders, coming especially from among the Mande speaking peoples of the old Mali empire, who in dispersion were known as Dyula, Yarse, and Wangara. These traders became a special class "whose members could carry their religion around with them." [18]

Those known as Dyula were members of "highly dispersed corporations, specializing in commerce," who "created a wide-flung supra-tribal network of trade" and "were able to wield considerable economic influence within the various states and communities in which they operated." [19]   They also attracted attention to their religion by "their practice of the outward Muslim devotions and...their confidence in the superior spiritual power of Islam in healing the sick, ensuring the fertility of women and crops, and in averting the dangers of witchcraft and sorcery...." [20]

As early as the fifteenth century a number of kingdoms had developed in the region of the middle and upper Volta in close association with the expansion of trade in gold and kola nuts between the Niger bend to the north and the forest region to the south. The Mande traders, whose ancestors had become Muslims through contact with the Berbers and their desert trade, now followed this opportunity for trade further south, among the "Voltaic" peoples in what is now the northern part of the modern Republic of Ghana. Some chiefs became Muslim, although continuing to base their local authority on traditional foundations. In other cases the rulers adopted certain outward characteristics of Islam without necessarily considering themselves Muslim, [21]   while those who found Islam incompatible with the traditional role of chief allowed relatives and associates to become Muslim. [22]   Muslims were considered to have special powers, useful to the chiefs; thus it might be said that, "if you want to wage war and you cannot find a Mallam [Muslim holy man], it is impossible for you to do so." [23]   Islam provided a new source of power, especially relevant to commercial affairs and international relations, as it had at an earlier time in the development of such kingdoms as Mali and Songhai. Thus Islam survived and even spread by "adapting itself to African categories of thought, Muslim clans being accorded their defined place in the social structure...." [24]

Turning to the eastern or Nilotic Sudan, the area now known as the Republic of the Sudan, we find a history of Islamic development quite different from that which we have seen further west. Relationships with Egypt go back to ancient times, with influences moving in both directions. The kingdom of Meroë, emerging in the third century B.C., combined Egyptian and Hellenistic influences with indigenous African traditions. In the fourth century A.D., the Nubians became dominant and in the sixth century were converted to Monophysite Christianity by missionaries from Egypt. The Arab

Muslims who conquered Egypt in 642 met the Nubians just south of the first Nile cataract at Aswan. After some inconclusive fighting an agreement was reached between the Muslim governor of Egypt and the Nubian king providing for nonaggression from either side, and for the exchange of goods. This agreement, surprisingly enough, remained the basis of relationships for some 600 years!

Although there were occasional clashes and some Arab penetration, no basic change took place until the thirteenth century, when dynastic struggles within Nubia coincided with a growing expansionist attitude on the part of the Mamluk rulers of Egypt. In 1275 the Egyptians defeated the Nubians and installed a puppet king. Further dynastic struggles weakened Nubia and opened it to settlement by Arab nomads encouraged to move out of Egypt by the Mamluks, who found them hard to handle. In 1317 a Muslim became king and from this time on Islam gained ground rapidly, not so much by direct proselytism as by intermarriage.

South of Nubia there was another kingdom, Alwa, with its capital near present-day Khartoum. Although Christianity was the state religion, it had probably not penetrated very deeply within the population as a whole. Muslim traders had been in the kingdom at least since the ninth century [25] but had no apparent effect on the local residents. After the Islamization of the Nubian kingdom in the fourteenth century, Alwa was cut off from outside influence and Arab tribes began to infiltrate the area. It finally fell in 1504, and Christianity had been replaced by Islam by the end of the sixteenth century.

The kingdom of Sennar, which followed Alwa in the area where the Blue and White Niles join, was dominated by a Black aristocracy known as the Funj, possibly of Shilluk origin. [26] Their first king became a Muslim about 1520, perhaps in order to ease political and commercial relations with Egypt. Sufi teachers from Arabia were brought in; they "created centers of religious enthusiasm" from which Muslim belief and practice spread gradually. [27]

In the Nilotic Sudan, in contrast to the situation further west, Islamization generally meant Arabization. "More than for most other Muslim peoples of Africa, for the Sudanese to be a Muslim is to be an Arab." [28] Intermarriage between Arab men and non-Arab women produced children who were considered Arabs. Further intermarriage between these children and other non-Arabs led to a situation in which an Arab identity was claimed by people with a very small percentage of actual Arab ancestry. In other cases groups with no Arab ancestry may have invented Arab genealogies which came to be accepted. The Arabic language generally replaced the indigenous languages except, interestingly enough, in Nubia, the area nearest Egypt, where the people maintained their separate ethnic identity and language after becoming Muslims. In spite of the fact that a large portion of the Nilotic Sudan had become nominally Muslim by the sixteenth century, Islamization was so superficial that a Muslim author can say that "Islam did not make any major advances until...the nineteenth century." [29]

The Muslims of East Africa are almost totally cut off from those of West Africa and even of the Nilotic Sudan by Christian Ethiopia, which, however, also has an Arabian background. It was probably in the seventh century B.C. that the Habashat and related groups from South Arabia crossed over to the African side. By the third century B.C. they had a well-established kingdom in what is now Eritrea and northwestern Ethiopia, with the capital at Axum. The Semitic settlers incorporated many of the earlier, "Hamitic-speaking", residents into their political and cultural system. In the middle of the fourth century A.D. the king of Axum was converted to Monophysite Christianity and by 500 A.D. this was the dominant religion of the people.

When Muhammad's early followers were being persecuted in Mecca it was to Axum that he sent them for refuge. Perhaps it was because of this early friendly contact that, while the Persian empire was destroyed and the Byzantine empire greatly reduced by early Muslim conquests, there was apparently no serious thought of conquering Axum. However, Muslims did gradually establish themselves along the African shores of the Red Sea, especially at Zeila. This area was peripheral to the Axumite kingdom, whose center was in the interior highlands, but its control by Muslims did have the effect of largely cutting off the Christian kingdom from the outside world. This situation, combined with the threat of the still-"pagan" Beja nomads to the north, encouraged a southward reorientation of the Semitic-speaking Christians. During the course of several centuries, by settlement, conversion, and conquest, they spread over the whole plateau area, incorporating the indigenous Agao peoples.

At the same time that Christianity was gradually becoming dominant in the highlands, Islam was spreading from the coast through the lowlands and into some of the eastern and southern highlands. It appears that Muslim rulers had established themselves in eastern Shoa, not far from the site of the present Addis

Ababa, no later than the twelfth century. [30]   Serious hostilities began about 1325, with the sultanate of Ifat, which dominated the area from the coast at Zeila to eastern Shoa, as the chief protaganist on the Muslim side. The fortunes of battle shifted back and forth until the sultanate finally was defeated in 1415. The struggle was resumed in 1527 under the Imam Ahmad, known as "Gran," a charismatic leader who believed himself appointed by God to wage the *jihad* against Christian Ethiopia. Within ten years Ahmad was in control of at least three-fourths of Ethiopia and the Christian king himself was a fugitive. Large numbers of people became Muslims in order to save their lives; destruction was widespread. In 1542, however, a Portuguese force came to the assistance of the king and when Ahmad was killed in battle his army collapsed. Most of the population returned to their former Christian allegiance and the kingdom was reestablished, though with weakened central control. The Muslim centers had also been weakened by this tremendous expenditure of energy. The major beneficiaries were the Galla, who moved into both Muslim and Christian territories, many eventually to be converted by both religions.

The Galla, in turn, were being pushed by the Somalis, whose original home was on the coast of the Gulf of Aden in the northern part of present-day Somalia. There they had been in contact with traders from Arabia since before the beginning of the Muslim era. Within a couple of hundred years of the rise of Islam, Muslim traders were settling on the coast, marrying Somali women, and forming a commercial-political-religious aristocracy of mixed ancestry. To this day certain Somali clans trace their origins to Arab immigrants; they do not, however, consider themselves Arabs. [31] By the twelfth century the Somalis were pushing south and west from the Gulf of Aden, perhaps partly because of the stimulus associated with the Arab-Muslim presence. By the sixteenth century the Somalis had all become Muslim. Many of them supported the *jihad* of the Iman Ahmad, probably because they needed more living space as much as for religious reasons. Although this attempt to conquer the highlands failed, expansion southward was more successful, leading eventually to their present wide distribution in the easternmost part of Africa.

Generally speaking, Islam in Ethiopia and neighboring areas entered a period of political weakness in the sixteenth century. The pagan Galla overran previously Muslim areas and the Muslim Somali had not consolidated their position. The main continuing centers of Islamic culture, the coastal cities and Harrar, had little political power.

From these centers, however, Islam expanded gradually, especially among the Galla, who were moving into the highland areas of the ancient Christian kingdom. In 1668 an attempt was made to control the situation by forbidding Muslims to own land in Christian areas. The result, however, was to encourage commercial activity which widened the scope of Muslim contacts and thus actually made for the spread of Islam.[32] Muslims were in touch with surrounding countries and thus presented themselves as members of a more universal faith than Christianity, which had become ingrown, parochial, and associated with Amharic nationalism. Islam appealed to groups such as the Galla partly because they were looking for help in their conflict with the Amhara.

In southern Ethiopia some of the formerly pagan kingdoms of the Sidama peoples were converted. The agents of their conversion are clearly indicated by the fact that their word for "merchant" is also the word for "Muslim."[33] A number of formerly Christian nomad tribes in what is now northern Eritrea became Muslim through the influence of traders and "holy families" and also because of neglect by the Christian Church.[34] Even in the Christian highlands conversions to Islam were fairly frequent.[35]

Further south along the East African coast (the "land of Zanj"), we again find an Islam which developed in relationship to trade. The commerce of the Indian ocean had been bringing southern Arabia and East Africa into contact with each other for many centuries; such contacts became more significant after the rise of Islam. There are accounts of Arab writers dating from as early as the tenth century A.D., which tell of adventures on the coast of "Zanj" (or "Zangebar"). From the African side we have the story of a sultan and his six sons from Shiraz in Persia who sailed in seven ships, landing at seven points on the East African coast. The story, as recorded in the Kilwa chronicle, tells of one who landed at Kilwa, married the daughter of the local chief, and founded a dynasty.[36] This story no doubt reflects the fact that merchant-adventurers from Arabia and Persia did settle on the East African coast and in some cases established themselves as rulers of towns by means of matrimonial alliances. In three or four generations their descendants were physically indistinguishable from their neighbors and used the tongue of their mothers as their first language; they maintained, however, the Muslim faith of their fathers and identified themselves with their immigrant ancestors.

Movement across the sea thus made its contribution to the new community on the East African coast, but some of the accounts probably exaggerate the numbers of Arabs or Persians involved. Neither the archeological nor the documentary evidence supports the view that there was large-scale colonization. In fact, some of the Muslim coastal towns may have developed as indigenous African responses to the possibilities of overseas trade. Their inhabitants were to some extent alienated from the traditional communities; as individual entrepreneurs, they could not accept open-ended responsibility for all their relatives. Yet some common basis for an ordered community had to be found. The Arab and Persian traders with whom they were in contact had a religion which seemed to meet this need, which, in fact, had arisen in a very similar situation in Mecca. It would not be surprising if African leaders themselves saw in Islam an answer to their individual and communal needs, as well as a basis for contact with the wider world over the seas.

The early accounts suggest that Zanzibar may have been the site of the first significant Muslim community along the east African coast. Al-Masudi, writing between 915 and 945 speaks of an island "in the Zanj sea" with "a mixed population of Muslims and Zanj idolaters."[37] The earliest archeological evidence is an inscription in a mosque on the island of Zanzibar dated A.H. 500 (A.D. 1107)[38] Another important early center was Kilwa, further to the south. Writing of a trip taken in 1331, Ibn Battuta speaks of the people of Kilwa as "of very black complexion," and also as devout Muslims.[39] The idea of a "Zanj" political empire with Kilwa as the capital is not supported by evidence, but perhaps there was a kind of trading "empire."

Out of the contacts and interactions of adventurers, traders, and local peoples a new society developed by the thirteenth century, Muslim in faith and largely African in racial composition. The Swahili language reflects the nature of this society, for it is thoroughly African (Bantu) in grammatical structure but has borrowed 20 to 30 per cent of its vocabulary from Arabic[40] and, to a lesser extent, from Persian and other sources. These borrowings have been largely of technical terms, especially those related to commerce, religion, and literate culture.

The culture associated with the Swahili language was limited to the coastal towns, of which there are said to have been thirty-seven in the fifteenth century, some of which had grown quite wealthy from trade.[41] This society had a minimal influence on neighboring groups; even the inland trade was largely in the hands of people from the interior who came to the coast. Thus the Swahili community did not expand outward, but grew by drawing to itself new migrants from overseas and from the interior.

Vasco da Gama's visit to the east coast of Africa in 1498 may be said to have signaled the end of the "classical" period of Swahili culture. Within a few years the Portuguese had gained control of much of the coast, disrupting the lines of commerce and largely destroying the earlier prosperity. In the late sixteenth century disaster also struck out of the African interior in the form of marauding bands of Zimba who wiped out several of the towns. A little later the Galla struck from the north and the Somali moved down the coast. As a result of these events the Swahili culture survived largely on a few offshore islands. The ruins of Gedi in the north and Kilwa in the south, and of many places between, are mute testimonies to the achievements of the first phase of east African Islam.

To sum up, the first phase of Muslim expansion in sub-Saharan Africa covered approximately the period from 1000 to 1600. It was largely due to contacts made by traders crossing the desert or the sea and its strongest centers were commercial towns on the desert fringes and the coast. Islam appealed primarily to those whose activities involved contacts beyond the local area—especially merchants and rulers. It also influenced some whose traditional lives had been disrupted by war or slavery. The masses of the rural population were hardly affected, except insofar as Islam provided access to new powers which supplemented the traditional. As a result of the first phase, then, there were Muslim individuals and Muslim towns but, with a few exceptions, such as the Tokolor and the Somali at opposite ends of the continent, no Muslim peoples.

In general, the seventeenth and early eighteenth centuries were a period of Islamic recession, associated with weakness in centralized authority. Changing trade patterns, however, due in part to the appearance of Europeans along the coast, drew Muslims into new areas—thus spreading at least a minimal influence and preparing for further advances.

The second phase of African Muslim history, beginning in the eighteenth century, is characterized by the transition from a class religion to a religion of whole peoples. Contributing to this popularization was the spread of the Sufi ("mystical") orders, *jihads* conducted by leaders who took seriously Islam's claim to be the basis of social and political organization, and changes associated with European penetration of Africa.

In Africa, as in other areas of Islamic expansion, Sufism played a major role, appealing to many who did not respond to traditional orthodox Islam, a rather austere system focusing on legal requirements and allowing slight opportunity for the expression of personal feeling. Sufism arose, at least in part, as a counterbalance to legal orthodoxy, providing the opportunity for a more emotional and directly personal relationship between the believer and God, and also for a close-knit community on the human level.

The Muslim doctrines of the absolute unity and otherness of God would appear to allow little room for mysticism. Developed in certain ways, however, these very doctrines provide the basis for mystical belief. Islam puts such emphasis on the unique power and truth of God that one is led to conclude that nothing is "really real" except God. All temporal things depend on Him at every moment for their continued existence. The only source of power is God; all actions are ultimately acts of God. This belief that only God is real can be very easily transposed into the idea that all that is real is God. God the wholly other becomes God the totally present. This is the transposition that took place in some forms of Sufism.

It was not until the time of the great Persian scholar Al-Ghazali (1059-1111) that orthodoxy was reconciled with mysticism. After an experience of acute doubt, Al-Ghazali discovered the foundation of orthodox belief and practice in his own personal relationship with God. Obedience was not simply an external conformity to the commandments of an austere God but the expression of a personal relationship with God present in the heart of man.

This reconciliation of orthodoxy and mysticism provided the context in which the Sufi *turuq* (plural of *tariqa*), "ways," arose in the period from 1100 to 1400. Their doctrines, rules, and methods were transmitted from one generation to another through "chains" of teachers. In the fifteenth century these "ways" became the bases of communal organizations whose members gave their personal allegiance to the community leader. [42] Local centers of these orders came to be the closest Islamic equivalents to "local churches" and their leaders the closest equivalent to "clergy." [43]

The most widespread of all the orders is the Qadariyya, traditionally founded by Abd al Qadar al-Jilani who lived from 1077 to 1166; the order, however, did not spread widely until the fifteenth century. [44] An important early Qadariyya representative in Africa was al-Maghili, who, like Al-Ghazali, combined orthodox legal scholarship with mysticism. His visit to Mali and the Hausa states in the late fifteenth century has already been noted. Further west the Kounta family of Mauretania was influential in the spread of the Qadariyya in the period from the sixteenth through the eighteenth centuries. Those initiated into the order formed small cells of relatively well-educated people, in touch with each other and with centers of Islamic learning. Serving as scribes, teachers, and dispensers of charms, they had considerable influence and were responsible for many conversions. [45]

Another order, especially important in West Africa, is the Tijaniyya, founded by Ahmad ben Muhammad at-Tijani, who was born in southern Algeria in 1737 but spent his later years in Fez, Morocco, where he died in 1815. He claimed to have been visited by Muhammad himself and given authority to found a new order. Through him salvation was guaranteed to all his followers—in fact, to all who performed services for him. [46] Exclusive loyalty was demanded but ritual obligations were relatively simple; because salvation was assured through the leader there was little need for time-consuming devotional practices. Asceticism was not necessary either; with salvation guaranteed, one may enjoy the comforts and pleasures of this world. [47] Thus the order, though based on a mystical link between Muhammad and the founder, did little to encourage actual mystical practices among its adherents. Its popular expression was largely communal, with a strong tendency toward political involvement.

In the Nilotic Sudan the *feki* combined the roles of legal scholar and Sufi master, establishing centers from which Islamic faith and practice influenced the "pagan" environment. [48] The Qadariyya and the Shadhiliyya, another old order, were the most influential. In the nineteenth century several new orders were inspired by the work of the reformer Ahmad Ibn Idris (1760-1837), a Moroccan who moved to the Hijaz. The most important of these in the Sudan was that known as the Mirghaniyya or Khatmiyya. In this, and other "new orders," like the Tijaniyya, more emphasis was placed on loyalty to the leader (*shaikh*), through whom salvation was assured, than on any distinctively mystical beliefs or practices. [49]

The Qadariyya also became the leading order in Ethiopia, having entered Harrar sometime around 1500. In the nineteenth century the new, more politically active orders gained influence among certain groups; for instance, the Salihiyya spread in Somalia, while the Tijaniyya, coming from West Africa, has been active among the Galla of the Jimma area. [50]

Along the east African coast, south of Somalia, the orders have not had the same social and political significance as elsewhere in Africa but have been important in the spread of Islam to the interior. The two most important orders are the Qadariyya and Shadhiliyya; the "new orders" of the nineteenth century have made little impact.

An important aspect of the second phase of Muslim expansion in West Africa was the emergence of men from within the Sufi orders become leaders of *jihads* (holy wars) aimed at the purification and spread of Islam. Their ethnic origin was generally from among the Tolkolor and the Fulbe. The Tokolor, whose homeland is along the Senegal River, are probably descended in part from the people of Takrur who were the first West Africans to be significantly influenced by Islam. They are somewhat mixed with other groups; in fact, it has been said that "they are not so much a people as a hierachized class society."[51] The Fulbe (also known as "Fulani" and "Peul"), who speak essentially the same language as Tokolor, are even more of a mixture; "they are a class society whose only common factor is language."[52] Through nomadic wanderings with their much esteemed long-horn cattle, they became widely dispersed throughout the western and central Sudan. In some places they settled down to agriculture or came to dominate and assimilate already settled groups. Some of them were very devout Muslims, others only nominal believers, if that. In spite of their great diversity and wide distribution, they have maintained a strong sense of ethnic identity.

The term "Torodbe" refers to the educated or clerical class of Muslims among the Tokolor and Fulbe, associated with the Sufi brotherhoods, originally the Qadariyya, who were accepted by traditional rulers in the western and central Sudan as representatives of an important supplementary source of power. This diffused group became the principal agents of a "revolution" which sought, with varying degrees of success, to change Islam from a primarily ritualistic class cult into a pattern of life for the whole community.

The "revolution" began in the far western Sudan, in the Tokolor homeland, known as the Futa Toro, and a little further south in the Futa Jalon, an area now in the Republic of Guinea, into which Fulbe nomads had been moving. Around 1725 the latter began an attempt to take control of the Futa Jalon from the previous inhabitants. Although most Fulbe were only nominally Muslim to start with, their leaders were devout members of the clerical class, affiliated with the Qadariyya order, who gave the revolution the character of a *jihad* against "pagans." The struggle was protracted, but in 1776 the Fulbe established what has been described as an "aristocratic religious republic" [53] under an elected *imam* or *almani* who functioned as both religious and political leader in the classic Muslim pattern.

A similar revolution of Muslims against pagan rulers took place in Futa Toro, beginning later but achieving success just about the same time, 1776. A new noble class was formed by the Torodbe, who elected the *imam* (*almani*) from among themselves. [54]

The most famous *jihad* was that of Uthman dan Fodio, a Torodbe, whose family had lived for some time in Hausa territory. He began his career as a Sufi (Qadariyya) preacher around 1774 and then was inspired by news of the Islamic revolutions in the west to make a similar effort among the Hausa, whose rulers were nominally Muslim but permitted many activities that were clearly non-Islamic. As Uthman's teacher put it, "they supposed, when they adopted the enlightenment of prayer and fasting and pronounced the unity of God, that they were Muslims, but undoubtedly they were not." [55] Uthman and his associates found this relaxed and compromising form of Islam, coexisting with other forms of belief and practice, intolerable and the proper object of a *jihad* aimed at the establishment of a truly Islamic society.

In 1804, Uthman was forced to flee from his home; he considered this event as his *hijra* and from that time "regarded himself as the chosen instrument for the execution of the decrees of the Divine will." [56] He took the title of the old Caliphs, "commander of the faithful" (*amir al-mu'minin*), and gathered a group of followers from among the Fulbe clerics of Hausaland. Fulbe nomads who earlier had migrated to the area also rallied to his cause, more out of communal than religious loyalty, for most were not devout Muslims. He also attracted recruits from the Tokolor and Fulbe centers to the west.

By 1810 Uthman's forces were in control of the Hausa states. They also established their rule over the Nupe and part of the Yoruba to the south and over the Adamawa region to the east in what is now the Cameroons. They captured part of the kingdom of Kanem and some Fulbe even passed Lake Chad and established themselves in Darfur. Thus an Islamic revolution which began in the far west reached three-fourths of the way across the continent into areas where the primary Islamic influence had been from Egypt.

After these startling victories Uthman retired from active political leadership, dividing the territory between his brother and his son. Actually, the centralized power was rather slight; Uthman's descendants in the newly built city of Sokoto were recognized as having religious more than political authority. To a considerable extent the result of the revolution was the substitution of Fulbe for Hausa rulers in the various city-states. There was some attempt at religious reformation, bringing about better observation of the *shari'a* in the cities. The rural population was at first left almost entirely untouched and allowed to continue the traditional practices. The spread of the Sufi orders, however, provided a type of Islam with which these people could identify. Although Uthman was of the Qadariyya order, members of his family later changed their affiliation to the Tijaniyya, perhaps finding it more congenial to religio-political activism.

Uthman's *jihad* inspired new activity back in the west. Sheikh Hamadu of Masina was initiated into the Qadariyya order, participated in early stages of Uthman's conquests, then returned home and opened a Qur'an school. He came into conflict with the authorities and proclaimed a *jihad*. The Fulbe as well as the Muslims of such towns as Jenne supported him and by 1815 he had established himself as ruler of a distinctively Islamic state. A serious effort was made to convert the inhabitants and to enforce a pattern of life based on the *shari'a*.

Another leader was al-Hajj Umar, born in Futa Toro in the 1790s into a family of clerics. In 1826 he made the pilgrimage and while in the Hijaz became a Tijaniyya teacher. On his return journey he visited Muhammed Belo, the son of Uthman dan Fodio, and Sheikh Hamadu. He then settled in the Futa Jalon and worked to spread the Tijaniyya order. About 1852 he proclaimed his *jihad* and won considerable support in Futa Toro. Growing French power kept him from establishing himself in this area so he moved eastward conquering a large area—including the Islamic state of Masina. He seems to have used the framework of the *jihad* as an excuse for simple conquest and self-aggrandizement more than either Hamadu or Uthman. Certainly Masina, the most truly Muslim state in the area, could not properly be the object of a *jihad*.

Umar's attempts to force Islam on "pagan" groups had little permanent result, but by uprooting people and destroying traditional institutions he helped to produce a situation in which there was need for a new center of loyalty. Umar was largely responsible for the spread of the Tijaniyya order in the western Sudan, replacing the Qadariyya in many areas. Allegiance to this order provided a new basis for communal solidarity between the diverse peoples who were thrown together as a result of war and slave raiding. Because of his hostility to the French he also helped to identify Islam with resistance to the growing European encroachment.

Further disruptions took place as a result of the temporary conquests of Samori in the west and of Rabih in the Chad area in the last part of the nineteenth century. With them the *jihad* had further degenerated into an excuse for destructive raids which made little distinction between Muslims and non-Muslims. Their contribution to Islam was twofold: on the negative side, the destruction of the traditional basis of society, and on the positive, making Islam more widely "available." By their conflict with the Europeans they also helped to identify Islam with opposition to colonial rule.

The appeal of the Sufi brotherhoods, combined with both the positive and negative influences of the *jihad* in the western and central Sudan, lead in the nineteenth century to the "massive conversion of the savanna farmers" who had previously resisted Islam. [57] Thus it can be said that "the events of the nineteenth century upset the historical equilibrium established between Islam and African religions and loaded the scale against the latter more effectively than at any previous stage of history." [58]

As noted earlier, in the Nilotic Sudan, Islam, though widespread, had little real effect on people's lives before the nineteenth century. By the middle of that century the area had come under the control of the Khedives of Egypt, Muhammad Ali and his successors. These rulers, of Turkish rather than Egyptian origin, had little concern for the welfare of the people of Egypt and less for that of the Sudanese. The slave trade dominated the scene; all other economic activity declined.

It was this situation that set the stage for a Muslim revolution. Muhammad Ahmad (b. 1843), a teacher and Sufi leader, was deeply disturbed by the sufferings of his people. In 1881 he became convinced that he himself was the awaited deliverer, the *mahdi*, whose mission was to establish a new social order, with a pure, unified, reformed Islam replacing one that was easy-going, corrupted by traditional practices, and divided by the multiplicity of Sufi orders.[59] The people, in despair over the conditions they faced, responded to his religio-political appeal. The *mahdi* gave to his followers the name used in early Islam by Muhammad's associates in Medina,

ansar ("helpers"). As in early Islam, tribal divisions were transcended. The Sufi orders were abolished and replaced by what was
intended to be a more inclusive brotherhood.

Soon the *mahdi* was strong enough to proclaim a *jihad* against the
corrupt Turkish-Egyptian rulers who were to him Muslim only in
name. At first the government did not take him very seriously; by
the time it did, it was too late. In January 1885 the capital,
Khartoum, fell and the *mahdi* was in control of the country. When
he died in June of the same year, leadership passed to his designated *khalifa* (successor), who tried to consolidate his rule but gradually lost control of the situation. The British, who now were the real
rulers of Egypt, invaded the country and were in control by 1898; in
theory the government was a "condominium" with Egypt. Thus at
the close of the nineteenth century the Muslims of the Nilotic Sudan
were divided among themselves and dominated from the outside.

Early in the nineteenth century Islam was spreading in Ethiopia,
but for many, here as elsewhere, it was not a vital faith so much as a
religion adopted for commercial or political reasons. No great leader
arose to reform Islam and proclaim a *jihad*; in fact, it was the
Christians who were aroused against the threat of Islam.

The traditionally Christian people of the highlands already had
the consciousness of belonging to a community that transcended
local loyalties without destroying them. In a sense they already had
what Islam offered to many other Africans and thus saw in Islam not
a resource but a threat. Therefore, in the last half of the nineteenth
century, they engaged in a series of wars which had something of
the characteristics of "crusades" or Christian "holy wars." Many
Muslims, including Somalis, were brought into the empire. Although after 1889 efforts to convert them by force ceased, they
found themselves in a country dominated by the Christian Amhara,
and thus, to some extent, "second-class citizens." In some areas,
Muslims "voluntarily" became Christians.[60] On the positive side,
however, the establishment of centralized rule over a large area
made possible greater contact between various Muslim groups and
thus encouraged an upgrading of the level of orthodox knowledge
and practice beyond Harrar and the coastal cities.[61]

In Somalia Sheikh (or Sayyid) Muhammad Abdille Hassan (1864-
1920) led an attempt at a Muslim "revolution" somewhat resembling the earlier revolutions further west. While on pilgrimage
to Mecca, Sheikh Muhammad joined the militant and puritanical
Salihiyya order.[62] In 1899 he came into conflict with the British administration and proclaimed a *jihad* against it. He also fought the

Ethiopians and Italians who, like the British, were attempting to establish foreign Christian control over the Somalis. Sheikh Muhammad's influence was based not only on military power but also on his ability to compose poems which powerfully aroused the combined religious and patriotic devotion of the Somalis. For twenty years, until his death in 1920, he managed to keep up a running battle with the British and Ethiopians. He did not establish any organization which survived him but remains to the present a national hero. [63]

On the east coast no revolution marked the beginning of the second phase of Muslim history. Instead, there was renewed stimulus from overseas, primarily from southern Arabia. Under the leadership of Arabs from 'Uman, the Portuguese were defeated late in the seventeenth century. New Arab migrations took place, reinforcing and remolding the Arabic elements of the Swahili culture. The man who came closest to bringing the whole coast under one political system was Sayyid Sa'id ibn Sultan who ruled in Muscat ('Uman) from 1806 to 1840, when he moved his capital to Zanzibar and from this vantage point dominated the coast until his death in 1856. It cannot be said, however, that he "ruled" the coast. His ambitions were essentially economic; he is quoted as having once said, "I am nothing but a merchant." [64] Under his leadership and that of his sons some of the old prosperity returned, through the extension of trade.

The demand for ivory and slaves led to more frequent penetration of the interior providing a basis for Muslim expansion. Traders settling along the main route from Bagamoyo on the coast opposite Zanzibar through Tabora in what is now central Tanzania to Ujiji on Lake Tanganyika formed the nuclei of Muslim communities. By the middle of the nineteenth century they had crossed the lake and reached the Lualaba River in what is now Zaïre. Other routes running to Lake Nyasa and Lake Victoria spread Islam in these areas. The disruption and movements of peoples connected with the slave trade produced a situation in which there was need for the kind of supertribal identity provided by Islam, and for the kind of local commmunity encouraged by the Qadariyya order.

The spread of Islam in East Africa was more a matter of individual conversion than it was in the west. Swahili traders "did not become part of the social structure" as did the Dyula traders, [65] and the conversion of chiefs was not as common. Thus, with certain exceptions, such as among the Yao, "Islam did not penetrate existing communities but created a new community." [66]

The encounter with European influence can best be understood as a continuation of the second phase of Islamic history in Africa. By contributing to the breakdown of traditional societies, the European pressure brought more Africans to the point where a religion such as Islam bacame appealing. It also inadvertently provided, in many areas, a context conducive to Islamic growth.

There was, of course, a large element of European hostility toward Islam, the heritage of centuries of conflict in the Mediterranean area which inclined Europeans to see Islam as a threat which must be contained. While there may have been little hope of converting those already Muslim, many Europeans certainly had the aim of preventing the further spread of Islam by encouraging the spread of Christianity. Aside from more sincerely religious motivations, there was undoubtedly the belief that European political and economic influence would be greater among Christians than among Muslims. Of course, religious and other motivations were not clearly distinguished in the minds of most colonists; they found it difficult to separate Christianity and European culture. In this their attitude was close to that of orthodox Muslims, for whom Islam is not simply a "religion," but a whole culture, a way of life.

The conflict, then, was not only between two religions but between two cultures, each of which believed in its own inherent superiority, but one of which had the power and resources to enforce its will. Even though there was little hope of converting Muslims, there was an attempt to impose European culture, especially by the French, who had a strong belief in their obligation to "raise" the indigenous peoples by imparting to them the "benefits" of French culture.

The colonial regimes gave their support to Christian schools, perhaps more for cultural than for purely religious reasons. Not surprisingly, Muslims hesitated to send their children to these schools, which meant that in many areas the non-Muslims "advanced" much more rapidly—from the European point of view. The Westernized elite that was prepared to move into governmental and commercial posts tended to be non-Muslim, sometimes even in predominantly Muslim areas. Those Muslims who did receive "Western" educations were likely to become culturally Westernized.

The conflict faced by those who saw both the advantages and dangers of Western education is presented in fictional form by

Cheikh Hamidou Kane. After noting what can be learned in the French schools, a chief says,

> But learning, they would also forget. Would what they would learn be worth as much as what they would forget? I should like to ask you: can one learn this without forgetting that, and is what one learns worth what one forgets? [67]

Along with these negative factors, however, it can also be said that in certain ways Islam profited from colonialism. We have already observed how the spread of Islam has been closely related to the development of trade; the colonial era provided new opportunities for activities of this type. Islam has thrived on movement and opportunities for new contacts; the development of communications under colonial rule expanded these possibilities. Islam in Africa has been very largely an urban phenomenon; cities grew rapidly in the colonial period. Of course, the colonial governments did not build roads and cities and encourage trade in order to spread Islam; such a result was the opposite of what most of them desired. The fact is, however, that the very nature of Islam put it in a position to take advantage of opportunities inadvertently provided by the colonialists.

We have noted that Islam provides significant resources for those who have lost their traditional "roots." The disruptions associated with the establishment of colonial rule, the movement associated with new economic opportunities, and especially the growth of urban areas, produced a large number of people needing a new basis of social integration. Islam, as a religion that was universal in outlook yet strongly rooted in Africa and readily available in many areas, naturally had an appeal to such persons. As in earlier times with kings and merchants, now with larger groups Islam met the needs of those whose interests and contacts transcended the local scene.

The fact that Muslims tended to have more than local interests contributed in another way to Islamic development under colonialism. Although most Europeans did not have a particularly positive attitude toward Islam, they did recognize that it had certain characteristics which could be useful to them. When Europeans first arrived they found a number of literate Muslims who had experience in travel, trade, and record-keeping which made their services valuable. In spite of feelings of hostility, Europeans generally recognized Muslims as members of a widespread literate culture and religion which, while not believed to be as "high" as their own, at least had some points of contact with it and was more "respectable" than "paganism." Thus, a very large number of the Africans first employed by Europeans as guides, agents, clerks and minor officials were Muslims. Some non-Muslims, seeing this, drew the reasonable conclusion that they would be treated with more respect and perhaps have more opportunities for advancement if they were Muslims. This was primarily in the early stages of colonialism; at a later period, as noted above, non-Muslims tended to accept more readily the educational opportunities which were available and thus to be better prepared for the more attractive positions.

The fact that chiefs were more likely to be Muslims than their subjects also gave Islam a certain advantage under the colonial system. This was especially true in British territories where "indirect rule" was established, above all in northern Nigeria. Muslim chiefs were confirmed and sometimes strengthened, in terms of their local authority, by the colonial regime. Because the chief was Muslim it was assumed—sometimes quite incorrectly—that his people were also Muslim. It was further assumed that Muslim law prevailed in the area and should be enforced. Although Muslim law was considered less "civilized" than Western law, at least it was a written law that could be applied consistently over large areas. In general, the colonialist desire to have things organized and orderly tended to be in Islam's favor. After all, it was more "orderly" to have a written law that was applicable over large areas than a confusing variety of local, unwritten traditions.

In many parts of Africa there was a rapid spread—almost an "explosion"—of Islam, during the colonial period. [68] In some areas this may have been because Islam was seen as a way of resisting Western political and cultural domination while in others it was because colonial policies unintentionally favored it. Perhaps in a complex way both the European hostility toward Islam and the European use of Muslims and Muslim institutions for their own purposes contributed to Islamic growth. Being Muslim could be a way of gaining advantages under the colonial system and at the same time expressing a certain distance from Western culture. It was a way of being part of a worldwide community which received grudging respect from Europeans while providing an alternative center of loyalty and a basis for an independent dignity. The pressure of a new alien culture and religion tended to strengthen the sense of identity with a culture and religion that, although also originally alien, had become an accepted part of the local scene.

In spite of the French attempt to replace traditional culture and education with their own, Islam made notable progress in the French-controlled areas; two different ways in which this occurred can be illustrated by the Wolof of Senegal and the Mossi of Upper Volta.

The Wolof are close neighbors of some of the earliest Islamic communities in sub-Saharan Africa, but Islam had grown only gradually among them up until the last half of the nineteenth century. Contrary to the more usual situation, the common people appear to have become Muslim more readily than their rulers. [69] The first known Muslim king was Lat-Dyor, whose conversion around 1870 was associated with the disruptions accompanying the establishment of French rule.

The naturalization of Islam among the Wolof is especially associated with the work of Amadou Bamba Mbake (1850-1927), who served for a time as Lat-Dyor's chief *qadi* (legal authority). Although initiated in the Qadariyya order, he was more interested in the practical than the theoretical elements of Sufism. [70] At first he may have hoped to play a political role, perhaps as leader of a new *jihad*, but this was not possible in light of the establishment of French authority. Instead, after a "call" at about the age of forty, he began to develop his own independent order, the Muridiyya, in which the emphasis was placed not so much on learning or ritual as on agricultural labor. Those who submitted to him or to one of his disciples and worked on their peanut farms were assured of paradise, even if they did not follow all the usual Muslim regulations. [71] Those who worked for themselves rather than on the farm of a *sheikh* were expected to give generously of their produce or income. Some Murids believe that work takes the place of prayer, but this is an extreme view, not generally accepted. [72] There is, however, a great emphasis on the sanctity of physical labor, especially in agriculture. This led to considerable financial success, largely from peanut cultivation and marketing carried out under the centralized management of the headquarters of the order.

The followers of Amadou Bamba believe that he was directly in touch with God; he may even have been in some sense divine. One of the most impressive mosques in sub-Saharan Africa has been built over his grave at Touba. Every good Murid is expected to make a pilgrimage here once a year; in practice this may appear to replace the pilgrimage to Mecca, although such a heresy is not officially supported. [73]

The French attitude toward the order was ambiguous; on the one hand, they appreciated the enterprise shown, which contributed significantly to the economy of the country, while, on the other hand, they were suspicious of the development of such a center of indigenous power. Again on the positive side, however, they appreciated the way the leaders maintained order and kept their followers from social or political agitation. To some extent the brotherhood was used in "a form of indirect rule." [74] In independent Senegal the leaders of the Muridiyya are generally credited with significant political influence; interestingly enough, they have given their support to President Senghor, a Catholic.

The Muridiyya provides for a kind of collective security based on agriculture and under the authority of a sacred leader, which has clear affinities with traditional African systems and also meets contemporary needs. It can be seen as "a national reaction of the Wolof people to a revolutionary upheaval in traditional society and as a vehicle for the partial reconstruction of a destroyed social and political order." [75]

The Muridiyya has helped to make possible the reintegration of the Wolof on an Islamic basis. The question has been raised, however, as to whether this process is more accurately described as the "Islamization of the Wolof" or the "Wolofization of Islam." [76] Some have seen the Muridiyya as so heretical as to be practically outside the realm of Islam, but according to the most recent extensive study it does "not depart very radically from the Sufi tradition of Islam either in organizational forms or in beliefs." [77] It may perhaps be seen as a Muslim equivalent of some of the "independent churches" of African Christianity.

The spread of Islam among the Mossi of Upper Volta has been much less spectacular. As noted previously, they were objects of a *jihad* as early as 1498. While they successfully resisted Islam as a military and political threat, they had no objection to the settlement among them of Muslim traders or refugees from the north, known locally as Yarse. Many of these adopted the local language and became essentially Mossi Muslims. Their close association with the court encouraged conversions among the nobles. Some kings became Muslims, although this was considered incompatible with certain traditional responsibilities. Thus Islam remained for them a personal matter; as rulers they still maintained contact with the royal ancestors. [78]

When the French invaded the country late in the nineteenth century, the Muslims were among their most vigorous opponents. It is said that after the French occupation Muslims went about telling the Mossi that "as soon as all the blacks become Muslims, the whites will leave." [79]

The breakdown of traditional authority and the development of communications seems to have been largely responsible for the considerable growth of Islam during the time that the Mossi were under French rule. Those who traveled and worked away from home discovered the advantages of Islam. The attitude of the chiefs was also important; in areas where they favored Islam—without necessarily adopting it themselves—there were many converts, but in areas where the chiefs saw Islam as a threat to traditional life, there were relatively few. [80]

Islam also spread in the formerly British-controlled territories, such as northern Nigeria. When they arrived, the British found Muslim ruling houses of Fulani (Fulbe) origin. These rulers were maintained in power; in fact, this was where the famous British policy of "indirect rule" was first clearly articulated. Within the territories of these rulers Islamic law was upheld by the colonial administration. Thus, "indirectly," the British power was placed behind Islam as the official religion of Northern Nigeria. Added to the usual factors of increased movement of people and growing urbanization, this encouraged the spread and consolidation of Islam. Thus Greenburg states that "conversation to Islam has progressed at an accelerated pace since the British took control in 1907." [81] At that time half of the Hausa may still have been "pagan," but by the time British rule ended in 1960 the number who could be so identified was probably no more than twenty per cent, [82] and was declining rapidly. Thus the process of transformation from a society in which Islam was a class religion to one which was totally Muslim, started by the *jihad* leaders of the early nineteenth century, was brought closer to realization under colonial rule in the twentieth century.

In southwestern Nigeria a Fulani dynasty had come into control of the northern part of Yoruba territory. The Yoruba also had a long tradition of urban living which provided a natural context for the spread of Islam. In spite of this, there was relatively little popular movement toward Islam until after the British occupation in the late nineteenth century. When it did come, the movement was more an individual than a communal matter; thus among the Yoruba it is quite common to find Muslims, Christians, and traditional believers in the same family, enjoying friendly relations with each other.

In British-controlled East Africa, Islam continued to be especially identified with the Swahili-speaking Muslims of the coastal towns and offshore islands. The upper classes of these communities preferred to be known as "Arabs" or "Shirazi." During the period of colonial rule, these designations were more widely adopted. Thus in Zanzibar and Pemba the name "Shirazi" was adopted by "the whole pre-nineteenth century population." [83] This term is only vaguely associated with the actual city of Shiraz in Iran; it suggests a "distant and glorious homeland" [84] with an ancient Muslim history.

The Yao of southern Tanzania, eastern Malawi, and northern Mozambique are a notable East African example of the movement into Islam of a whole people rather than of individuals or families. The Yao had been involved in the inland trade from the port of Kilwa and thus had long been familiar with Islam in a superficial way. Late in the nineteenth century, as a result of the disruptions associated with the slave trade and then with the establishment of European rule, the Yao began to spread along the trade routes and, at the same time, to become Muslims. Thus, as in other cases, movement is associated with the adoption of Islam, in this case the movement of a people as a whole rather than of isolated individuals. Through becoming Muslim, they have been able to maintain their communal identity in a new situation. This has not, however, led to far-reaching changes in their customs. It is interesting that a book on the Yao hardly mentions Islam except as a label by which the people identify themselves. [85] The function of Islam for the Yao seems to be that of providing for a distinctive identity and a basis for relationships with the outside world without requiring extensive internal changes in the society.

A different pattern of Muslim development took place in Uganda. Islam first entered from the coast in the mid-nineteenth century through the activities of traders and, as in West Africa, appealed to rulers seeking contact with the outside world. In 1876 Egyptian forces from the Sudan added a further Islamic influence. What might have been the start of a development similar to that which occurred in many West African kingdoms was forestalled, however, by the arrival of Anglican and Roman Catholic missionaries. Three religiously based political parties arose, competeing for the allegiance of the country, with the support of different foreign powers. After a confusing series of maneuvers, the British-supported Anglican party emerged victorious. The Muslim party retained certain rights but did not participate significantly in political power of educational and economic development. As the inherited religion of one portion of the community, Islam did not spread rapidly; from 1911 to the mid-sixties the percentage of

Muslims in the total population is said to have increased from two per cent to a little over five per cent. [86]

In Zaïre, the former Belgian Congo, there exists an interesting extension of east coast Islam. By the middle of the nineteenth century Arab and Swahili merchants had crossed Lake Tanganyika, reached the Lualaba River, and established centers for their trade in ivory and slaves. Tippu Tib, a man of mixed Arab and African ancestry, gained control of a large part of this trade and excercised a certain amount of political authority, theoretically as the representative of the sultan of Zanzibar. When Henry M. Stanley and others began to explore the area and to establish centers of trade and authority on behalf of Leopold's "Congo Free State," they found themselves in a somewhat ambiguous relationship with the Arab traders. On the one hand, the latter were of considerable help to the Europeans while at the same time there was clearly competition between the two. An attempt to resolve the problem was made in 1887, in a curious arrangement by which Tippu Tib became governor of the eastern Congo, on behalf of Leopold. In 1892 this alliance of convenience broke up and the "Free State" forces engaged in a successful military action against the "Arabs," which was justified before world opinion as an "anti-slavery campaign."

The end of "Arab" domination left a number of communities of Muslims scattered through the eastern Congo; the most important centers were Kasongo and Stanleyville (now known again by its traditional name, Kisangani). These communities were composed of a mixture of people from the east coast with their Congolese associates.

The Belgian government was the most hostile of all colonial governments in its attitude toward Islam, seeing in it a threat to its "civilizing" and "Christianizing" mission. Permission was granted for the construction of a few mosques but Muslim schools were illegal. The headquarters of Congo Islam was actually Ujiji, across Lake Tanganyika in British-controlled territory. [87] Isolation and official disapproval kept Islam from growing significantly in most parts of the Congo. It is probably the one country in Africa where the expansion of Islam was consistently and successfully opposed by a colonial government.

In solidly Muslim countries, such as Somalia, nationalist developments had strong Muslim associations. In many other countries, however, the nationalist leaders were primarily those with "Western" educations; for reasons already noted, such people were predominantly non-Muslims. Even those who were Muslim tended to have become somewhat "secularized." Thus it was that in some areas, notably northern Nigeria, Muslims were not overly anxious for independence, fearing that it would lead to domination by non-Muslims better prepared for administrative positions.

Since independence, differences between the Muslim "north" and the non-Muslim "south" have been partially responsible for civil strife in Nigeria, Chad, and the Republic of the Sudan. The basic problems may not be religious so much as ethnic and economic, but the religious aspect cannot be ignored.

In the Republic of the Sudan, where the conflict has been going on much of the time since independence, the Muslim, Arabic-speaking, northern two-thirds of the country has seen the problem as one of national unity, believing that European imperialism, working through Christian missionaries, has been trying to divide the country. On the other hand, the southern third, with a Christian-educated elite, has felt itself subjected to an "internal imperialism," seeking to impose Arabic language and culture as well as Muslim faith. It is to be hoped that the recent reconciliation will be permanent.

In the northern part of the country, Islam is associated with nationalism and politics, but the Muslims are not at all united. The Islamic revolution of the nineteenth century, which attempted to establish religious unity, actually produced another competing group, made up of the followers of the *mahdi* and led by his descendants. Their political arm, the Umma party, has promoted a moderately reformist Muslim program. The other major party is associated with the Khatmiyya order. Even the Communists have provided prayer rugs at their headquarters and have sought to emphasize the affinities between Communism and Islam.[88] Perhaps this is one reason why the Sudan had the largest Communist party in the Arab world until the attempted coup of 1971.

It may be asked whether a new "third phase" of African Muslim ·history has now begun. If so, it probably is associated more with "secularization" than with independence as such. In some areas, such as in western Nigeria, among the Yoruba, Islam is spreading as the personal faith of individuals more than as a total communal way of life. The "new Muslims" may be very devout personally, even going on pilgrimage to Mecca, yet identify themselves politically, economically, and culturally with non-Muslims. Political alliances cross religious lines in other areas, such as Senegal, which has a large Muslim majority but a Christian president. Secularization, in these cases, involves the disassociation of political loyalties from religious considerations.

A greater degree of secularization is found in the small but growing minority of younger and better-educated Muslims in various parts of Africa, for whom "Islam" is an identifying label that has little observable relationship to any distinctively Islamic behavior. In areas of mixed religious affiliation, these people frequently find their vocational and political associations among non-Muslims. Clearly it is too soon to say how widely or rapidly either of these attitudes will spread, but they certainly point to the possibility of an Islam quite different both from that of the first phase, when it was a class cult, and from that of the second phase, when it was a basis for communal integration.

As a matter of fact, the "three phases" are not simply chronological; they exist along side each other in contemporary Africa. There are places where Islam is still primarily the cult of chiefs and merchants, others in which it is closely associated with communal identity, while throughout Africa there is a small but growing number of individuals for whom it is essentially a matter of personal religious faith, with little class or communal significance. As we look now at the contemporary beliefs and practices of African Muslims we will observe this variety in the forms of Islamic commitment.

The message of the prophet Muhammad was that of the uniqueness and power of God, who demanded and deserved man's total gratitude and loyalty, to be manifested through worship and obedience. This message, according to Muslim belief, was not new; it had been proclaimed by numerous earlier prophets, beginning with Adam. Muhammad differed from previous prophets, not in the message proclaimed, but because this time the message was completely and correctly recorded in a book, the Qur'an, and because a faithful community, the Ummah, was established on the basis of the message. This community, in order to exist and prosper in the world had of necessity to be political as well as religious. Thus, the work of Muhammad as administrator, statesman, and warrior was not a "fall" or aberration, as some Western interpreters have supposed, but was essential to the completion of his work as prophet.

It has been persuasively argued by Watt that, in a sociological sense, the success of Islam in Arabia was associated with the transition from a tribal society, based on kinship, to an urban commercial society, based on more impersonal relationships. Islam provided an ideology appropriate for this transition and a new community, based, not on natural ties, but on the common loyalty of individuals to the one God and His messenger. [89]

It is reasonable to suppose that Islam may prove to be relevant, both ideologically and sociologically, in other societies in the midst of a similar transition from homogeneous, localized groups based on kinship, to urbanized, commercial societies with greater individual specialization, wider horizons, and more varied contacts. Islam may not only be relevant to societies already in the process of such transition, it may serve to stimulate or accelerate such a process.

Such considerations may be especially helpful in understanding the spread of Islam in an area such as sub-Saharan Africa, where the earliest contacts were due less to military conquest than to commercial penetration. Watt believes that, to a significant extent, the growth of Islam in West Africa is due to the fact that the situation there has been similar to that in Arabia in the time of Muhammad, in which kinship structures were being disturbed and a new basis for community was needed. [90]

Islam, of course, is a religion; but it is a religion that is ideally a whole way of life. Belief is expressed through behavior, to the point that it can be said that, in Africa, at least, "Islam is primarily a distinctive way of performing religious acts, observing specific taboos and social customs." [91] The "Five Pillars" of Islam relate belief to individual and communal practice.

The first pillar affirms belief in the absolute unity and authority of God: "there is no god but God." It also relates belief to history in the words, "Muhammad is the messenger of God." The first pillar involves not simply intellectual assent to these propositions but a bearing witness to them, a kind of "pledge of allegiance."

In African traditional religions there has generally been belief in the "supreme God," often associated with the sky, who is the ultimate source of power. He is not usually addressed directly, however, except in cases of emergency. Lesser spirits or gods are more immediately available to man. Thus, African religion is often described as "polytheism." The lesser gods, however, are probably not to be thought of as being on the same level of reality as the supreme God. There is only one ultimate source of power and authority—God—who may be manifested in or through many lesser centers of power, natural and supernatural.

Thus, in theory, the Muslim affirmation of the oneness of God is not difficult for most Africans to accept, but in practice it involves a considerable shift of emphasis from a number of localized centers of power to one universal center. Allah is usually identified with the traditional supreme God; the other deities are demoted to good or evil spirits, more clearly distinguished from God than they were traditionally. A practical problem arises, however, from the fact that among most African peoples there was little or no direct worship of the supreme God; he was approached through lesser spirits. This is probably one reason why traditional forms persist among many peoples who have long been officially Muslim. Belief in only one God is relatively easy to accept but limiting worship to one source of power, especially one seldom worshipped in the past, may seem very unwise. Thus local beliefs and customs do not suddenly disappear but continue as added "insurance" within the context of the more universal system of Islam.

The figure of Muhammad relates the eternal truth to historical time. It has been said that "with Islam time entered the African world." [92] This is going too far; Africans traditionally have had a sense of "ancestral time." It is to this ancestral time that they tend to assimilate the figure of Muhammad, often thinking of him as in some sense an "original ancestor." [93] It is suggested that in East Africa Muhammad "fulfills in a sense the role of secondary spirits in African religion, an intermediary between God and human beings." [94] He is the one to whom God has most fully communicated his "vital force." [95]

The anniversary of the birth of Muhammad is an important celebration for many African Muslims. A Swahili poem, translated by Harries, gives expression to popular devotion in the following lines:

> and when you mention His Birth
> it is traditional for those present to stand up
>
> On the day of the Birth (miracles) were many
> that was the foundation of this religion
> by that it was strengthened and by that it survives. [96]

Devotion to the family of the prophet is an aspect of Islam that appeals to many Africans but the Shi'ite form of such devotion, which limits religious authority to descendents of the prophet, is present only in immigrant communities.

The second pillar of Islam is that of prayer, specifically the ritual prayers to be said five times a day. These prayers are not only occasions for approaching God, they provide an "outward and visible sign" of Islamic loyalty. A Muslim is often defined as "one who prays"—in a ritual sense—and a Muslim community is identified by the fact that it has a mosque, a "place of prayer." In West Africa this may simply be a cleared area, marked off from its surroundings, with an indication of the direction of Mecca. In East Africa some kind of building is thought to be essential, but frequently it is indistinguishable on the outside from an ordinary dwelling. (Fig. 10) There are, however, impressive mosques in African cities, both east and west. Some mosques are built on sites sacred to the traditional religion. [97]

Friday prayer at the congregational mosques is widely observed and, in cities, may serve to bring together persons of diverse ethnic background, thus affirming Muslim brotherhood. In some parts of West Africa, however, Muslims have split into different congregations along ethnic lines, [98] while in East Africa a major controversy arose over the proper "quorum" for Friday prayers. [99]

Few African Muslims, other than professional religionists, regularly observe the five daily prayers. [100] Actually, the idea of regular ritual prayer, regardless of any obvious immediate need, is alien to most traditional African practice, in which prayer normally has been related to particular emergencies or to occasional festivals. It is not surprising, therefore, that African Muslims continue to call upon God for specific needs, following traditional custom. Such prayers may address God by his local name rather than as "Allah," as in the following case, quoted from the Nupe:

> The harvest is cleared: Soko, protect us from fire; Soko, protect us from smallpox; Soko, protect us from the heat that dries up everything. [101]

Of course it would be affirmed that Soko and Allah are the same, but the use of the former in occasional prayers and the latter in ritual prayers suggests some difference in context and attitude.

The third pillar, alms, or *zakat*, is not especially prominent in African Islam. In areas where rulers attempted to establish a strictly Islamic society, as among the Hausa, *zakat* used to be collected as a tax. Even here, however, it became totally voluntary after British rule was established. [102] In some areas *zakat* may be collected at special times during the Muslim year [103] or on the occasion of the visit of a *sheikh*, "as a contribution to his traveling expenses." [104] For many African Muslims the obligatory *zakat* has been confused with or replaced by the voluntary *sadaka*. The latter is also associated with offerings or sacrifices made in memory of the dead, at rainmaking ceremonies, and on other occasions. [105]

The fast of Ramadan is probably the most widely and strictly observed of all the pillars, in Africa as well as elsewhere in the Muslim world. It is a way of affirming and maintaining communal identity, a "badge" or external evidence of loyalty to Islam, like the wearing of a turban or some other distinctive article of clothing. A typical view is that "a man who does not pray is a poor Muslim, yet he is nevertheless a Muslim so long as he fasts Ramadan." [106]   Generally the less devout at least try to give the appearance of fasting, especially in such strict areas as northern Nigeria. In some other places, however, the attitude is more relaxed and a partial observance is considered satisfactory.

The final pillar is pilgrimage to Mecca. Most African Muslims undoubtedly consider themselves released from this obligation by the pr[...] hat it [...]ly binding on those for whom it is physically [...]ly possible. Enough do go, however, to provide some [...] the worldwide expanse of Islam. As in the past, the [...]rves as a means for the diffusion of Islamic ideas and [...]. Those who have been on pilgrimage tend to strengthen [...]nivers[a]l aspects of Islam, both orthodox and modernizing, [...]gainst the local.

The traditional land route from West Africa through the Nilotic Sudan is still followed by less affluent pilgrims who must "work their way." Often such a trip requires a number of years; some pilgrims even settle permanently along the route.

The development of modern communication, of course, has made the trip relatively easy for those with means. "A good number of instructed and practicing Muslims believe that since God permitted the invention of cars and airplanes, it is normal for one to profit from them." [107]   Considerable numbers now fly from such places as Nigeria where the pilgrimage appears to be especially popular among recently converted Yoruba.

In some towns there are associations in which people pool their money and then draw lots to see who will go on pilgrimage, a practice which is hardly orthodox! [108]   In other cases, the pilgrimage has been undertaken for reasons that are at least as much commerical as religious; I was even told of a "Christian" Yoruba who went to Mecca as a smuggler and then presumed to use the title *al-hajj*, designating one who has performed the pilgrimage!

Although the Muslims of the Nilotic Sudan and East Africa are nearer to Mecca than are those of West Africa, it is not clear that any more make the pilgrimage. [109]   In Buurri al-Lamaab, a suburb of Khartoum, fifty-five men and nineteen women out of a total population of 2,379 in 1959 had been to Mecca; this is probably somewhat above average. [110]

Islam is better understood as a system of social obligations than as a system of belief. The obligations of orthodox Islam are enshrined in the *shari'a*, a word usually translated as "law" but actually meaning a whole way of life. The *shari'a* is an eternal pattern, based on the Word of God as infallibly interpreted by the consensus of the community of believers. Thus it is one in all times and places and not subject to change. Even if it should seem to conflict with the practical needs of the community it can not be changed. This does not mean, however, that it is universally obeyed; in fact, it often seems to be more of an ideal pattern of how life ought to be lived than a basis for the practical regulation of life. When the eternal ideal conflicts with temporal reality, the former is not changed to make it "relevant"; it is kept as an ideal, uncorrupted by the world of change. In Buurri al-Lamaab, when villagers state that the life of the Prophet is a sufficient and perfect guide to the conduct of one's life," they mean that "it should be adapted to modern times, not modern times adapted to the way of the Prophet"; but this is not "a matter of actual practice. [111]   Thus, in general, "reverence for the law assumes an importance which is quite disproportionate to observance." [112]

Two of the four "orthodox schools of law" (*Madhhab*) predominate in Africa: the Maliki in the whole Sudan area and the Shafi'i along the east coast. In recent years, however, differences between these schools have had much less effect on actual practice than have differences in the policies of the political authorities. The British, in general, allowed—or even encouraged—the application of Muslim law in predominantly Muslim areas. As indicated earlier, in some cases the British preference for predictable and orderly procedure led to increased enforcement of some aspects of Muslim law, especially in northern Nigeria. In West Africa the British usually treated Islamic law as a variety of "native law and custom" which made it possible to accept the various local compromises between traditional law and the *shari'a* which had developed. In East Africa, on the other hand, Islamic law was generally treated as a distinct system to be applied only to persons or communities clearly identified as Muslim. [113]   This difference perhaps reflects the somewhat more foreign "flavor" of Islam in East Africa as contrasted with West Africa.

The French, on the whole, were less inclined to stand behind the enforcement of the *shari'a*; their preference was clearly to establish French law in all the areas they controlled. Muslim law was not recognized at all by the Belgian government; when cases arose among those who wished to abide by this law they settled the matter in more or less secret courts of their own. [114]

The Islamic criminal law is now enforced hardly anywhere in the Muslim world; northern Nigeria was until recently one of the few exceptions, but in 1959 a new criminal code was adopted there. [115] Laws relating to property matters are somewhat more widely observed, but it is in the area of family law that the *shari'a* is most effective. Even in this, however, traditional customs frequently prevail over the strict application of the *shari'a*, especially in rural areas. It is said that among the Yao one of the few questions of Islamic law that is taken seriously is whether or not it is legal to eat hippopotamus meat. [116]

We should not suppose, however, that the *shari'a* has no effect upon African life. Although it certainly is not adopted all at once by a group that becomes Muslim and few, if any, African peoples are totally governed by it, there is no doubt but what a gradual transformation takes place in which individuals, families and communities move *toward* the Islamic standards. As Trimingham reminds us, "We should not approach Muslim society by taking the ideal standard of Islamic law as our basis and thinking of it as corrupted by local custom but should take ancestral custom and see how it has been modified by Islam." [117]

One of the most significant problems has to do with inheritance. In traditional African society land is the major resource and is normally under some form of group control. To divide land according to Muslim rules of inheritance would lead to fragmentation and in some cases to economic disaster. For this reason a compromise may be worked out, whereby the land remains intact according to traditional custom while movable personal property is divided according to Muslim law.

In general, Islam promotes a gradual transformation from the extended to the nuclear family. This change, of course, is more acceptable in the cities than in rural areas. Where matrilineal succession has been the rule there is a gradual shift to the patrilineal—though remnants of the old may linger for a long time.

The relative position of women is probably not greatly effected by the change from traditional customs to Islamic law. Women are not usually veiled or secluded except in a few very strict families. In some areas their opportunity for independent action may be diminished; on the other hand, the *shari'a* provides for inheritance by women (though this may not be enforced). As an example of the position of women, it is said that among the Nupe "Women are as free as men and legally as fully qualified; the veiling of women is unknown; and though the Nupe do not admit women to the mosque or other religious observances, girls of the upper class are often taught the Qur'an." [118]

Polygamy is traditional in most African societies and is accepted by Islam, with a limit of four wives. This is generally quite adequate, except for some chiefs, who usually are able to find legal subterfuges. Thus Islam probably does little directly either to increase or decrease the number of plural marriages. Changing economic conditions, however, tend to discourage polygamy and in some cases such changes are chronologically associated with the spread of Islam.

Islam makes divorce very easy for the man but practically impossible for the woman; whether or not this weakens the woman's position depends on what the traditional customs were.

Traditional Muslim education begins in the "Qur'an school," in which boys—and a few girls—memorize large portions of the Qur'an—ideally the whole of it. This, of course, is in Arabic, which is not the native language of most sub-Saharan Muslims. In fact, the classical Arabic of the Qur'an is quite different even from the colloquial Arabic spoken in the Niiotic Sudan. Thus, relatively little understanding accompanies memorization. We should note, however, that the recitation of the Arabic Qur'an, even without understanding, is a central act of Muslim piety, for these are the very words, in fact, the very sounds, which have existed for all eternity with God and were communicated to Muhammad. Their recitation thus brings one, in a unique way, into direct and immediate contact with God and His Prophet. Through memorization and recitation of the Qur'an "power is gained in this world and reward in the next." [119]

Beyond the Qur'an school, the traditional higher Islamic studies lead to a greater command of classical Arabic, some attempt to understand the Qur'an through the study of commentaries and, above all, a study of the authoritative law books of the Maliki or Shafi'i school. There is generally a high regard in African Islam for literate culture and for the scholar. With some exceptions, however, African Islamic scholars have very limited resources available and their information is somewhat miscellaneous and uncoordinated. [120]

In recent years efforts have been made to combine Islamic and Western-style education, but these have not been widely effective.

In general, two educational systems, traditional and modern, exist side by side with only minimal influence on each other.

Islam in Africa, as elsewhere, has no formally identified "clergy," but there are those with varying degrees of education who meet popular religious needs. They may be known by such titles as *mwallimu* (Hausa), *mwalimu* (Swahili), *wadad* (Somalia), and *feqi* (Nilotic Sudan). They serve as teachers, leaders in ritual, conductors of weddings and funerals, personal advisors, and, frequently, diviners and healers. Typically they are affiliated with a Sufi order.

The Sufi or "mystical" orders and brotherhoods are widespread in African Islam; in fact, in some areas the majority of adult males have at least a nominal affiliation with an order. For instance, it is said that approximately seventy per cent of the Muslims of the former Belgian Congo were associated with the Qadariyya order.[121] In Buurri al-Lamaab, on the other hand, the "great majority of men...belong to no religious brotherhood at all." [122]

For those who are members, the primary significance of the orders is often not so much in the mystical devotion as such as in the communal identity provided. Islam, of course, is a community, *ummah*, on a world scale; every Muslim is a brother to every other Muslim. But this universal brotherhood is too abstract to be a practical focus of identity for most Muslims. A more immediate, available, localized brotherhood is required than is available in the orthodox mosque which is a place of prayer, not a "congregation" of people. The mosque does not have "members," it is not a "fellowship." Those who pray together at a mosque do not necessarily have any more relationship with each other than with brother Muslims in distant places. In fact, of course, they are usually neighbors and often friends, but this has no inherent relationship to their common use of a mosque. The Sufi brotherhood, on the other hand, is a community, corresponding somewhat to a congregation, and available as a replacement for some of the traditional communal ties. Among the Somali, for instance, membership in the brotherhood cuts "across clan and tribal loyalties, seeking to substitute the status of brother in religion for that of clansman..."[123] In southern Somalia communal agricultural settlements, known as *jama'a*, have been especially attractive to de-tribalized people of varying backgrounds.[124] On the other side of the continent, the Muridiyya has encouraged communal agricultural settlements among the Wolof of Senegal. However, the brotherhoods can also have the effect of dividing members from nonmembers, thus creating tensions. This appears to be especially true in the Nilotic Sudan. [125]

Although the primary significance of the orders may be in their communal aspects, they do meet a need for personal emotional expression. The *dhikr*—literally "remembrance"—involves the repetition of certain words and phrases, leading, in some cases, to an ecstatic condition; often it takes on the characteristics of traditional African dancing, including the use of drums, and may fulfill "the same function as revivalism in the Christian world." [126] Extreme emotionalism in the *dhikr* appears to be more characteristic of the Nilotic Sudan and East Africa than of the western and central Sudan. [127]

In the Nilotic Sudean and the eastern "horn," the Sufi orders have been closely associated with reverence for saints, whose many tombs are centers of popular devotion. Although, properly speaking, Muslims do not pray *to* the saints but rather approach God *through* them, on the popular level this distinction may not be clearly maintained. According to Trimingham the tomb of the saint is a more significant symbol of the faith of the Muslims of the Nilotic Sudan than is the mosque; "the cult of the saints, both alive or dead, is their religion." [128] It is to the saints that the ordinary believer turns in times of sickness or other special need. Visitations to the tombs are made especially by women, sometimes while the men are participating in other ceremonies. [129]

The cult of saints is of less importance in the western Sudan and in Swahili-speaking East Africa. In parts of west Africa spirit possession cults such as *komo* and *bori* are prominent; while in Ethiopia and neighboring countries there is the *zar* cult. Although clearly un-Islamic and opposed by the strictly orthodox, these cults are generally tolerated. Women, who are not so involved in orthodox Islamic activities, tend to be especially attracted to the spirit cults. Thus a kind of "dualism" of religion may develop, as suggested by the following statement by Baba of Karo, a Hausa woman: "The work of the *Malams* is one thing, the work of *bori* experts is another, each has his own kind of work and they must not be mixed up." [130]

Islamic festivals bring the community together in celebration. Often they incorporate traditional African features and thus affirm ties with the local past as well as with universal Islam. The New Year festivities, for instance, often include popular observances that are questionable from an orthodox Muslim perspective. In some West African societies, for instance, the New Year is celebrated by bathing and erotic play, which are apparently associated with a concern for fertility. [131]

The birthday of the prophet is widely observed, frequently with readings and recitations dealing with the life of the prophet. The end of Ramadan (*id al-fitr*) is celebrated with rejoicing, new clothes, and, in some areas dancing and drumming through the night. [132]

The "Great Festival" (*id al kabir*) comes at pilgrimage time and involves the sacrifice of a ram. It may also have communal significance, as among the Nupe, where it "serves as a display of kingship," and thus "in mobilizing the religious community it mobilizes also the population of the Moslem state, so that the religious appeal blends with the confirmation of political allegiance. [133]

Traditional beliefs regarding the nature of the human soul or spirit are largely preserved among African Muslims but views of life after death are radically changed. The Muslim concept of judgment, issuing in individual reward or punishment, is quite different from traditional views of communal immortality. The idea that a believer will be separated in the future life from his unbelieving ancestors is one of the points on which Islam is furthest removed from traditional concepts in Africa as in seventh century Arabia.

Belief in witchcraft, divination, and magical practices does not disappear with the coming of Islam. In fact, there is evidence that the dislocation associated with Islamization (though not necessarily caused by it) creates new fears which are expressed and dealt with in these terms. In the urban conditions under which many Muslims live, large numbers of practitioners flourish, frequently combining traditional, Islamic, and Western methods in an attempt to deal with the fears and hostilities of the city. Muslim "clergy" themselves often function very much as traditional healers but with new powers, especially those associated with the written or spoken words of the Qur'an, used for "magical" purposes. The chief *imam* of a Yoruba city told me that, besides for leading the community in prayer, it was his responsibility to deal with the physical and emotional troubles of the people. He has many Arabic texts available for use in varying situations of need. He also has protective "charms" in his own house; when asked why this was necessary for one who trusted in God he responded "we accept wisdom from all sources." His father was a practitioner of Ifa, the traditional form of Yoruba divination, and while the *imam* does not practice Ifa, he believes it has a certain validity; as he put it, "Ifa is Islam confused."

For the African Muslim old customs are not so much disrupted as reintegrated; "they can still serve a vital function; but now between him and the unknown stands more than his old custom." [134] As Lewis points out, "dualism" and "parallelism" are not adequate terms for a situation in which the traditional and Islamic "are seen as merging in a single Muslim way of life...." [135]

The African tradition encourages a kind of "catholicity" in religious thought and practice. It looks with favor on any power, new or old, that may be available for the healing and enhancing of man's life, especially in the communal context. An attempt to relate rather than to separate is characteristic of the African religious perspective; "the respect for everything human and a spirit of religious tolerance are the striking characteristics of present day Africans, whether Moslem or non-Moslem." [136]

For example, it is said of Muslim chiefs in Sierra Leone that
"They keep up the ancestral cult and the *poro* for they are part of the body of custom they have to maintain, they support Islam to the extent of becoming adherents, and they encourage Christian missions out of appreciation of their work in education and social welfare...." [137]

In like manner, a Nupe chief is quoted as saying:
There are three benefits, Islam, Christianity, and the kuti (traditional "medicine"). Some of us have chosen one, others the other. One may be stronger than the rest, but this we do not know. [138]

In general, Islam in Africa has not set itself strongly against the traditional life but rather has infiltrated this life and changed it gradually from within. Compromise is justified as a temporary expedient, even by some who are personally orthodox. Islam appeals as the basis of a more comprehensive personal or social identity within which the old still finds a place. Movement from tradition to orthodox Islam takes place in a series of small changes, none of which individually causes substantial disruption of personal or communal habits, although the end result may be radically different from the starting place. Even orthodox Islam in Africa, however, is still "African" because it has "grown up" in Africa and thus has an African rather than a foreign flavor. As Trimingham says, "Islam in Africa has developed cultural patterns that are at one and the same time African and Islamic." [139]

Perhaps the most interesting and challenging question now facing African Islam is whether it will also be able to penetrate modern and secular life and participate in the development of new cultural patterns appropriate to a changing society.

NOTES

1. J. Spencer Trimingham, *A History of Islam in West Africa.* London: Oxford University Press, 1962, p. 43.
2. *Ibid.*, p. 52 f.
3. *Ibid.*, p. 61 f.

4. J. C. Froelich, *Les Musulmans d'Afrique noire*. Paris: Editions d'Orient, 1962, p. 27.

5. Trimingham, *A History of Islam in West Africa*, p. 86.

6. Froelich, *Les Musulmans*, p. 41 f.

7. J. O. Hunwick, in I. M. Lewis (ed.), *Islam in Tropical Africa.* London: Oxford University Press, 1966, p. 301.

8. Jean Rouch, *La Religion et la Magie Songhay*. Paris: Presses Universitaires de France, 1960, p. 14.

9. Although Takrur originally referred to an area along the Senegal River, it came to be used by Arabs as a general designation for the Islamic areas of the western Sudan.

10. Hunwick, in Lewis, *Islam in Tropical Africa*, p. 307.

11. Trimingham, *A History of Islam in West Africa*, p. 102.

12. Ta'rikh al-fatlash, pp. 208-210, quoted by Hunwick, in Lewis, *Islam in Tropical Africa*, p. 311.

13. Norbert Tapiero, in James Kritzeck and William H. Lewis (eds.), *Islam in Africa*. New York: Van Nostrand-Reinhold Company, 1969, p. 61.

14. Joseph Greenberg, *The Influence of Islam on Sudanese Religion*. Seattle: University of Washington Press, 1946, p. 6.

15. Trimingham, *A History of Islam in West Africa*, p. 131.

16. *Ibid.*

17. *Ibid.*, p. 141.

18. *Ibid.*, p. 143.

19. I.M. Lewis, in I.M. Lewis (ed.), *Islam in Tropical Africa*, p. 24f.

20. *Ibid.*, p. 26.

21. Nehemia Levtzion, *Muslims and Chiefs in West Africa*. London: Oxford University Press, 1968, p. 55.

22. *Ibid.*, p. 113.

23. *Ibid.*, p. 52.

24. Trimingham, *A History of Islam in West Africa*, p. 160.

25. J. Spencer Trimingham, *Islam in the Sudan*. London: Frank Cass and Co., Ltd., 1949, p. 73.

26. *Ibid.*, p. 75.

27. Norman Daniel, in Kritzeck and Lewis, *Islam in Africa*, p. 203.

28. I. M. Lewis, *Islam in Tropical Africa*, p. 5.

29. Mahmud Brelvi, *Islam in Africa*. Lahore: Institute of Islamic Culture, 1964, p. 156.

30. J. Spencer Trimingham, *Islam in Ethiopia*. London: Oxford University Press, 1952, p. 58.

31. See I. M. Lewis, *The Modern History of Somaliland,* London: Weidenfeld and Nicolson, 1965, p. 20 ff; and *Peoples of the Horn of Africa*. London: International African Institute, 1955, pp. 45, 47, 140.

32. Trimingham, *A History of Islam in West Africa*, p. 103.

33. *Ibid.*, p. 140.

34. *Ibid.*, p. 112.
35. *Ibid.*, p. 111 f.
36. G. S. P. Freeman-Grenville, *The East African Coast.* London: Oxford University Press, 1962, p. 222.
37. *Ibid.*, p. 14.
38. John Gray, *History of Zanzibar.* London: Oxford University Press, 1962, p. 13.
39. Freeman-Grenville, *The East African Coast*, p. 31.
40. G. S. P. Freeman-Grenville, *The Medieval History of the Coast of Tanganyika.* Berlin: Akademie-Verlag, 1962, p. 27.
41. Gervase Mathew and Roland Oliver (eds.), *History of East Africa.* London: Oxford University Press, 1963, p. 113.
42. J. Spencer Trimingham, *The Sufi Orders in Islam.* London: Oxford University Press, 1971, p. 103.
43. *Ibid.*, p. 71.
44. *Ibid.*, pp. 40-41.
45. Froelich, *Les Musulmans*, p. 64.
46. Jamil M. Abun-Nasr, *The Tijaniyya.* London: The Oxford University Press, 1965, p. 22.
47. *Ibid.*, p. 48 ff.
48. Trimingham, *Islam in the Sudan*, p. 197.
49. Trimingham, *The Sufi Orders in Islam*, p. 118.
50. Trimingham, *Islam in Ethiopia*, p. 246.
51. J. Spencer Trimingham, *Islam in West Africa.* London: Oxford University Press, 1959, p. 131, footnote 1.
52. *Ibid.*, p. 11.
53. Trimingham, *A History of Islam in West Africa*, p. 170.
54. *Ibid.*, p. 172.
55. Quoted in Trimingham, *A History of Islam in West Africa*, p. 142.
56. *Ibid.*, p. 198.
57. Tapiero in Kritzeck and Lewis, *Islam in Africa*, p. 66.
58. Trimingham, *Islam in West Africa*, p. 58.
59. Daniel in Kritzeck and Lewis, *Islam in Africa*, p. 204.
60. Trimingham, *Islam in Ethiopia*, p. 140, footnote 1.
61. *Ibid.*, pp. 142f, 180, 200.
62. Lewis, *The Modern History of Somaliland*, p. 65f.
63. *Ibid.*, p. 84f.
64. De Gobineau, *Trois Ans en Asie.* Paris, 1905, p. 99. Quoted in Reginald Coupland, *East Africa and Its Invaders*, London: Oxford University Press, 1956, p. 299.
65. J. Spencer Trimingham, *Islam in East Africa.* London: Oxford University Press, 1964, p. 55.
66. *Ibid.*, p. 67.
67. Cheikh Hamidou Kane, *Ambiguous Adventure*, tr., Katherine Woods. New York: Walker and Co., 1963.

68. See Vincent Monteil, *L'Islam Noir*. Paris: Editions du Seuil, 1964, p. 10f.
69. Donal B. Cruise O'Brien, *The Mourides of Senegal*. Oxford: Clarendon Press, 1971, p. 21.
70. Alphonse Gouilly, *L'Islam dans l'Afrique Occidentale Française*. Paris: Editions Larose, 1952, p. 118.
71. Cruise O'Brien, *The Mourides*, p. 56.
72. *Ibid.*, pp. 89, 149, 158.
73. *Ibid.*, p. 138.
74. *Ibid.*, p. 71.
75. *Ibid.*, p. 9.
76. Paul Marty, *L'Islam au Senegal*. p. 259f, quoted in Gouilly, *L'Islam dans l'Afrique Occidentale Francaise*, p. 121.
77. Cruise O'Brien, *The Mourides*, p. 81.
78. See Levtzion, *Muslims and Chiefs*, p. 172; Elliott Skinner in Lewis, *Islam in Tropical Africa*, p. 354.
79. Louis Tauxier, *Le Noir du Soudan*. Paris: Larose, 1912; quoted by Skinner in Lewis, *Islam in Tropical Africa*, p. 356.
80. Skinner in Lewis, *Islam in Tropical Africa*, p. 359.
81. Greenberg, *The Influence of Islam*, p. 359.
82. *Ibid.* Also see Trimingham, *Islam in West Africa*, p. 16.
83. Trimingham, *Islam in East Africa*, p. 32.
84. John Middleton and Jane Campbell, *Zanzibar*. London: Oxford University Press, 1965, p. 16.
85. J. Clyde Mitchell, *The Yao Village*. Manchester: Manchester University Press, 1956.
86. Trimingham, *Islam in East Africa*, p. 48.
87. Frank Schildknecht, in Kritzeck and Lewis, *Islam in Tropical Africa*, p. 237.
88. Daniel in Kritzeck and Lewis, *Islam in Africa*, p. 206.
89. See W. Montgomery Watt, *Islam and the Integration of Society*. London: Routledge and Kegan Paul, 1961, Ch. 1.
90. *Ibid.*, p. 137.
91. Trimingham, *Islam in West Africa*, p. 50.
92. *Ibid.*, p. 9.
93. See S. F. Nadel, *Nupe Religion*, Glencoe, Illinois: The Free Press, 1954, p. 276; and Schildknecht in Kritzeck and Lewis, *Islam in Africa*, p. 234.
94. Trimingham, *Islam in East Africa*, p. 79.
95. *Ibid.*, p. 78.
96. Lyndon Harries, *Swahili Poetry*. London: Oxford University Press, 1962, p. 111.
97. See Trimingham, *Islam in West Africa*, p. 109, and I. M. Lewis, *Islam in Tropical Africa*, p. 63f.
98. See M. Chailley in M. Chailley, *et al.*, *Notes et études*. Paris:

Université de Paris, 1962, p. 26ff, and Humphrey Fisher in Kritzeck and Lewis, *Islam in Africa*, p. 128f.

99. Trimingham, *Islam in East Africa*, p. 81f.

100. Trimingham, *Islam in West Africa*, p. 71; *Islam in the Sudan*, p. 123; Schildknecht, in Kritzeck and Lewis, *Islam in Africa*, p. 238. But see Monteil, *L'Islam Noir*, p. 107 and Harold Barclay, *Buurri al Lamaab*. Ithaca: Cornell University Press, 1964, p. 141ff, for different views.

101. Nadel, *Nupe Religion*, p. 238.

102. Greenberg, *The Influence of Islam*, p. 63.

103. Trimingham, *Islam in West Africa*, p. 74.

104. Schildknecht in Kritzeck and Lewis, *Islam in Africa*, p. 239.

105. See Greenberg, *The Influence of Islam*, p. 59; I.M. Lewis, *Islam in Tropical Africa*, p. 73.

106. Harold Barclay, "Muslim Religious Practice in a Village Suburb of Khartoum," *Muslim World*, vol. LIII (June, 1963), p. 205. Quoted in Barclay, *Buurri al Lamaab*, p. 140.

107. Monteil, *L'Islam Noir*, p. 112.

108. Chailley, *Notes et études*, p. 17; Barclary, *Buurri al Lamaab*, p. 153.

109. Trimingham, *Islam in Ethiopia*, p. 229; *Islam in the Sudan*, p. 124; *Islam in East Africa*, p. 91.

110. Barclay, *Buurri al Lamaab*, p. 152f.

111. *Ibid.*, p. 138f.

112. J. Spencer Trimingham, *The Influence of Islam Upon Africa*. New York: Frederick A. Praeger, 1968, p. 58.

113. J. N. D. Anderson in Kritzeck and Lewis, *Islam in Africa*, p. 43ff.

114. F. M. de Thier, *Singhitinii: La Stanleyville Musulmane*. Brussels: Publications du Centre pour l'Etude des Problèmes du Monde Musulman Contemporain, 1963, p. 78.

115. Anderson in Kritzeck and Lewis, *Islam in Africa*, p. 45.

116. *Ibid.*, p. 41.

117. Trimingham, *Islam in West Africa*, p. 125.

118. Nadel, *Nupe Religion*, p. 245.

119. Trimingham, *Islam in West Africa*, p. 158.

120. Nadel, *Nupe Religion*, p. 246f.

121. De Thier, *Singhitinii*, p. 68.

122. Barclay, *Buurri al Lamaab*, p. 179.

123. Lewis, *The Modern History of Somaliland*, p. 63f.

124. *Ibid.*, p. 64f. See also Lewis, *Peoples of the Horn of Africa*, p. 145, 151.

125. See Barclay, *Buurri al Lamaab*, pp. 181, 182.

126. Daniel in Kritzeck and Lewis, *Islam in Africa*, p. 203.

127. Trimingham, *Islam in West Africa*, p. 94.

128. *Ibid.*, pp. 105, 110.

129. Barclay, *Buurri al Lamaab*, p. 184.
130. Mary Smith, *Baba of Karo*, 1954, p. 222, quoted in Trimingham, *Islam in West Africa*, p. 43f.
131. See Nadel, *Nupe Religion*, p. 241.
132. Trimingham, *Islam in West Africa*, p. 79.
133. Nadel, *Nupe Religion*, p. 240.
134. Trimingham, *Islam in the Sudan*, p. 166.
135. Lewis, *Islam in Tropical Africa*, p. 75.
136. Tapiero in Kritzeck and Lewis, *Islam in Africa*, p. 75.
137. Trimingham, *Islam in West Africa*, p. 140.
138. Nadel, *Nupe Religion*, p. 253.
139. Trimingham, *Islam in West Africa*, p. 42.

BIBLIOGRAPHY

The following bibliography is divided into several categories for convenient reference. In cases where a book might well have been included in more than one category it has generally been placed in the category that appears first. Where a book appears without comment no particular judgment is implied; it is simply the case that the book is not sufficiently well known to those preparing the bibliography.

I. *General Books on African Religion*

This section includes books which deal with religion in all of sub-Saharan Africa or in a major portion thereof.

Beattie, John, and John Middleton, (eds.). *Spirit Mediumship and Society in Africa*. New York: Africana Publishing Corporation, 1969.
Thirteen essays by established experts on as many groups examining the specific nature and function of ecstatic possession and its relation to the needs of the societies in which it occurs. West, east, and south Africa are represented.

Bitek, Okot p'. *African Religions in Western Scholarship*. Kampala: East African Literature Bureau, 1970.
A Kenyan scholar's highly critical reaction to all previous studies of African religion, claiming that they have been written to gain points in the religious controversies of the West.

Dammann, Ernst. *Die Religionen Afrikas*. Stuttgart: Kohlammer, 1963. French edition: *Les Religions de l'Afrique*. Paris: Payot, 1964.

Deschamps, Herbert Jules. *Les religions de l'Afrique noir*. Paris: Presses Universitaires de France, 1954, 1965.
A brief survey by a scholar most familiar with the religions of the peoples of the formerly French-controlled parts of West Africa.

Forde, Daryll, (ed.). *African Worlds: Studies in the Cosmological Ideas and Social Values of African Peoples.* London and New York: Oxford University Press, 1954, 1968.

A collection of essays by competent anthropologically oriented authors on the world views of nine groups in various parts of Africa.

Fortes, Meyer, and G. Dieterlen (eds.). *African Systems of Thought.* New York: Oxford University Press, 1965.

A collection of essays by competent scholars on the content of African religion and philosophical thought, with a strong anthropological slant. The essays vary in quality and value.

Idowu, E. Bolaji, *African Traditional Religion: A Definition,* Maryknoll, N.Y.: Orbis Books, 1973.

This is the first serious book-length discussion of the *approach* to African religion in the context of the study of religion generally. It provides an excellent perspective, especially for understanding African concepts of God.

Jahn, Janheinz. *Muntu: An Outline of the New African Culture.* New York: Grove Press, 1961.

The author seeks to "translate" important philosophical concepts common to many African cultures. The work makes it possible for a person steeped with Western cultural values and biases both to understand and to give positive value to the African mind.

King, Noel Quinton. *Religions in Africa: A Pilgrimage into Traditional Religions.* New York: Harper, 1970.

Written in an informal, conversational style, this small book is generally accurate but provides little substance that is not more adequately stated elsewhere.

Mbiti, John S. *African Religions and Philosophy.* New York: Praeger, 1969; London: Heinemann, 1969.

The first general survey of African religion by an African scholar, based on wide reading as well as personal contacts. The information is most reliable on East Africa; that from other areas comes from sources of varying quality. The interpretation of time is stimulating but has been questioned by other African scholars.

————. *Concepts of God in Africa*. New York: Praeger, 1970.
A useful compendium of information drawn from sources of varying reliability, presented in somewhat of a "catalogue" style.

Mendelsohn, Jack. *God, Allah, and Ju Ju: Religion in Africa Today*. New York: Nelson, 1962; Boston: Beacon Press, 1965.
A journalistic account of the religious situation in Africa in the early sixties, written by a sympathetic but superficial observer. Some valuable material but should be used with discretion.

Middleton, John (ed.). *Gods and Rituals*. Garden City, N.Y.: The Natural History Press, 1967.
————. *Magic, Witchcraft and Curing*. Garden City, N.Y.: The Natural History Press, 1967.
————. *Myth and Cosmos*. Garden City, N.Y.: The Natural History Press, 1967.
These are collections of articles by competent anthropologists on aspects of religion in various parts of the world; approximately half the articles are on Africa.

————, and E. H. Winter (eds.). *Witchcraft and Sorcery in East Africa*. London: Routledge & Kegan Paul, 1963; New York, Praeger, 1963.
Generally competent essays by anthropologically oriented observers.

Parrinder, Edward Geoffrey. *African Mythology*. London: Paul Hamlyn, 1967.
————. *African Traditional Religion*. Westport, Conn.: Greenwood Press, 1970 (first published in 1953).
————. *Religion in Africa*. New York: Praeger, 1969.
————. *West African Psychology: A Comparative Study of Psychological and Religious Thought*. London: Lutterworth Press, 1951.
————. *West African Religion, illustrated from the beliefs and practices of the Akan, Ewe, Yoruba, Ibo, and Kindred Peoples*. London: Epworth Press, 1949, 1961.
————. *Witchcraft: European and African*. London: Faber & Faber, 1958, 1963; London: Penguin, 1963; New York: Barnes & Noble, 1963.
Parrinder has been a pioneer in the study of the history of religions in Africa. He is generally careful with facts and restrained in interpretations but has a tendency to generalize on the basis of the area of which he has direct personal knowledge, the forest region of West Africa.

Ranger, T. O., and I. N. Kimambo (eds.). *The Historical Study of African Religion*. Berkeley: University of California Press, 1972.

Sawyerr, Harry. *God: Ancestor or Creator*. London: Longman, 1970.
This book by a Sierra Leonian scholar deals with the concepts of God among the Mende, Akan, and Yoruba peoples of West Africa.

Smith, Edwin William (ed.). *African Ideas of God, a Symposium*. London: Edinburgh House Press, 1950; 1961; New York: Friendship Press, 1961. (2nd edition edited by E. G. Parrinder)
Still a useful collection though the essays, largely by persons of missionary background, are of varying quality.

Thomas, Louis-Vincent, and Rene Luneau. *Les religions d'Afrique noir: textes et traditions sacres*. Paris: Fayard, 1969.

Werner, Alice. *Myths and Legends of the Bantu*. London: Frank Cass and Co., Ltd., 1933, 1968.
A useful collection of stories, primarily from the southern and eastern Bantu areas, with minimal information on context and interpretation.

Willoughby, William Charles. *The Soul of the Bantu: A Sympathetic Study of the Magico-religious Practices and Beliefs of the Bantu Tribes of Africa*. Garden City: Doubleday, Doran, 1928.
An early study containing valuable information written from a missionary point of view.

Wilson, Monica. *Religion and the Transformation of Society*. Cambridge: Cambridge University Press, 1971.
An anthropologist who is an avowed Christian discusses the changes taking place in contemporary African religion, drawing primarily on her study of the Nyakusa.

II. *Books on Religion in Specific Areas*

This section includes works primarily on the traditional religion of particular groups or closely related groups. It also includes monographs which deal with religion in the context of the description of whole societies.

Abimbola, Wande. *Ifa Divination Poetry.* New York: NOK Publishers, 1977.
A collection of Ifa poems of the Yoruba, with explanations.

Abraham, Roy C. *The Tiv People.* Farnborough, England: Gregg Press, 1968. (reprint).

Abraham, W. E. *The Mind of Africa.* Chicago: University of Chicago Press, 1962.
An attempt by a Ghanaian scholar to state the fundamental philosophical foundation of African culture, with the Akan used as a "paradigm." Chapter 2 is the most useful for students of religion.

Arinze, Francis A. *Sacrifice in Ibo Religion.* Ibadan: Ibadan University Press, 1970.
A detailed study of the "heart" of Ibo religion by a Roman Catholic Ibo scholar.

Ashton, E. H. *The Basuto.* London: Oxford Univesity Press, 1952, 1957.
An anthropological account including some information on religion.

Balandier, Georges. *La Vie Quotidienne au Royaume de Kongo.* Paris: Hachette, 1965.

Barnette, Donald and Karari Njama. *Mau Mau from Within.* London: MacGibben and Kee, 1966.
Although not exclusively on religion, this book emphasizes the role which traditional Kikuyu beliefs played in the formation of Mau Mau ideology and ritual and also the influence of Biblical beliefs.

Bascom, William. *Ifa Divination: Communication Between Gods and Men in West Africa.* Bloomington: Indiana University Press, 1969.

Indispensable study of the Yoruba divination system,
with translations of many accompanying verses and
narratives.

Basden, G. T. *Among the Ibos of Nigeria*. New York: Barnes and
Noble, Inc., 1966 (orig. pub. 1921).
Detailed description of many phases of Ibo life at a
time they were feeling the first effects of the colonial
presence, but without special insight into the internal
dynamics of African traditional religion.

Bernardi, B. *The Mugwe, a Failing Prophet*. London: Oxford University Press, 1959.
A detailed account by a misssionary-anthropologist of
the religiopolitical leadership of the Meru of Kenya and
of its contemporary decline.

Burton, William Frederick Padwick. *Luba Religion and Magic in
Custom and Belief*. Tervuren: Musee Royale de l'Afrique Centrale, 1961.
The only available account in English of the religion of
the important Baluba people of the Congo. It includes
very useful material but is poorly organized and written
from a rather judgmental point of view.

Calame-Griaule, Genevieve. *Ethnologie et langage: La parole chez
les Dogon*. Paris: Editions Gallimard, 1965.

Callaway, Henry. *The Religious System of the Amazulu*. Nendeln,
Liechtenstein: Kraus Reprint Ltd., 1967 (orig. pub. 1870).
Religious texts in the Zulu language with English
translations.

Case Studies in Cultural Anthropology.
This is a series of small books on particular peoples,
including the Igbo, Yoruba, Nyoro, Lugbara, and Swazi
in Africa. All these are by competent authors and include
a chapter on religion. The series is published in New
York by Holt, Rinehart and Winston.

Crawford, J. R. *Witchcraft and Sorcery in Rhodesia*. London: International African Institute, 1967.
Careful study of contemporary wizardry and accusations of wizardry, paying attention to their social function. Sources drawn from 103 cases in government
written records.

Daneel, M. L. *The God of the Matopo Hills*. The Hague: Mouton & Co., 1970.
A brief account, based on personal experience, of the way the Shona deity, Mwari, is believed to speak through his oracle on contemporary problems.

Danquah, J. B. *The Akan Doctrine of God*. 2nd ed. London: Frank Cass & Co., Ltd., 1968.
The valuable insights of an Akan scholar are presented in the context of Western philosophy and are partially obscured by attempts to relate Akan names and concepts of God to those of the ancient Middle East.

Debrunner, Hans W. *Witchcraft in Ghana*. Accra: Presbyterian Book Depot, 1959, 1961.
A fairly objective presentation of factual materials but rather superficial in interpretation.

Dieterlin, G. L. H. M. *Essai sur la religion Bambara*. Paris: Presses Universitaires de France, 1951.

Doke, Clement M. *The Lambas of Northern Rhodesia*. London: George G. Harrap & Sons, 1931.
A significant portion of this book by a competent observer deals with religious beliefs and practices.

Douglas, Mary. *The Lele of the Kasai*. London: Oxford University Press, 1963.
An anthropological work primarily concerned with the problem of authority, including religious authority.

Doutreloux, Albert. *L'ombre des fetiches: Societe et culture Yombe*. Louvain & Paris: Nauwelaerts, 1967.

Downs, R. M. *Tiv Religion*. Ibadan: Ibadan University Press, n. d.

Edel, Mary. *The Chigga of Western Uganda*. London: Oxford University Press, 1957.
An anthropological account with one chapter on religion.

Ellis, Alfred B. *The Ewe-Speaking Peoples*. Chicago: Benin Press, 1965 (reprint).
———. *The Tshi-Speaking Peoples*. Chicago: Benin Press, 1964 (reprint).
———. *The Yoruba-Speaking Peoples*. Chicago: Benin Press, 1964 (reprint).

These books, originally published in the 1890s, were among the first serious accounts of West African religion by an outsider.

Ethnographic Survey of Africa.
   This is a series of competent compact volumes, each on one of the peoples of Africa—or, in some cases, a group of closely related peoples. Each volume includes information on religion as well as other aspects of communal life, and provides an extensive bibliography. The series as a whole is edited by Daryll Forde and published by the International African Institute of London. There is also a french series published by the Presses Universitaires de France of Paris.

Evans-Pritchard, E. E. *The Divine Kingship of the Shilluk of the Nilotic Sudan.* Cambridge: Cambridge University Press, 1948.
———. *Nuer Religion.* London: Oxford University Press, 1956.
   One of the best monographs on the religion of an African people. Well written by an anthropologist sympathetic to the study of religion and to the people about whom he writes.
———. *Witchcraft, Oracles and Magic Among the Azande.* Oxford: The Clarendon Press, 1937.
   This pioneer work is quoted by practically all subsequent writers on witchcraft and related phenomena.

Farrow, Stephen S. *Facts, Fancies and Fetich.* New York: Negro Universities Press, 1969 (orig. pub. 1926).
   In spite of the title, this is a relatively sympathetic study of Yoruba religion.

Field, M. J. *Religion and Medicine of the Ga People.* London: Oxford University Press, 1937, 1961.
   A widely quoted study by a psychiatrically oriented observer. It contains useful material, but some facts as well as interpretations can be questioned, so it must be used with care.
———. *Search for Security: An Ethno-psychiatric Study of Rural Ghana.* Evanston: Northwestern University Press, 1960, 1962.
   Analysis of the insecurities and psychological needs of patrons of rural shrines, including their treatment by the shrine priests. Extensive case histories by a clinical psychiatrist.

Fortes, Meyer. *Oedipus and Job in West African Religion.* Cambridge: The University Press, 1959.

An anthropologist uses the figures of Oedipus and Job
as paradigms in a discussion of the centrality of the
parent-child relationship in the religion of the Tallensi.

Fu-Kiau, A. *Le Mukongo et la Monde qui l'entourait: Cosmogonie
Kongo.* Kinshasa: Office Nationale de la Recherche et de Developpement, 1969.
A fascinating study of the world view of the BaKongo
people.

Gaba, Christian. *Scriptures of an African People: The Sacred Ut-
terances of the Anlo.* New York: NOK Publishers, 1973.
Annotated texts of the Anlo-Ewe people of Ghana and
Togo.

Gelfand, Michael. *An African's Religion: the Spirit of Nyajena;
Case History of a Karanga People.* Cape Town: Juta, 1966.
————. *The African Witch: With Particular Reference to Witchcraft
Beliefs and Practice Among the Shona of Rhodesia.* Edinburgh
and London: E. & S. Livingstone, 1967.
————. *Shona Religion, With Special Reference to the Makorekere.*
Cape Town: Juta, 1962.
————. *Shona Ritual: With Special Reference to the Chaminuka
Cult.* Cape Town: Juta, 1959.
————. *Witch Doctor, Traditional Medicine Man of Rhodesia.*
London: Harvill Press, 1965.
A doctor with long contact with the Shona people, Gel-
fand presents much valuable material in his books but
lacks the scholarly background for careful interpretation.

Goody, Jack (John Rankine). *Death, Property and the Ancestors.*
Stanford: Stanford University Press, 1962.
A sociological study of the mortuary institutions of the
LoDagaa people of upper Ghana, noting effects of
varying inheritance systems among them. Much in-
formation about the transition to ancestor status.

Griaule, Marcel *Coversations with Ogotemmeli.* London: Oxford
University Press, 1956.
A fascinating account of the complex world view of the
Dogon as recounted to Griaule by an elder. Some have
wondered whether Griaule's interest in the subject may
not have had an influence on the account.

Harwood, Alan. *Witchcraft, Sorcery and Social Categories Among
the Safwa.* London: Oxford University Press, 1970.

Harris, W.T., and Harry Sawyerr. *The Springs of Mende Belief and Conduct*. Freetown: Sierra Leone University Press, 1968.

Description of traditional religious concerns of the Mende of Sierra Leone from extensive notes made by an empathetic missionary. Emphasis is on morality and stability in Mende society, with much informaion about specific practices.

Herskovitz, Melville J. *Dahomey*. New York: J. J. Augustin, 1938. 2 vols.
A very influential anthropological study, including considerable information on religion.

Hobley, Charles W. *Bantu Beliefs and Magic*. London: Frank Cass, 1967 (reprint).
Contains useful information on the Akamba and Kikuyu but written from the paternalistic perspective of an earlier twentieth-century colonial administrator.

Idowu, E. Bolaji. *Olodumare: God in Yoruba Belief*. London: Longmans, 1962; New York: Praeger, 1963.
An excellent account by a Yoruba scholar well acquainted with the discipline of the history of religions.

Junod, Henri A. *The Life of a South African Tribe*. New Hyde Park, N.Y.: University Books, Inc., 1962. 2 vols. (first published in 1912, revised in 1926).
The second volume especially contains a great deal of information collected by a missionary observer familiar with anthropological methods. Although written in the style of the early twentieth century, it is still a valuable resource.

Kagame, Alexis. *La Philosophie Bantu-Rwandaise de l'Etre*. Brussels: Academie Royale des Sciences Coloniales, 1956.
A widely quoted and influential pioneer study by a Rwandaise Catholic scholar.

Kenyatta, Jomo. *Facing Mount Kenya*. New York: Vintage Books of Random House, 1962.
The way in which religion pervades life in an African society is made evident by this classic description of Kikuya culture—the first such study to be written by an African in an European language. A chapter on "Religion and Ancestor Worship" attempts to clear up some common Western misconceptions.

Krige, Eileen. *The Social System of the Zulus*. London: Longmans Green, 1936; reprinted Pietermaritzburg, South Africa; Shuter Shooter, 1936.
An anthropological account with some attention to religion.
————, and D. D. Krige. *The Realm of a Rain-Queen*. London: Oxford University Press, 1943.

Leakey, Louis S. B. *Mau-Mau and the Kikuyu*. New York: John Day and Co., n.d. (orig. pub. 1952).
A brief, clear and reasonably objective account of the traditional socioreligious system of the Kikuyu, its breakdown and the rise of Mau Mau.

Lienhardt, Godfrey. *Divinity and Experience, the Religion of the Dinka*. London: Oxford University Press, 1961.
A sympathetic and generally well-written account by a competent anthropologist.

Little, Kenneth L. *The Mende of Sierra Leone*. London: Routledge and Kegan Paul, 1951; revised, 1967.
An anthropological work with two chapters on religion.

Lucas, J. Olumide. *The Religion of the Yorubas*. Lagos: C.M.S. Bookshop, 1948.
Valuable information from a Yoruba scholar is largely obscured by the attempt to prove that present Yoruba religion has degenerated from a "purer faith" closely related to that of the ancient Egyptians. This theory is supported by the confident assertion of far-fetched linguistic connections.

Mair, Lucy P. *An African People in the Twentieth Century*. London: Routledge and Kegan Paul, 1934; New York: Russell and Russell, 1965.
An anthropological study of the Baganda with a chapter on religion.

Maupoil, E. *La Geomancie a l'ancienne Cote des Esclaves*. Paris: Institute d'Ethnologie, 1961.

Mbiti, John S. *Akamba Stories*. Oxford: Clarendon Press, 1966.

Melland, Frank H. *In Witch-Bound Africa*. London: Seeley, Service & Co., 1923; Frank Cass, 1967.
An early account of the Kaonde of Zambia, containing valuable information but lacking in scholarly competence.

Meyerowitz, Eva. *The Sacred State of the Akan.* London: Faber & Faber, 1951.

Middleton, John. *Lugbara Religion: Ritual and Authority Among an East African People.* London & New York: Oxford University Press, 1960, 1964.
A careful study by a well-trained anthropologist.

Nadel, S. F. *Nupe Religion.* Glencoe, Illinois: The Free Press, 1954.
A careful, comprehensive anthropological study.

Ojo, G. J. Afolabi. *Yoruba Culture: A Geographical Analysis.* London: University of Ife and University of London Press, Ltd., 1966.

Includes illuminating comments on the relation of environment to Yoruba religion, philosophy, and art by a Yoruba scholar.

Parrinder, E. G. *Religion in an African City.* London: Oxford University Press, 1953.
A detailed study of the interaction of traditional Yoruba religion, Islam, and Christianity in the city of Ibadan, Nigeria.

Parsons, Robert Thomas. *Religion in an African Society: A Study of the Religion of the Kono People of Sierra Leone in its Social Environment with Special Reference to the Function of Religion in That Society.* Leiden: E. J. Brill, 1964; New York: Humanities Press, n.d.

A scholarly anthropological account.

Raponda-Walker, André, and Roger Sillans. *Rites et croyances des peuples du Gabon.* Paris: Presence Africaine, 1962.
A useful but somewhat repetitious account, emphasizing ritual behavior, based on personal observation.

Rattray R. S. *Ashanti.* London: Oxford University Press, 1923.
———. *Religion and Art in Ashanti.* London: Oxford University Press, 1927.
These widely quoted works provide a detailed and generally sympathetic account by a British official with long experience in the area. Some of the interpretations have been questioned.

Reynolds, Barrie. *Magic, Divination and Witchcraft Among the Barotse of Northern Rhodesia.* Berkeley: University of California Press, 1963.
As it is largely based on court cases this account tends to emphasize the dramatic and the legalistic, although the importance of underlying attitudes is also recognized.

Richards, Audrey. *Chisungu.* London: Faber and Faber, 1956.
A detailed account of a girl's initiatory ceremony, based on the personal observation of an anthropologist.

Roscoe, John. *The Baganda.* London: Frank Cass, 1965. (orig. pub. 1911).
―――. *The Bagesu and Other Tribes.* Cambridge: The University Press, 1924.
―――. *The Bakitara or Banyoro.* Cambridge: The University Press, 1923.
―――. *The Banyankole.* Cambridge: The University Press, 1923.
―――. *The Northern Bantu.* London: Frank Cass, 1966 (reprint).
All of these books on peoples in what is now Uganda are based on early contacts. There is considerable information on religion but without much interpretation.

Rouch, Joan. *Essai sur la religion et magie Songhay.* Paris: Presses Universitaires de France, 1960.

Sangree, Walter H. *Age, Prayer and Politics in Tiriki, Kenya.* London, New York, Nairobi: East African Institute of Social Research and Oxford University Press, 1966.
Anthropological study of the role leadership patterns have played in maintaining indigenous stability and adaptability of the Tiriki, an Abaluyia Bantu group in Kenya, even with the introduction of Christianity and new political structures.

Schapera, Isaac. *The Khoisan Peoples.* London: Routledge and Kegan Paul, 1930.
An anthropological account of the Bushmen and Hottentots, including chapters on religion.

―――(ed.). *The Bantu Speaking Tribes of South Africa.* London: Routledge and Kegan Paul, 1937, 1956.
Chapters by different contributors deal with various aspects of traditional life, including religion.

Schebesta, Paul. *Les pygmies du Congo Belge.* Brussels: Institute Royal Colonial Belge, 1952.

Seligman, Charles G., and Brenda Z. *Pagan Tribes of the Nilotic Sudan.* London: G. Routledge and Sons, 1932.

Smith, Edwin W., and Andrew M. Dale. *The Ila-speaking Peoples of Northern Rhodesia.* New Hyde Park, N.Y.: University Books, 1968 (first published in 1920).
One of the best of the older studies, this book includes considerable material on religion.

Stayt, Hugh A. *The Bavenda.* London: Frank Cass, 1968 (first published in 1931).

Stefaniszyn, Bronislaw. *Social and Ritual Life of the Ambo of Northern Rhodesia.* London and New York: Oxford University Press, 1964.
Some useful information, based on personal observation but poorly written.

Talbot, P. Amaury. *Life in Southern Nigeria.* London: Frank Cass, 1967 (first published in 1923).
An account of beliefs and practices of the Ibibio people, written before 1914, in the style of that time.
———. *Some Nigerian Fertility Cults.* London: Frank Cass, 1967 (first published in 1927).
This brief but interesting book deals with the worship of the earth goddess and related cults among the Ibo and Kalabari (Ijaw) peoples.
———. *Tribes of the Niger Delta.* London: Frank Cass, 1967 (first published in 1932).
An account of the religion of the Kalabari (Ijaw) people and neighboring Ibo groups, based largely on material gathered before 1916.

Tauxier, L. *La religion Bambara.* Paris, 1927.

Tempels, Placide. *Bantu Philosophy.* Paris: Presence Africaine, 1959.
This widely quoted work by a Catholic missionary among the Baluba of the Congo grew out of the author's conviction that Christianity cannot be meaningfully taught to people except in relationship to their own world view. Tempels' interpretation of this view, though not universally accepted, has influenced much of the recent thinking on African religion.

Thomas, Elizabeth M. *The Harmless People*. New York: Alfred A. Knopf, 1959.
An anthropological account of the Bushmen in narrative form containing some material on religion.

Turnbull, Colin. *The Forest People*. Garden City, N.Y.: Natural History Press, 1961; New York: Simon and Schuster, n.d.
A well-written personalized account of the Bambuti pygmies by an anthropologist who lived among them and tried to look with them at their world. Religious practices are shown as inseparable from the whole of life.
————.*Wayward Servants*. Garden City, N.Y.: Natural History Press, 1965.
A more academic anthropological account of the Bambuti.

Turner, V. W. *Chihamba, The White Spirit: A Ritual Dance of the Ndembu*. Manchester: Manchester University Press, 1962.
————. *The Drums of Affliction*. Oxford: Clarendon Press, 1968.
————. *The Forest of Symbols*. Ithaca: Cornell University Press, 1967.
————. *Ndembu Divination*. Manchester: Manchester University Press, 1961.
These books are all based on the sympathetic observations of a competent anthropologist who does not hesitate to indulge in considerable symbolic interpretation.

Verger, Pierre. *Dieux d'Afrique*. Dakar: Institute Francais d'Afrique Noir, 1954.
————. *Notes sur le culte des Orisa et Vodun*. Dakar: Institute Francais d'Afrique Noir, 1957.
A detailed study of the Yoruba and Fon deities both in their homeland and in Brazil, with original texts.

Wagner, Gunter. *The Bantu of North Kavirondo*. Vol. I. *Family Structure and Magico-Religious Beliefs*. London: Oxford University Press, 1949.

Wilson, Monica. *Communal Rituals of the Nyakyusa*. London: Oxford University Press, 1959.
————. *Rituals of Kinship among the Nyakyusa*. London: Oxford University Press, 1956.
————. *Good Company: A Study of Nyakyusa Age Villages*. Boston: Beacon Press, 1963.

III. *Religion through Art and Literature*

The following list includes some of the best primary and secondary sources for a study of the religious meaning of African art and literature.

Achebe, Chinua. *Arrow of God.* New York: John Day, 1964; Anchor Books, 1962.
Set among the Ibo about 1920, this novel has a priest of the traditional religion as its hero.
———. *Things Fall Apart.* London: Heinemann, 1958.
This may be the best African novel to date; it is set in the early twentieth century and shows traditional Ibo life in its first encounter with Europeans.

Beier, Ulli. *African Mud Sculpture.* Cambridge, England: University Press, 1963.
A survey of sculpture in unfired mud or clay. Some references to religious uses and meanings.
———. *The Story of Sacred Wood Carvings From One Small Yoruba Town.* Lagos: Marine, 1957.
A case study of the religious carvings in one Yoruba village.
———. *African Poetry: An Anthology of Traditional African Poems.* Cambridge: The University Press, 1966.
———. *Contemporary Art in Africa.* London: Pall Mall Press, 1968.
———. *Introduction to African Literature.* London: Longmans, Green, 1967.

Biebuyck, Daniel (ed.). *Tradition and Creativity in Tribal Art.* Berkeley: University of California Press, 1969.
A number of useful articles. Robert Thompson's study of a master Yoruba potter fuses art and ritual considerations.

Brain, Robert, and Adam Pollock. *Bangwa Funerary Sculpture.* Toronto and Buffalo: University of Toronto Press, 1971.
Copiously illustrated study by two historians of a specific kind of sculpture in the context of a specific kind of ritual.

Cartey, Wilfred. *Whispers From a Continent.* New York: Random House, 1969.
A detailed interpretation of recent African literature

with some attention to religious themes, especially in
chapters 1, 2, and 6.

Elisofon, Eliot, and William Fagg. *The Sculpture of Africa. New*
York: Praeger, 1958.
A major survey with explanations that include references to the religious context and meaning of the works
of art.

Fagg, W. B. *African Tribal Images.* Cleveland: Cleveland Museum
of Art, 1968.
————. *Tribes and Forms in African Art.* New York: Tudor, 1965.
A survey with superb examples and some references
to religious meaning.

Fraser, D., and H. Cole (eds.). *African Art and Leadership.* Madi-
son: University of Wisconsin Press, 1972.
Articles by several experts, including one by Roy
Sieber on terracotta funerary portraits of dead leaders.

Goldwater, Robert. *Bambara Sculpture.* New York: Museum of
Primitive Art, 1960.
The basic survey which accounts for many of the
meanings of traditional Bambara art.

Griaule, Marcel. *Folk Art of Black Africa.* New York: Tudor Publishing Co., 1950.
A summary of Griaule's thoughts on African art and
its relation to myth, religion, etc.
————. *Masques Dogon.* Paris: Musée de Homme, 1938.
The study of one group's masking traditions and the
mythic bases for them.

Hughes, Langston (ed.). *Poems From Black Africa.* Bloomington:
Indiana University Press, 1963.
An anthology.

Kane, Hamidou. *Ambiguous Adventure.* Tr. Katherine Woods.
New York: Walker and Co., 1963.
Part autobiography, part fable, this work by a Sene-
galese Muslim deals with the encounter of Afro-Islamic
and French cultures.

Kjersmeier, Carl. *Centres de style de la sculpture negre Africaine.*
New York: Hackner Art Books, 1967 (first published in 1935).
The classic study that established the concept of

tribally based styles. Some references to religion.

Kyerematen, A. A. Y. *Panoply of Ghana*. London: Longmans, 1964; New York: Praeger, 1964.
Contains descriptions of a great number of chiefly attributes and is the best summary of these royal attributes.

Laye, Camara. *The Dark Child*. Tr. James Kirkup. London: Collins, 1955.
A semi-autobiographical novel of an Afro-Islamic childhood and youth in Guinea and France.

Leiris, Michel, and Jacqueline Delange. *African Art*. New York: Golden Press, 1968.
A beautifully done survey, with colored plates and interpretive text.

Moore, Gerald, and Ulli Beier. *Modern Poetry from Africa*. Baltimore: Penguin, 1963.
An anthology.

Mphahlele, Ezekiel. *The African Image*. New York Praeger, 1962.
An interpretation of Africa through its literature, by one who has contributed to this literature.
———. *African Writing Today*. Baltimore: Penguin, 1967.
An anthology.

Ngugi, James. *A Grain of Wheat*. London: Heinemann, 1967.
———. *The River Between*. London: Heinemann, 1965.
———. *Weep Not Child*. London: Heinemann, 1964.
These novels are set among the Gikuyu of Kenya. *The River Between* takes place in the early days of British penetration, *Weep Not Child* during the Mau Mau crisis of the 1950s and *A Grain of Wheat* at the time of independence, with flashbacks to the Mau Mau period. In all of them religious concerns have a significant place.

Nzouankeu, J. M. *Le souffle des ancêtres*. Yaounde, Cameroun: Editions CLD, 1965.
Four short stories in which there are encounters with divine beings.

Radin, Paul, and James J. Sweeney. *African Folktales and Sculpture*. New York: Pantheon, 1952, 1964.

Robbins, Warren M. *African Art in American Collections*. New York: Praeger, 1966.
Somewhat dated because of the great influx of sculpture in the past five years. References to religion are fairly casual.

Rutherford, Peggy (ed.). *African Voices*. New York: Grosset and Dunlap, 1961.
An anthology of writings.

Shaw, Thurston. *Igbo Ukwu*. London: Faber & Faber, 1970.
The basic report on major excavations in eastern Nigeria, one of which revealed the tomb of a ninth century priest-King.

Sieber, Roy. *Sculpture of Northern Nigeria*. New York: Museum of Primitive Art, 1961.
Survey of the arts of some of the groups in the Benue River basin including a description of ritual meanings.

Soyinka, Wole. *A Dance of the Forest*. London: Oxford University Press, 1963.
———. *The Interpreters*. London: A. Deutsch, 1965.
———. *Three Short Plays*. London: Oxford University Press, 1969.

Thompson, Robert F. *Black Gods and Kings: Yoruba Art at UCLA*. Los Angeles: University of California, 1971.
Brilliant review of Yoruba art and its cultural meanings.

Tutuola, Amos. *The Brave African Huntress*. London: Faber & Faber, 1958.
———. *My Life in the Bush of Ghosts*. London: Faber & Faber; New York: Grove Press, 1954.
———. *The Palm Wine Drunkard*. London: Faber & Faber; New York: Grove Press, 1952.
———. *Simbi and the Satyr of the Dark Jungle*. London: Faber & Faber, 1955.
Tutuola writes English with a distinctive Yoruba "accent." The line between this world and the supernatural is indistinct and modern details are incorporated into traditional mythological context.

Wassing, Rene S. *African Art: Its Background and Traditions*. New York: H. N. Abrams, 1968.
An anthropologist's description, but with a section on religious arts.

Willett, Frank. *Ife in the History of West African Sculpture*. New York and London: Thames and Hudson, 1967.
Survey of the art of the ancient religious capitol of the Yoruba and related forms.

———. *African Art, An Introduction*. New York: Praeger, 1971.
An excellent survey with stimulating interpretations.

IV. *Islam in Africa*

Abu Nasr, Jamil M. *The Tijaniyya*. London: The Oxford University Press, 1965.

Atterbury. A. P. *Islam in Africa*. New York and London: G. P. Putnam's Sons, 1899.
An early, judgmental treatment of value only for a study of the history of Christian attitudes toward Islam.

Brelvi, Mahmud. *Islam in Africa*. Lahore: Institute of Islamic Culture, 1964.
Expresses the point of view of a Pakistani Muslim; unfortunately it is poorly organized and contains many factual errors.

Cruise O'Brien, Donal B. *The Mourides of Senegal*. Oxford: Clarendon Press, 1971.
A comprehensive anthropological study of a significant modern African Sufi order.

Fisher, Humphrey J. *Ahmaddiyyah: A Study in Contemporary Islam on the West African Coast*. London: Oxford University Press, 1963.

Froelich, Jean Claude. *Les Musulmans dans l'Afrique noire*. Paris: Editions de l'Oriente, 1962.
A well written sympathetic account with some new insights but largely a repetition of material presented in more original works.

Gouilly, Alphonse. *L'Islam dans l'Afrique Occidentale Francaise.* Paris: Larouse, 1952.
A careful, scholarly account based on personal contacts.

Greenberg, J. *The Influence of Islam on a Sudanese Religion.* New York: J. J. Augustin, 1947.
A brief scholarly treatment of the effect of Islam on the traditional religion of the Hausa people.

Harris, Lyndon P. *Islam in East Africa.* London: Universities' Mission to Central Africa, 1954.

Kritzeck, James, and William H. Lewis (eds.). *Islam in Africa.* New York: Van Nostrand-Reinhold, 1969.
A collection of essays by competent scholars, dealing with important general themes and regional particularities of African Islam.

Levtzion, Nehemia. *Muslims and Chiefs in West Africa: A Study of Islam in the Middle Volta Basin in the Pre-Colonial Period.* Oxford: Clarendon Press, 1968.
A careful and useful study of the significant role of chiefs in the expansion of Islam in one African area.

Lewis, I. M. (ed.). *Islam in Tropical Africa.* London: Oxford University Press, 1966.
A brief general survey by the editor and scholarly essays on particular aspects of Islam in various parts of Africa.

Monteil, Vincent. *L'Islam Noir.* Paris: Editions du Seuil, 1964.
A competent study by a sympathetic French scholar.

Nordenstam, Tore. *Sudanese Ethics.* Uppsala: The Scandinavian Institute of African Studies, 1968.
A descriptive study of the traditional Sudanese Muslim concept of "virtue," based on extensive interviews with three students.

Trimingham, John Spencer. *A History of Islam in West Africa: The Report of a Survey Undertaken in 1961.* Glasgow: Edinburgh House Press, 1962.
———. *The Influence of Islam Upon Africa.* New York: Praeger, 1968.

————. *Islam in East Africa*. New York: Friendship Press, 1962; London: Oxford University Press, 1964.

————. *Islam in Ethiopia*. London & New York: Oxford University Press, 1952; New York: Barnes & Noble, 1965.

————. *Islam in the Sudan*. London: Oxford University Press, 1949; Barnes & Noble, 1965.

————. *Islam in West Africa*. London: Oxford University Press, 1959, 1961.

Trimingham provides more useful information on Islam in African than anyone else writing in English. The books are based on careful study and are generally reliable, if rather pedantic in style. The early works (through 1955) have some tendency to be judgmental; the later ones generally avoid this.

V. *Christianity in Africa*

These books deal with the churches established as the result of European and American missionary activity and with the African-initiated groups sometimes known as "independent churches" or "prophet movements." Some also deal with the relationships of Christianity with traditional religion and/or Islam.

Ajayi, Jacob F. Ade. *Christian Missions in Nigeria 1841-91: The Making of a New Elite*. London: Longmans, 1965.

An analysis of Christian missionary activity which considers its impact on society and provides more sympathetic treatment of Africans than that of earlier missionary writers. The Missionary Research Library considers it "a superb study."

Anderssen, Efraim. *Messianic Popular Movements in the Lower Congo*. London: Kegan Paul, 1958.

A careful and detailed account of the origins and development of Kimbanguism and related movements.

Ayandele, E. A. *The Missionary Impact on Modern Nigeria 1842-1914: A Political and Social Analysis*. London: Longmans, Green, 1966.

Ayandale sees Nigerian History as the response to three groups of intruders. More important than administrators and traders were the missionaries. He writes of good and bad effects of this impact.

Baëta, Christian Gonsalves. *Prophetism in Ghana: A Study of Some 'Spiritual' Churches.* London: SCM Press, 1962.
A useful study by a Ghanaian scholar of independent churches in Ghana.

———— (ed.). *Christianity in Tropical Africa.* London: Oxford University Press, 1968.
Papers presented by leading Africanists are gathered under three topics: Historical Perspectives, Analytic Perspectives and Trends and Prospects; each part is introduced with a summary of the seminar discussion. A valuable introduction to issues faced in the Africanization of the church.

Barrett, David Brian. *Schism and Renewal.* London: Oxford University Press, 1968.
An attempt to correlate information on independent churches all over Africa and to make appropriate generalizations as to why they have arisen. A significant work, although some of the interpretations have been criticized.

Beetham, T. A. *Christianity and the New Africa.* London: Pall Mall Press, 1967. New York: Frederick A. Praeger, 1967.
Can Christianity planted during the colonial era survive in the independent Africa? Mr. Beetham considers both the obstacles to survival and the changes required to answer with a qualified affirmative.

Bittremieux, Leo. *La société secrète des Bakhimba au Mayombe.* Brussels: Institute Royal Colonial Belge, 1936.

Daneel, M. L. *Old and New in Southern Shona Independent Churches.* Vol. I. The Hague: Mouton, 1971.

Desai, Ram (ed.). *Christianity in Africa as Seen by Africans.* Denver: Alan Swallow, 1962.
A severe critique of Christian missions and Christianity in Africa, with the introduction by an Indian and other chapters by Africans. Much of its criticism is true but it should not be read for a balanced evaluation.

Dickson, Kewsi, and Paul Ellingworth (eds.). *Biblical Revelation and African Beliefs.* Maryknoll, N. Y.: Orbis Books, 1969.
A collection of essays by African Christian theologians, with more emphasis on African belief than on Biblical revelation. Several of the essays provide significant new insights.

Groves, Charles Pelham. *The Planting of Christianity in Africa.*
4 volumes. London: Lutterworth Press, 1948-1958, 1964. New
York: Humanities Press.
An essential work on Christianity in Africa because it
is the only one that treats the continent as a whole in the
full sweep of Christian history. Whatever is lost in detail
is made up for by sensitive interpretation and readable
style.

Hastings, Adrian. *Church and Mission in Modern Africa.* New York:
Fordham University Press, 1967.
A Roman Catholic's assessment of the issues faced by
the church in modern Africa, from an East African perspective.

Hayward, Victor E. W. (ed.). *African Independent Church Movements.* London: Edinburgh House Press, 1963.
A research pamphlet, with bibliography, dealing with
such issues as polygamy, ghosts, ancestors, and healing,
sharpened for traditional Christianity by the independent churches.

Idowu, E. Bolaji. *Towards an Indigenous Church.* London: Oxford
University Press, 1965.
A brief, forceful statement, from a Nigerian perspec-
tive, on the direction the church in Africa must go to be-
come both distinctively Nigerian and more profoundly
Christian.

Kale, S. I., and H. Hogan. *Christian Responsibility in an Independent Nigeria.* Lagos: Christian Council of Nigeria, n.d.
A study conducted at the achievement of independence to determine issues confronting the nation and the
fitting Christian response.

Karefa-Smart, John and Rena. *The Halting Kingdom.* New York:
Friendship Press, 1959.
A sympathetic brief discussion of the weaknesses of
the African church written for American church study
groups by a distinguished Sierra Leonean and his
American-born wife.

Lanternari, Vittorio. *The Religions of the Oppressed: A
Study of Modern Messianic Cults.* New York: Knopf, 1963; New
American Library (Mentor Books), 1965.

A worldwide survey including a section on Kimbanguism which contains serious errors.

Mbiti, John S. *New Testament Eschatology in an African Background*. London: Oxford University Press, 1971.
Kenyan Christian scholar discusses critically the way
in which New Testament eschatological concepts have
been presented among the Akamba of Kenya and makes
positive suggestions.

Mitchell, Robert C., and Harold W. Turner. *A Comprehensive
Bibliography of Modern African Religious Movements*. Evanston:
Northwestern University Press, 1966.
An indispensable guide to communities of faith which
represent independence from missionary ties and indigenization of both Christianity and Islam as well as the
resurgence of traditional religious forms. Up-dating has
occurred in the *Journal of Religion in Africa*.

M'Timkulu, Donald. *Beyond Independence: The Face of the New
Africa*. New York: Friendship Press, 1970.
A brief survey, written as a study book for American
churches.

Mulago, Vincent. *Un visage Africaine du Christianisme*. Paris: Pre-
sence Africaine, 1962.
A Zaïrian Catholic scholar emphasizes the positive re-
lationships between the traditional African and the
Christian perspectives, focusing on groups in Rwanda,
Burundi and eastern Zaïre. There is a brief summary in
English.

Murphree, Marshall Warne. *Christianity and the Shona*. London:
The Athlone Press, 1969.
A careful and useful study by an anthropologist who
grew up in the area, discussing Catholic, Protestant, and
Independent Christianity and Traditional religion as
interrelated elements of a religious spectrum.

Northcott, Cecil. *Christianity in Africa*. London: S.C.M. Press,
1963. Philadelphia: Westminster Press, 1963.
A brief, simple, loving, and critical introduction written to help Christians to understand the difficult situation Christianity faces in Africa.

Ogot, Bethwell A., and F. B. Welbourn. *A Place to Feel at Home*.
London: Oxford University Press, 1966.

A very good study of two independent churches in
Kenya.

Oliver, Roland. *The Missionary Factor in East Africa.* London:
Longmans, Green and Co., 1952.
A historical study of Christian missions from 1856 to
1949 in the area of Uganda, Kenya, and Tanganyika
which considers their influence both on the growth of
European interest and on the subsequent history of East
Africa.

Oosthuizen, G. C. *Post Christianity in Africa: A Theological and
Anthropological Study.* London: C. Hurst and Co., 1968. Grand
Rapids: William E. Eerdman's, 1968.
A careful study of independent religious movements.
Seeing these largely as the result of failures in traditional
Christian witness. Oosthuizen's critique is theologically
analytical but weaker in sympathetic understanding.

Pauw, Berthold Adolf. *Religion in a Tswana Chiefdom.* London: Oxford University Press, 1960, 1964.

Peel, John D. Y. *Aladura:A Religious Movement Among the Yoruba.* London: Oxford University Press, 1968.

Sawyerr, Harry. *Creative Evangelism.* London: Lutterworth Press,
1968.
A contribution toward the development of evangelism
and worship which meet African needs, by a Sierra
Leone Angelican theologian.

Sundkler, Bengt Gustaf M. *Bantu Prophets in South Africa.* London:
Lutterworth Press, 1948; London: Oxford University Press, 1961.
In the first edition, one of the earliest studies of independent churches, which has influenced later studies;
detailed and competent.
————. *The Christian Ministry in Africa.* London: S.C.M. Press,
1960.
An intimate and comprehensive portrait of the African
pastor that communicates much about the essential
nature of the African church.

Tanner, Ralph E. S. *Transition in African Beliefs: Traditional Religion and Christian Change.* Maryknoll, N. Y.: Maryknoll Publications, 1967.
A sober assessment of the difficulty with which
Catholic faith makes functional religious sense among

the Sukuma of Tanzania, written with close understanding of their traditional culture as this appears to
recent observation.

Taylor, John V. *Christians of the Copperbelt.* London: S.C.M.
  Press, 1961.
A careful effort sponsored by the World Council of
Churches to understand in depth the environment and
response of the church in the Copperbelt towns of North-
ern Rhodesia (now Zambia). Historical and social, with a
section treating some independent churches.
———. *The Growth of the Church in Buganda.* London: S.C.M.
  Press, 1958.
A social, historical, and theological study similar to
and precedent to *Christians of the Copperbelt*, written
from an intimate and sensitive relationship.
———. *The Primal Vision: Christian Presence Amid
  African Religion.* London: S.C.M. Press, 1963; Philadelphia:
  Fortress Press, 1964.
The author emphasizes the positive values of the Afri-
can traditional religion from a Christian perspective.

Trimingham, John Spencer. *The Christian Approach to Islam in the
  Sudan.* London & New York: Oxford University Press, 1948.
———. *Christian Church and Islam in West Africa.* London: S.C.M.
  Press, 1955; New York: Friendship Press, 1955.

Turner, Harold W. *African Independent Church.* 2 volumes. Oxford: Clarendon Press, 1966.
A very careful, comprehensive and sympathetic study
of the "Church of the Lord, Aladura," which has spread
from Nigeria to neighboring countries.

Webster, James Bertin. *The African Churches Among the Yoruba,
  1881-1922.* Oxford: Clarendon Press, 1964.
A careful historical study, finding causes of the African church movement in the ethnocentrism of missionaries.

Welbourne, Frederick B. *East African Christian.* London: Oxford
  University Press, 1965.
An introduction to the social forces and problems confronting the East African Christian, aimed at helping
theological students there to understand themselves and
to press on in further study of their own culture. Ele-
mentary and attractive.

————. *East African Rebels: A Study of Some Independent Churches.* London S.C.M. Press, 1961.
A competent study of several independent churches.

Williamson, Sihey George. *Akan Religion and the Christian Faith.* Accra: Shane Universities Press, 1965.
A valuable study of the impact of European Christianity on the Akan religion which argues cogently that Christianity should have separated itself more from its Western identity (even though that helped its expansion to be more sensitive to Akan perceptions.

VII. *Afro-American Religion*

These books deal with religious movements among people of African descent in the Caribbean and Brazil.

Barrett, Leonard E. *The Rastafarians: A Study in Messianic Cultism in Jamaica.* Puerto Rico: Institute of Caribbean Studies, University of Puerto Rico, 1968.

Bastide, Roger. *Les Religions Africaines au Brésil; vers une Sociologie des Interpenetrations de Civilisations.* Paris: Presses Universitaires de France, 1960.
An analysis of Afro-Brazilian cults based largely on observations made in the city of Salvador, Bahia, by a French sociologist. As the title suggests, Bastide is primarily concerned with the phenomenon of acculturation as illustrated by the African presence in Brazilian society.
————. *O Candombe da Bahia, rito Nago.* Sao Paulo: Companhia Editora Nacional, 1961.
A specialized study of Afro-Brazilian cultic practice in which Yoruba-speaking rites are predominant as observed in and around the city of Salvador by a French sociologist who has good contacts in both the *candomble* and sociological communities of Bahia.

Carneiro, Edson. *Candombles da Bahia.* 3rd edition. Rio de Janeiro: Conquista, 1961.
A study of Afro-Brazilian cults as practiced today in the city of Salvador. Although written by a Brazilian sociologist, it is largely descriptive rather than analytic.

There is some historical information about the development of the cultic practices from colonial times. An appendix provides descriptive information about Afro-Brazilian cults in and around Rio de Janeiro, pointing out differences from normative Bahian practice.

Courlander, Harold. *The Drum and the Hoe: Life and Lore of the Haitian.* California: Berkley: University of California Press, 1960.

Deren, Maya. *Divine Horsemen: The Living Gods of Haiti.* London & New York: Thames & Hudson, 1953.

Herskovits, Melville J. *Life in a Haitian Valley.* New York: Octagon Books, 1937.

McGregor, Pedro. *The Moon and Two Mountains.* London: Souvenir Press, 1966.
The only book-length study of Afro-Brazilian cults in the English language, but cannot be recommended. It is an unscholarly narrative which confuses genuinely Afro-Brazilian rites and communities with the spiritualist movement based on the thought of Ailan Vardec and unrelated popular faith healers.

Metraux, Alfred. *Voodoo in Haiti.* London: A. Deutsch, 1959; New York: Oxford University Press, 1959.

Simpson, George Eaton. *Religious Cults of the Caribbean: Trinidad, Jamaica, and Haiti.* Puerto Rico: Institute of Caribbean Studies, 1970.

Williams, John Joseph. *Psychic Phenomena of Jamaica.* New York: Dial Press, 1934.

VIII. *Journals*

The following are some of the journals in which articles on African religion are most likely to appear.

Africa. London: Oxford University Press.
Cahiers des religions Africaines. Kinshasa: Centre d'études des religions Africaines, Université de Zaïre.
Dini na Mila: Revealed Religion and Traditional Custom. Kampala: Makerere University.
Ghana Bulletin of Theology. Legon: University of Ghana.
Journal of Religion in Africa. Leiden: E. J. Brill.
Orita: Ibadan Journal of Religious Studies. Ibadan: Ibadam University Press.

The Contributors

Newell S. Booth, Jr., has his Ph.D. from Boston University and is now Professor of Religion at Miami University, Oxford, Ohio, where he teaches courses on African Religion and Islam and participates in an interdisciplinary course on African Civilization. Among his publications are "Islam and Ancestry in East Africa," *Vidya*, Spring, 1967; "The Historical and the Non-Historical in Islam," *The Muslim World*, LX, 2, 1970; "Time and Change in African Traditional Thought," *Journal of Religion in Africa*, VII, 2, 1975; and "Civil Religion in Traditional Africa," *Africa Today*, Oct.–Dec., 1976.

Donald G. S. M'Timkulu has his Ph.D. from the University of Natal and is now Professor of Sociology at Renison College, University of Waterloo, where he teaches courses on "Race and Culture" with special reference to Africa south of the Sahara, and participates in an interdisciplinary programme on "Third World Studies". He was formerly the first Secretary-General of the All Africa Conference of Churches and later African Area Specialist, U. S. Department of Health, Education and Welfare. His most recent book is *Beyond Independence: The Face of the New Africa*, Friendship Press, 1971.

John M. Janzen has his Ph.D. from the University of Chicago in Anthropology. He has taught at Bethel College, N. Newton, Kansas; McGill University, Montreal, Canada, and presently is Associate Professor in Anthropology at the University of Kansas. He has fieldwork experience in Central Africa in the Lower Zaïre and Bandundu provinces, where he has focused on social, economic, and expressive implications of ascriptive and voluntary organization. His publications include: "Kongo Religious Renewal: Iconoclastic and Iconorthostic," *Canadian Journal of African Studies*, V, 135–143; "The Dynamics of Therapy in the Lower Zaïre," *Proceedings of the*

IXth International Congress of Anthropology and Ethnology, The Hague, Mouton; and, with Wyatt MacGaffey, *An Anthology of Kongo Religion*, University of Kansas, 1974.

3) Kongo Religious Renewal: Iconoclastic and Iconorthostic," *Canadian Journal of African Studies*, V, 135-143.

4) "The Dynamics of Therapy in the Lower Zaïre," *Proceedings of the IXth International Congress of Anthropology and Ethnology*, The Hague, Mouton, Forthcoming, 1974.

Kipng'eno Koech received his early education in his homeland of Kenya. He holds an A.B. degree from Indiana Central College, an M.A. from Antioch and has studied at the Union Graduate School, Dayton, Ohio. He taught Swahili at Wilberforce University and Wright State University and worked with the Dayton Board of Education. He is now a lecturer at the University of Nairobi.

Roy Sieber. Dr. Sieber received his Ph.D. from the University of Iowa and is now Professor of Fine Arts at the University of Indiana. He has done extensive field work in Africa and is the author of *African Textiles & Decorative Arts*, the *Sculpture of Northern Nigeria*, as well as numerous articles.

Leonard E. Barrett is Associate Professor of Religion, Temple University, Philadelphia, Pennsylvania. He received his Ph.D. from Temple in religion and anthropology and has published numerous articles in this area. He is the author of *The Rastafarians: A Study in Messianic Cultism in Jamaica* and *Soul-Force: African Heritage in Afro-American Religion*.

Fred Gillette Sturm received his Ph.D. from Columbia University and has done research at the Institute of Brasilian Studies (Vanderbilt University), the Escola de Portugues (Campinas, Brasil), and the University of Sao Paulo where he was a Fulbright research fellow. He has served as professor on three universities faculties in Brasil and is an honorary member of the Instituto Brasileiro de Filosofia. He taught at The Western College, Oxford, Ohio, and is now Professor of Philosophy, University of New Mexico.

Charles S. Brown received his A.B. from Morehouse College, his M.Div. from United Theological Seminary and his Th.D. from Boston University. He has served in churches in Rhode Island,

Massachusetts and Ohio, and has been active in community affairs. He is now Associate Professor of Church and Society at United Theological Seminary, Dayton, Ohio.

Yvonne Reed Chappelle received her B.A. from Allegheny College and an M.A. from American University. From 1961 to 1963 she was Executive Secretary of the High Commission for the Inga Dam Project in the Republic of the Congo (now Zaïre). She has taught French and Lingala and was Director of the Bolinga Black Cultural Resources Center at Wright State University, Dayton, from 1971 to 1973. At present she resides in Silver Springs, Maryland.

Calvin H. Reber, Jr. is Vera B. Blinn Professor of Missions at United Theological Seminary, Dayton, Ohio, where he teaches courses in world religions and the world-wide relationships of Christianity. He secured his Ph.D. from Columbia University under its joint program in religion with Union Theological Seminary. Between 1939-1951 he served as a missionary to China. He spent his 1962-63 sabbatical on an American Association of Theological Schools Fellowship in West Africa studying religion and the church there. Other publications are "Africa—the Bruised Continent," *Torch*, April 1965, and "Distinctive Marks of the Church in Africa," *United Theological Seminary Bulletin* LXIII, (March 1964), pp. 22–29.

George B. Thomas has his S.T.M. degree from Boston University. He was a missionary in Zaïre (Congo) from 1960 to 1963 and has had several lecture-study experiences in East and West Africa. He is now Professor of Theological Ethics at the Interdenominational Theological Center, Atlanta, Georgia, where he teaches interdisciplinary courses linking African religions to socio-religious movements in America. He is also Project Director of Religious Heritage of The Black World. Among his publications are "The Relationship of the Congo with Other African States" (Chapters VI, X) *Congo Profile*, (ed.) J. Davis and L.E. Griswold, World Division of the Board of Missions, Methodist Church Publication, 1965; and "The Relevance of African Religion to Christianity in America," to be edited by John Mbiti, and published in East Africa.

Supplementary Bibliography

Abimbolo, Wande, *Ifa Divination Poetry.* New York, NOK Publishers, 1973. A collection of Ifa poems, with explanations.

Gaba, Christian, *Scriptures of an African People: The Sacred Utterances of the Anlo.* New York: NOK Publishers, 1973. Annotated ritual texts of the Anlo-Ewe people of Ghana and Togo.

Ilogu, Edmund, *Christianity and Igbo Culture.* New York: NOK Publishers, 1974. The relationship of traditional religions and Christianity as seen by a Igbo clergyman.

Janzen, John and Wyatt MacGaffey, *An Anthology of Kongo Religion.* Lawrence, Kansas: University of Kansas Press, 1974. A collection of religious documents from the Bakongo of Zaïre.

Julles-Rosette, Bennetta, *African Apostles: Ritual and Conversion in the Church of John Maranke.* Ithaca, New York: Cornell University Press, 1975. This account combines sociological analysis and a personal story of conversion.

Mbiti, John S., *The Prayers of African Religion.* Maryknoll, New York: Orbis Books, 1976. A collection from various sources, with comments.

McVeigh, Malcolm J., *God in Africa: Conceptions of God in African Traditional Religion and Christianity.* Cape Cod, Mass.: Claude Stark, 1974. An interpretation of Edwin Smith's understanding of African religion.

Merriam, Alan P., *An African World: The Basongye Village of Lupupa Ngye.* Bloomington: Indiana University Press, 1974. An anthropological study with considerable attention to religion.

p'Bitek, Okot, *Religion of the Central Luo.* Nairobi: East African Literature Bureau, 1971.

Ray, Benjamin C., *African Religions: Symbol, Ritual and Community.* Englewood Cliffs, N.J.: Prentice-Hall, 1976. A survey, interpreting specific ethnographic information in terms of symbols, rituals and community.

Setiloane, Gabriel M., *The Image of God Among the Sotho-Tswana.* Rotterdam: A.-A. Balkema, 1976. A sensitive account of a dual heritage, traditional and Christian.

Shorter, Aylward, *Prayer in the Religious Traditions of Africa.* London: Oxford University Press, 1975.

Sundkler, Bengt, *Zulu Zion.* London: Oxford University Press, 1976. A personally oriented supplement to Sundkler's pioneer work.

West, Martin, *Bishops and Prophets in a Black City.* Capetown: David Philip, 1975. A timely study of African churches in Soweto.

Zahan, Dominique, *The Bambara.* Leiden: E. J. Brill, 1974. A part of the series on "Iconography of Religions"; brief, but well done.

Symbols, 71f, 81, 87, 89, 93f, 96,
142f, 154f, 300

Taboo (tabu), 120f, 167, 328
Takrur, 298, 312, 339
Talbot, P. Amaury, 179
Tanzania, 298, 317, 324
Tapiero, Norbert, 339, 340, 343
Tauxier, Louis, 341
Taylor, John V., 264, 265, 273
taylor, Nicholas, G.J.B., 246
Tempels, Placide, 6, 11, 33, 36, 64,
65, 66, 249, 252, 254
tenda, 222, 226, 237
terreiros, 222, 226, 229, 230, 237
Theology, 242, 271, 292
Theuws, Theodore, 59, 64, 65, 66, 67
Thomas, George B., *article,* 275-296
Thompson, George, 259
Thunder, 171, 172, 173, 224
Tijaniyya, 311, 314
Tillich, Paul, 176, 181
Timbuktu, 299, 300, 301
Time, 7f, 329
Tippu Tib, 325
Tiv, 76, 77
Tokolor, 300, 309, 312f
Torodbe, 312f
Torres de Freitas, Byron, 222, 236
Townsend, H., 259, 266
Trade, traders, 297, 298, 299, 302,
303, 304, 306f, 308, 309, 317, 319,
324, 325
Trimingham, J. Spencer, 333, 336,
338, 339, 340, 341, 342, 343
Trinidad, 195, 206-208
tro, 166
Tsav, 76, 77
Tupí-Guaraní, 219, 225, 235
Ture, Muhammad, 300f
Turnbull, Colin, 1, 10
Turner, Victor W., 66
Twi, 153, 155
Twins, 41, 58, 61, 70, 71, 89, 162,
171, 173, 226

ubuntu, 15, 25
Uganda, 264, 265, 266, 324f
Ujiji, 317, 325

ulama, 300, 301
Ultimate, 34, 39, 146, 162, 165, 176f,
328
Uman, 317
Umar, al-hajj, 314
Umbanda, 221, 235, 236
Umbrella, 153, 155
United Brethren Church, 262f
Upper Volta, Republic of, 322
Uthman dan Fodio, 313f

Van Avermaet, E., 65, 66
Van Gennep, A., 85
Vansina, Jan, 66, 113
Van Wing, J., 83, 114, 115, 294
Ven, Henry, 262, 265, 267f
Verger, Pierre, 175, 178, 179, 180,
181
Verhulpen, Edmond, 64
vevers, 200, 202
vidye, bavidye, 48, 52f, 56, 58, 59,
60, 62, 63
Vidye Mukulu, 59f
Vital-force, 6, 19, 39, 185, 189, 194,
211
vodun ("Voodoo"), 166, 167, 169,
174, 175, 176, 191, 192, 193, 195,
198f, 200, 203, 204, 205, 206, 207,
211
Volta River, 303

Wallace, Antony, F.C., 189, 214
Washington, Booker T., 265
Water, 41, 42, 86, 90, 103, 118, 143,
172, 173, 231f, 293
Watt, J., 115
Watt, J. Montgomery, 327f, 341
Webster, J.B., 274
Weeks, John A., 83, 114
White
skin color, 73, 87, 190, 245, 248,
265, 285
symbolic color, 82, 85, 87, 89-93
passim, 124, 134, 154, 163, 165,
201, 204, 223, 232
Whole, Wholeness, 7, 8, 9, 10, 33,
49, 54, 88, 292
Williams, John J., 215
Willett, Frank, 157

Witchcraft, witches, 42, 45, 50, 73, 84, 95, 97, 99-104 *passim*, 109, 147, 189, 190, 191f, 194, 207, 303. 337
Witch-doctor
  See Doctor, traditional
Wolof, 321f, 335
Work, 26, 58, 321
Worship, 20, 21, 30, 43, 71, 74f, 111. 120, 167, 168, 169, 175, 230f, 270, 288, 327, 329
Wright, R., 184, 214

Xango, 221, 222, 223, 224, 226, 233
  See also Shango

Yang, C.K., 1, 10
Yao, 317, 324

Yarse, 302, 322
Yemoja, 174
Yemowo, 164
Yevhe, Yehwe, 172, 179
Yoruba, 9, 147, 159-181, passim, 204f, 217, 218f, 222, 223, 224, 229, 234, 237, 258f, 262, 313, 323, 326, 331, 337

Zaïre, 31, 33, 69, 74, 86, 93, 151, 270, 317, 325
Zambia, 33
Zanj, 298, 307f.
Zanaibar, 308, 317, 324, 325
Zulu(s) 13-30
Zulu National Baptist Church, 29
  See also Shembites